ULTIMATE X-MEN
RETURN TO WEAPON X

WRITER
MARK MILLAR

PENCILS
ADAM KUBERT
W/ TOM RANEY
& TOM DERENICK

INKS
ART THIBERT
W/ SCOTT HANNA,
JOE KUBERT,
DANNY MIKI
& LARY STUCKER

COLORS
**TRANSPARENCY
DIGITAL**
W/ RICHARD ISANOVE
& DAVID STEWART

LETTERS
**RICHARD
STARKINGS
& COMICRAFT'S
WES'N'SAIDA!**

ASSISTANT EDITOR
PETE FRANCO
EDITOR
MARK POWERS

COLLECTIONS EDITOR
JEFF YOUNGQUIST
ASSISTANT EDITOR
JENNIFER GRUNWALD
BOOK DESIGN
**ROSHELL & COMICRAFT'S
ERIC ENG WONG**

EDITOR IN CHIEF
JOE QUESADA
PUBLISHER
DAN BUCKLEY

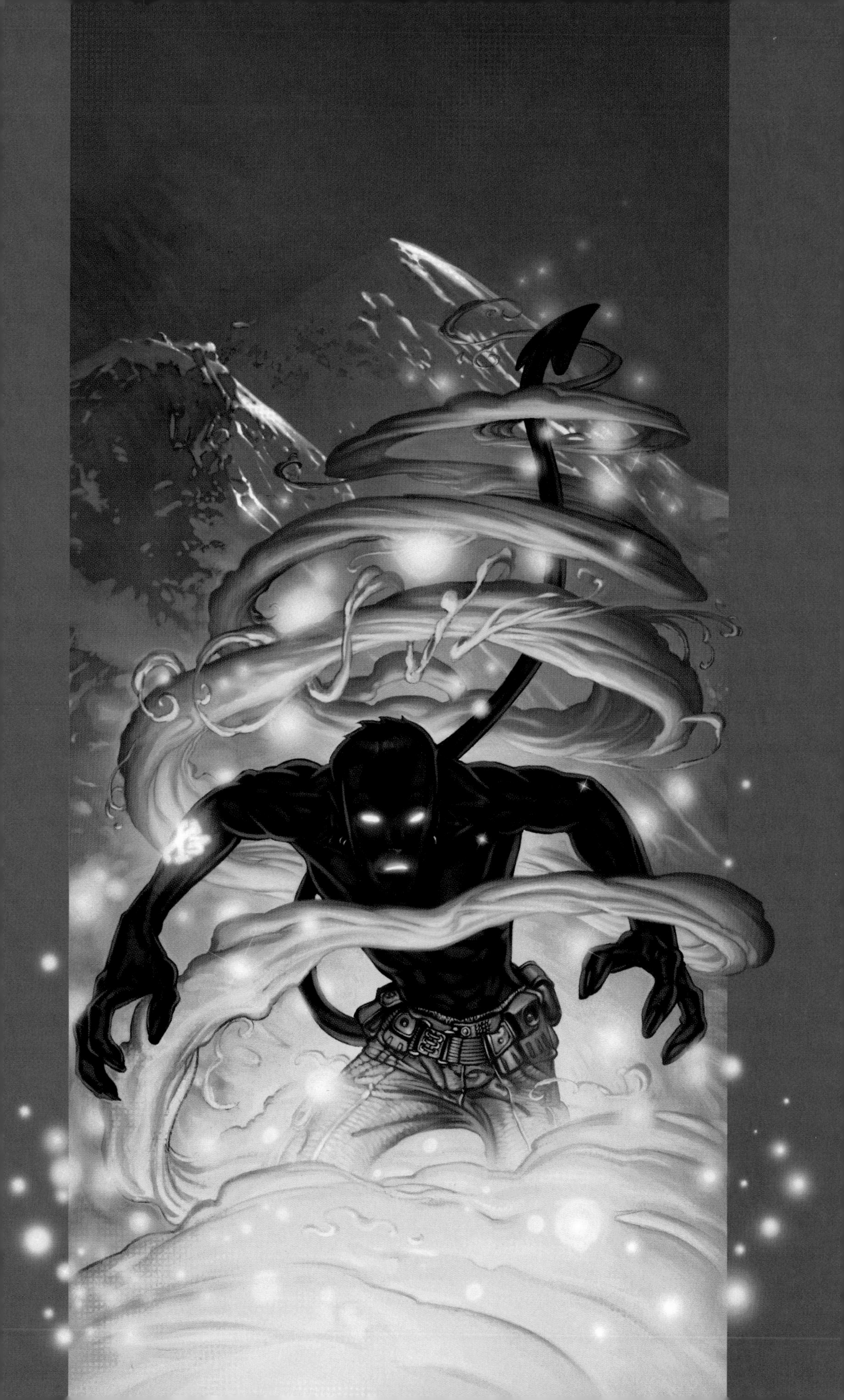

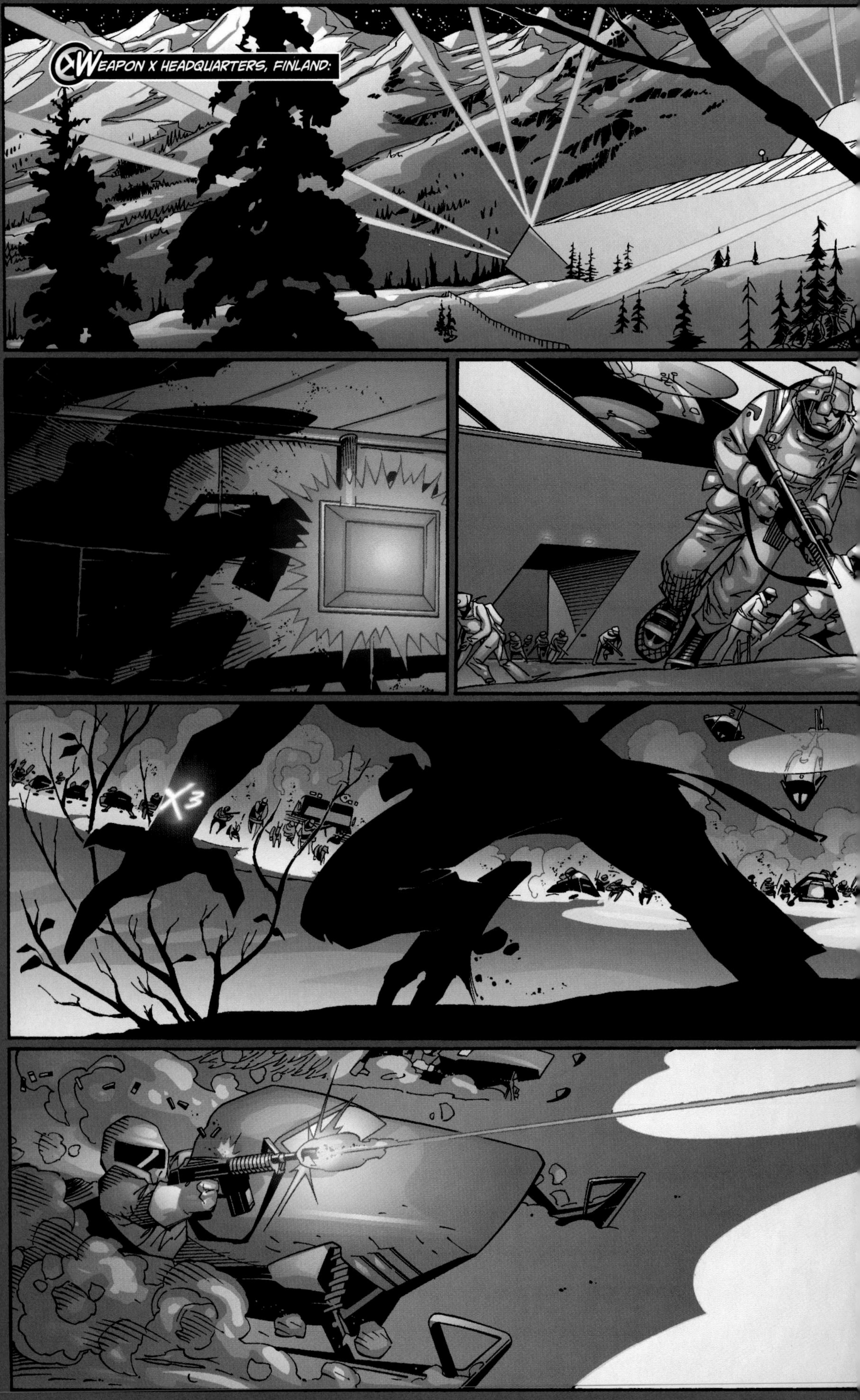
WEAPON X HEADQUARTERS, FINLAND:
X3

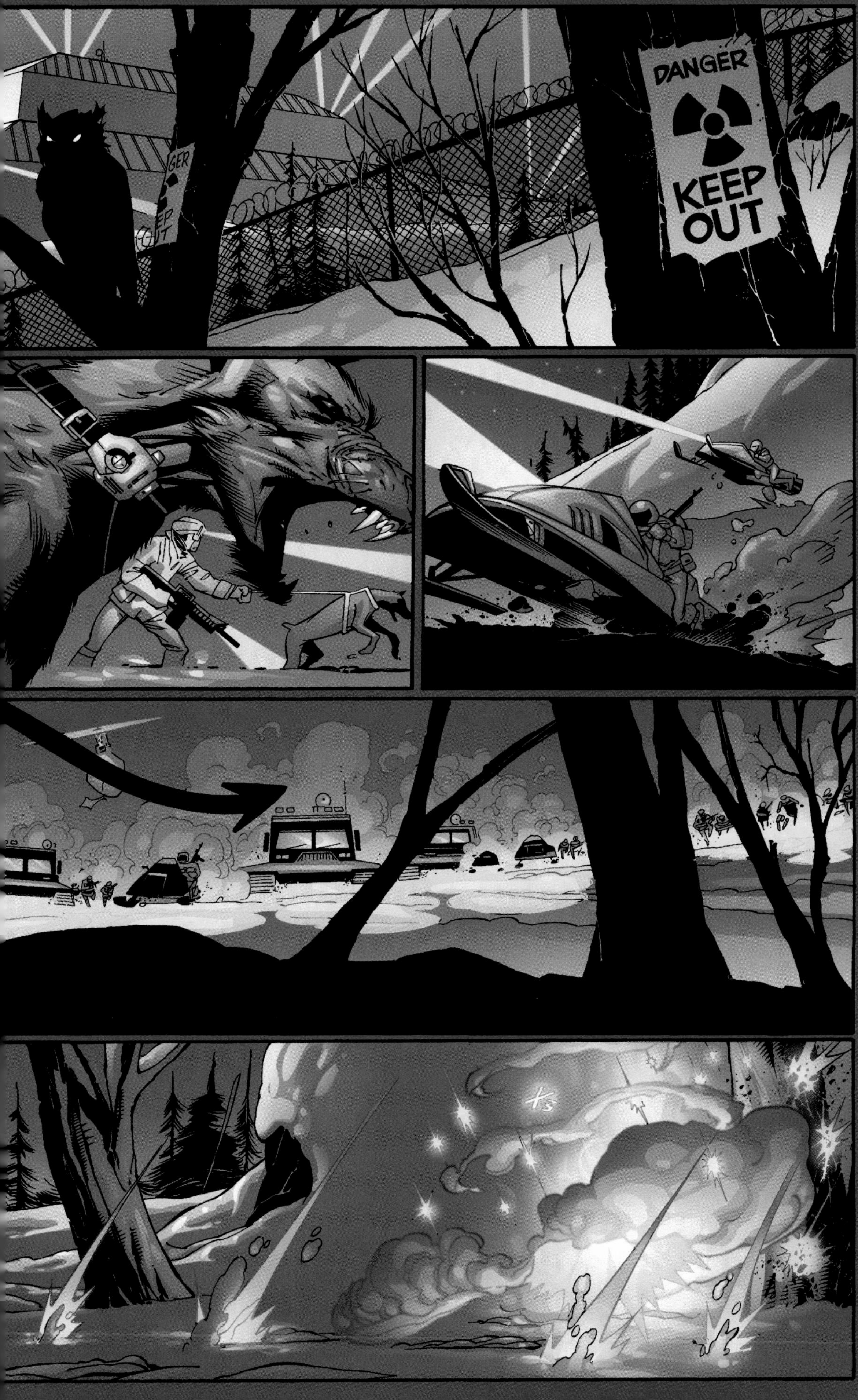
DANGER
KEEP OUT

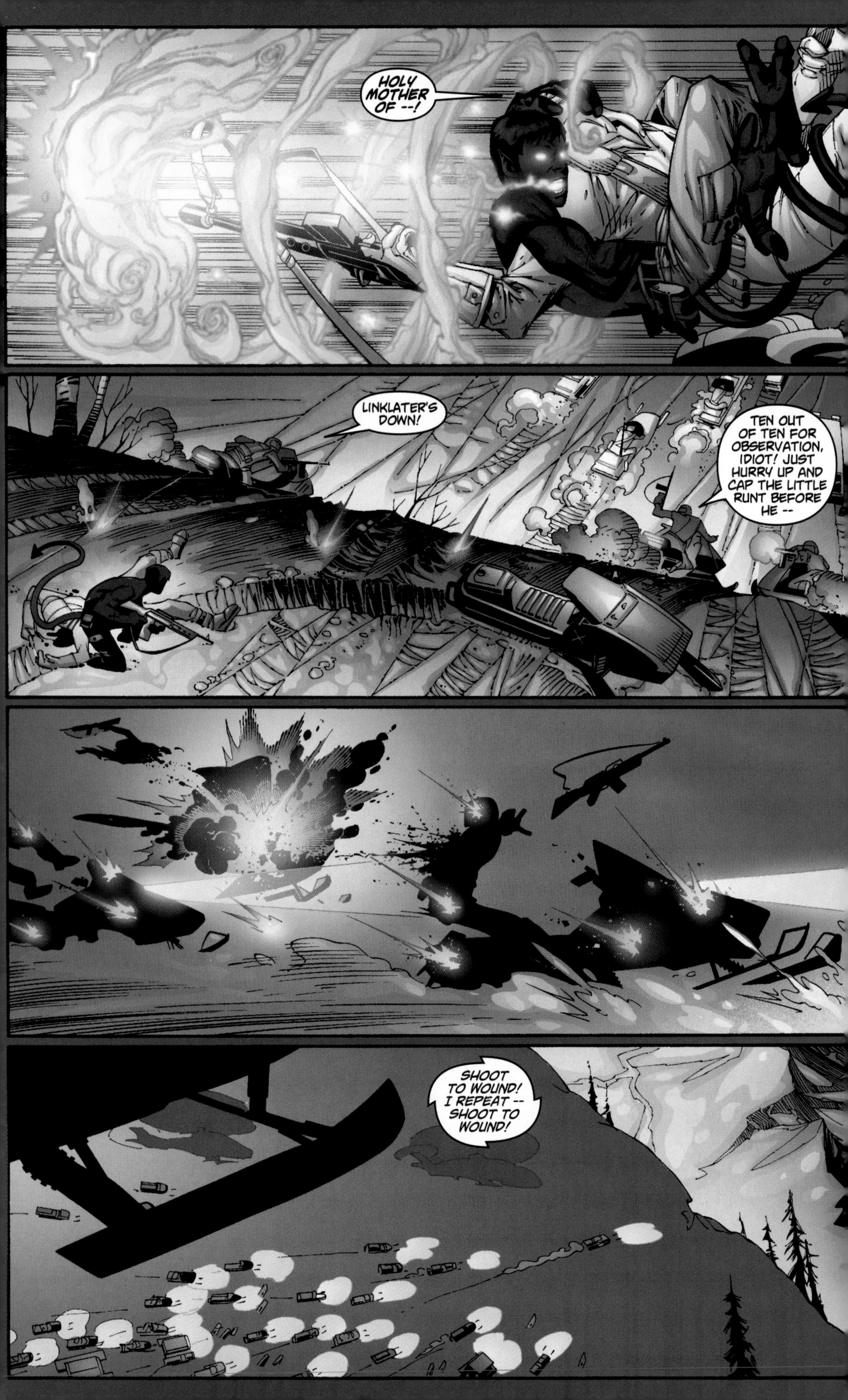
HOLY MOTHER OF --!
LINKLATER'S DOWN!
TEN OUT OF TEN FOR OBSERVATION, IDIOT! JUST HURRY UP AND CAP THE LITTLE RUNT BEFORE HE --
SHOOT TO WOUND! I REPEAT -- SHOOT TO WOUND!

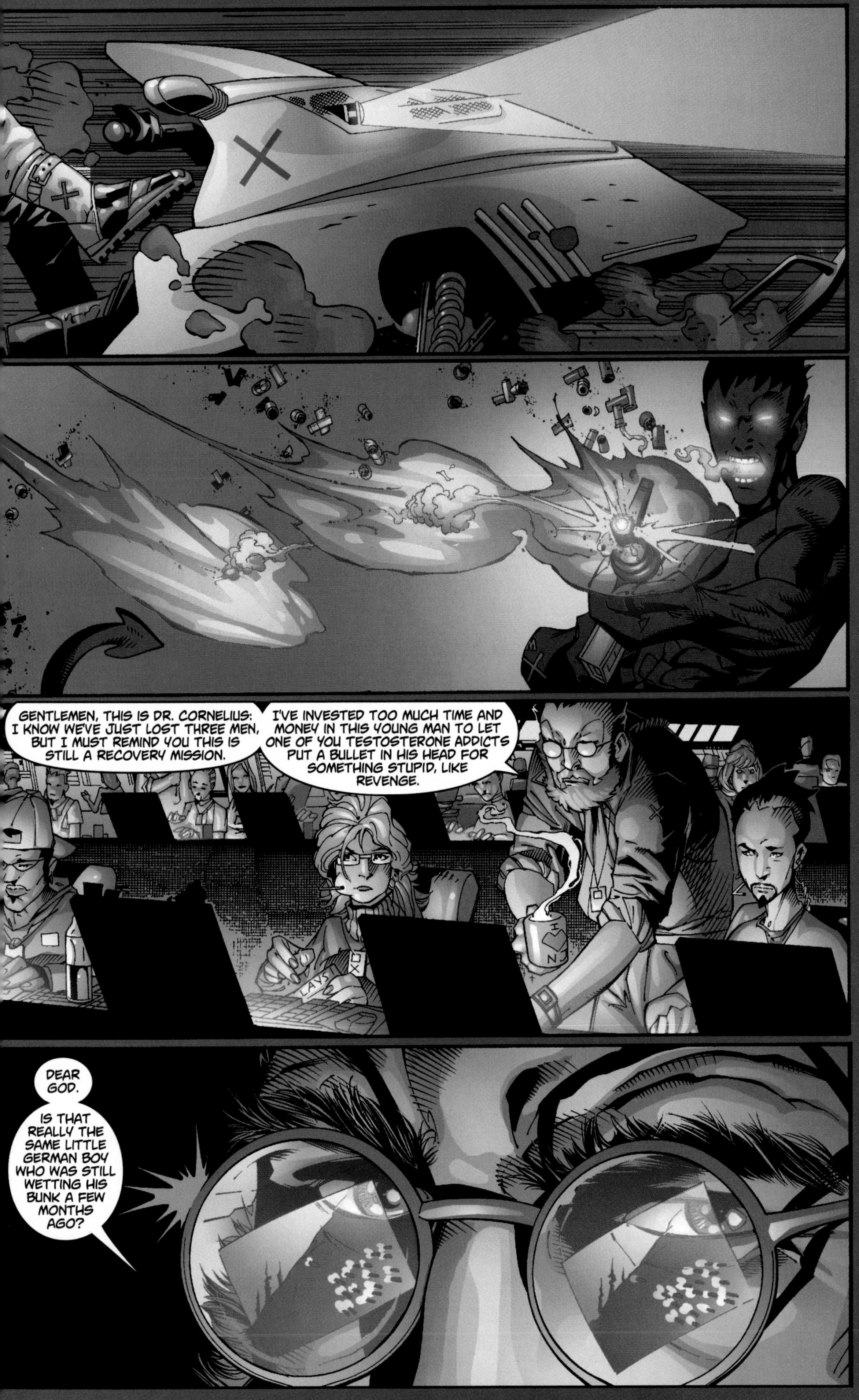
GENTLEMEN, THIS IS DR. CORNELIUS: I KNOW WE'VE JUST LOST THREE MEN, BUT I MUST REMIND YOU THIS IS STILL A RECOVERY MISSION.
I'VE INVESTED TOO MUCH TIME AND MONEY IN THIS YOUNG MAN TO LET ONE OF YOU TESTOSTERONE ADDICTS PUT A BULLET IN HIS HEAD FOR SOMETHING STUPID, LIKE REVENGE.
LAYS
I ♡ NJ
DEAR GOD.
IS THAT REALLY THE SAME LITTLE GERMAN BOY WHO WAS STILL WETTING HIS BUNK A FEW MONTHS AGO?

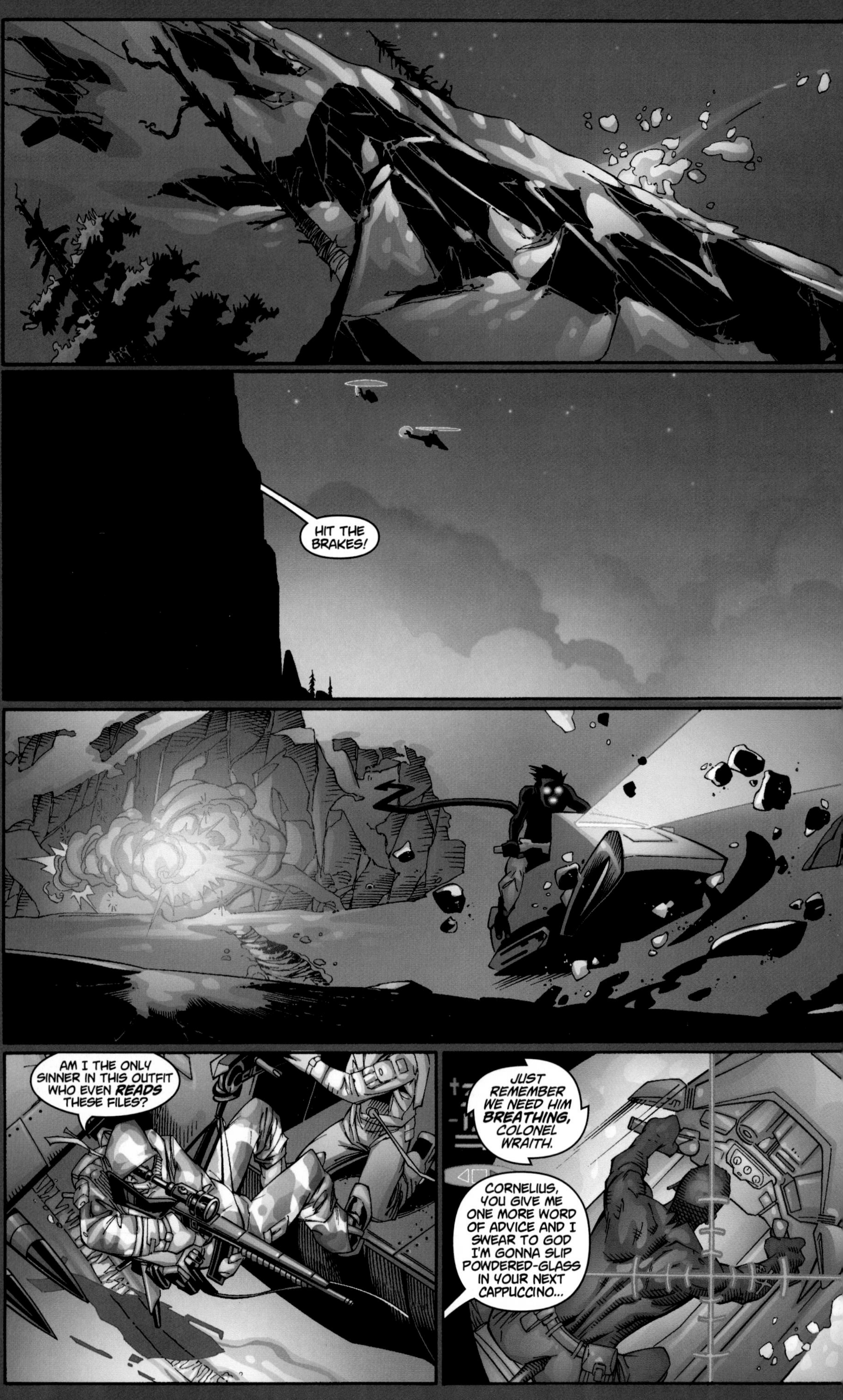
HIT THE BRAKES!
AM I THE ONLY SINNER IN THIS OUTFIT WHO EVEN READS THESE FILES?
JUST REMEMBER WE NEED HIM BREATHING, COLONEL WRAITH.
CORNELIUS, YOU GIVE ME ONE MORE WORD OF ADVICE AND I SWEAR TO GOD I'M GONNA SLIP POWDERED-GLASS IN YOUR NEXT CAPPUCCINO...

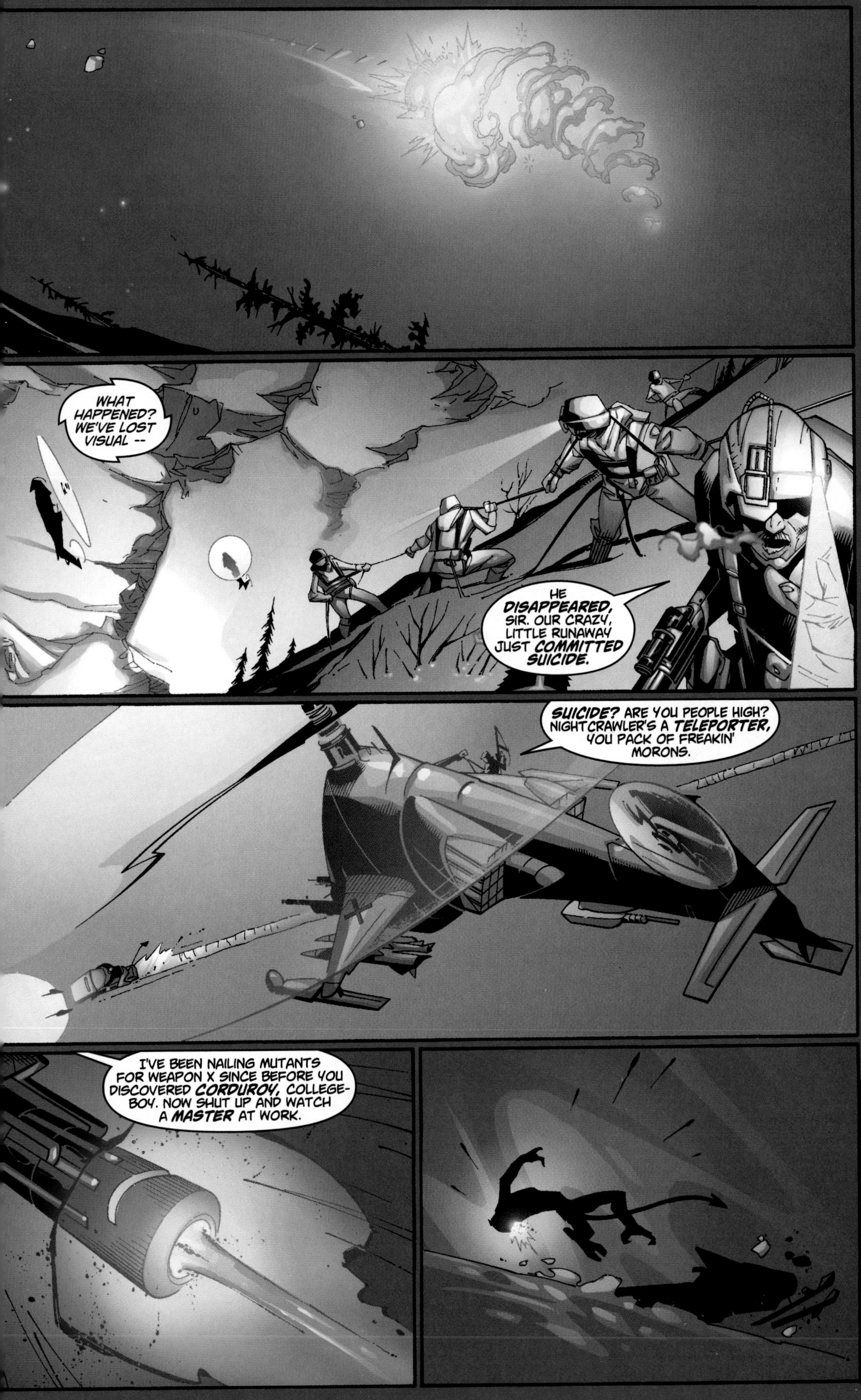
WHAT HAPPENED? WE'VE LOST VISUAL --
HE DISAPPEARED, SIR. OUR CRAZY, LITTLE RUNAWAY JUST COMMITTED SUICIDE.
SUICIDE? ARE YOU PEOPLE HIGH? NIGHTCRAWLER'S A TELEPORTER, YOU PACK OF FREAKIN' MORONS.
I'VE BEEN NAILING MUTANTS FOR WEAPON X SINCE BEFORE YOU DISCOVERED CORDUROY, COLLEGE-BOY. NOW SHUT UP AND WATCH A MASTER AT WORK.

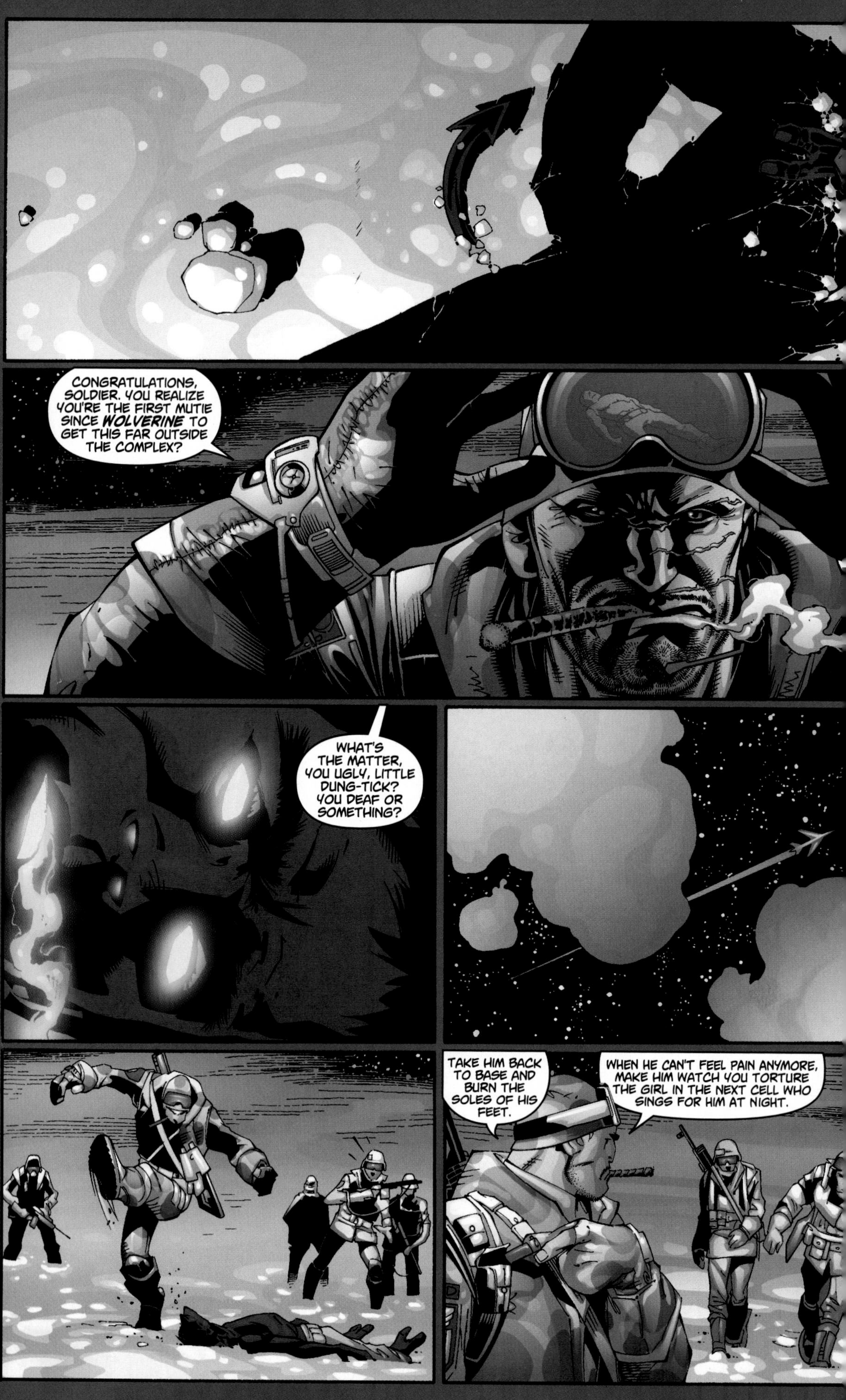
CONGRATULATIONS, SOLDIER. YOU REALIZE YOU'RE THE FIRST MUTIE SINCE WOLVERINE TO GET THIS FAR OUTSIDE THE COMPLEX?
WHAT'S THE MATTER, YOU UGLY, LITTLE DUNG-TICK? YOU DEAF OR SOMETHING?
TAKE HIM BACK TO BASE AND BURN THE SOLES OF HIS FEET.
WHEN HE CAN'T FEEL PAIN ANYMORE, MAKE HIM WATCH YOU TORTURE THE GIRL IN THE NEXT CELL WHO SINGS FOR HIM AT NIGHT.

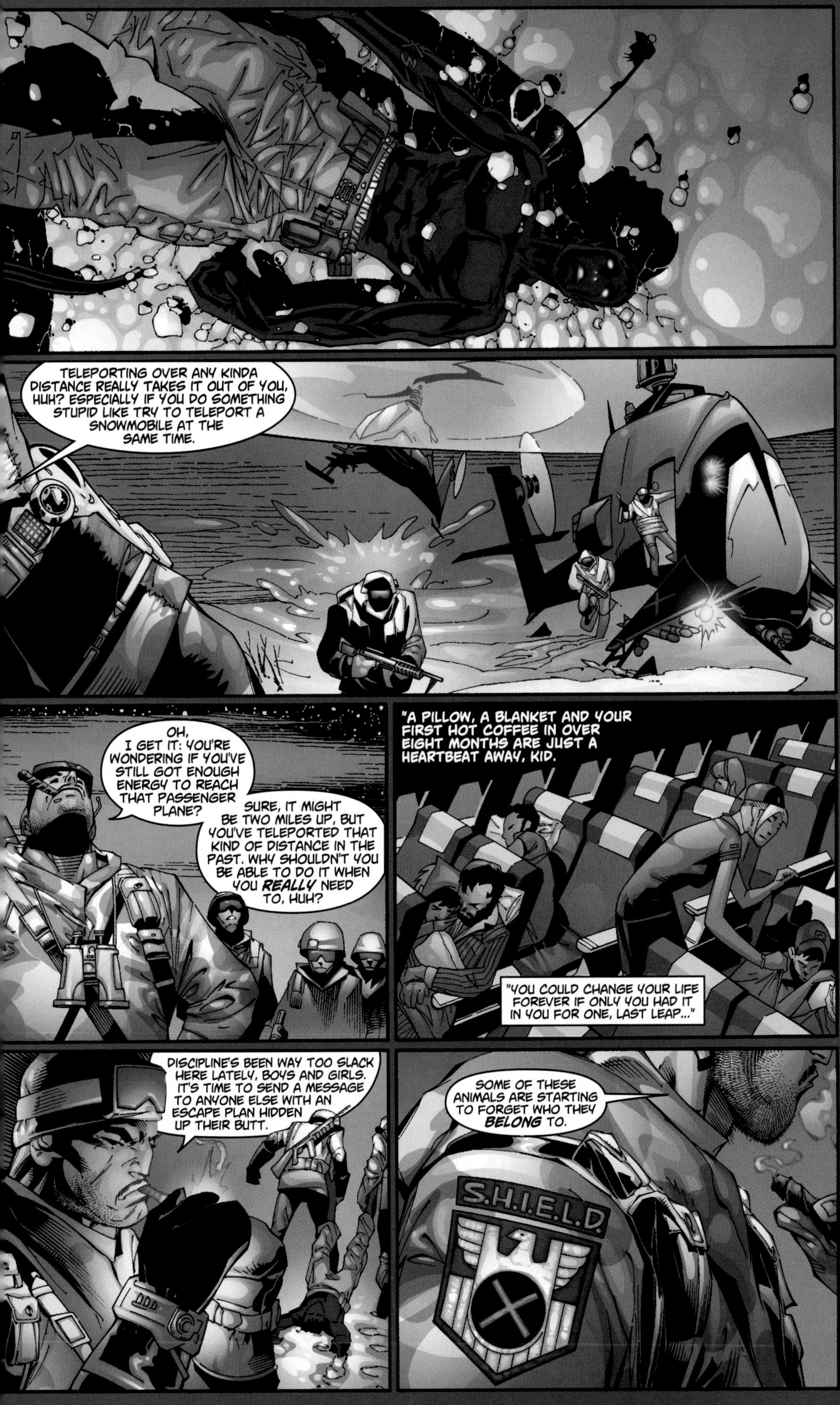
TELEPORTING OVER ANY KINDA DISTANCE REALLY TAKES IT OUT OF YOU, HUH? ESPECIALLY IF YOU DO SOMETHING STUPID LIKE TRY TO TELEPORT A SNOWMOBILE AT THE SAME TIME.
OH, I GET IT: YOU'RE WONDERING IF YOU'VE STILL GOT ENOUGH ENERGY TO REACH THAT PASSENGER PLANE?
SURE, IT MIGHT BE TWO MILES UP, BUT YOU'VE TELEPORTED THAT KIND OF DISTANCE IN THE PAST. WHY SHOULDN'T YOU BE ABLE TO DO IT WHEN YOU REALLY NEED TO, HUH?
"A PILLOW, A BLANKET AND YOUR FIRST HOT COFFEE IN OVER EIGHT MONTHS ARE JUST A HEARTBEAT AWAY, KID.
"YOU COULD CHANGE YOUR LIFE FOREVER IF ONLY YOU HAD IT IN YOU FOR ONE, LAST LEAP..."
DISCIPLINE'S BEEN WAY TOO SLACK HERE LATELY, BOYS AND GIRLS. IT'S TIME TO SEND A MESSAGE TO ANYONE ELSE WITH AN ESCAPE PLAN HIDDEN UP THEIR BUTT.
SOME OF THESE ANIMALS ARE STARTING TO FORGET WHO THEY BELONG TO.
S.H.I.E.L.D.

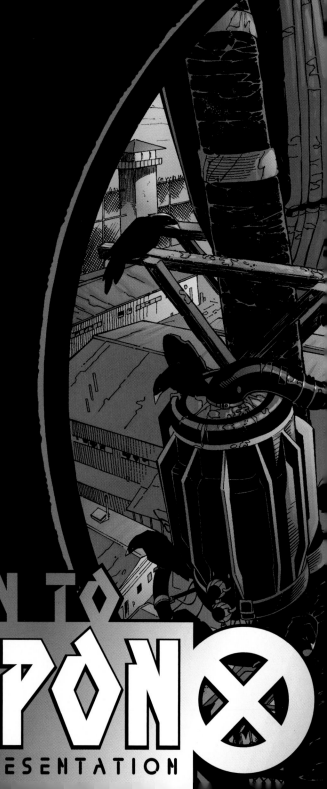

MARK MILLAR
writer

ADAM KUBERT
pencils

ART THIBERT
inks

RICHARD ISANOVE
colors

**RICHARD STARKINGS
& COMICRAFT'S
WES ABBOTT**
letters

PETE FRANCO
assistant editor

MARK POWERS
editor

JOE QUESADA
editor in chief

BILL JEMAS
president

RETURN TO WEAPON X

A STAN LEE PRESENTATION

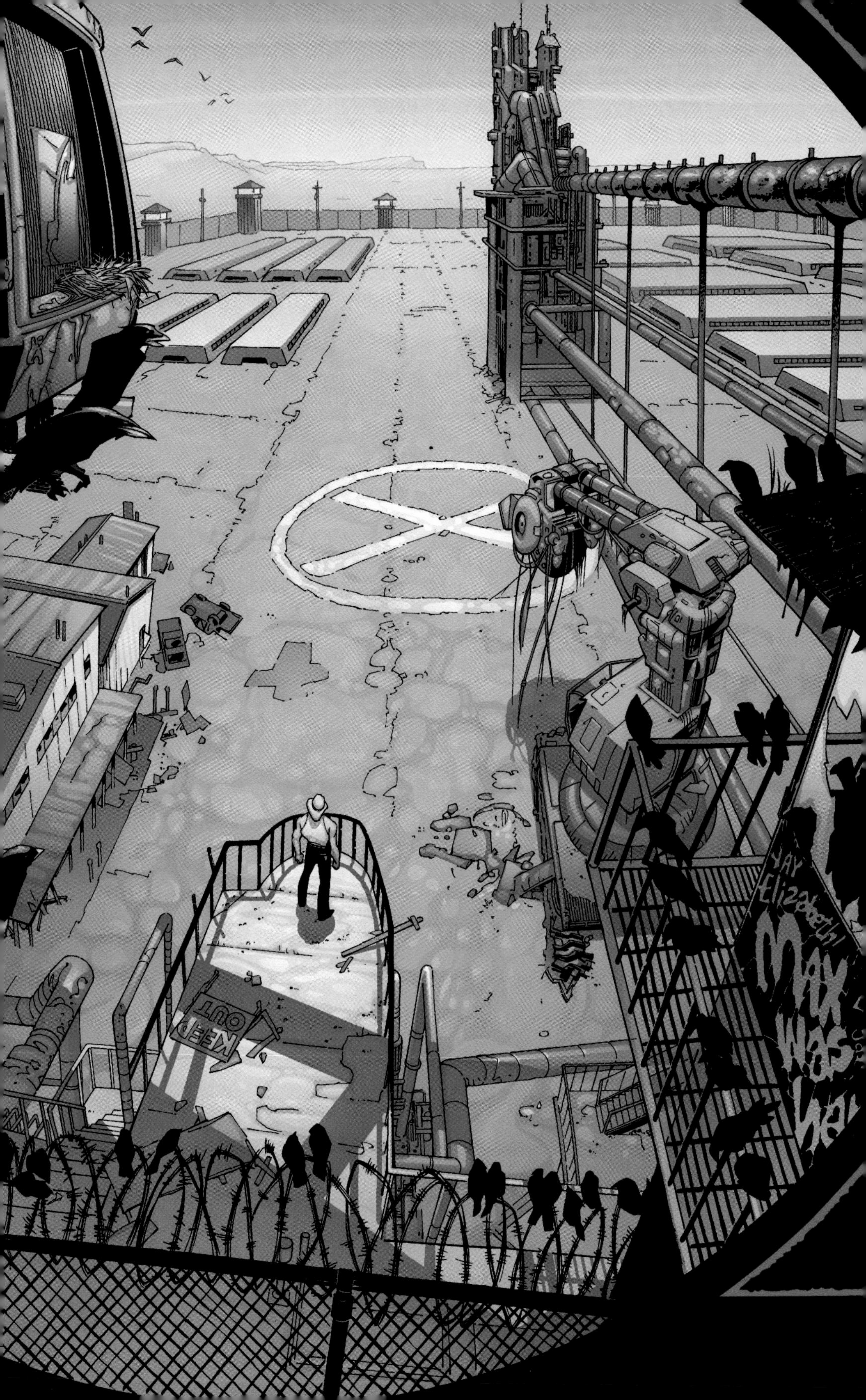
KEEP OUT
JAY
Elizabeth!!
Max was

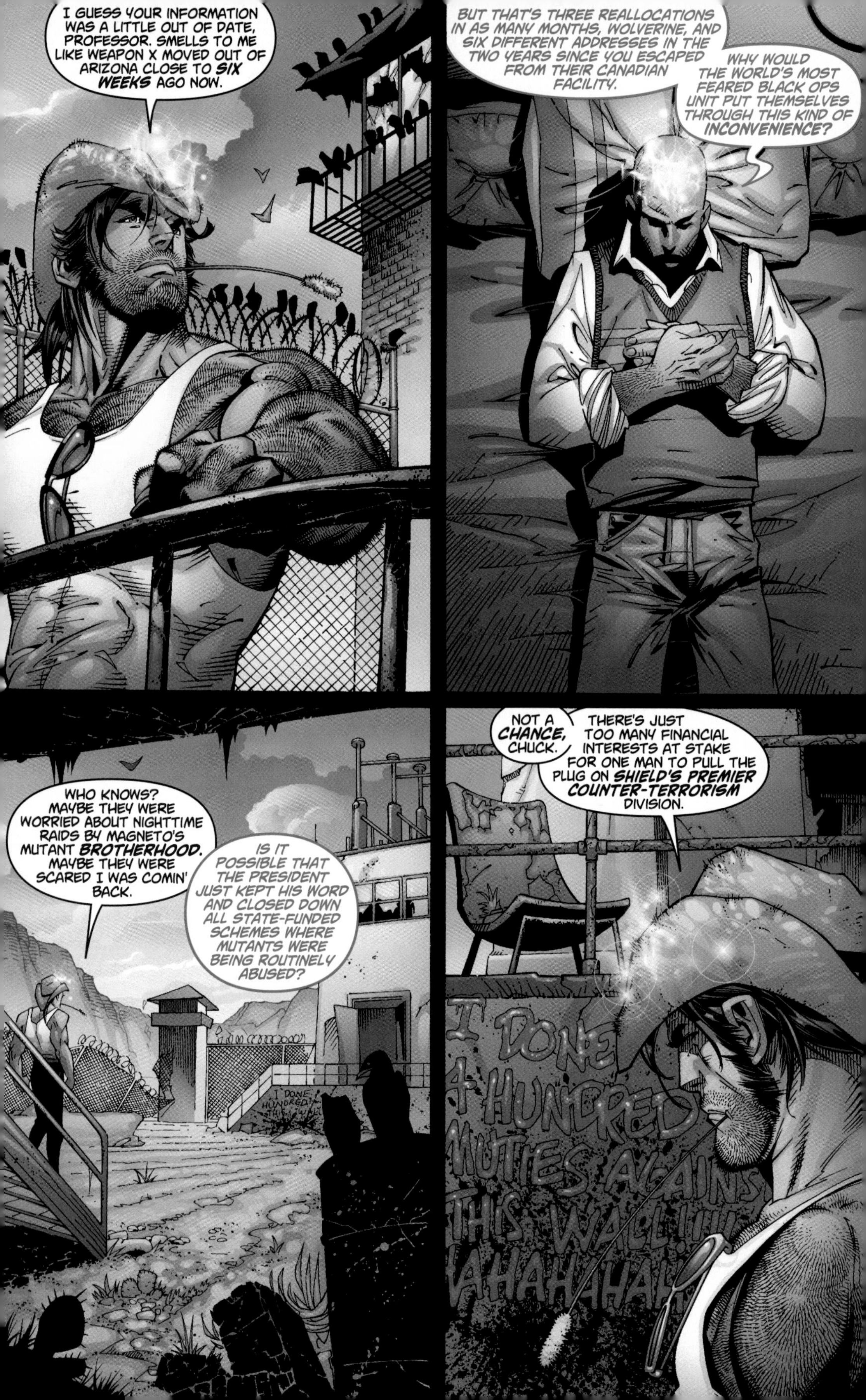
I GUESS YOUR INFORMATION WAS A LITTLE OUT OF DATE, PROFESSOR. SMELLS TO ME LIKE WEAPON X MOVED OUT OF ARIZONA CLOSE TO **SIX WEEKS** AGO NOW.
BUT THAT'S THREE REALLOCATIONS IN AS MANY MONTHS, WOLVERINE, AND SIX DIFFERENT ADDRESSES IN THE TWO YEARS SINCE YOU ESCAPED FROM THEIR CANADIAN FACILITY.
WHY WOULD THE WORLD'S MOST FEARED BLACK OPS UNIT PUT THEMSELVES THROUGH THIS KIND OF **INCONVENIENCE?**
WHO KNOWS? MAYBE THEY WERE WORRIED ABOUT NIGHTTIME RAIDS BY MAGNETO'S MUTANT **BROTHERHOOD.** MAYBE THEY WERE SCARED I WAS COMIN' BACK.
IS IT POSSIBLE THAT THE PRESIDENT JUST KEPT HIS WORD AND CLOSED DOWN ALL STATE-FUNDED SCHEMES WHERE MUTANTS WERE BEING ROUTINELY ABUSED?
NOT A **CHANCE,** CHUCK.
THERE'S JUST TOO MANY FINANCIAL INTERESTS AT STAKE FOR ONE MAN TO PULL THE PLUG ON **SHIELD'S PREMIER COUNTER-TERRORISM** DIVISION.
I DONE 4 HUNDRED MUTIES AGAINS THIS WALL!!!! AHAHAHAH

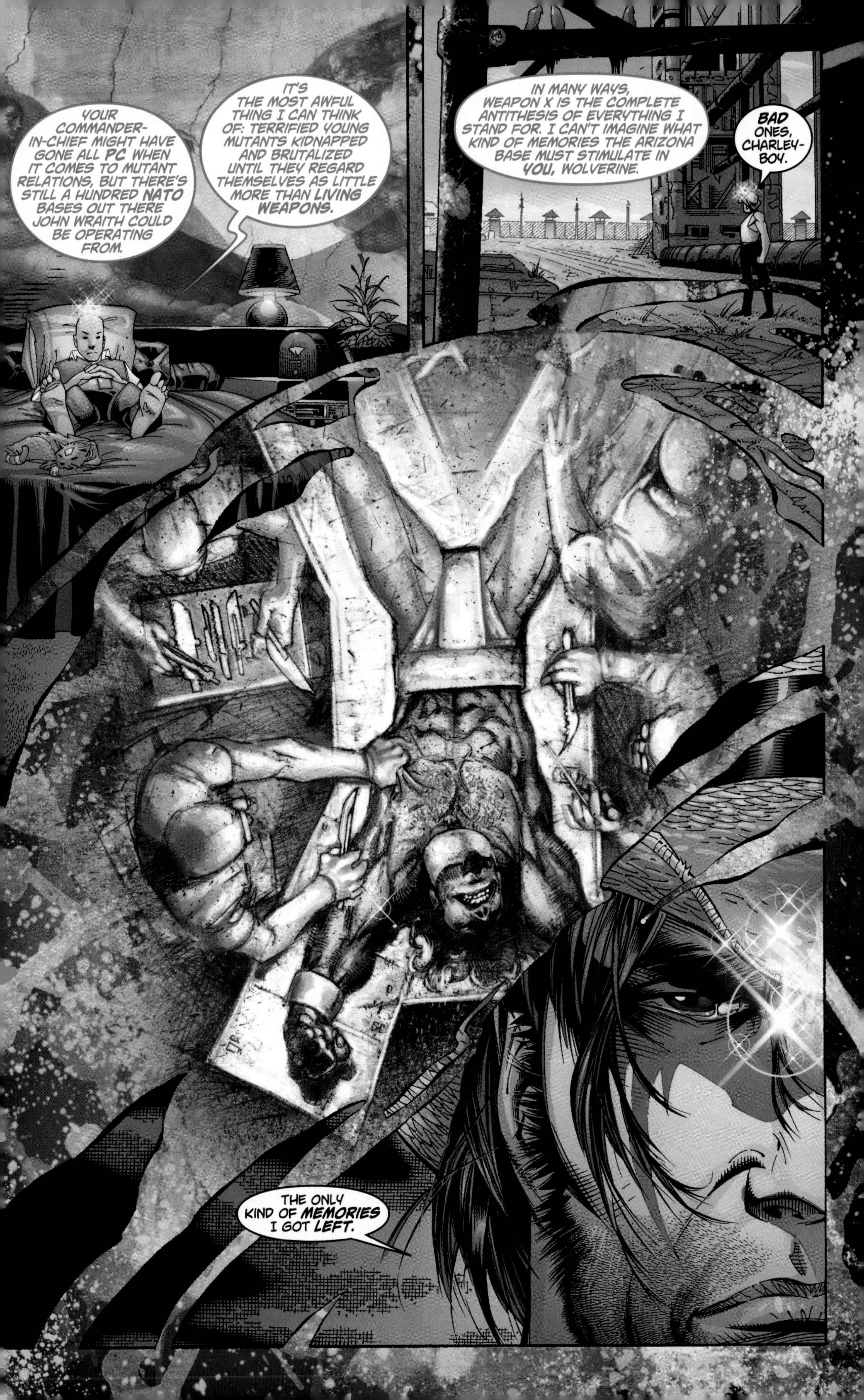
YOUR COMMANDER-IN-CHIEF MIGHT HAVE GONE ALL PC WHEN IT COMES TO MUTANT RELATIONS, BUT THERE'S STILL A HUNDRED NATO BASES OUT THERE JOHN WRAITH COULD BE OPERATING FROM.
IT'S THE MOST AWFUL THING I CAN THINK OF: TERRIFIED YOUNG MUTANTS KIDNAPPED AND BRUTALIZED UNTIL THEY REGARD THEMSELVES AS LITTLE MORE THAN LIVING WEAPONS.
IN MANY WAYS, WEAPON X IS THE COMPLETE ANTITHESIS OF EVERYTHING I STAND FOR. I CAN'T IMAGINE WHAT KIND OF MEMORIES THE ARIZONA BASE MUST STIMULATE IN YOU, WOLVERINE.
BAD ONES, CHARLEY-BOY.
THE ONLY KIND OF MEMORIES I GOT LEFT.

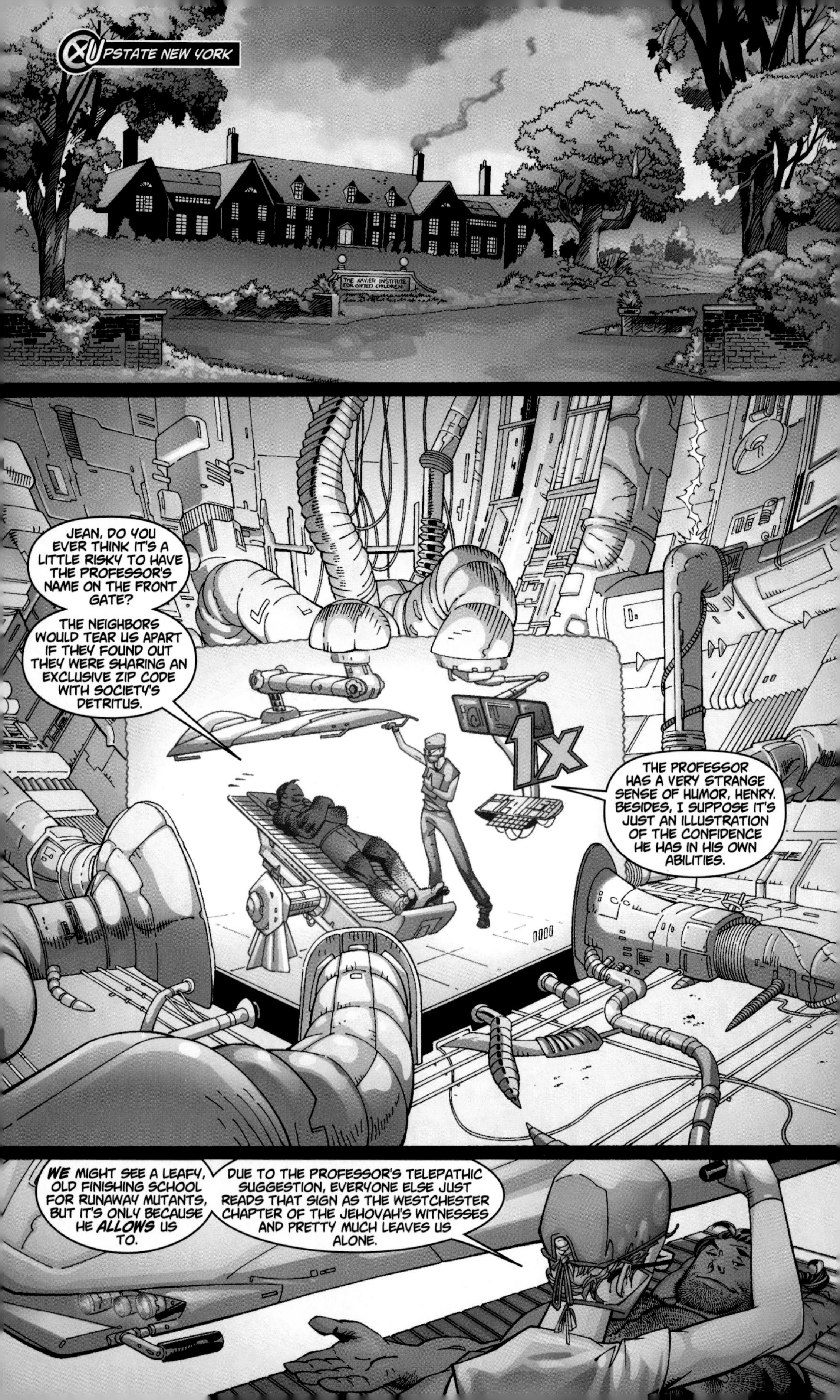
UPSTATE NEW YORK
THE XAVIER INSTITUTE FOR GIFTED CHILDREN
JEAN, DO YOU EVER THINK IT'S A LITTLE RISKY TO HAVE THE PROFESSOR'S NAME ON THE FRONT GATE?
THE NEIGHBORS WOULD TEAR US APART IF THEY FOUND OUT THEY WERE SHARING AN EXCLUSIVE ZIP CODE WITH SOCIETY'S DETRITUS.
1X
THE PROFESSOR HAS A VERY STRANGE SENSE OF HUMOR, HENRY. BESIDES, I SUPPOSE IT'S JUST AN ILLUSTRATION OF THE CONFIDENCE HE HAS IN HIS OWN ABILITIES.
WE MIGHT SEE A LEAFY, OLD FINISHING SCHOOL FOR RUNAWAY MUTANTS, BUT IT'S ONLY BECAUSE HE ALLOWS US TO.
DUE TO THE PROFESSOR'S TELEPATHIC SUGGESTION, EVERYONE ELSE JUST READS THAT SIGN AS THE WESTCHESTER CHAPTER OF THE JEHOVAH'S WITNESSES AND PRETTY MUCH LEAVES US ALONE.

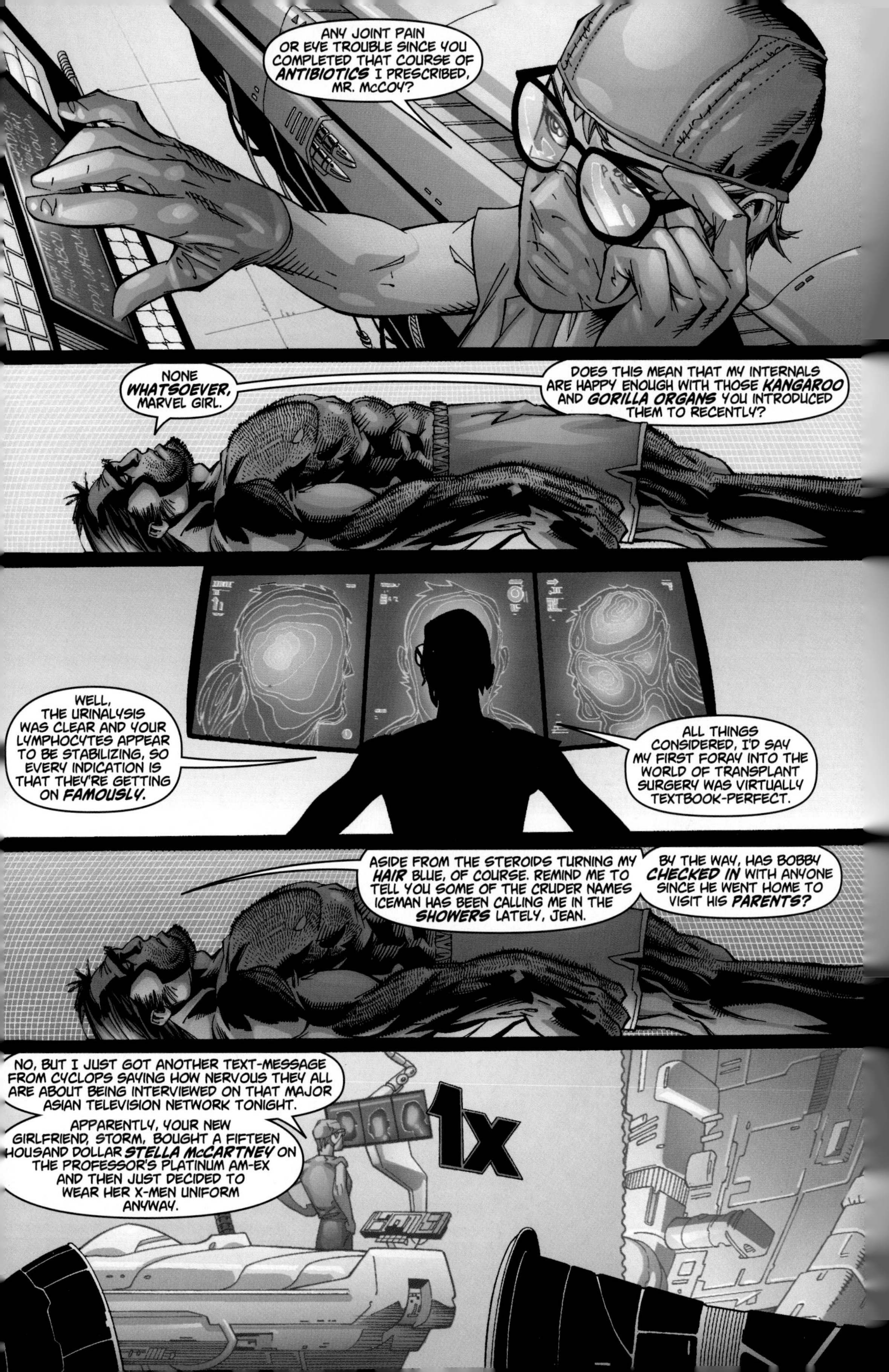
ANY JOINT PAIN OR EYE TROUBLE SINCE YOU COMPLETED THAT COURSE OF ANTIBIOTICS I PRESCRIBED, MR. McCOY?
NONE WHATSOEVER, MARVEL GIRL.
DOES THIS MEAN THAT MY INTERNALS ARE HAPPY ENOUGH WITH THOSE KANGAROO AND GORILLA ORGANS YOU INTRODUCED THEM TO RECENTLY?
WELL, THE URINALYSIS WAS CLEAR AND YOUR LYMPHOCYTES APPEAR TO BE STABILIZING, SO EVERY INDICATION IS THAT THEY'RE GETTING ON FAMOUSLY.
ALL THINGS CONSIDERED, I'D SAY MY FIRST FORAY INTO THE WORLD OF TRANSPLANT SURGERY WAS VIRTUALLY TEXTBOOK-PERFECT.
ASIDE FROM THE STEROIDS TURNING MY HAIR BLUE, OF COURSE. REMIND ME TO TELL YOU SOME OF THE CRUDER NAMES ICEMAN HAS BEEN CALLING ME IN THE SHOWERS LATELY, JEAN.
BY THE WAY, HAS BOBBY CHECKED IN WITH ANYONE SINCE HE WENT HOME TO VISIT HIS PARENTS?
NO, BUT I JUST GOT ANOTHER TEXT-MESSAGE FROM CYCLOPS SAYING HOW NERVOUS THEY ALL ARE ABOUT BEING INTERVIEWED ON THAT MAJOR ASIAN TELEVISION NETWORK TONIGHT.
APPARENTLY, YOUR NEW GIRLFRIEND, STORM, BOUGHT A FIFTEEN HOUSAND DOLLAR STELLA McCARTNEY ON THE PROFESSOR'S PLATINUM AM-EX AND THEN JUST DECIDED TO WEAR HER X-MEN UNIFORM ANYWAY.
1x

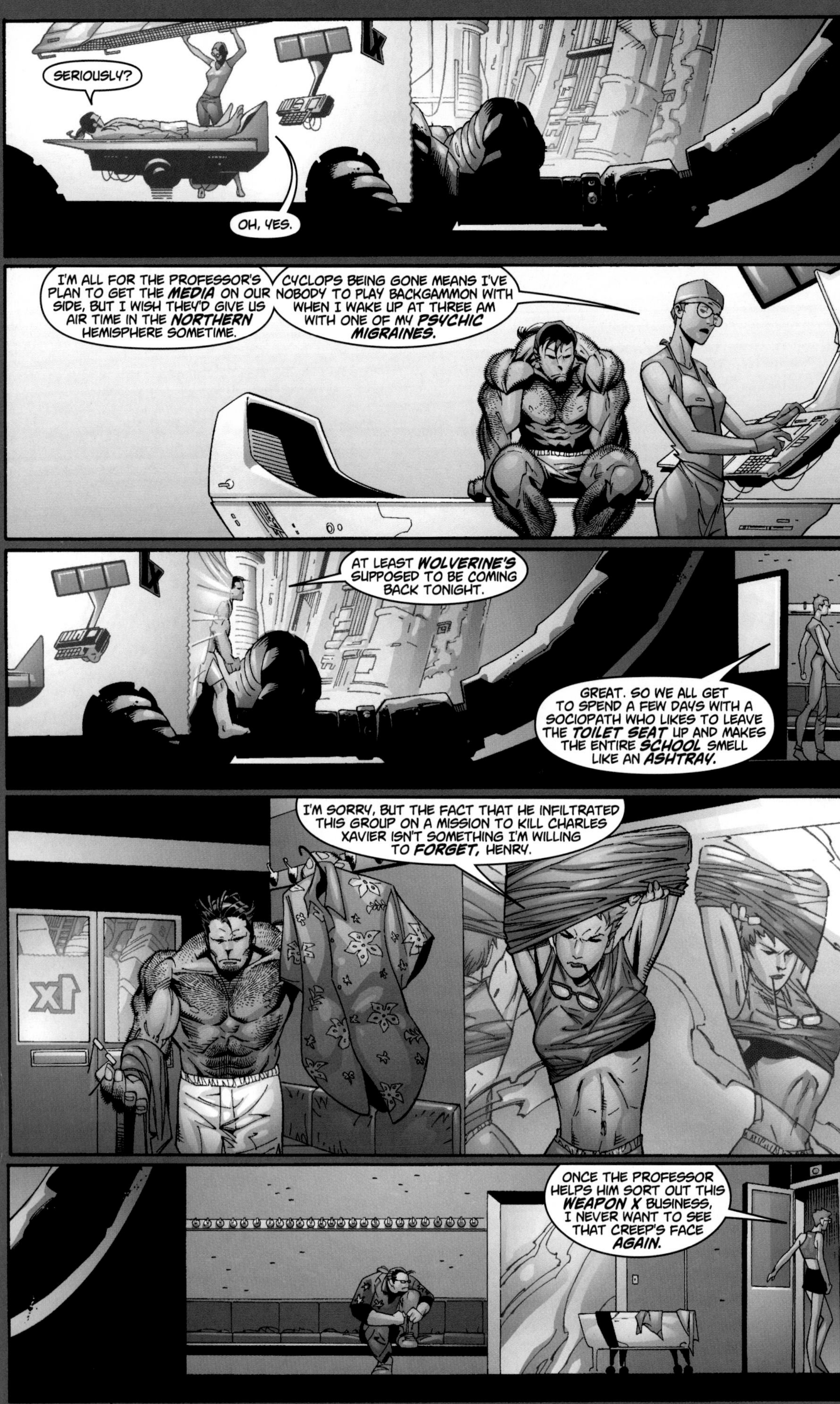
SERIOUSLY?
OH, YES.
I'M ALL FOR THE PROFESSOR'S PLAN TO GET THE MEDIA ON OUR SIDE, BUT I WISH THEY'D GIVE US AIR TIME IN THE NORTHERN HEMISPHERE SOMETIME.
CYCLOPS BEING GONE MEANS I'VE NOBODY TO PLAY BACKGAMMON WITH WHEN I WAKE UP AT THREE AM WITH ONE OF MY PSYCHIC MIGRAINES.
AT LEAST WOLVERINE'S SUPPOSED TO BE COMING BACK TONIGHT.
GREAT. SO WE ALL GET TO SPEND A FEW DAYS WITH A SOCIOPATH WHO LIKES TO LEAVE THE TOILET SEAT UP AND MAKES THE ENTIRE SCHOOL SMELL LIKE AN ASHTRAY.
I'M SORRY, BUT THE FACT THAT HE INFILTRATED THIS GROUP ON A MISSION TO KILL CHARLES XAVIER ISN'T SOMETHING I'M WILLING TO FORGET, HENRY.
ONCE THE PROFESSOR HELPS HIM SORT OUT THIS WEAPON X BUSINESS, I NEVER WANT TO SEE THAT CREEP'S FACE AGAIN.

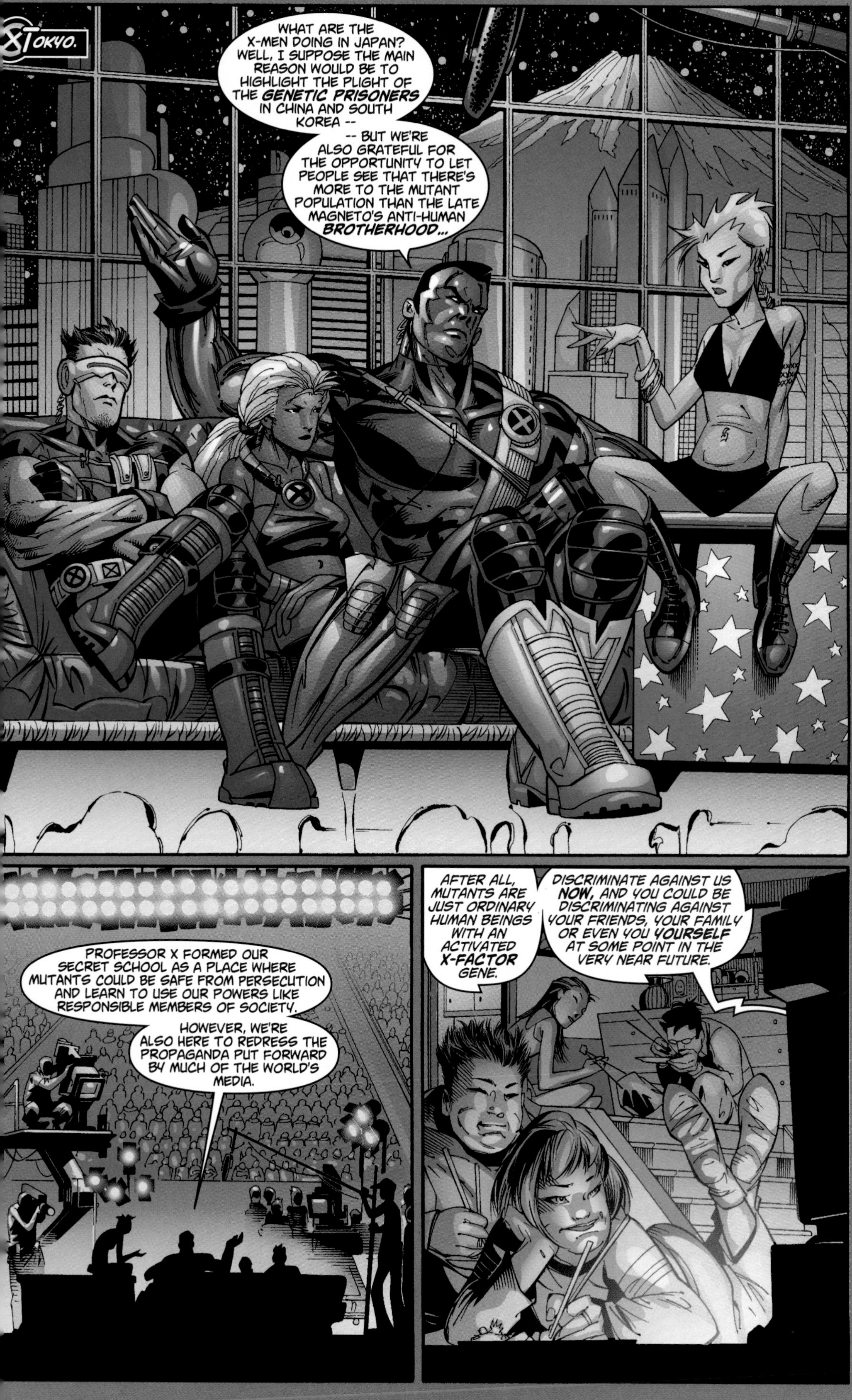

TOKYO.
WHAT ARE THE X-MEN DOING IN JAPAN? WELL, I SUPPOSE THE MAIN REASON WOULD BE TO HIGHLIGHT THE PLIGHT OF THE GENETIC PRISONERS IN CHINA AND SOUTH KOREA --
-- BUT WE'RE ALSO GRATEFUL FOR THE OPPORTUNITY TO LET PEOPLE SEE THAT THERE'S MORE TO THE MUTANT POPULATION THAN THE LATE MAGNETO'S ANTI-HUMAN BROTHERHOOD...
PROFESSOR X FORMED OUR SECRET SCHOOL AS A PLACE WHERE MUTANTS COULD BE SAFE FROM PERSECUTION AND LEARN TO USE OUR POWERS LIKE RESPONSIBLE MEMBERS OF SOCIETY.
HOWEVER, WE'RE ALSO HERE TO REDRESS THE PROPAGANDA PUT FORWARD BY MUCH OF THE WORLD'S MEDIA.
AFTER ALL, MUTANTS ARE JUST ORDINARY HUMAN BEINGS WITH AN ACTIVATED X-FACTOR GENE.
DISCRIMINATE AGAINST US NOW, AND YOU COULD BE DISCRIMINATING AGAINST YOUR FRIENDS, YOUR FAMILY OR EVEN YOU YOURSELF AT SOME POINT IN THE VERY NEAR FUTURE.

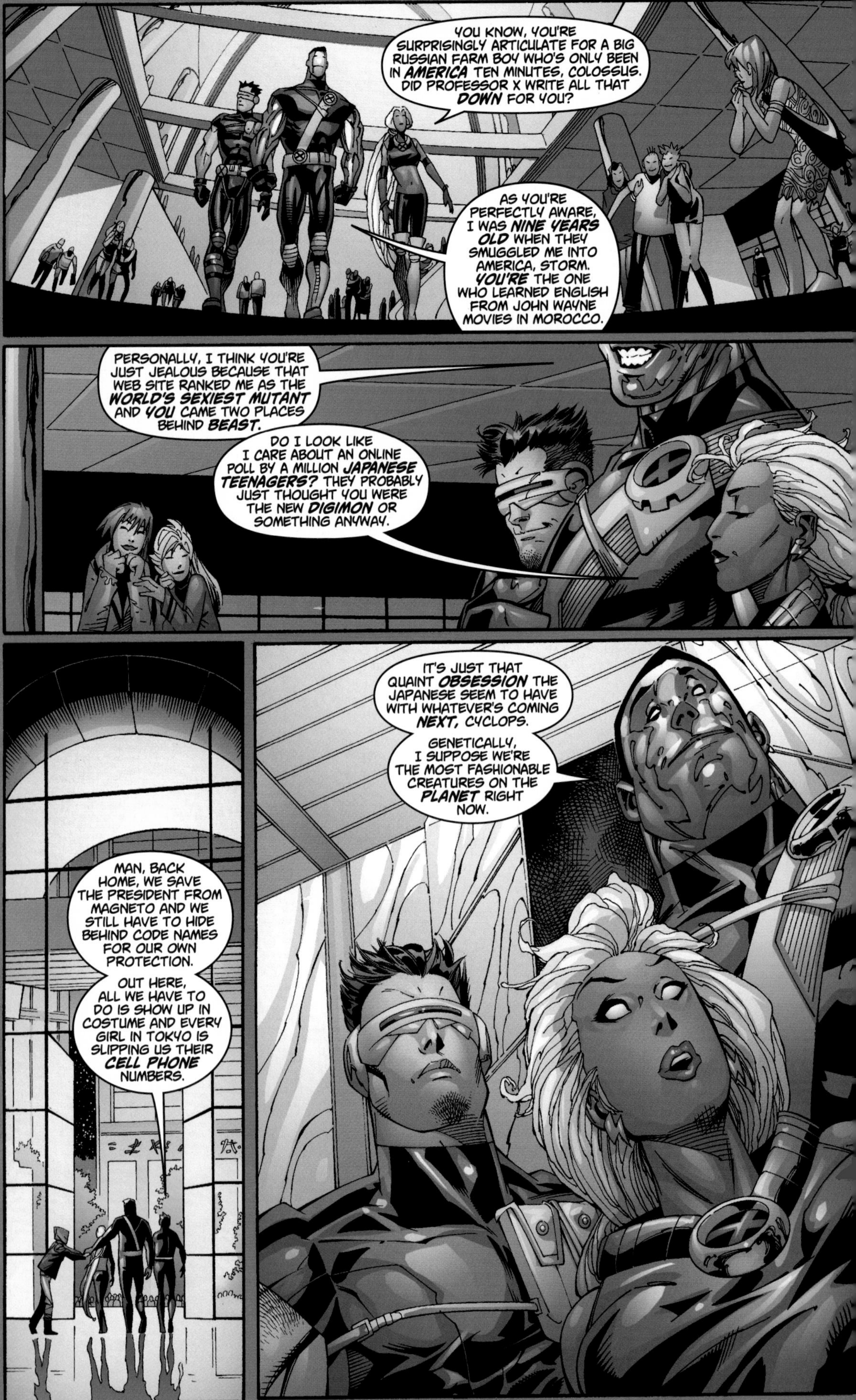

YOU KNOW, YOU'RE SURPRISINGLY ARTICULATE FOR A BIG RUSSIAN FARM BOY WHO'S ONLY BEEN IN AMERICA TEN MINUTES, COLOSSUS. DID PROFESSOR X WRITE ALL THAT DOWN FOR YOU?
AS YOU'RE PERFECTLY AWARE, I WAS NINE YEARS OLD WHEN THEY SMUGGLED ME INTO AMERICA, STORM. YOU'RE THE ONE WHO LEARNED ENGLISH FROM JOHN WAYNE MOVIES IN MOROCCO.
PERSONALLY, I THINK YOU'RE JUST JEALOUS BECAUSE THAT WEB SITE RANKED ME AS THE WORLD'S SEXIEST MUTANT AND YOU CAME TWO PLACES BEHIND BEAST.
DO I LOOK LIKE I CARE ABOUT AN ONLINE POLL BY A MILLION JAPANESE TEENAGERS? THEY PROBABLY JUST THOUGHT YOU WERE THE NEW DIGIMON OR SOMETHING ANYWAY.
MAN, BACK HOME, WE SAVE THE PRESIDENT FROM MAGNETO AND WE STILL HAVE TO HIDE BEHIND CODE NAMES FOR OUR OWN PROTECTION.
OUT HERE, ALL WE HAVE TO DO IS SHOW UP IN COSTUME AND EVERY GIRL IN TOKYO IS SLIPPING US THEIR CELL PHONE NUMBERS.
IT'S JUST THAT QUAINT OBSESSION THE JAPANESE SEEM TO HAVE WITH WHATEVER'S COMING NEXT, CYCLOPS.
GENETICALLY, I SUPPOSE WE'RE THE MOST FASHIONABLE CREATURES ON THE PLANET RIGHT NOW.

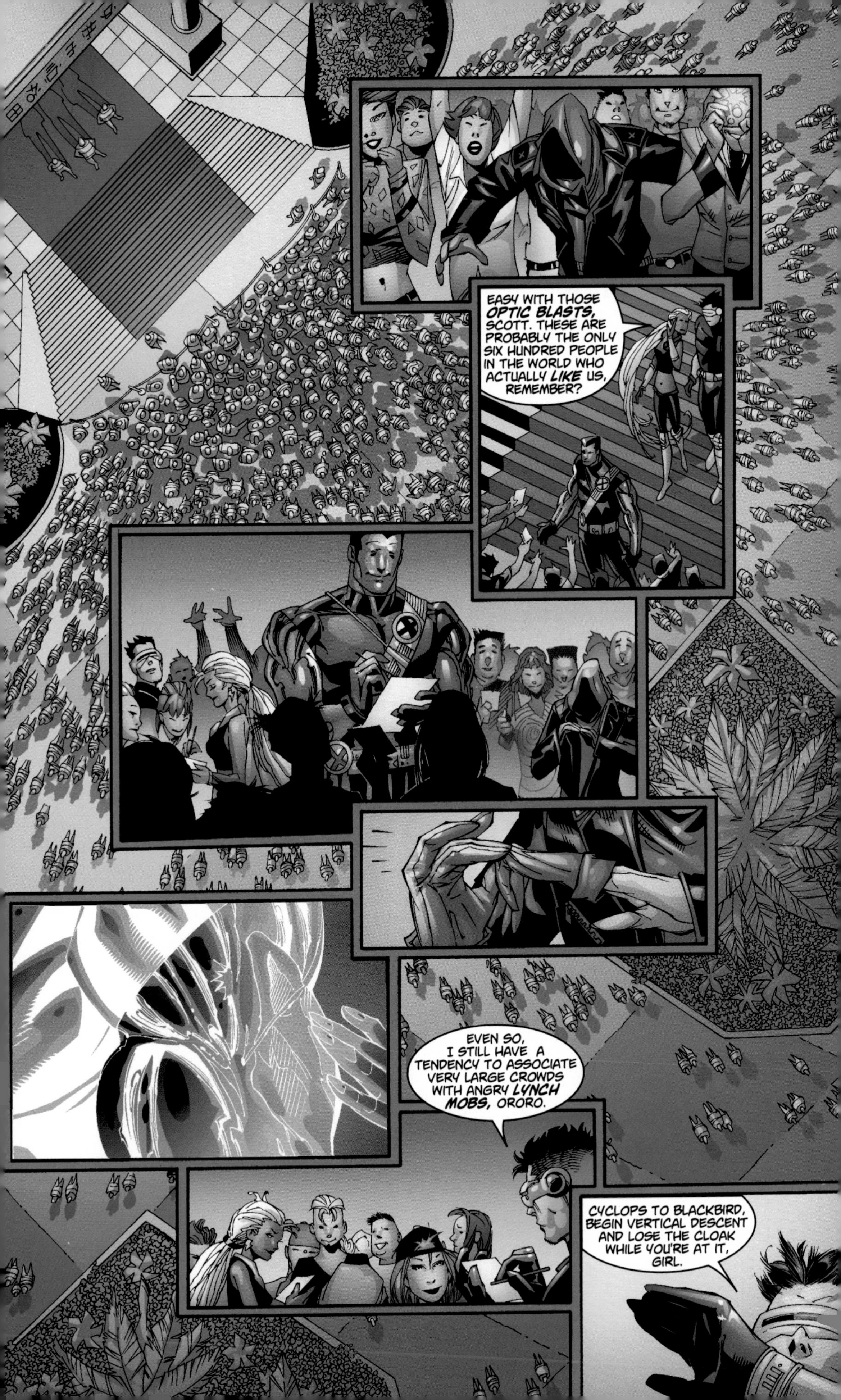
EASY WITH THOSE OPTIC BLASTS, SCOTT. THESE ARE PROBABLY THE ONLY SIX HUNDRED PEOPLE IN THE WORLD WHO ACTUALLY LIKE US, REMEMBER?
EVEN SO, I STILL HAVE A TENDENCY TO ASSOCIATE VERY LARGE CROWDS WITH ANGRY LYNCH MOBS, ORORO.
CYCLOPS TO BLACKBIRD, BEGIN VERTICAL DESCENT AND LOSE THE CLOAK WHILE YOU'RE AT IT, GIRL.

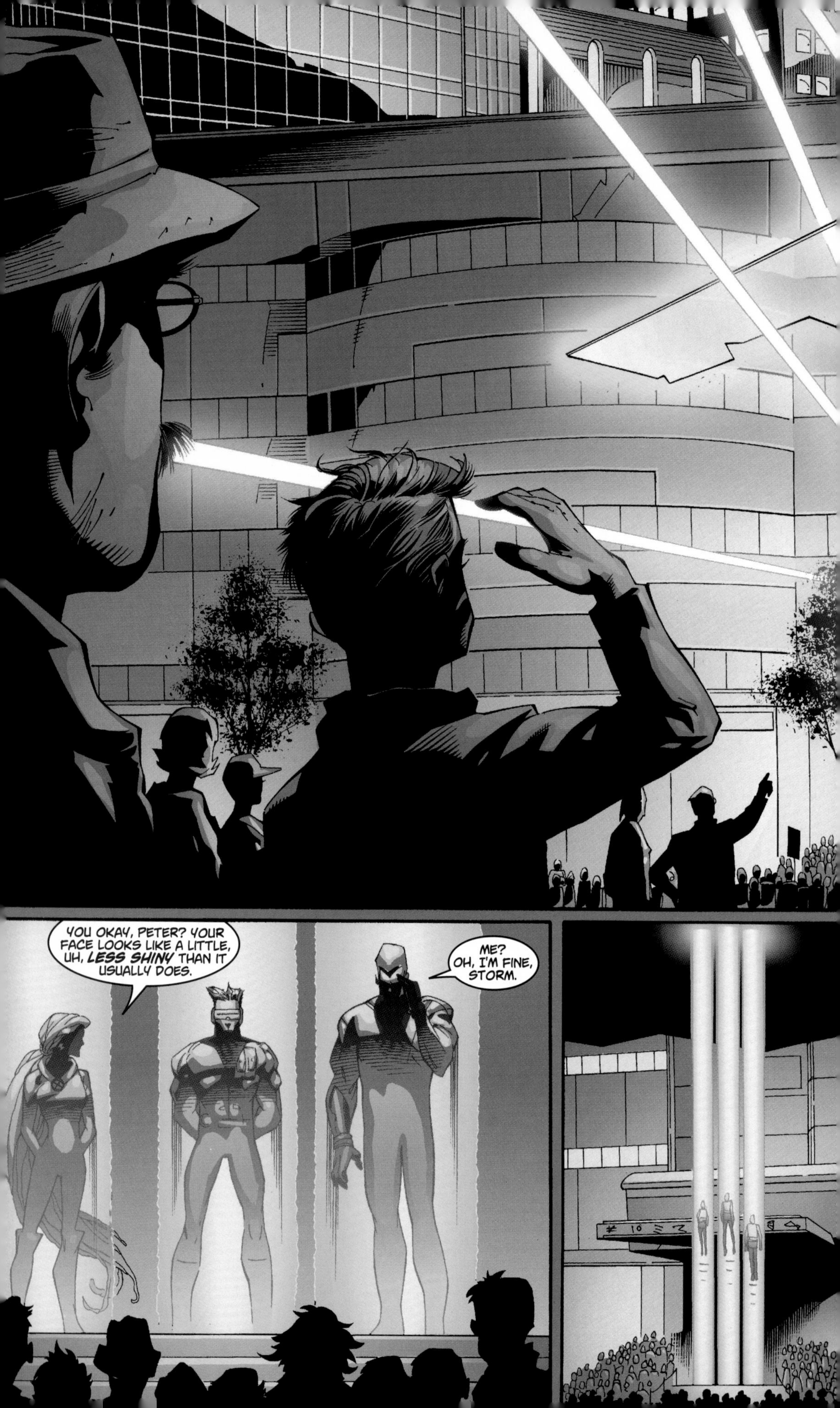
YOU OKAY, PETER? YOUR FACE LOOKS LIKE A LITTLE, UH, **LESS SHINY** THAN IT USUALLY DOES.
ME? OH, I'M FINE, STORM.

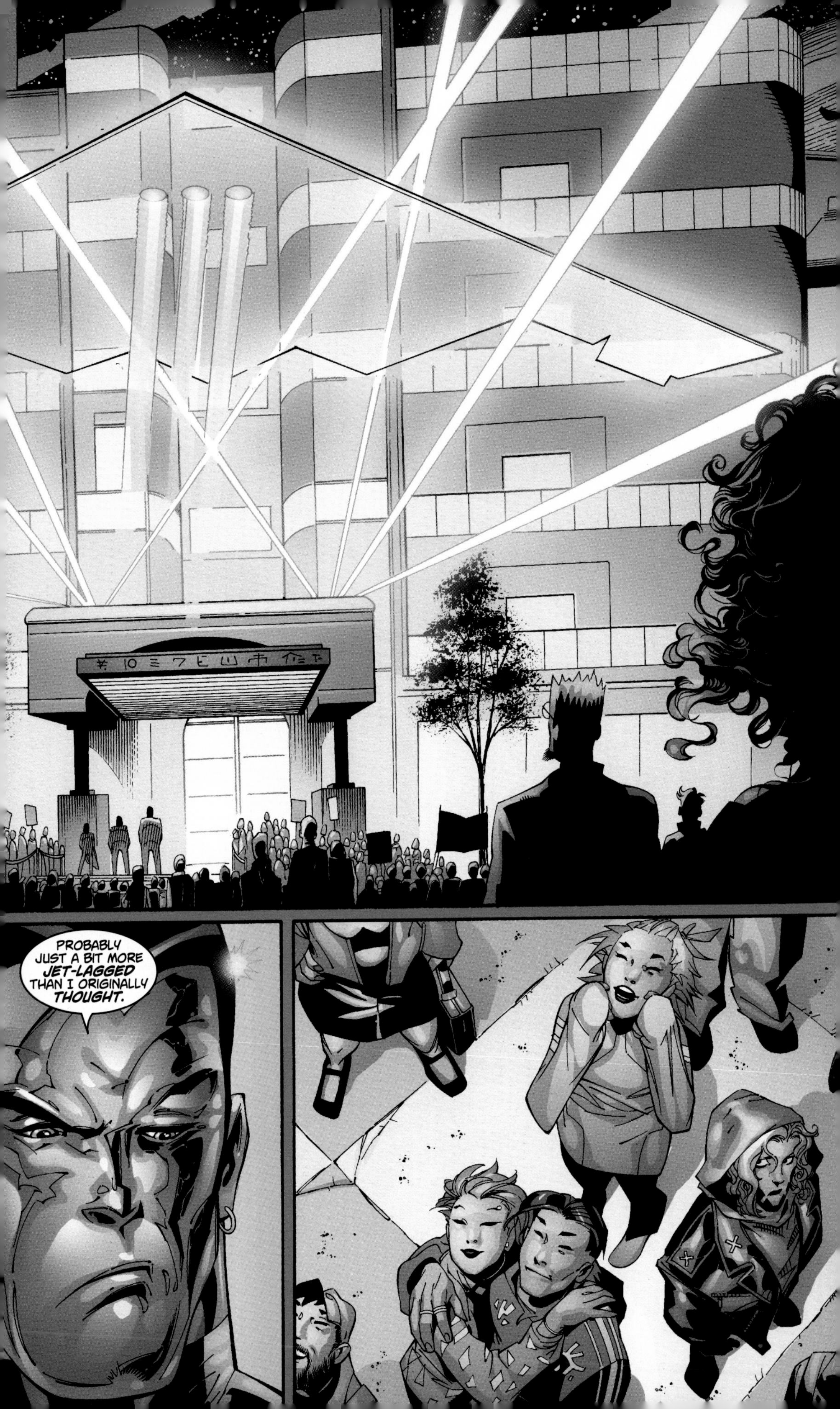
PROBABLY JUST A BIT MORE JET-LAGGED THAN I ORIGINALLY THOUGHT.

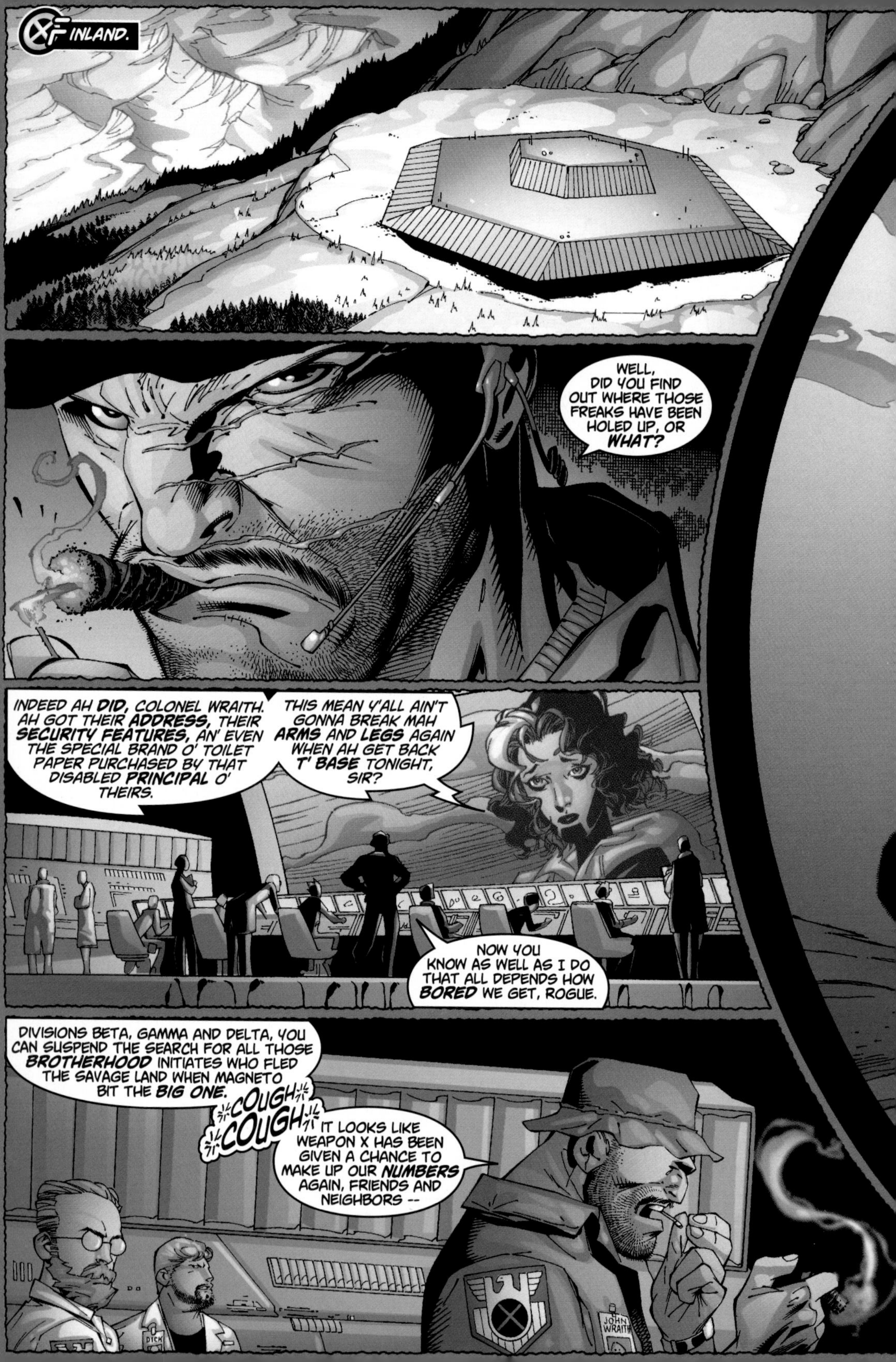
FINLAND.
WELL, DID YOU FIND OUT WHERE THOSE FREAKS HAVE BEEN HOLED UP, OR WHAT?
INDEED AH DID, COLONEL WRAITH. AH GOT THEIR ADDRESS, THEIR SECURITY FEATURES, AN' EVEN THE SPECIAL BRAND O' TOILET PAPER PURCHASED BY THAT DISABLED PRINCIPAL O' THEIRS.
THIS MEAN Y'ALL AIN'T GONNA BREAK MAH ARMS AND LEGS AGAIN WHEN AH GET BACK T' BASE TONIGHT, SIR?
NOW YOU KNOW AS WELL AS I DO THAT ALL DEPENDS HOW BORED WE GET, ROGUE.
DIVISIONS BETA, GAMMA AND DELTA, YOU CAN SUSPEND THE SEARCH FOR ALL THOSE BROTHERHOOD INITIATES WHO FLED THE SAVAGE LAND WHEN MAGNETO BIT THE BIG ONE.
COUGH COUGH
IT LOOKS LIKE WEAPON X HAS BEEN GIVEN A CHANCE TO MAKE UP OUR NUMBERS AGAIN, FRIENDS AND NEIGHBORS --
DICK
JOHN WRAITH

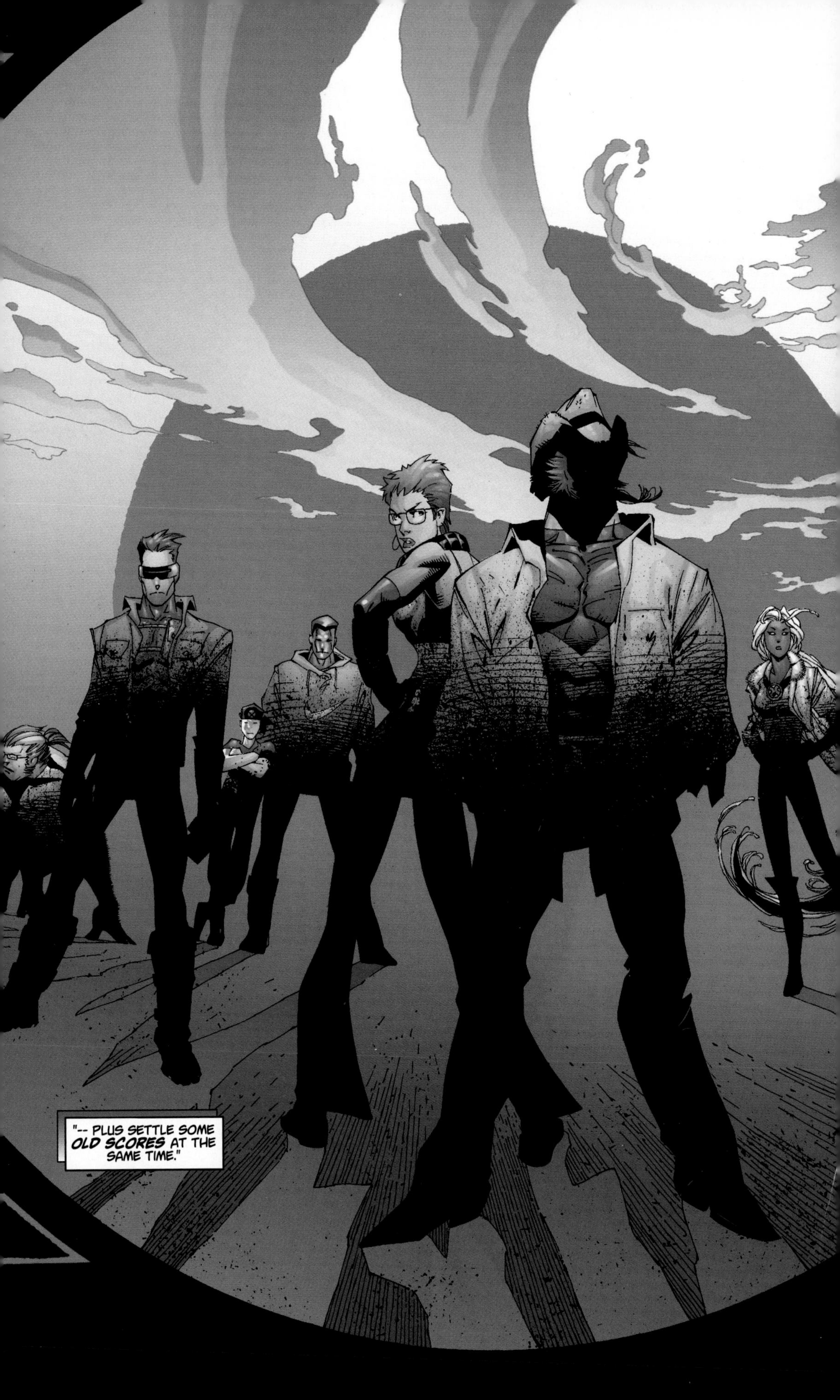
"-- PLUS SETTLE SOME OLD SCORES AT THE SAME TIME."

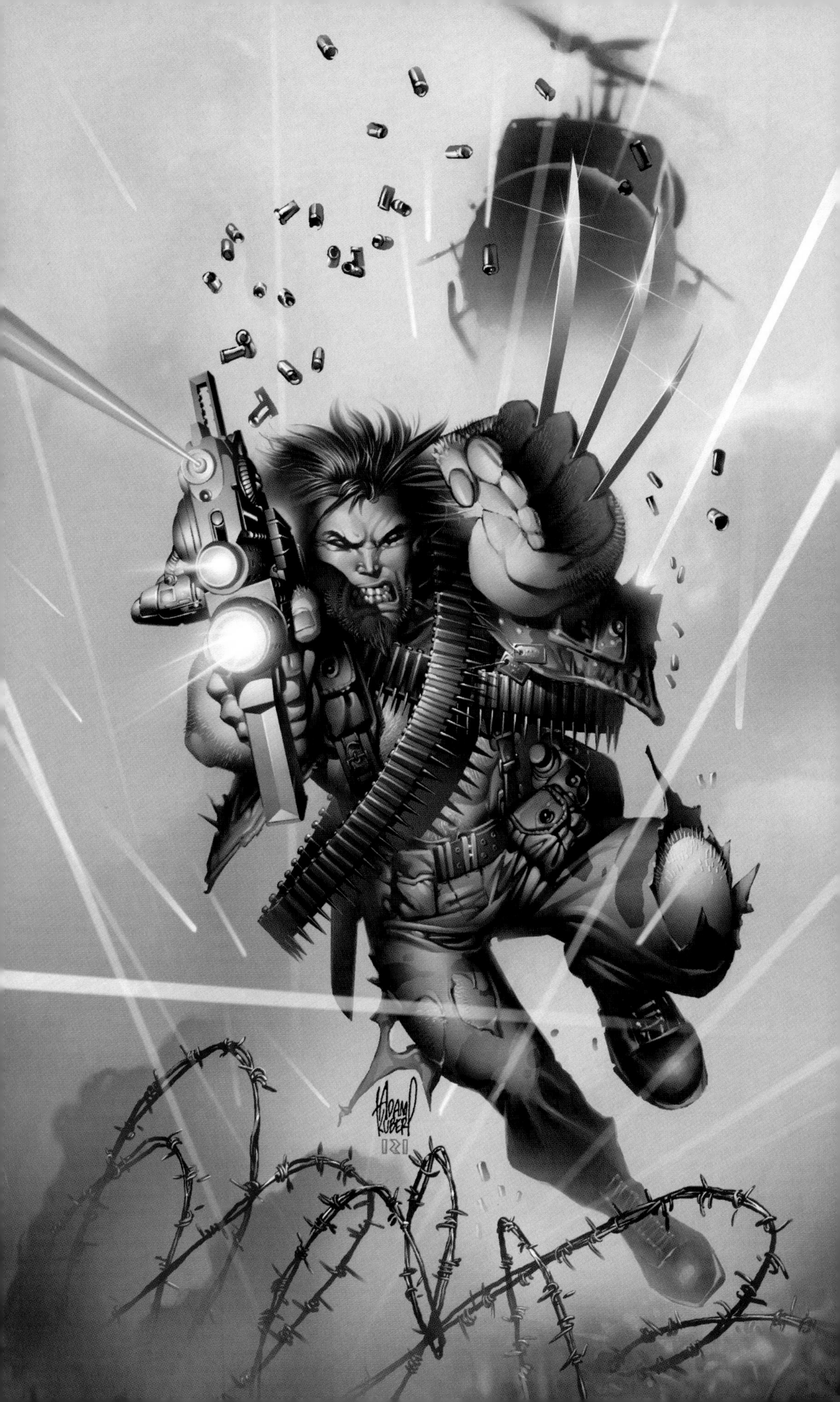
ADAM KUBERT

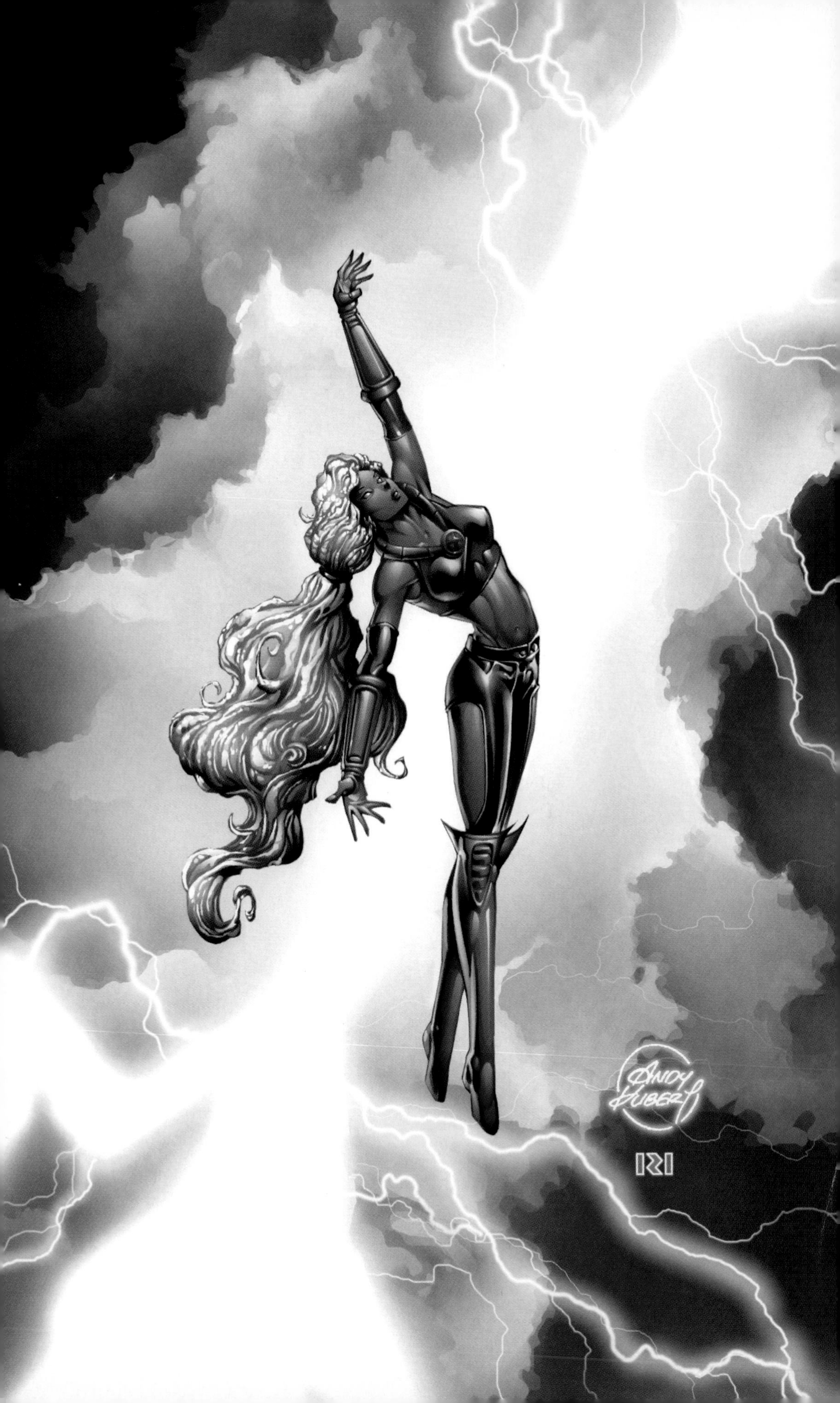
ANDY KUBERT

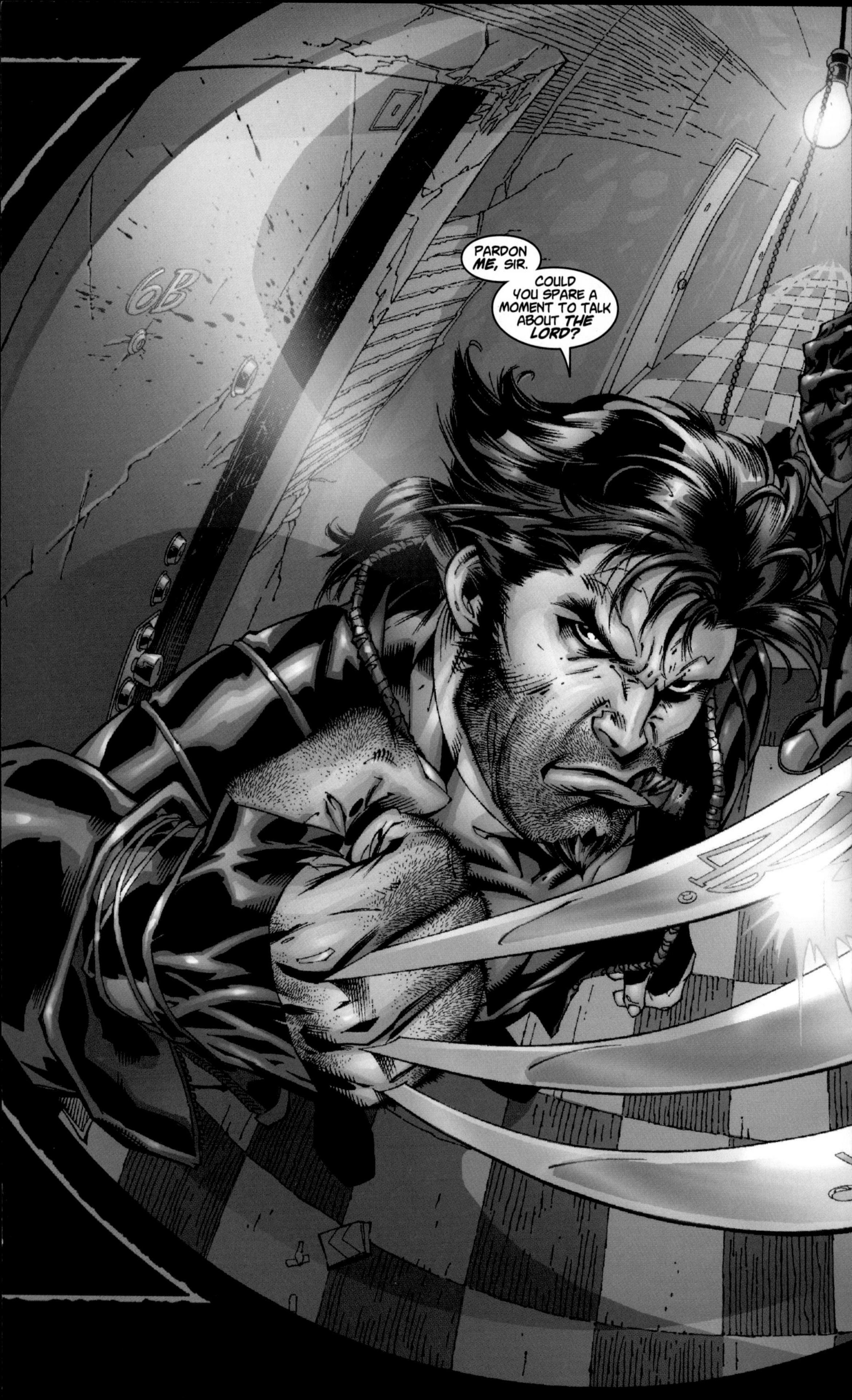
PARDON ME, SIR.
COULD YOU SPARE A MOMENT TO TALK ABOUT THE LORD?

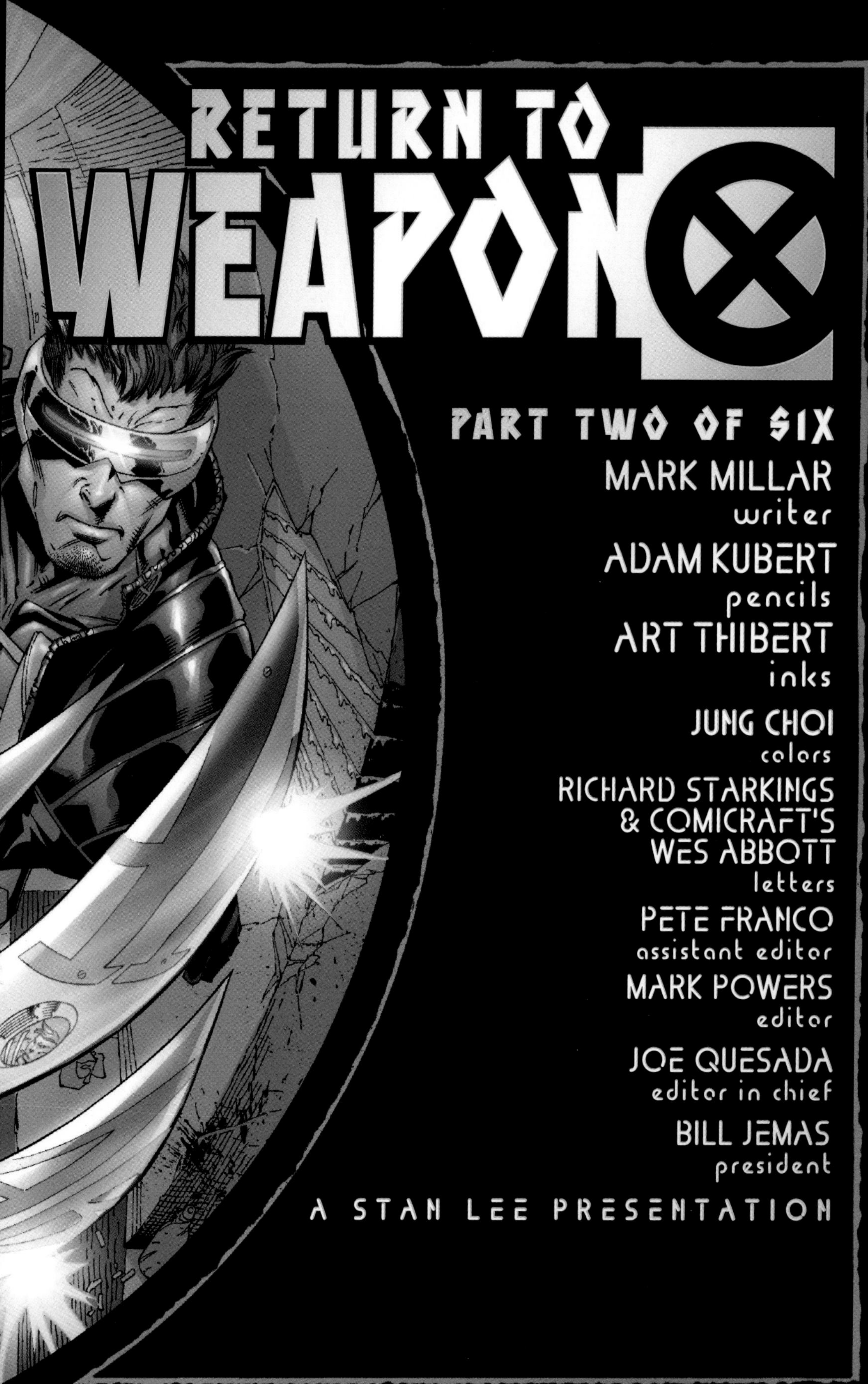

RETURN TO WEAPON X

PART TWO OF SIX

MARK MILLAR
writer

ADAM KUBERT
pencils

ART THIBERT
inks

JUNG CHOI
colors

RICHARD STARKINGS
& COMICRAFT'S
WES ABBOTT
letters

PETE FRANCO
assistant editor

MARK POWERS
editor

JOE QUESADA
editor in chief

BILL JEMAS
president

A STAN LEE PRESENTATION

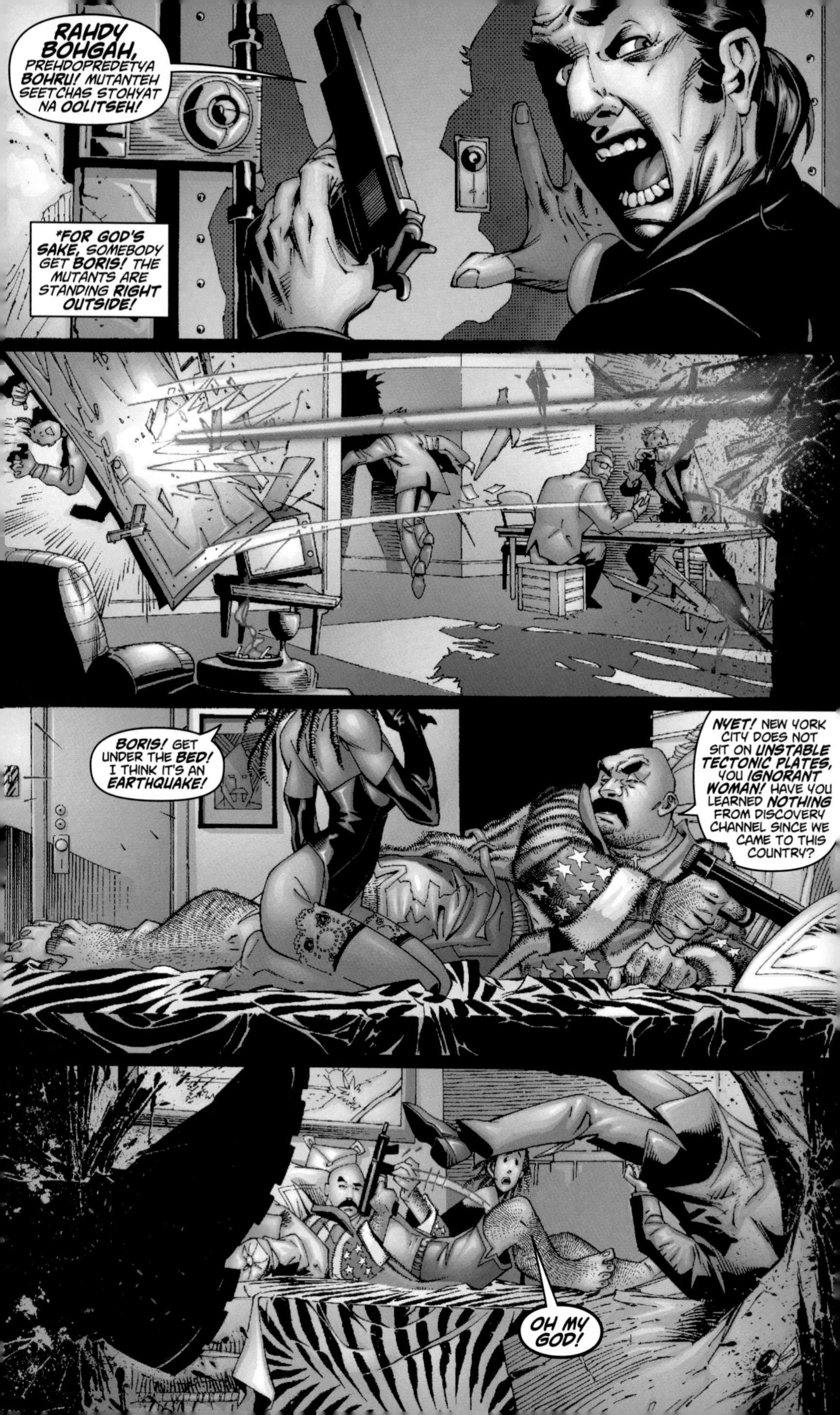
RAHDY BOHGAH, PREHDOPREDETYA BOHRU! MUTANTEH SEETCHAS STOHYAT NA OOLITSEH!
*FOR GOD'S SAKE, SOMEBODY GET BORIS! THE MUTANTS ARE STANDING RIGHT OUTSIDE!
BORIS! GET UNDER THE BED! I THINK IT'S AN EARTHQUAKE!
NYET! NEW YORK CITY DOES NOT SIT ON UNSTABLE TECTONIC PLATES, YOU IGNORANT WOMAN! HAVE YOU LEARNED NOTHING FROM DISCOVERY CHANNEL SINCE WE CAME TO THIS COUNTRY?
OH MY GOD!

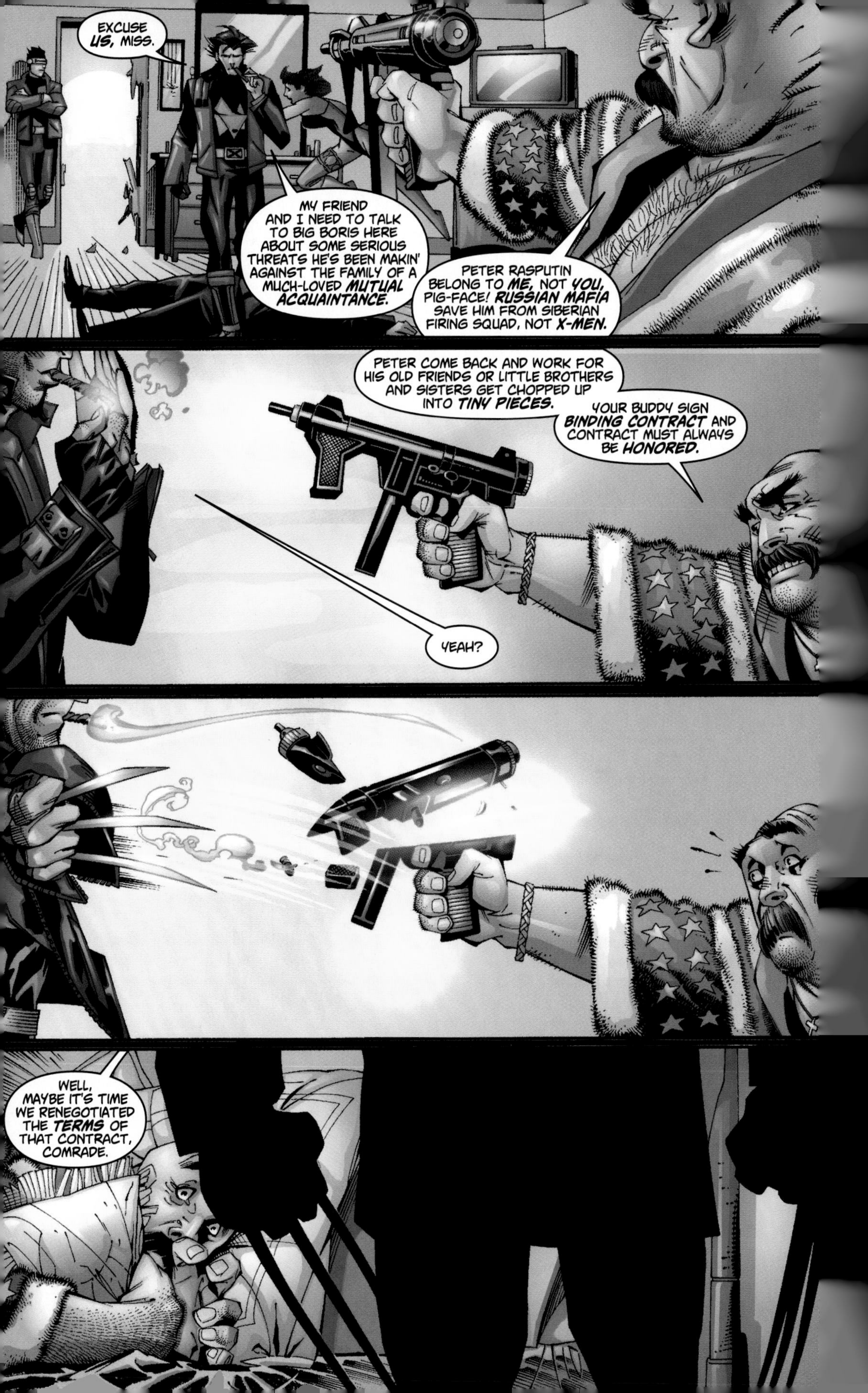
EXCUSE US, MISS.
MY FRIEND AND I NEED TO TALK TO BIG BORIS HERE ABOUT SOME SERIOUS THREATS HE'S BEEN MAKIN' AGAINST THE FAMILY OF A MUCH-LOVED MUTUAL ACQUAINTANCE.
PETER RASPUTIN BELONG TO ME, NOT YOU, PIG-FACE! RUSSIAN MAFIA SAVE HIM FROM SIBERIAN FIRING SQUAD, NOT X-MEN.
PETER COME BACK AND WORK FOR HIS OLD FRIENDS OR LITTLE BROTHERS AND SISTERS GET CHOPPED UP INTO TINY PIECES.
YOUR BUDDY SIGN BINDING CONTRACT AND CONTRACT MUST ALWAYS BE HONORED.
YEAH?
WELL, MAYBE IT'S TIME WE RENEGOTIATED THE TERMS OF THAT CONTRACT, COMRADE.

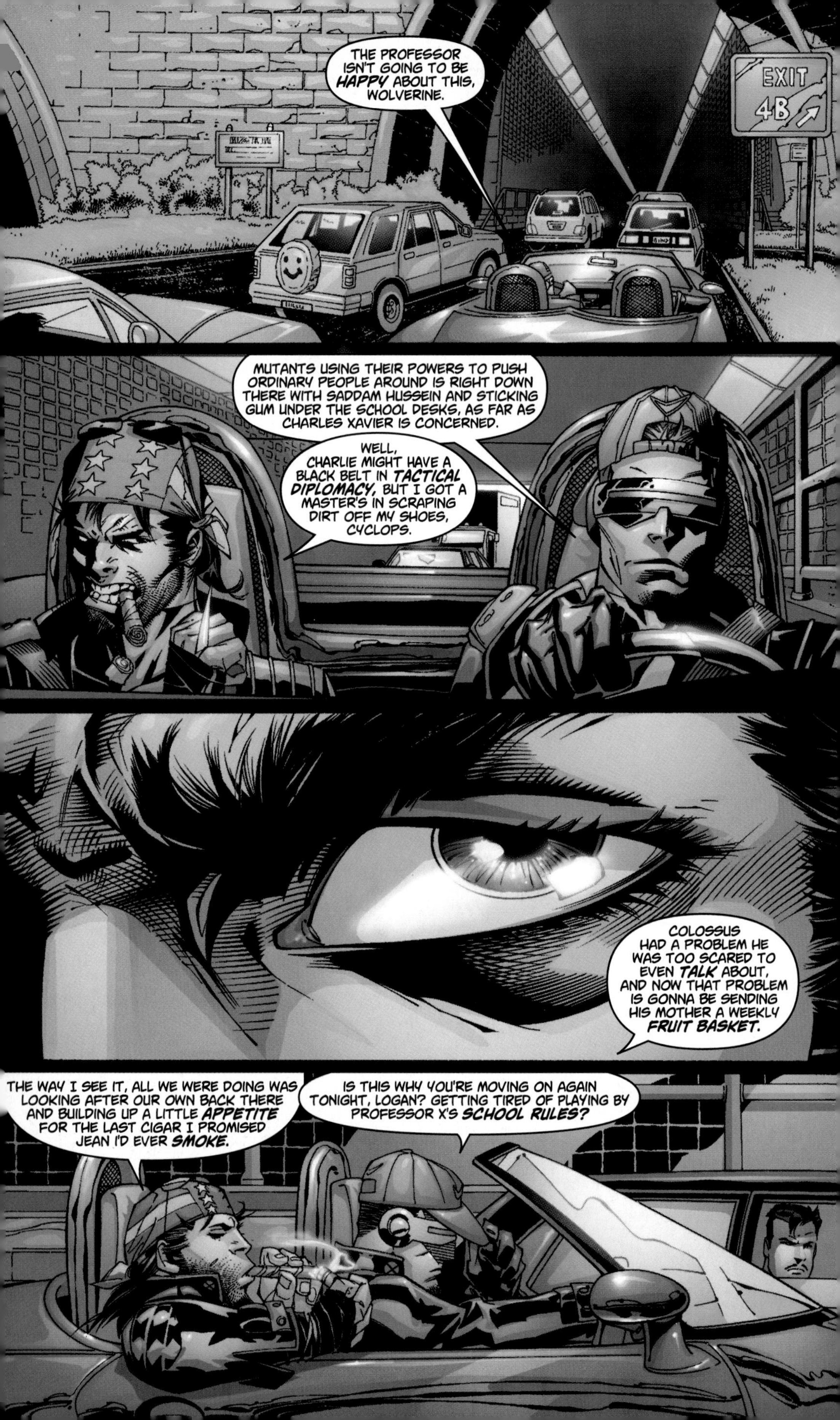
THE PROFESSOR ISN'T GOING TO BE HAPPY ABOUT THIS, WOLVERINE.
EXIT 4B
MUTANTS USING THEIR POWERS TO PUSH ORDINARY PEOPLE AROUND IS RIGHT DOWN THERE WITH SADDAM HUSSEIN AND STICKING GUM UNDER THE SCHOOL DESKS, AS FAR AS CHARLES XAVIER IS CONCERNED.
WELL, CHARLIE MIGHT HAVE A BLACK BELT IN TACTICAL DIPLOMACY, BUT I GOT A MASTER'S IN SCRAPING DIRT OFF MY SHOES, CYCLOPS.
COLOSSUS HAD A PROBLEM HE WAS TOO SCARED TO EVEN TALK ABOUT, AND NOW THAT PROBLEM IS GONNA BE SENDING HIS MOTHER A WEEKLY FRUIT BASKET.
THE WAY I SEE IT, ALL WE WERE DOING WAS LOOKING AFTER OUR OWN BACK THERE AND BUILDING UP A LITTLE APPETITE FOR THE LAST CIGAR I PROMISED JEAN I'D EVER SMOKE.
IS THIS WHY YOU'RE MOVING ON AGAIN TONIGHT, LOGAN? GETTING TIRED OF PLAYING BY PROFESSOR X'S SCHOOL RULES?

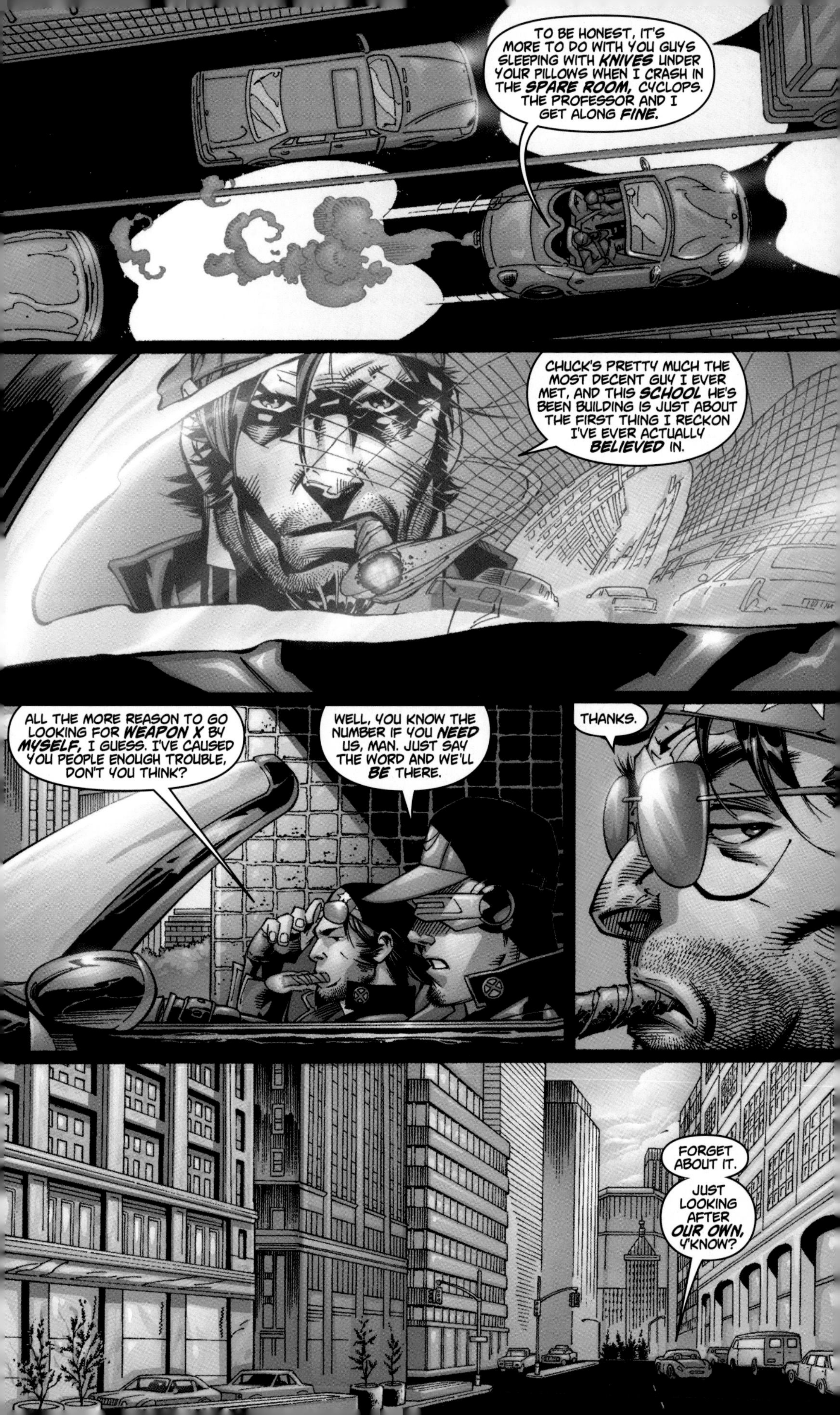

TO BE HONEST, IT'S MORE TO DO WITH YOU GUYS SLEEPING WITH KNIVES UNDER YOUR PILLOWS WHEN I CRASH IN THE SPARE ROOM, CYCLOPS. THE PROFESSOR AND I GET ALONG FINE.
CHUCK'S PRETTY MUCH THE MOST DECENT GUY I EVER MET, AND THIS SCHOOL HE'S BEEN BUILDING IS JUST ABOUT THE FIRST THING I RECKON I'VE EVER ACTUALLY BELIEVED IN.
ALL THE MORE REASON TO GO LOOKING FOR WEAPON X BY MYSELF, I GUESS. I'VE CAUSED YOU PEOPLE ENOUGH TROUBLE, DON'T YOU THINK?
WELL, YOU KNOW THE NUMBER IF YOU NEED US, MAN. JUST SAY THE WORD AND WE'LL BE THERE.
THANKS.
FORGET ABOUT IT.
JUST LOOKING AFTER OUR OWN, Y'KNOW?

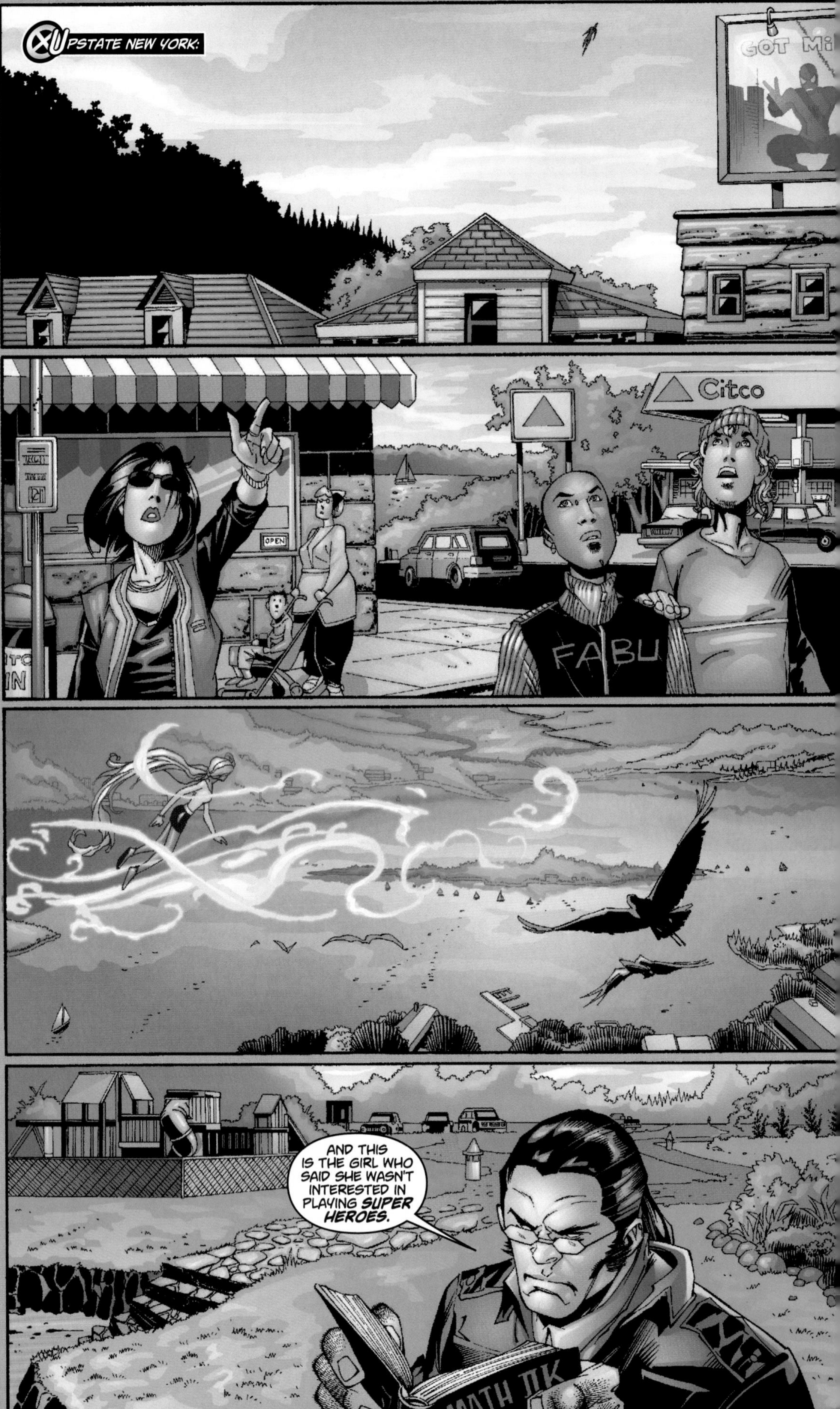
UPSTATE NEW YORK:
GOT MI
Citco
OPEN
FABU
AND THIS IS THE GIRL WHO SAID SHE WASN'T INTERESTED IN PLAYING SUPER HEROES.
MATH IIK

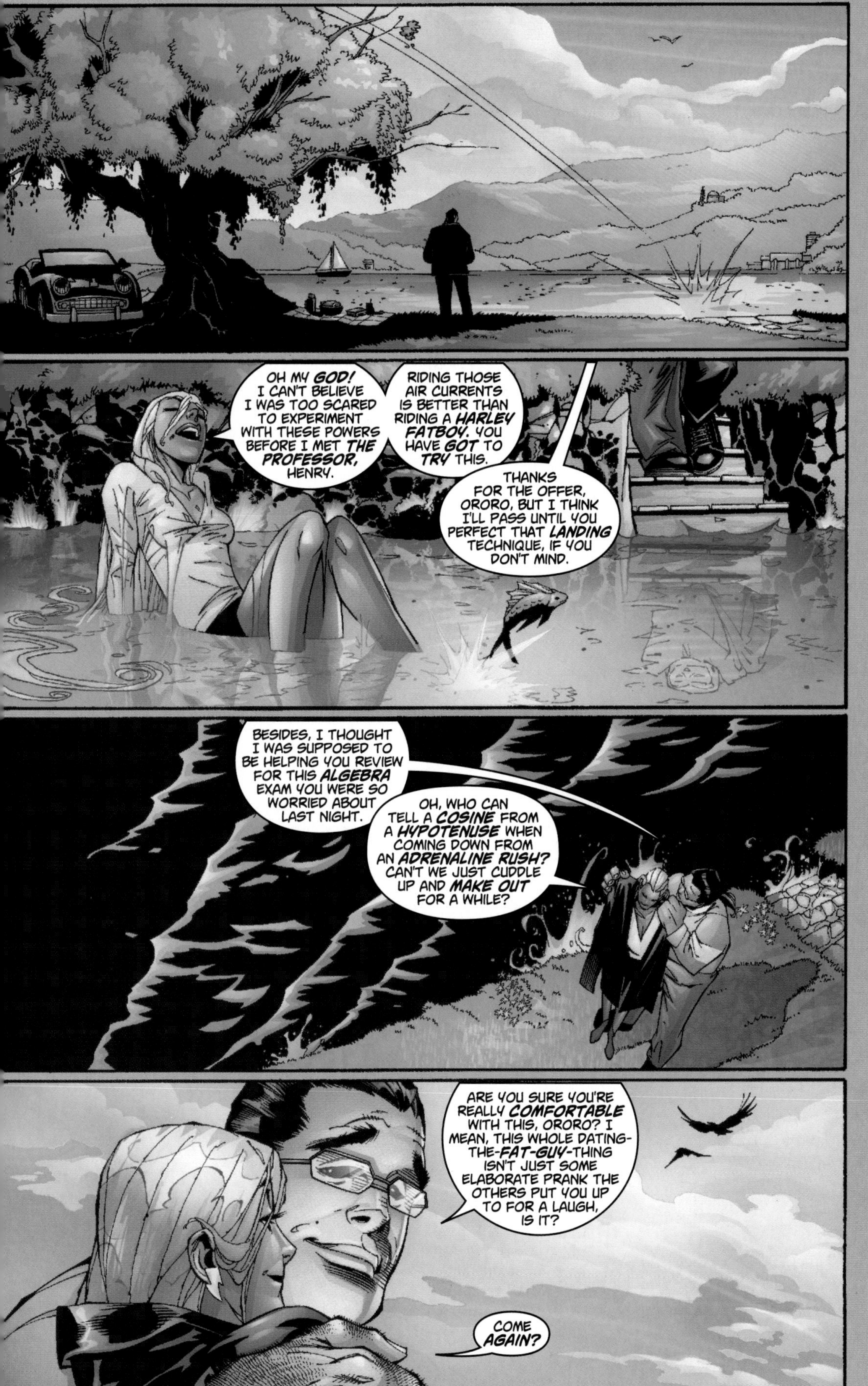
OH MY GOD! I CAN'T BELIEVE I WAS TOO SCARED TO EXPERIMENT WITH THESE POWERS BEFORE I MET THE PROFESSOR, HENRY.
RIDING THOSE AIR CURRENTS IS BETTER THAN RIDING A HARLEY FATBOY. YOU HAVE GOT TO TRY THIS.
THANKS FOR THE OFFER, ORORO, BUT I THINK I'LL PASS UNTIL YOU PERFECT THAT LANDING TECHNIQUE, IF YOU DON'T MIND.
BESIDES, I THOUGHT I WAS SUPPOSED TO BE HELPING YOU REVIEW FOR THIS ALGEBRA EXAM YOU WERE SO WORRIED ABOUT LAST NIGHT.
OH, WHO CAN TELL A COSINE FROM A HYPOTENUSE WHEN COMING DOWN FROM AN ADRENALINE RUSH? CAN'T WE JUST CUDDLE UP AND MAKE OUT FOR A WHILE?
ARE YOU SURE YOU'RE REALLY COMFORTABLE WITH THIS, ORORO? I MEAN, THIS WHOLE DATING-THE-FAT-GUY-THING ISN'T JUST SOME ELABORATE PRANK THE OTHERS PUT YOU UP TO FOR A LAUGH, IS IT?
COME AGAIN?

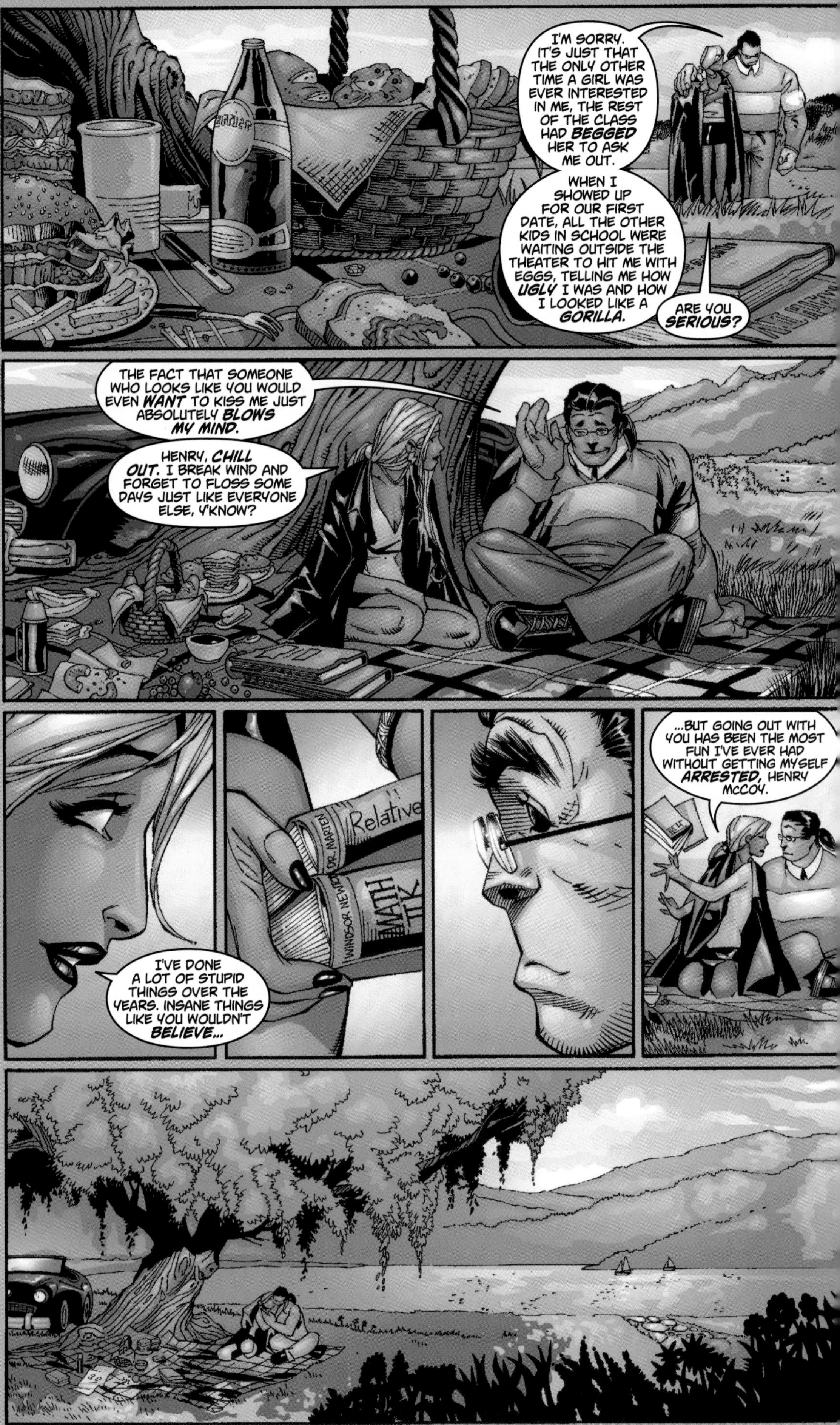
I'M SORRY. IT'S JUST THAT THE ONLY OTHER TIME A GIRL WAS EVER INTERESTED IN ME, THE REST OF THE CLASS HAD BEGGED HER TO ASK ME OUT.
WHEN I SHOWED UP FOR OUR FIRST DATE, ALL THE OTHER KIDS IN SCHOOL WERE WAITING OUTSIDE THE THEATER TO HIT ME WITH EGGS, TELLING ME HOW UGLY I WAS AND HOW I LOOKED LIKE A GORILLA.
ARE YOU SERIOUS?
THE FACT THAT SOMEONE WHO LOOKS LIKE YOU WOULD EVEN WANT TO KISS ME JUST ABSOLUTELY BLOWS MY MIND.
HENRY, CHILL OUT. I BREAK WIND AND FORGET TO FLOSS SOME DAYS JUST LIKE EVERYONE ELSE, Y'KNOW?
I'VE DONE A LOT OF STUPID THINGS OVER THE YEARS. INSANE THINGS LIKE YOU WOULDN'T BELIEVE...
Relative
DR. MARTEN
WINDSOR NEWTON
MATH
...BUT GOING OUT WITH YOU HAS BEEN THE MOST FUN I'VE EVER HAD WITHOUT GETTING MYSELF ARRESTED, HENRY McCOY.

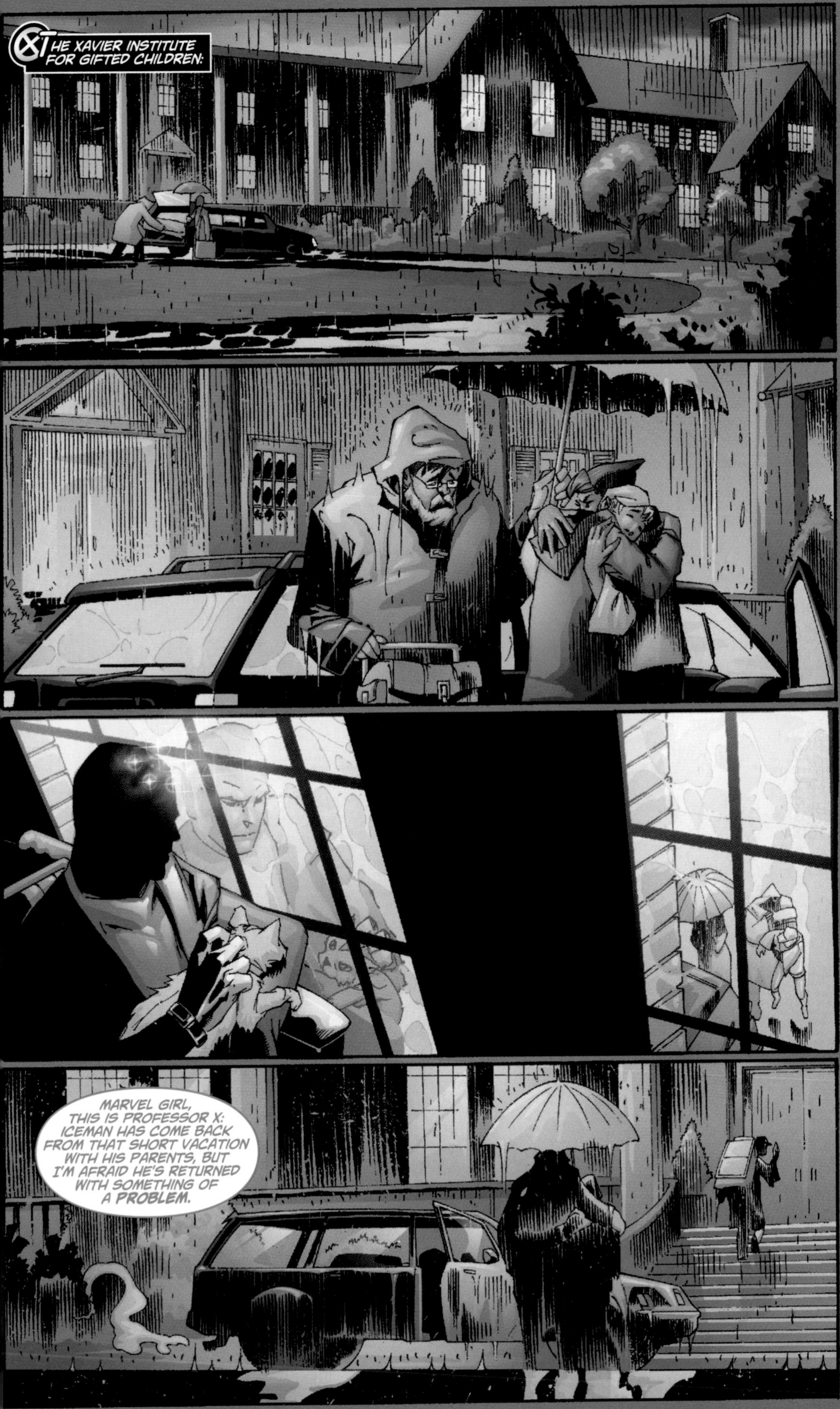
THE XAVIER INSTITUTE FOR GIFTED CHILDREN:
MARVEL GIRL, THIS IS PROFESSOR X: ICEMAN HAS COME BACK FROM THAT SHORT VACATION WITH HIS PARENTS, BUT I'M AFRAID HE'S RETURNED WITH SOMETHING OF A PROBLEM.

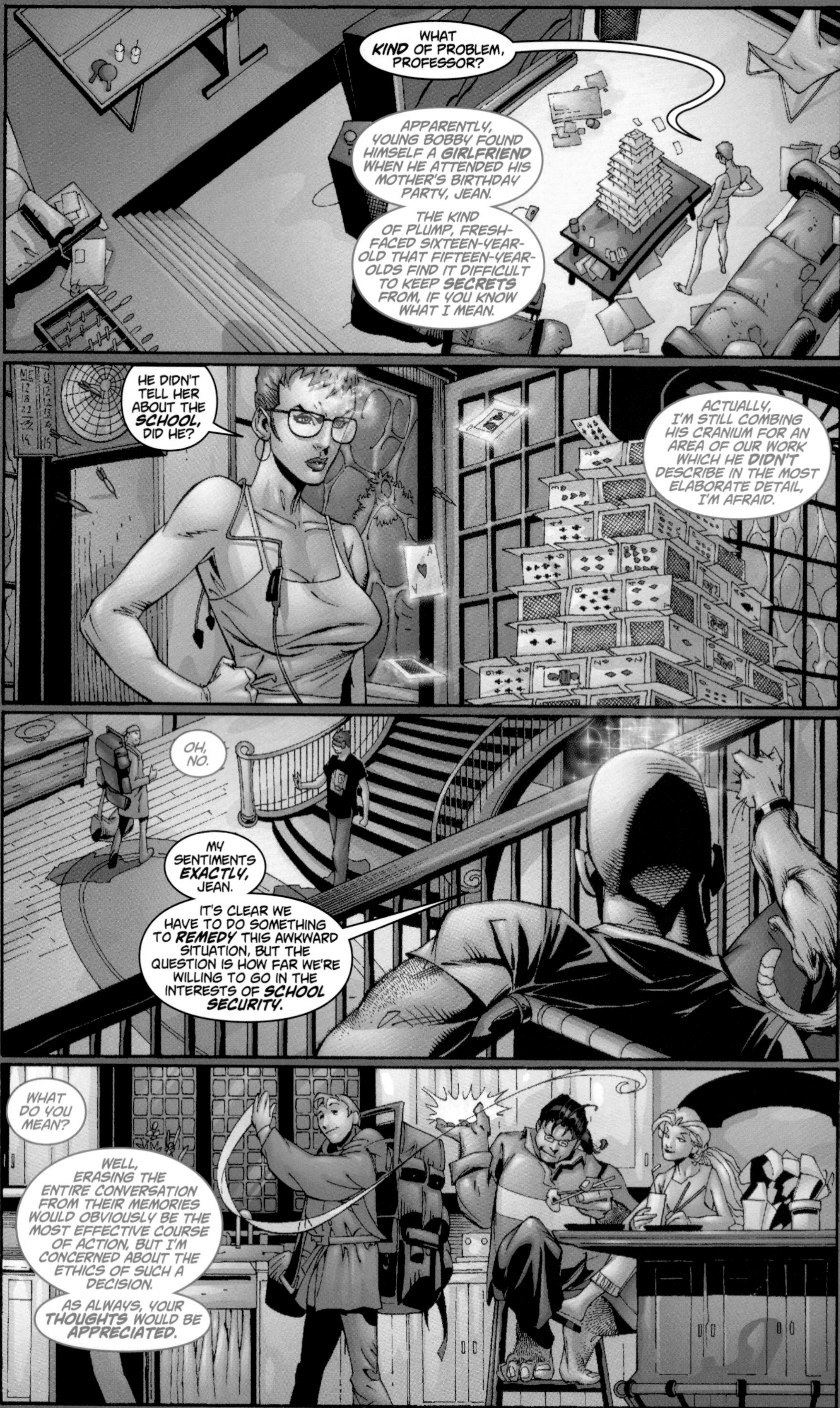
WHAT KIND OF PROBLEM, PROFESSOR?
APPARENTLY, YOUNG BOBBY FOUND HIMSELF A GIRLFRIEND WHEN HE ATTENDED HIS MOTHER'S BIRTHDAY PARTY, JEAN.
THE KIND OF PLUMP, FRESH-FACED SIXTEEN-YEAR-OLD THAT FIFTEEN-YEAR-OLDS FIND IT DIFFICULT TO KEEP SECRETS FROM, IF YOU KNOW WHAT I MEAN.
HE DIDN'T TELL HER ABOUT THE SCHOOL, DID HE?
ACTUALLY, I'M STILL COMBING HIS CRANIUM FOR AN AREA OF OUR WORK WHICH HE DIDN'T DESCRIBE IN THE MOST ELABORATE DETAIL, I'M AFRAID.
OH, NO.
MY SENTIMENTS EXACTLY, JEAN.
IT'S CLEAR WE HAVE TO DO SOMETHING TO REMEDY THIS AWKWARD SITUATION, BUT THE QUESTION IS HOW FAR WE'RE WILLING TO GO IN THE INTERESTS OF SCHOOL SECURITY.
WHAT DO YOU MEAN?
WELL, ERASING THE ENTIRE CONVERSATION FROM THEIR MEMORIES WOULD OBVIOUSLY BE THE MOST EFFECTIVE COURSE OF ACTION, BUT I'M CONCERNED ABOUT THE ETHICS OF SUCH A DECISION.
AS ALWAYS, YOUR THOUGHTS WOULD BE APPRECIATED.

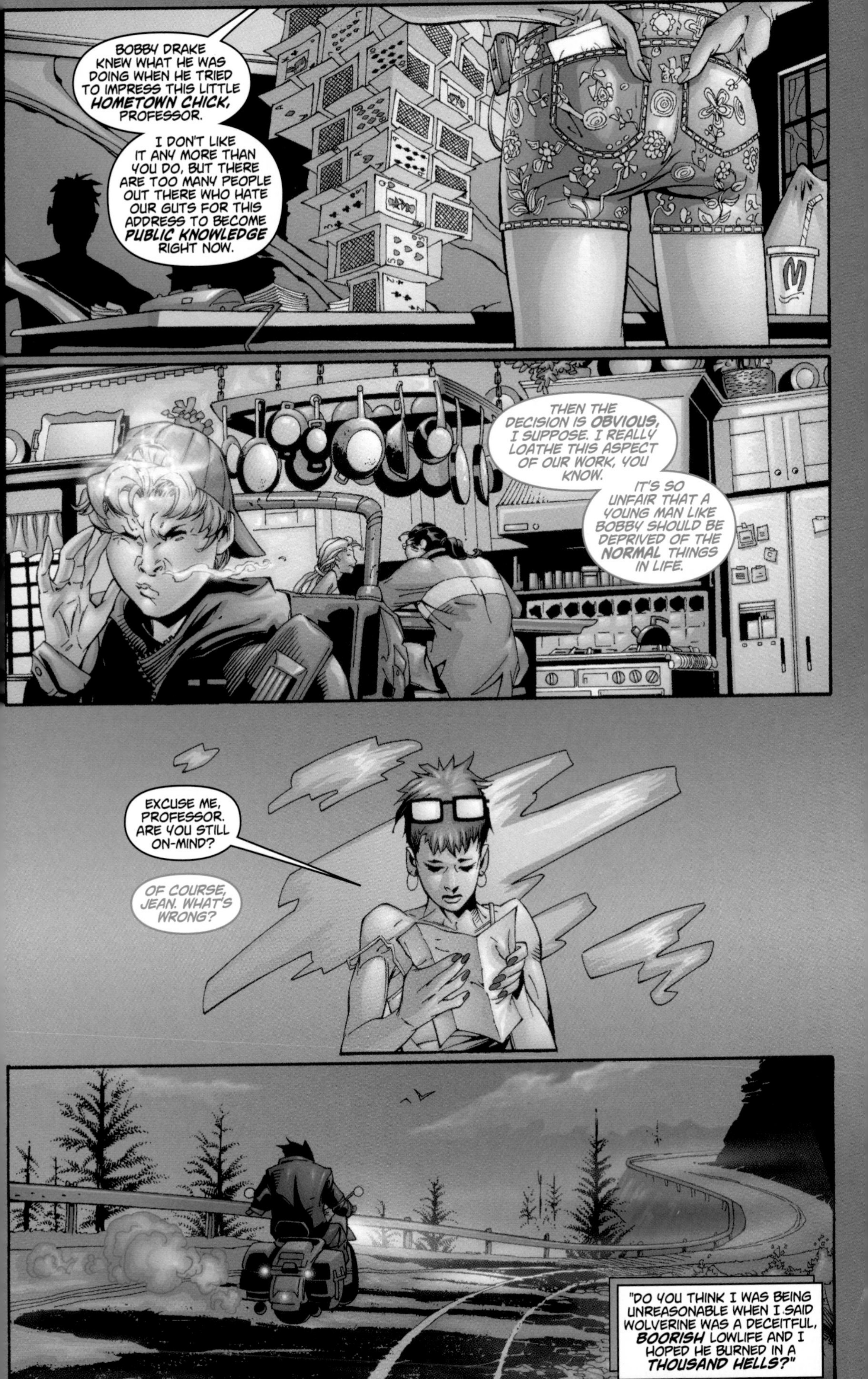
BOBBY DRAKE KNEW WHAT HE WAS DOING WHEN HE TRIED TO IMPRESS THIS LITTLE **HOMETOWN CHICK,** PROFESSOR.
I DON'T LIKE IT ANY MORE THAN YOU DO, BUT THERE ARE TOO MANY PEOPLE OUT THERE WHO HATE OUR GUTS FOR THIS ADDRESS TO BECOME **PUBLIC KNOWLEDGE** RIGHT NOW.
*THEN THE DECISION IS **OBVIOUS,** I SUPPOSE. I REALLY LOATHE THIS ASPECT OF OUR WORK, YOU KNOW.*
*IT'S SO UNFAIR THAT A YOUNG MAN LIKE BOBBY SHOULD BE DEPRIVED OF THE **NORMAL** THINGS IN LIFE.*
EXCUSE ME, PROFESSOR. ARE YOU STILL ON-MIND?
OF COURSE, JEAN. WHAT'S WRONG?
"DO YOU THINK I WAS BEING UNREASONABLE WHEN I SAID WOLVERINE WAS A DECEITFUL, **BOORISH** LOWLIFE AND I HOPED HE BURNED IN A **THOUSAND HELLS?"**

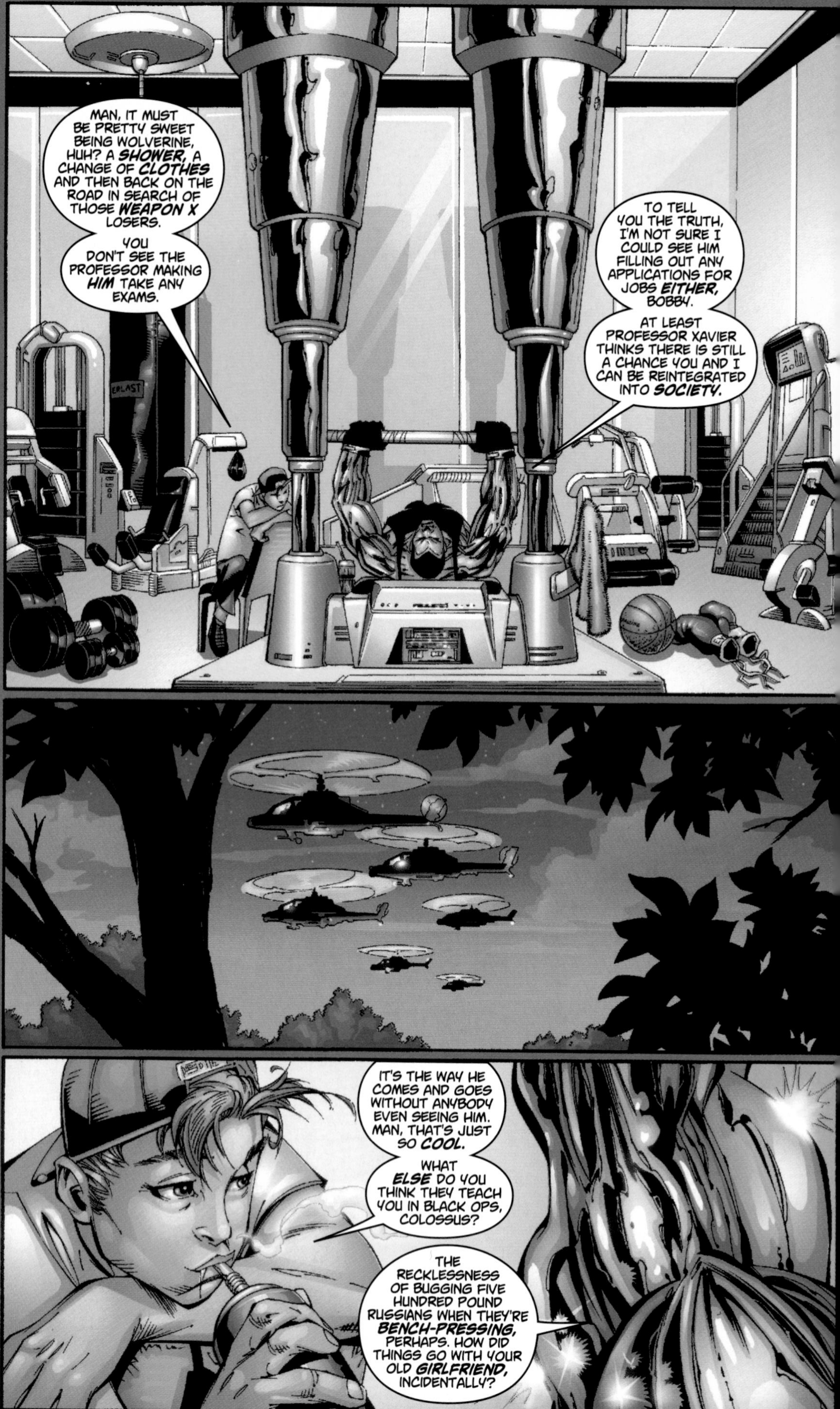

MAN, IT MUST BE PRETTY SWEET BEING WOLVERINE, HUH? A SHOWER, A CHANGE OF CLOTHES AND THEN BACK ON THE ROAD IN SEARCH OF THOSE WEAPON X LOSERS.
YOU DON'T SEE THE PROFESSOR MAKING HIM TAKE ANY EXAMS.
TO TELL YOU THE TRUTH, I'M NOT SURE I COULD SEE HIM FILLING OUT ANY APPLICATIONS FOR JOBS EITHER, BOBBY.
AT LEAST PROFESSOR XAVIER THINKS THERE IS STILL A CHANCE YOU AND I CAN BE REINTEGRATED INTO SOCIETY.
IT'S THE WAY HE COMES AND GOES WITHOUT ANYBODY EVEN SEEING HIM. MAN, THAT'S JUST SO COOL.
WHAT ELSE DO YOU THINK THEY TEACH YOU IN BLACK OPS, COLOSSUS?
THE RECKLESSNESS OF BUGGING FIVE HUNDRED POUND RUSSIANS WHEN THEY'RE BENCH-PRESSING, PERHAPS. HOW DID THINGS GO WITH YOUR OLD GIRLFRIEND, INCIDENTALLY?

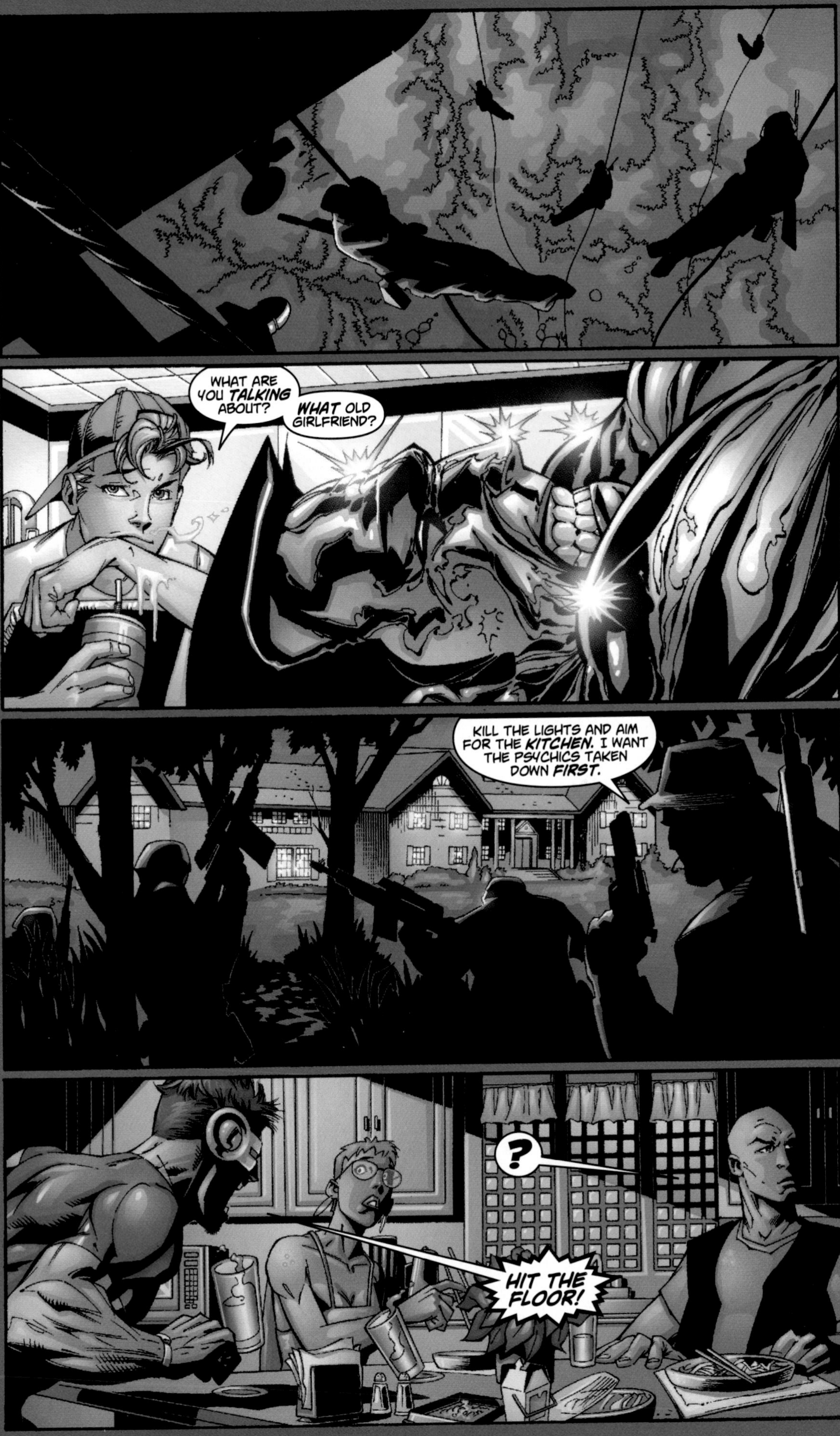
WHAT ARE YOU TALKING ABOUT?
WHAT OLD GIRLFRIEND?
KILL THE LIGHTS AND AIM FOR THE KITCHEN. I WANT THE PSYCHICS TAKEN DOWN FIRST.
?
HIT THE FLOOR!

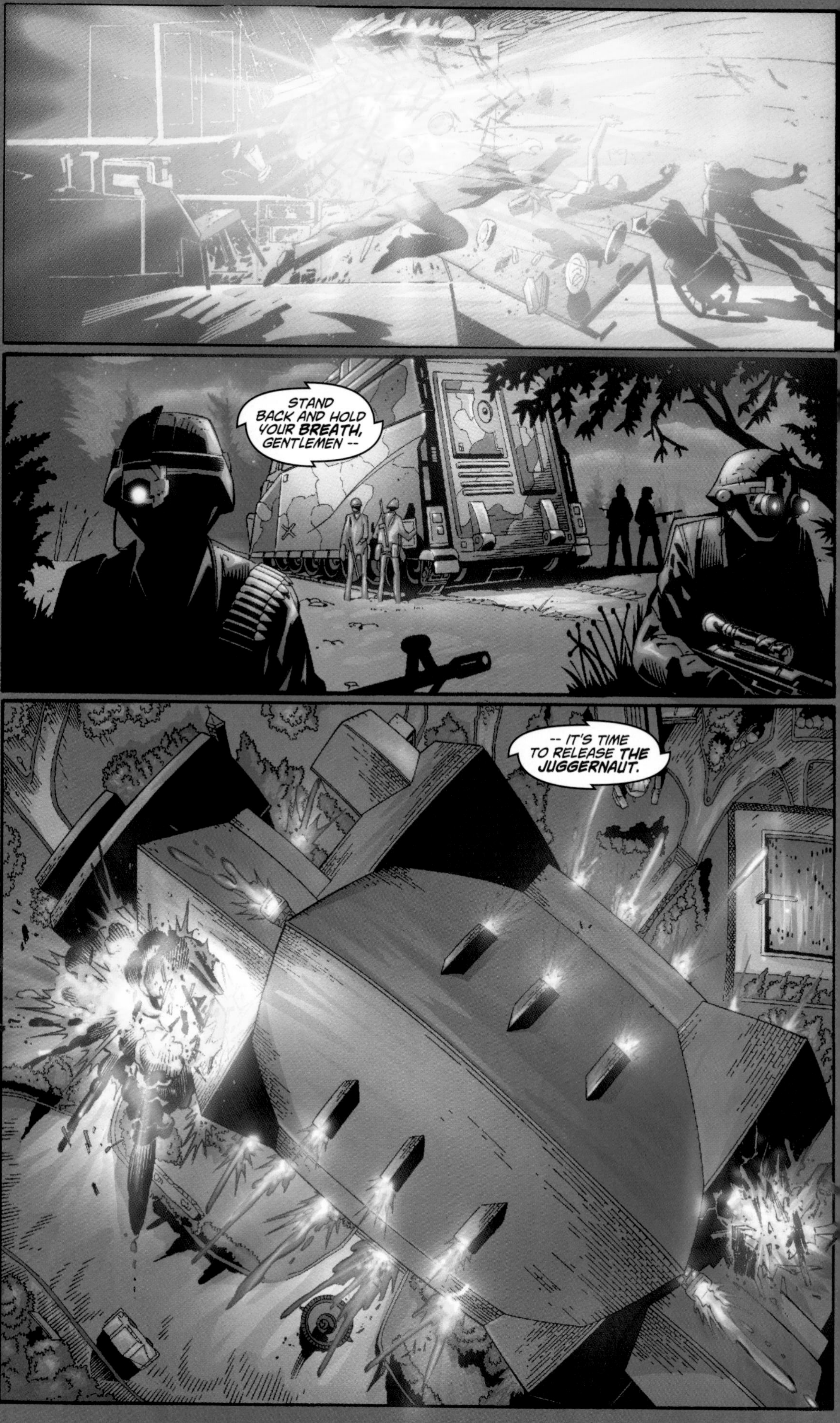
STAND BACK AND HOLD YOUR BREATH, GENTLEMEN --
-- IT'S TIME TO RELEASE THE JUGGERNAUT.

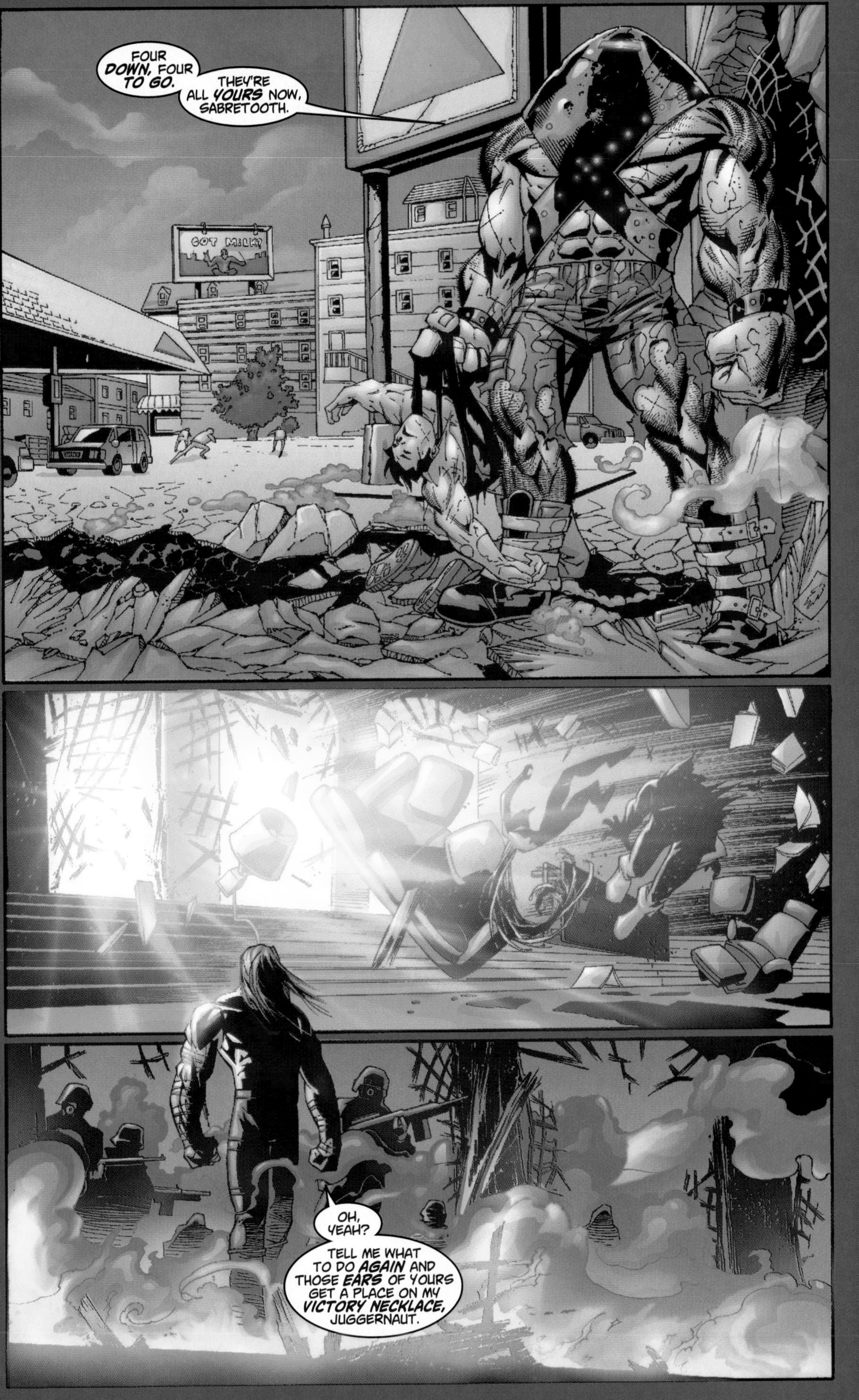
FOUR DOWN, FOUR TO GO.
THEY'RE ALL YOURS NOW, SABRETOOTH.
GOT MILK?
OH, YEAH?
TELL ME WHAT TO DO AGAIN AND THOSE EARS OF YOURS GET A PLACE ON MY VICTORY NECKLACE, JUGGERNAUT.

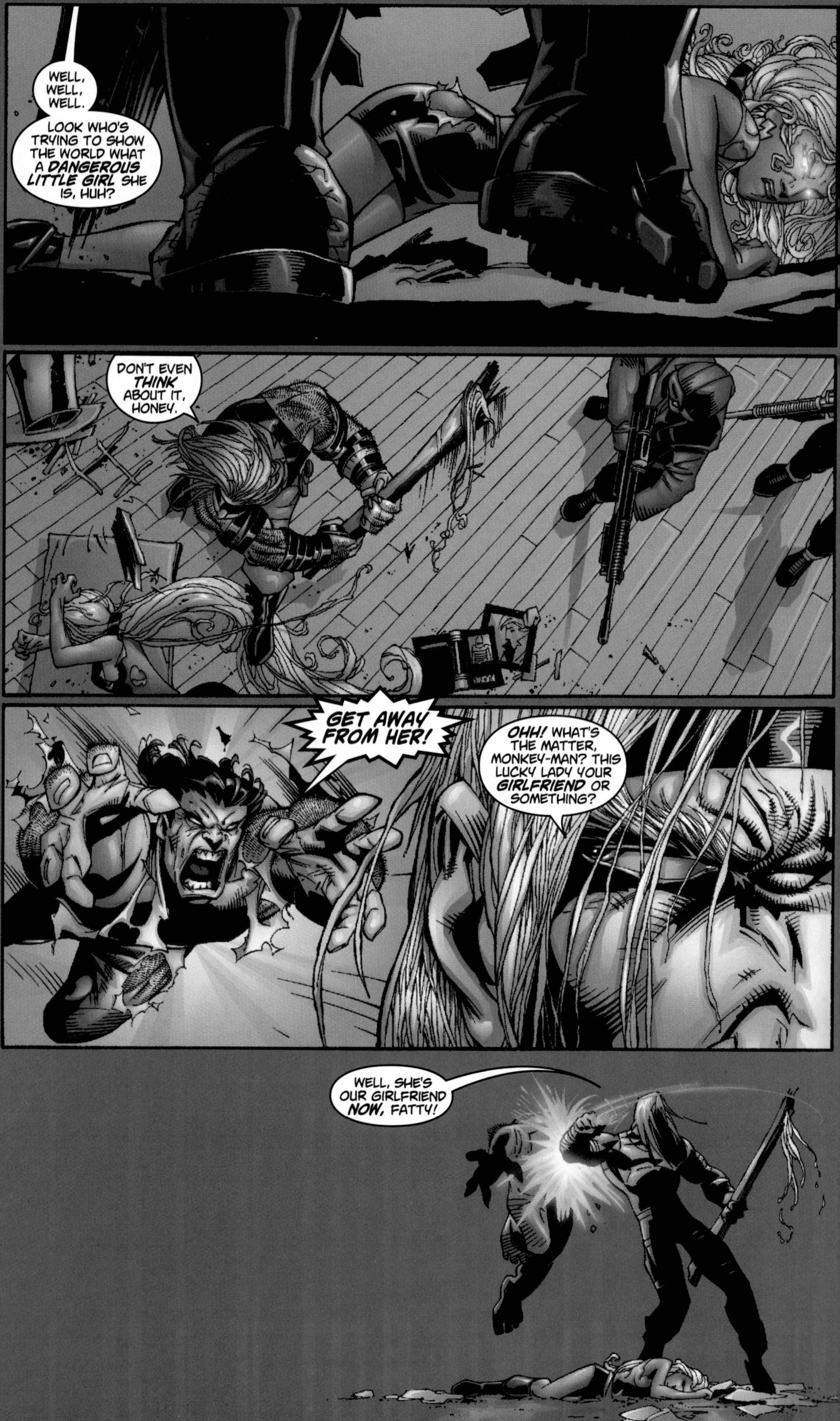
WELL, WELL, WELL.
LOOK WHO'S TRYING TO SHOW THE WORLD WHAT A DANGEROUS LITTLE GIRL SHE IS, HUH?
DON'T EVEN THINK ABOUT IT, HONEY.
GET AWAY FROM HER!
OHH! WHAT'S THE MATTER, MONKEY-MAN? THIS LUCKY LADY YOUR GIRLFRIEND OR SOMETHING?
WELL, SHE'S OUR GIRLFRIEND NOW, FATTY!

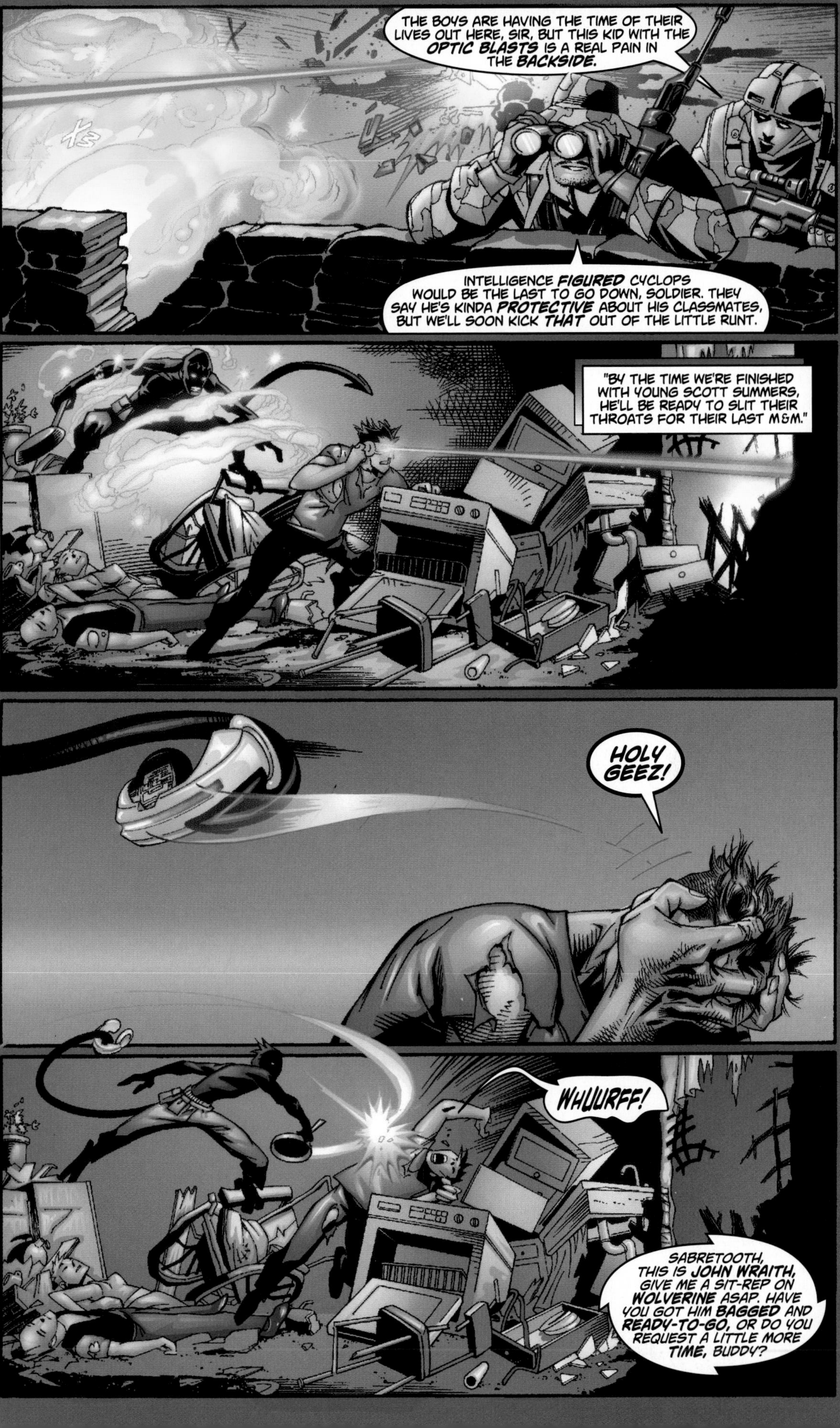
THE BOYS ARE HAVING THE TIME OF THEIR LIVES OUT HERE, SIR, BUT THIS KID WITH THE OPTIC BLASTS IS A REAL PAIN IN THE BACKSIDE.
INTELLIGENCE FIGURED CYCLOPS WOULD BE THE LAST TO GO DOWN, SOLDIER. THEY SAY HE'S KINDA PROTECTIVE ABOUT HIS CLASSMATES, BUT WE'LL SOON KICK THAT OUT OF THE LITTLE RUNT.
"BY THE TIME WE'RE FINISHED WITH YOUNG SCOTT SUMMERS, HE'LL BE READY TO SLIT THEIR THROATS FOR THEIR LAST M&M."
HOLY GEEZ!
WHUURFF!
SABRETOOTH, THIS IS JOHN WRAITH, GIVE ME A SIT-REP ON WOLVERINE ASAP. HAVE YOU GOT HIM BAGGED AND READY-TO-GO, OR DO YOU REQUEST A LITTLE MORE TIME, BUDDY?

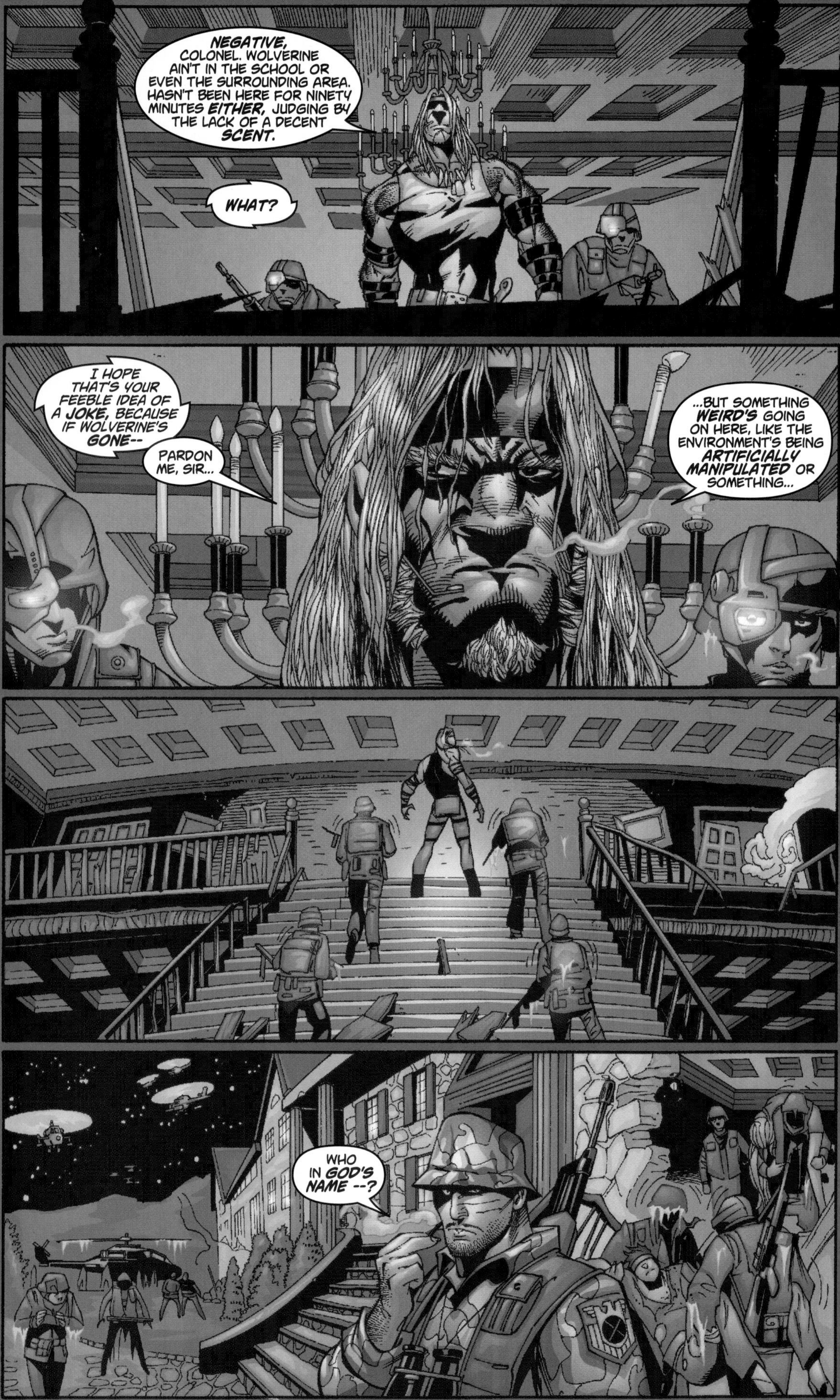
NEGATIVE, COLONEL. WOLVERINE AIN'T IN THE SCHOOL OR EVEN THE SURROUNDING AREA. HASN'T BEEN HERE FOR NINETY MINUTES EITHER, JUDGING BY THE LACK OF A DECENT SCENT.
WHAT?
I HOPE THAT'S YOUR FEEBLE IDEA OF A JOKE, BECAUSE IF WOLVERINE'S GONE--
PARDON ME, SIR...
...BUT SOMETHING WEIRD'S GOING ON HERE, LIKE THE ENVIRONMENT'S BEING ARTIFICIALLY MANIPULATED OR SOMETHING...
WHO IN GOD'S NAME --?

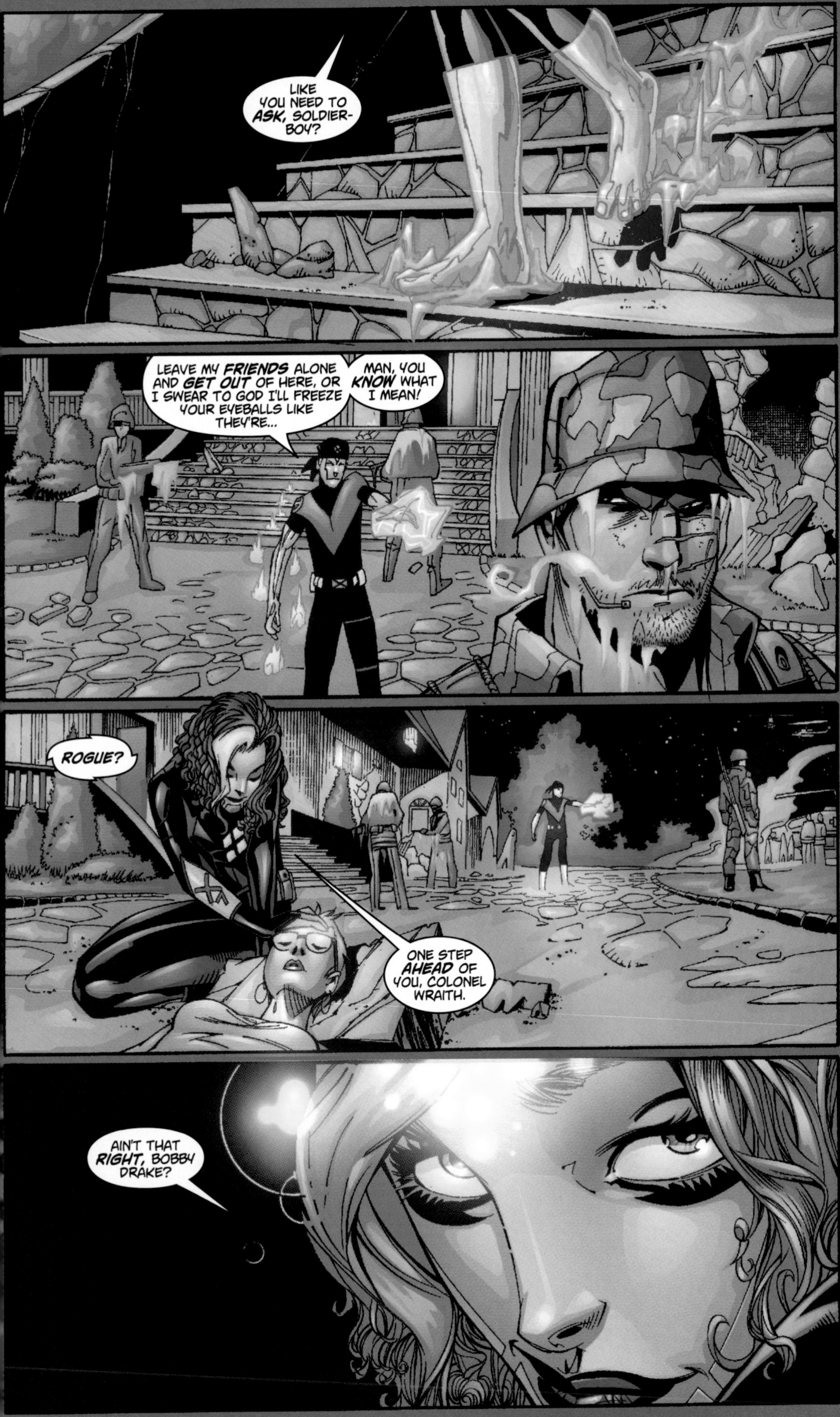
LIKE YOU NEED TO ASK, SOLDIER-BOY?
LEAVE MY FRIENDS ALONE AND GET OUT OF HERE, OR I SWEAR TO GOD I'LL FREEZE YOUR EYEBALLS LIKE THEY'RE...
MAN, YOU KNOW WHAT I MEAN!
ROGUE?
ONE STEP AHEAD OF YOU, COLONEL WRAITH.
AIN'T THAT RIGHT, BOBBY DRAKE?

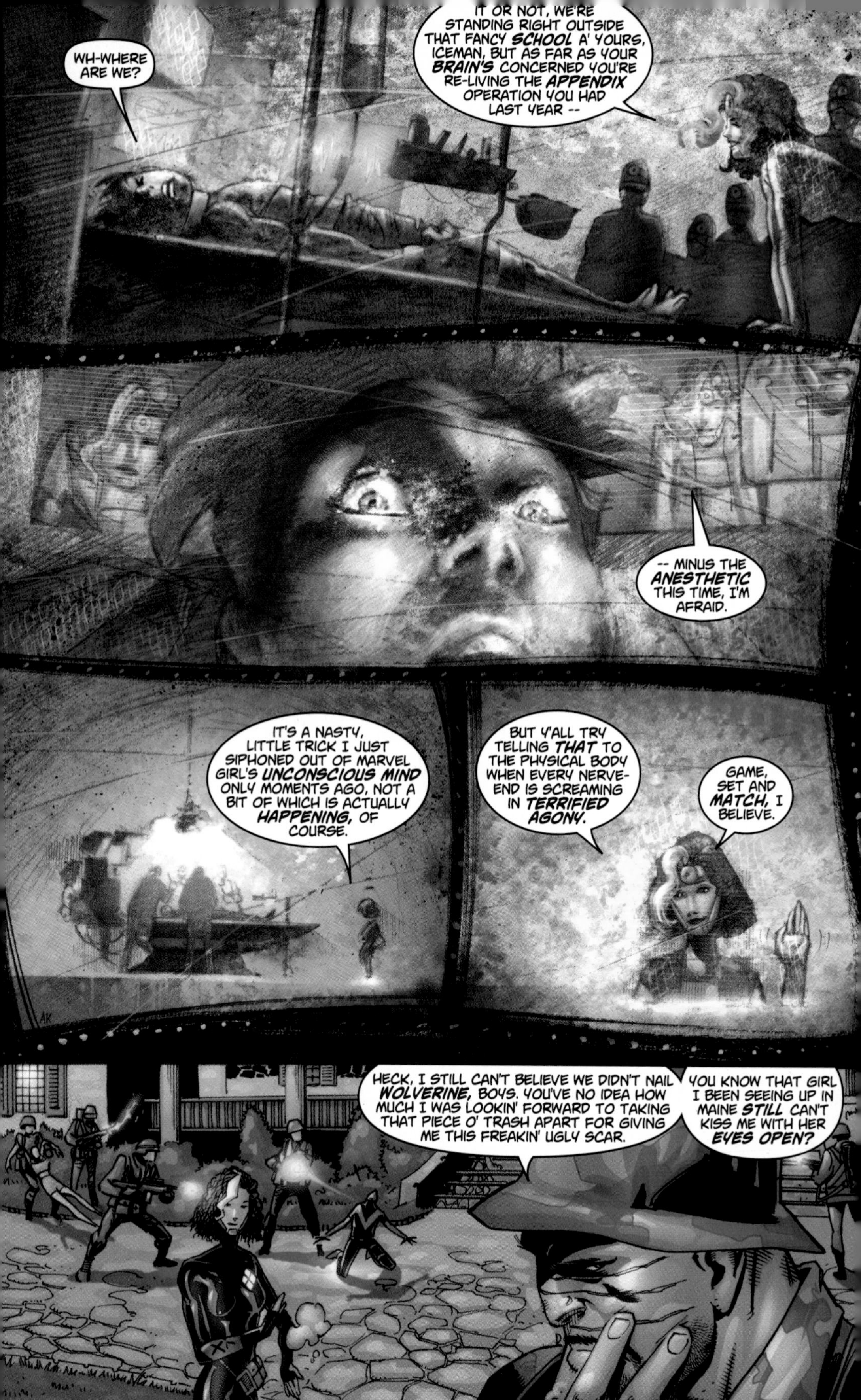
WH-WHERE ARE WE?
IT OR NOT, WE'RE STANDING RIGHT OUTSIDE THAT FANCY SCHOOL A' YOURS, ICEMAN, BUT AS FAR AS YOUR BRAIN'S CONCERNED YOU'RE RE-LIVING THE APPENDIX OPERATION YOU HAD LAST YEAR --
-- MINUS THE ANESTHETIC THIS TIME, I'M AFRAID.
IT'S A NASTY, LITTLE TRICK I JUST SIPHONED OUT OF MARVEL GIRL'S UNCONSCIOUS MIND ONLY MOMENTS AGO, NOT A BIT OF WHICH IS ACTUALLY HAPPENING, OF COURSE.
BUT Y'ALL TRY TELLING THAT TO THE PHYSICAL BODY WHEN EVERY NERVE-END IS SCREAMING IN TERRIFIED AGONY.
GAME, SET AND MATCH, I BELIEVE.
AK
HECK, I STILL CAN'T BELIEVE WE DIDN'T NAIL WOLVERINE, BOYS. YOU'VE NO IDEA HOW MUCH I WAS LOOKIN' FORWARD TO TAKING THAT PIECE O' TRASH APART FOR GIVING ME THIS FREAKIN' UGLY SCAR.
YOU KNOW THAT GIRL I BEEN SEEING UP IN MAINE STILL CAN'T KISS ME WITH HER EYES OPEN?

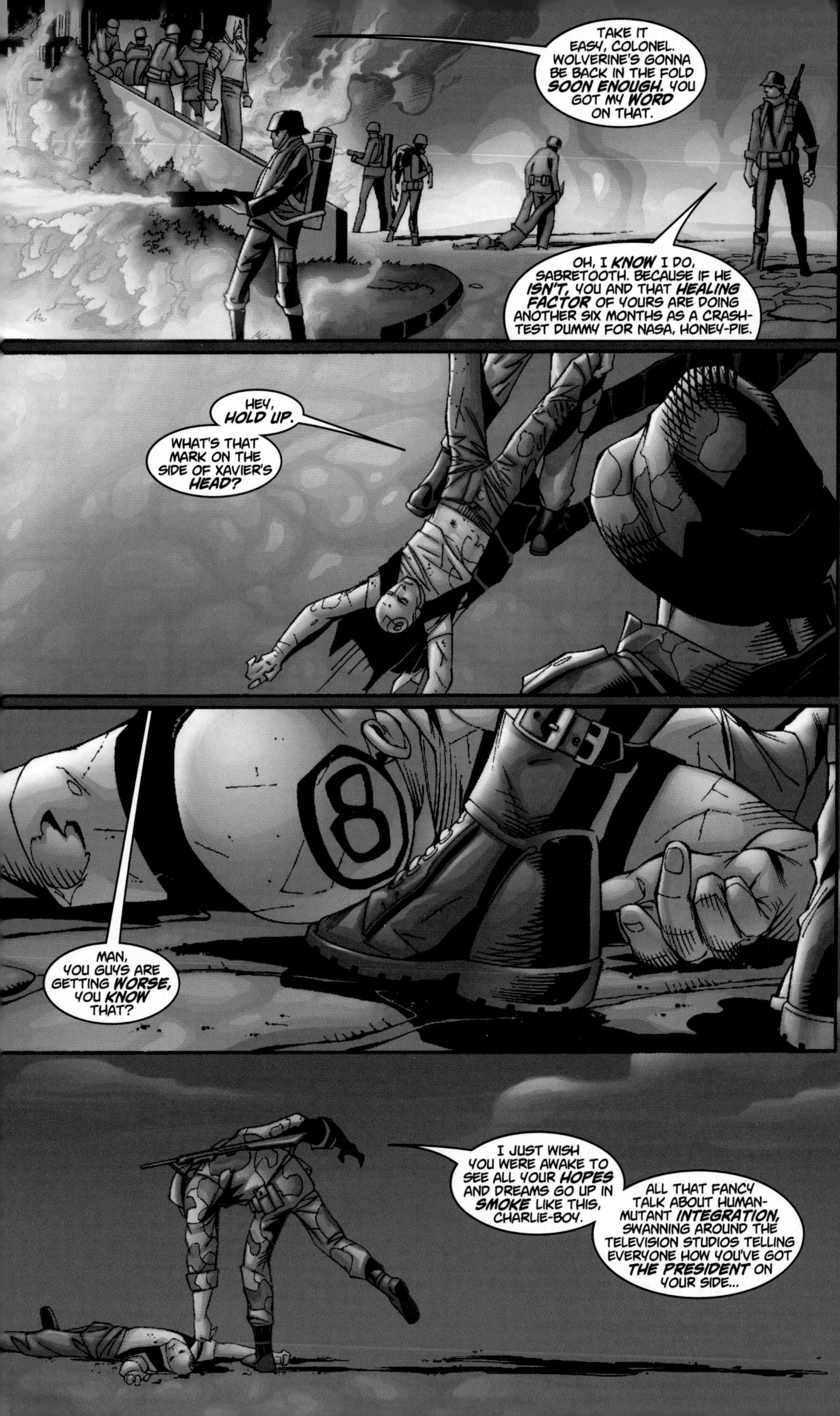
TAKE IT EASY, COLONEL. WOLVERINE'S GONNA BE BACK IN THE FOLD SOON ENOUGH. YOU GOT MY WORD ON THAT.
OH, I KNOW I DO, SABRETOOTH. BECAUSE IF HE ISN'T, YOU AND THAT HEALING FACTOR OF YOURS ARE DOING ANOTHER SIX MONTHS AS A CRASH-TEST DUMMY FOR NASA, HONEY-PIE.
HEY, HOLD UP.
WHAT'S THAT MARK ON THE SIDE OF XAVIER'S HEAD?
MAN, YOU GUYS ARE GETTING WORSE, YOU KNOW THAT?
I JUST WISH YOU WERE AWAKE TO SEE ALL YOUR HOPES AND DREAMS GO UP IN SMOKE LIKE THIS, CHARLIE-BOY.
ALL THAT FANCY TALK ABOUT HUMAN-MUTANT INTEGRATION, SWANNING AROUND THE TELEVISION STUDIOS TELLING EVERYONE HOW YOU'VE GOT THE PRESIDENT ON YOUR SIDE...

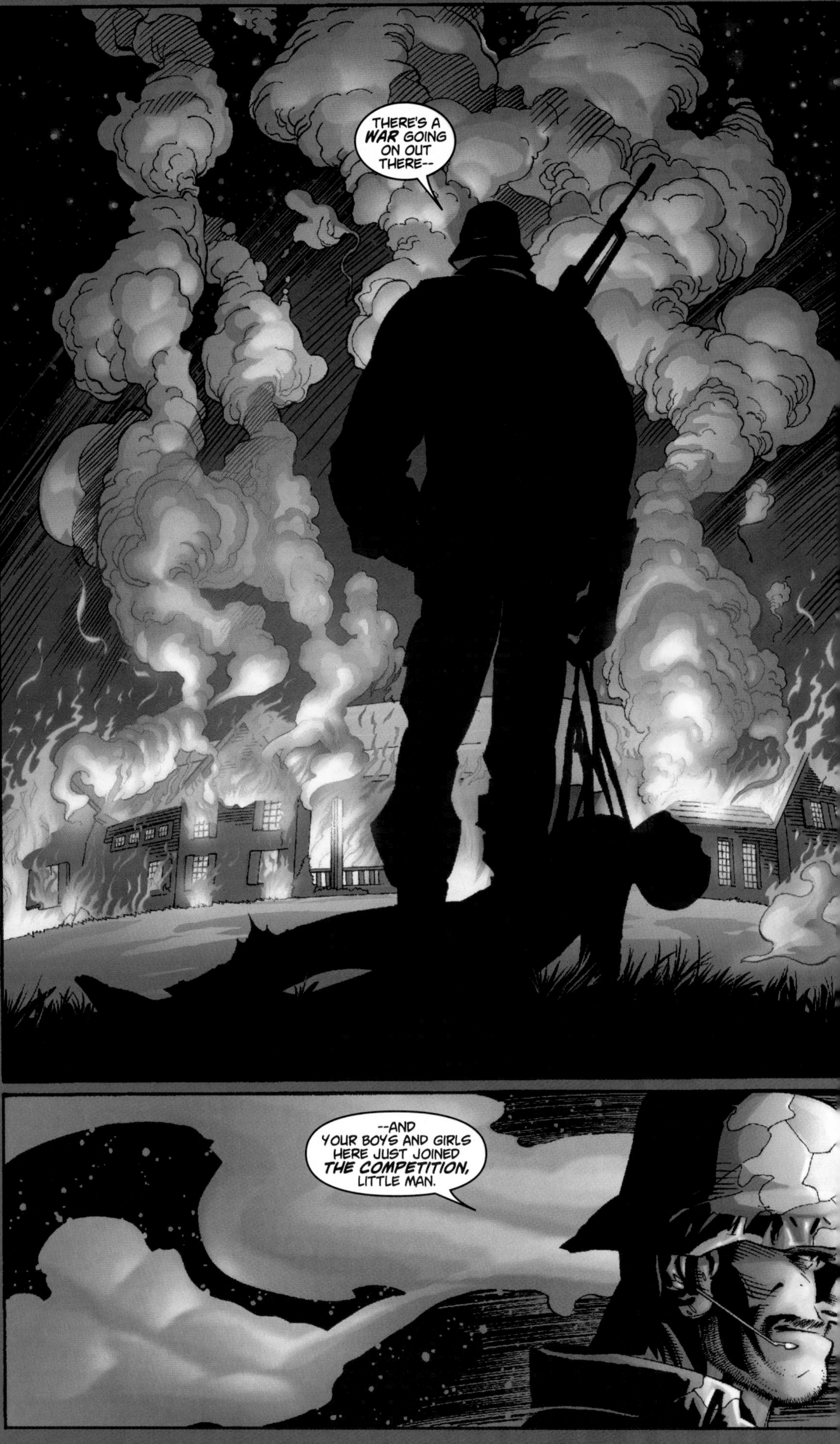
THERE'S A WAR GOING ON OUT THERE--
--AND YOUR BOYS AND GIRLS HERE JUST JOINED THE COMPETITION, LITTLE MAN.

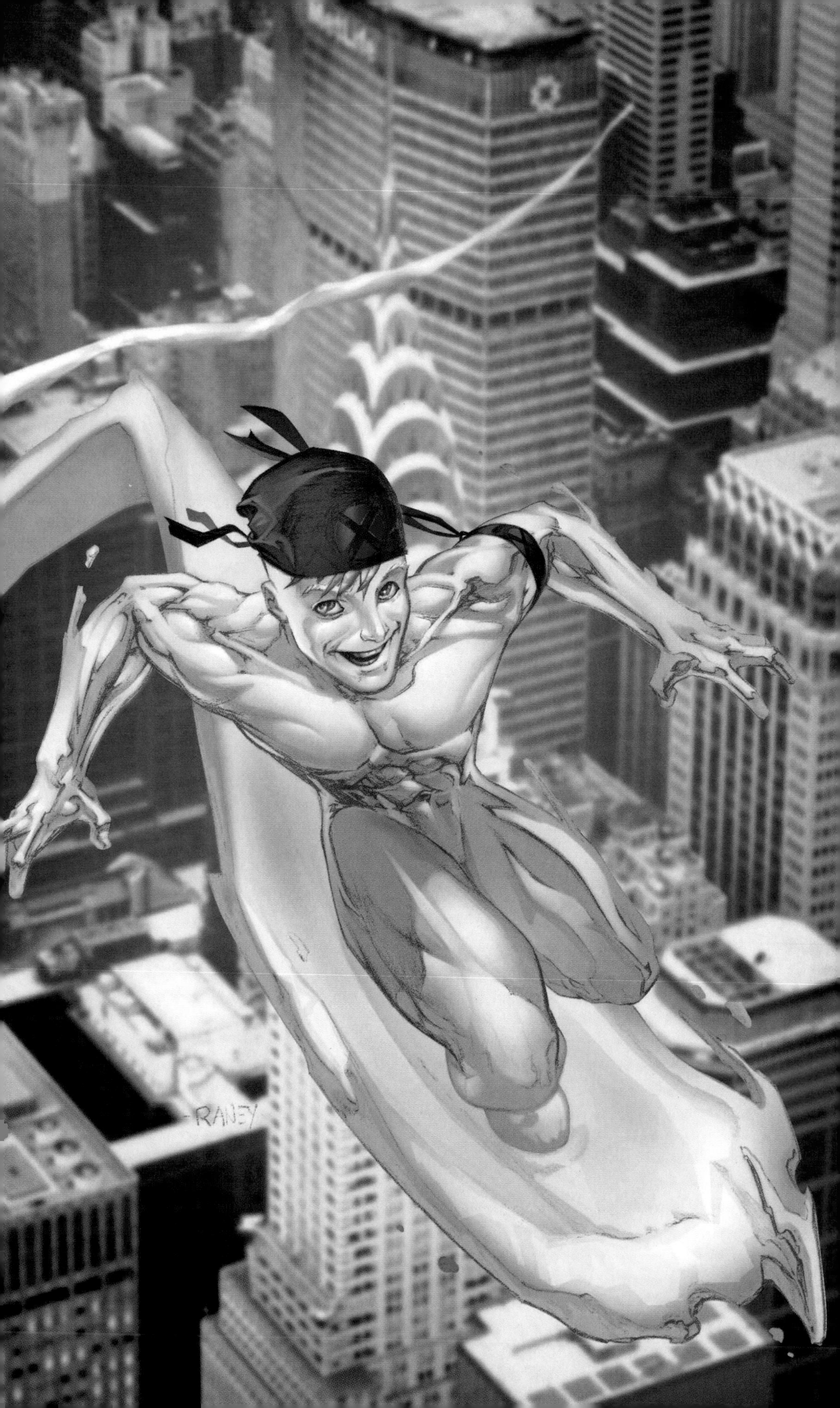
RANEY

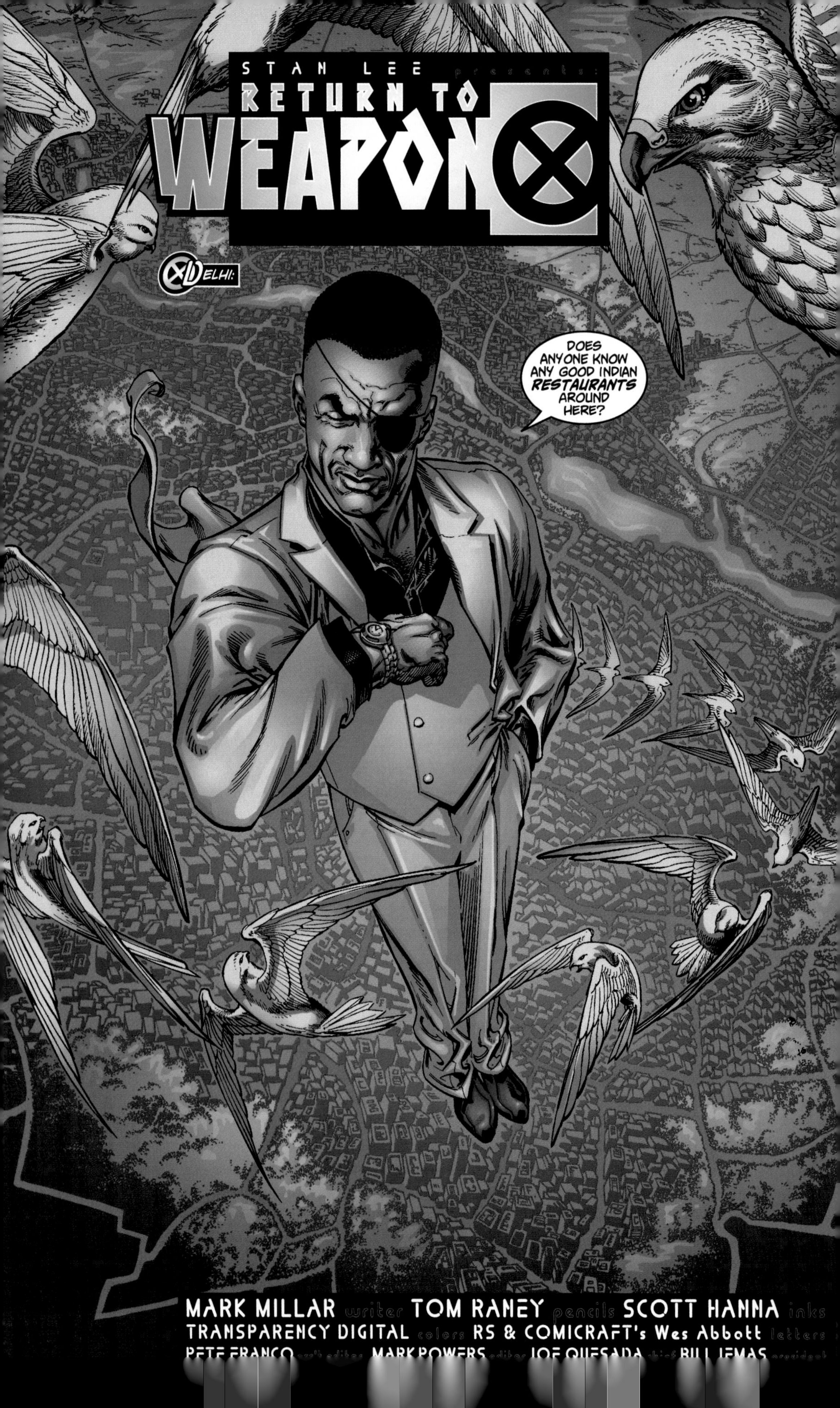
STAN LEE presents:
RETURN TO WEAPON X
DELHI:
DOES ANYONE KNOW ANY GOOD INDIAN RESTAURANTS AROUND HERE?
MARK MILLAR writer TOM RANEY pencils SCOTT HANNA inks
TRANSPARENCY DIGITAL colors RS & COMICRAFT's Wes Abbott letters
PETE FRANCO MARK POWERS JOE QUESADA BILL JEMAS

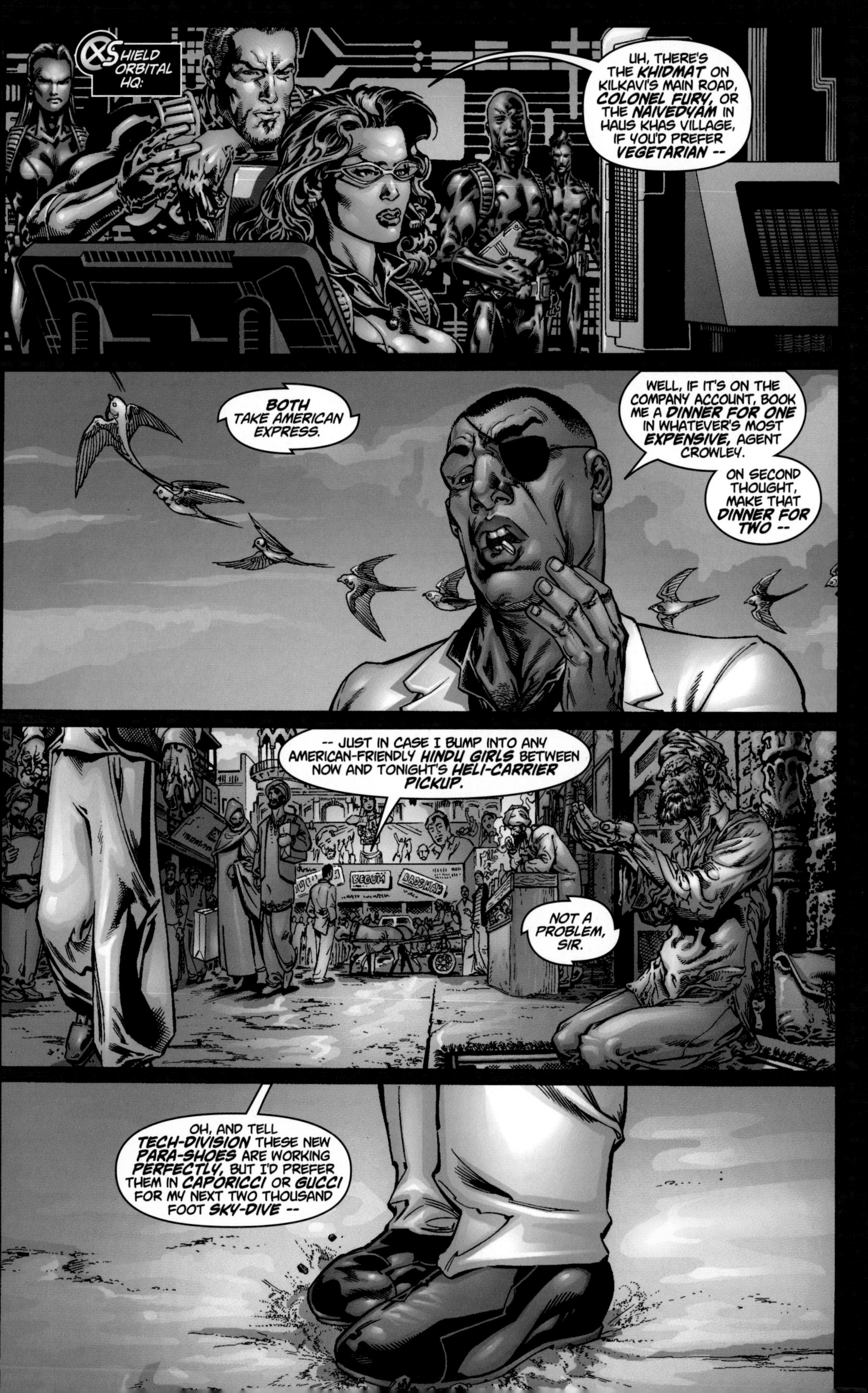
SHIELD ORBITAL HQ:
UH, THERE'S THE KHIDMAT ON KILKAVI'S MAIN ROAD, COLONEL FURY, OR THE NAIVEDYAM IN HAUS KHAS VILLAGE, IF YOU'D PREFER VEGETARIAN --
BOTH TAKE AMERICAN EXPRESS.
WELL, IF IT'S ON THE COMPANY ACCOUNT, BOOK ME A DINNER FOR ONE IN WHATEVER'S MOST EXPENSIVE, AGENT CROWLEY.
ON SECOND THOUGHT, MAKE THAT DINNER FOR TWO --
-- JUST IN CASE I BUMP INTO ANY AMERICAN-FRIENDLY HINDU GIRLS BETWEEN NOW AND TONIGHT'S HELI-CARRIER PICKUP.
BEGUM
BADSHAH
NOT A PROBLEM, SIR.
OH, AND TELL TECH-DIVISION THESE NEW PARA-SHOES ARE WORKING PERFECTLY, BUT I'D PREFER THEM IN CAPORICCI OR GUCCI FOR MY NEXT TWO THOUSAND FOOT SKY-DIVE --

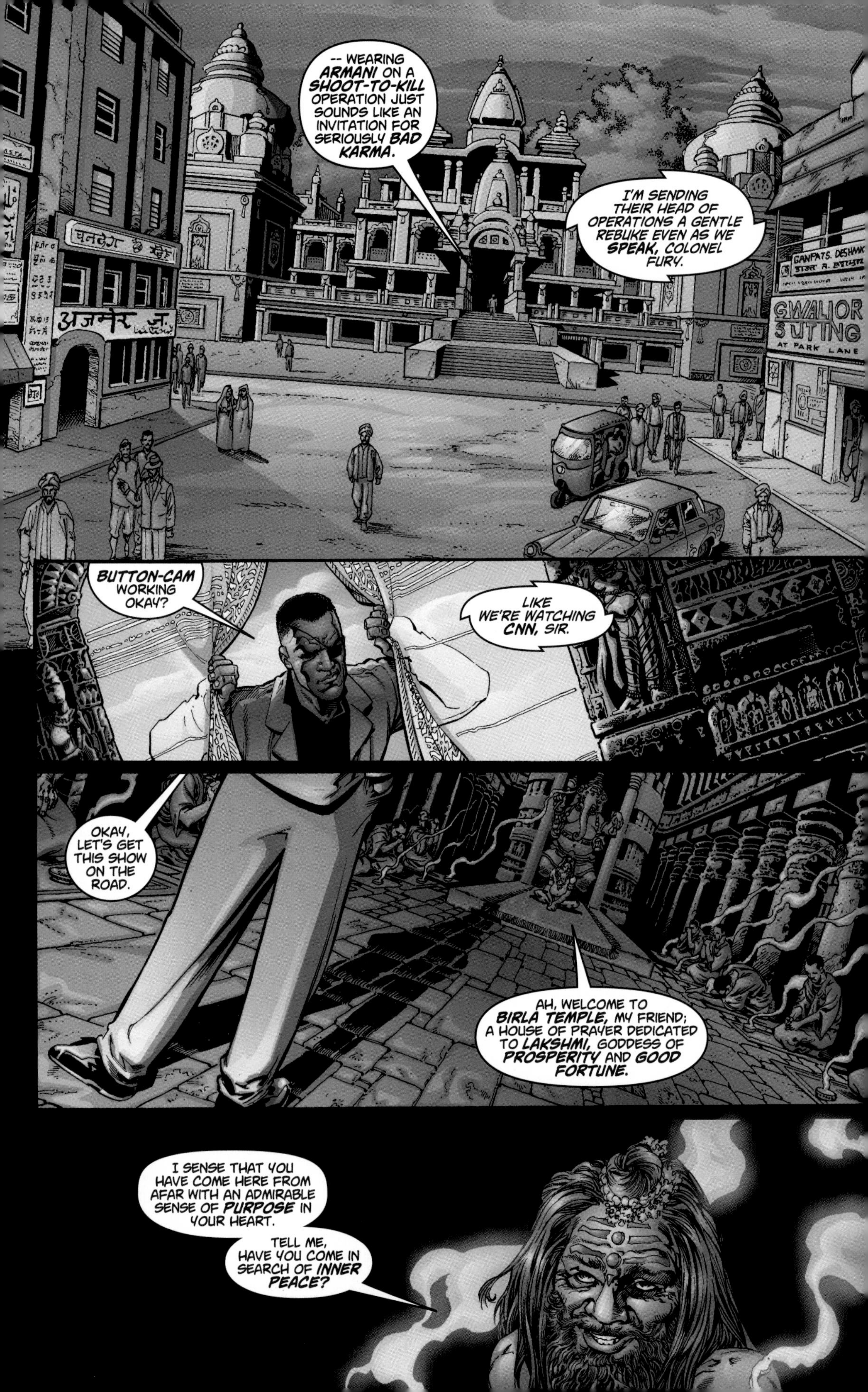
-- WEARING ARMANI ON A SHOOT-TO-KILL OPERATION JUST SOUNDS LIKE AN INVITATION FOR SERIOUSLY BAD KARMA.
I'M SENDING THEIR HEAD OF OPERATIONS A GENTLE REBUKE EVEN AS WE SPEAK, COLONEL FURY.
GWALIOR SUTING
AT PARK LANE
GANPATS. DESHMK
अजमेर ज.
BUTTON-CAM WORKING OKAY?
LIKE WE'RE WATCHING CNN, SIR.
OKAY, LET'S GET THIS SHOW ON THE ROAD.
AH, WELCOME TO BIRLA TEMPLE, MY FRIEND; A HOUSE OF PRAYER DEDICATED TO LAKSHMI, GODDESS OF PROSPERITY AND GOOD FORTUNE.
I SENSE THAT YOU HAVE COME HERE FROM AFAR WITH AN ADMIRABLE SENSE OF PURPOSE IN YOUR HEART.
TELL ME, HAVE YOU COME IN SEARCH OF INNER PEACE?

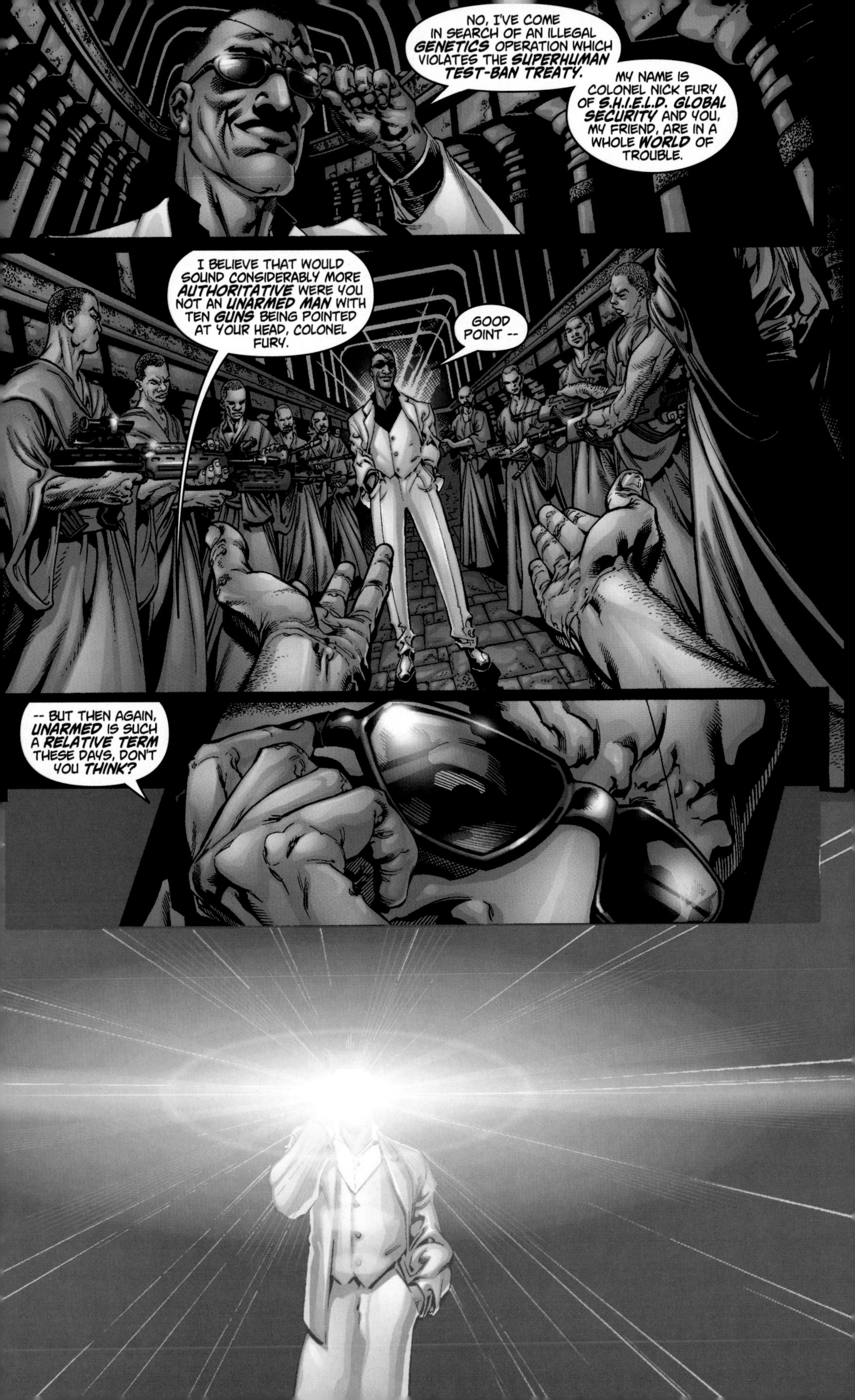
NO, I'VE COME IN SEARCH OF AN ILLEGAL GENETICS OPERATION WHICH VIOLATES THE SUPERHUMAN TEST-BAN TREATY.
MY NAME IS COLONEL NICK FURY OF S.H.I.E.L.D. GLOBAL SECURITY AND YOU, MY FRIEND, ARE IN A WHOLE WORLD OF TROUBLE.
I BELIEVE THAT WOULD SOUND CONSIDERABLY MORE AUTHORITATIVE WERE YOU NOT AN UNARMED MAN WITH TEN GUNS BEING POINTED AT YOUR HEAD, COLONEL FURY.
GOOD POINT --
-- BUT THEN AGAIN, UNARMED IS SUCH A RELATIVE TERM THESE DAYS, DON'T YOU THINK?

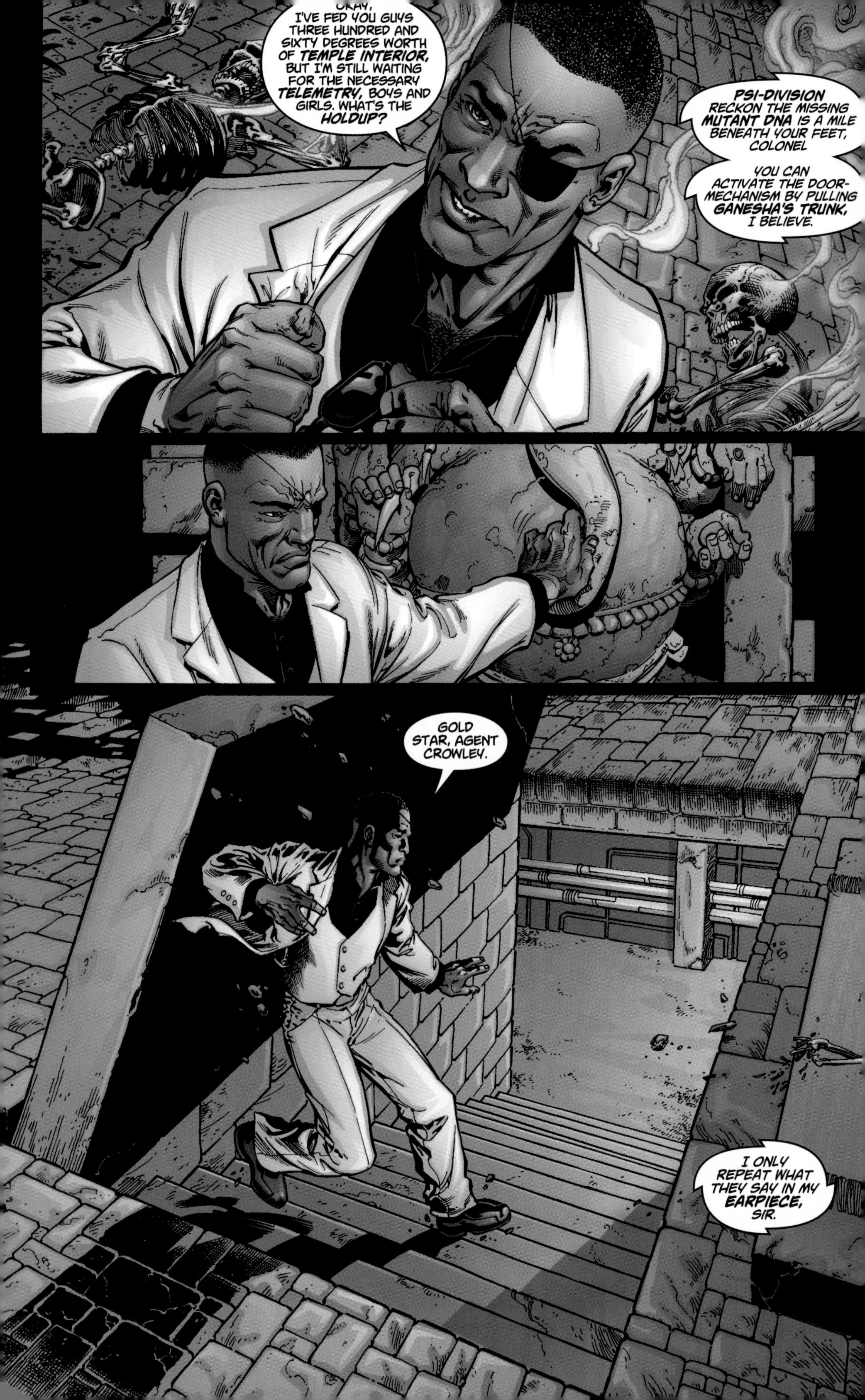
I'VE FED YOU GUYS THREE HUNDRED AND SIXTY DEGREES WORTH OF TEMPLE INTERIOR, BUT I'M STILL WAITING FOR THE NECESSARY TELEMETRY, BOYS AND GIRLS. WHAT'S THE HOLDUP?
PSI-DIVISION RECKON THE MISSING MUTANT DNA IS A MILE BENEATH YOUR FEET, COLONEL
YOU CAN ACTIVATE THE DOOR-MECHANISM BY PULLING GANESHA'S TRUNK, I BELIEVE.
GOLD STAR, AGENT CROWLEY.
I ONLY REPEAT WHAT THEY SAY IN MY EARPIECE, SIR.

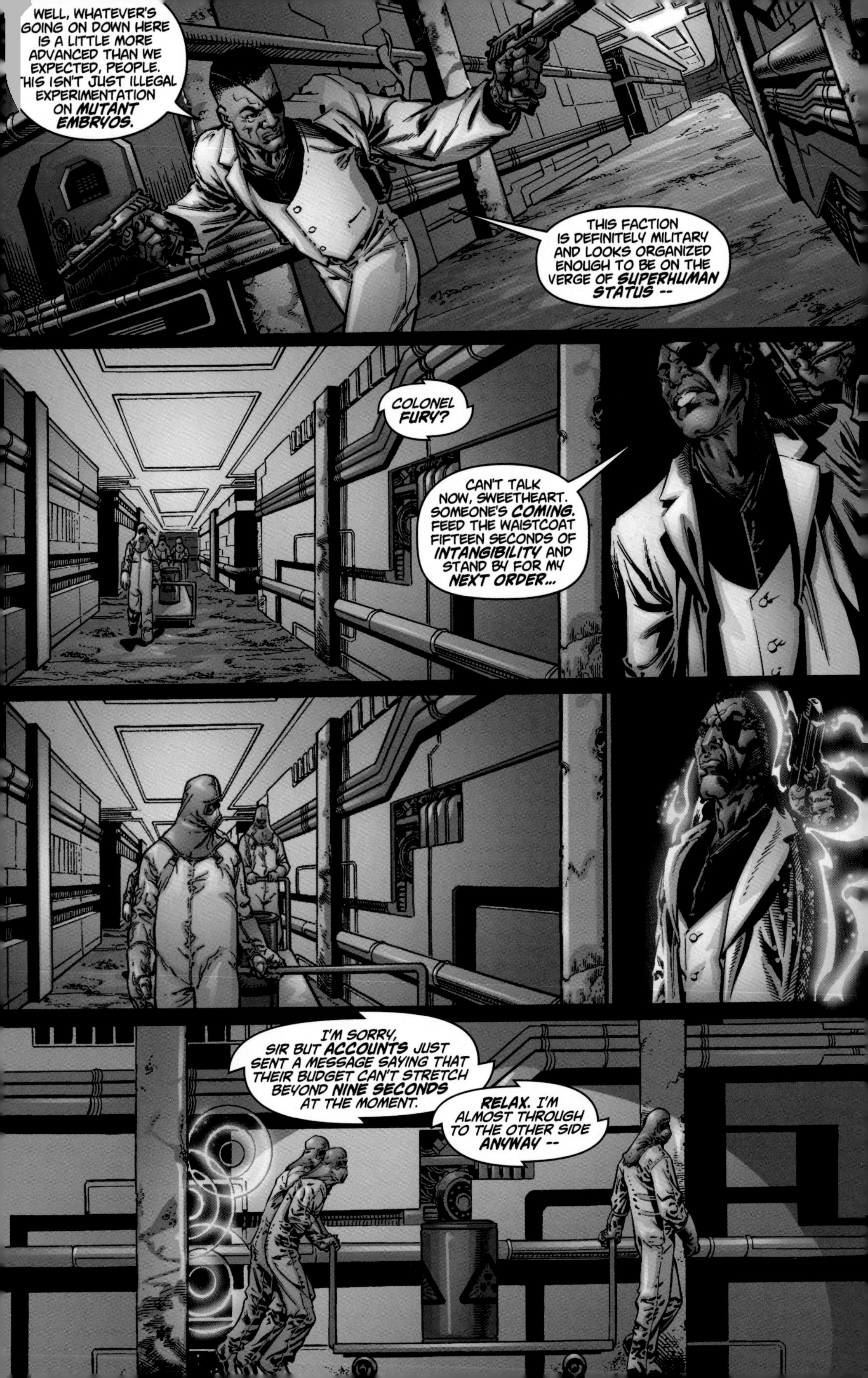
WELL, WHATEVER'S GOING ON DOWN HERE IS A LITTLE MORE ADVANCED THAN WE EXPECTED, PEOPLE. THIS ISN'T JUST ILLEGAL EXPERIMENTATION ON MUTANT EMBRYOS.
THIS FACTION IS DEFINITELY MILITARY AND LOOKS ORGANIZED ENOUGH TO BE ON THE VERGE OF SUPERHUMAN STATUS --
COLONEL FURY?
CAN'T TALK NOW, SWEETHEART. SOMEONE'S COMING. FEED THE WAISTCOAT FIFTEEN SECONDS OF INTANGIBILITY AND STAND BY FOR MY NEXT ORDER...
I'M SORRY, SIR BUT ACCOUNTS JUST SENT A MESSAGE SAYING THAT THEIR BUDGET CAN'T STRETCH BEYOND NINE SECONDS AT THE MOMENT.
RELAX. I'M ALMOST THROUGH TO THE OTHER SIDE ANYWAY --

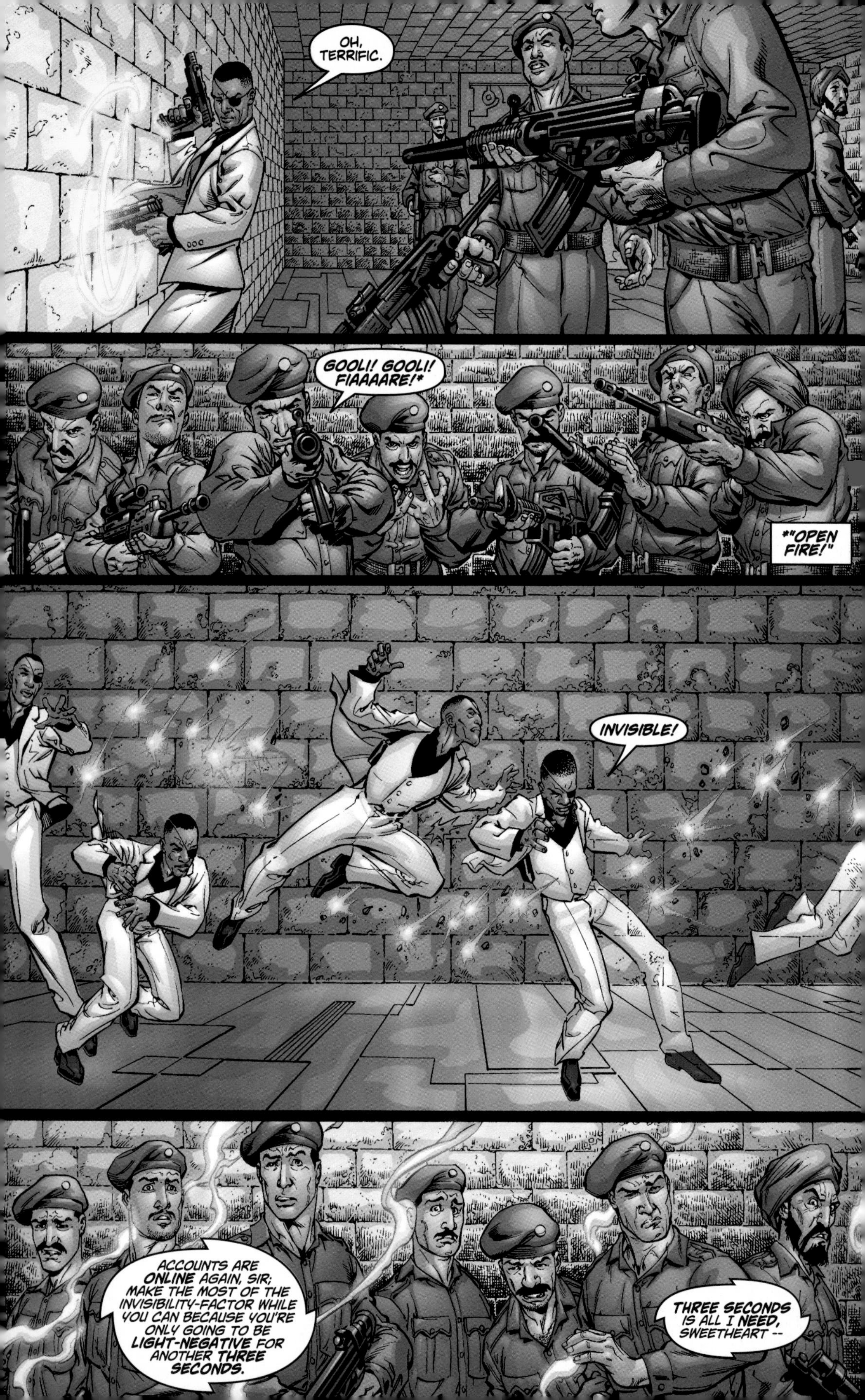
OH, TERRIFIC.
GOOLI! GOOLI! FIAAAARE!*
*"OPEN FIRE!"
INVISIBLE!
ACCOUNTS ARE ONLINE AGAIN, SIR; MAKE THE MOST OF THE INVISIBILITY-FACTOR WHILE YOU CAN BECAUSE YOU'RE ONLY GOING TO BE LIGHT-NEGATIVE FOR ANOTHER THREE SECONDS.
THREE SECONDS IS ALL I NEED, SWEETHEART --

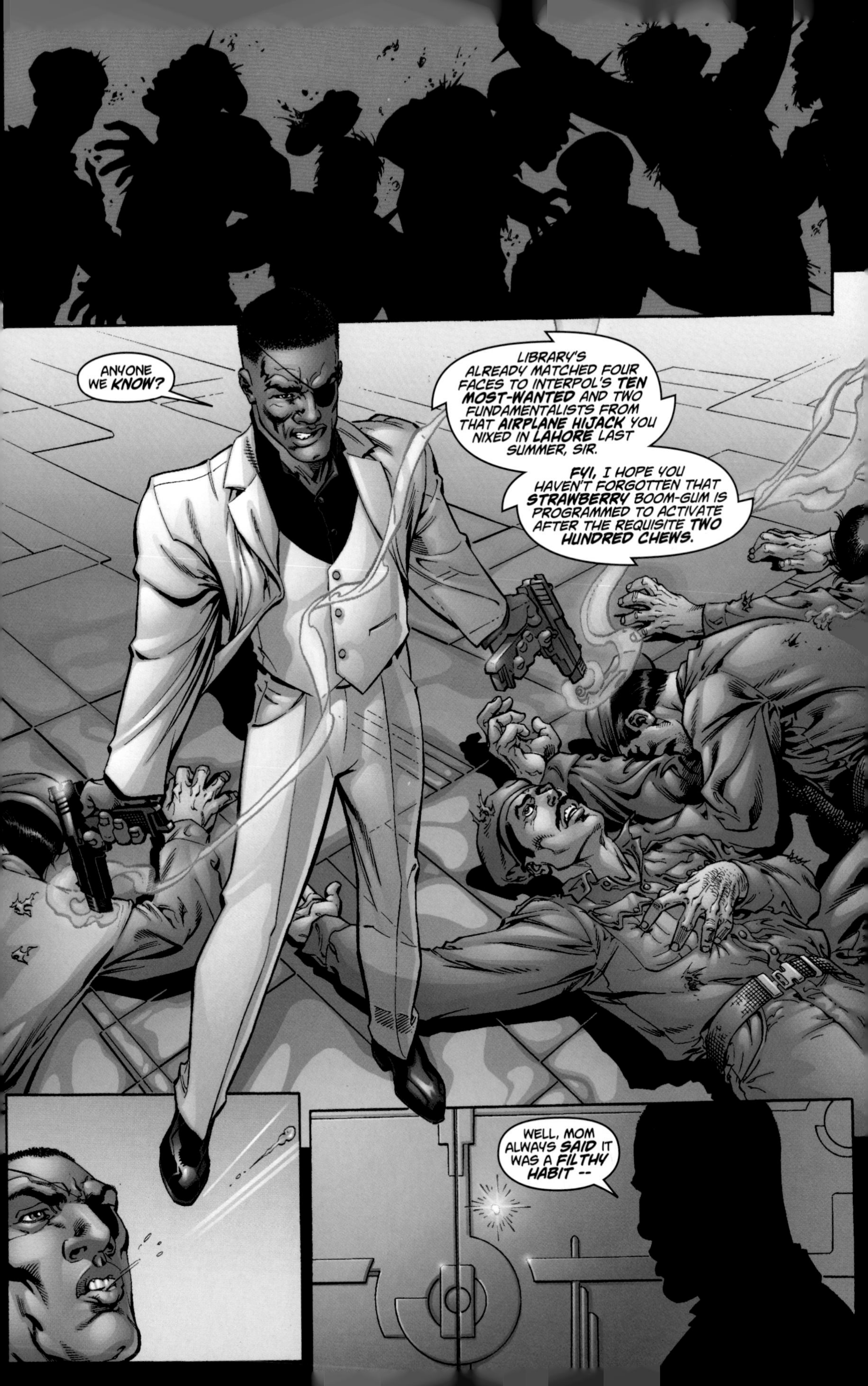
ANYONE WE **KNOW?**
LIBRARY'S ALREADY MATCHED FOUR FACES TO INTERPOL'S **TEN MOST-WANTED** AND TWO FUNDAMENTALISTS FROM THAT **AIRPLANE HIJACK** YOU NIXED IN **LAHORE** LAST SUMMER, SIR.
FYI, I HOPE YOU HAVEN'T FORGOTTEN THAT **STRAWBERRY** BOOM-GUM IS PROGRAMMED TO ACTIVATE AFTER THE REQUISITE **TWO HUNDRED CHEWS.**
WELL, MOM ALWAYS **SAID** IT WAS A **FILTHY HABIT --**

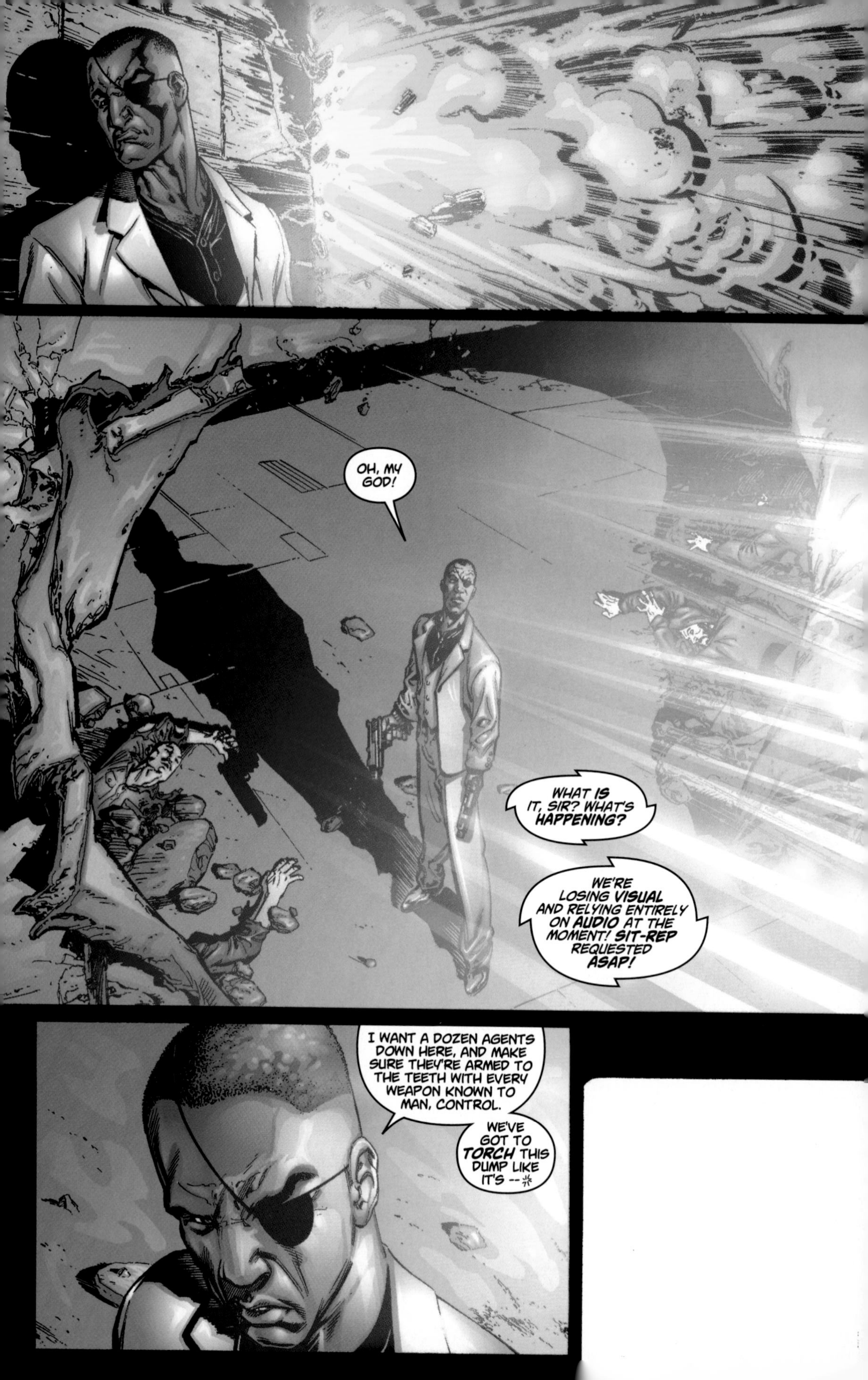
OH, MY GOD!
WHAT IS IT, SIR? WHAT'S HAPPENING?
WE'RE LOSING VISUAL AND RELYING ENTIRELY ON AUDIO AT THE MOMENT! SIT-REP REQUESTED ASAP!
I WANT A DOZEN AGENTS DOWN HERE, AND MAKE SURE THEY'RE ARMED TO THE TEETH WITH EVERY WEAPON KNOWN TO MAN, CONTROL.
WE'VE GOT TO TORCH THIS DUMP LIKE IT'S --

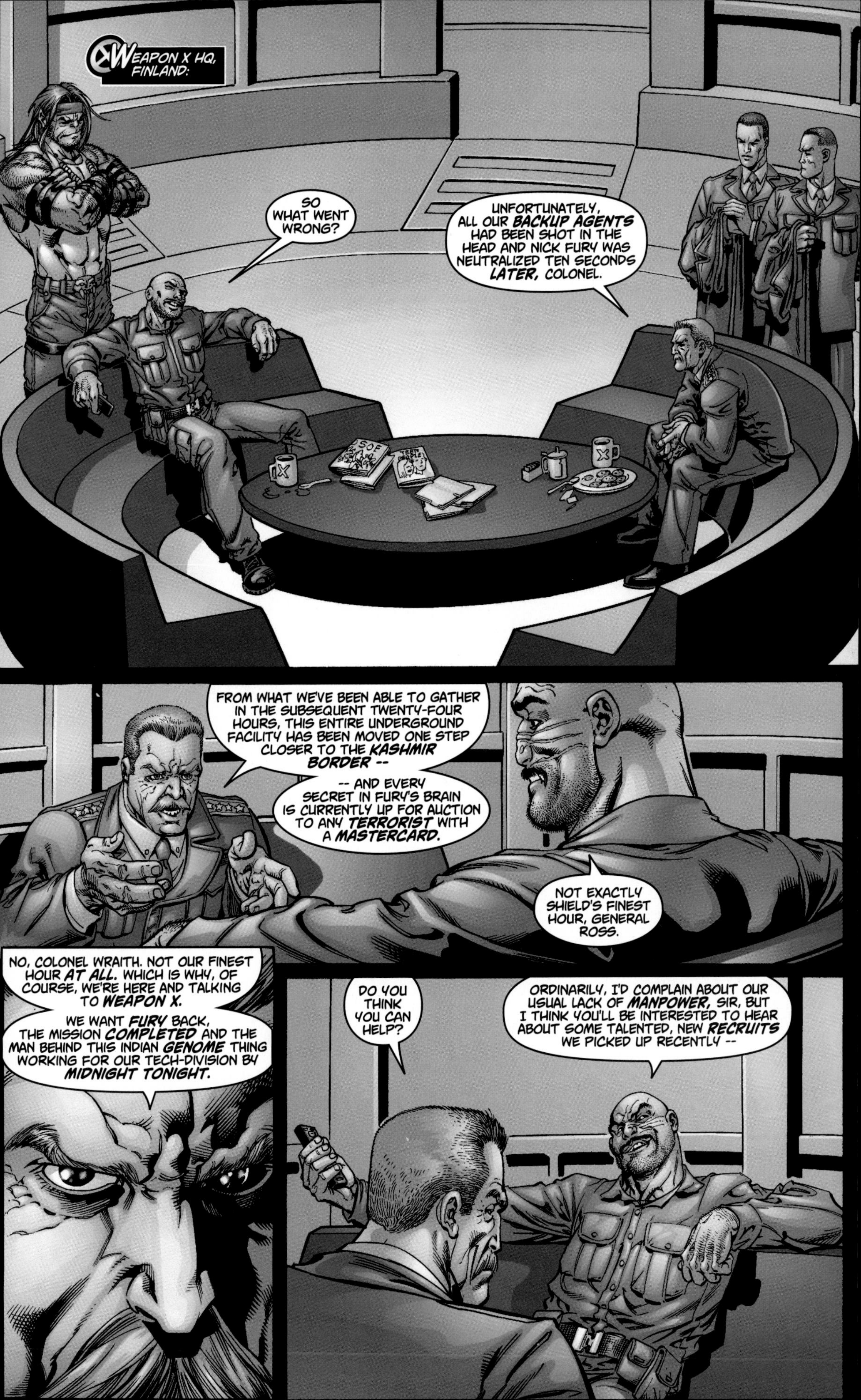
WEAPON X HQ, FINLAND:
SO WHAT WENT WRONG?
UNFORTUNATELY, ALL OUR BACKUP AGENTS HAD BEEN SHOT IN THE HEAD AND NICK FURY WAS NEUTRALIZED TEN SECONDS LATER, COLONEL.
FROM WHAT WE'VE BEEN ABLE TO GATHER IN THE SUBSEQUENT TWENTY-FOUR HOURS, THIS ENTIRE UNDERGROUND FACILITY HAS BEEN MOVED ONE STEP CLOSER TO THE KASHMIR BORDER --
-- AND EVERY SECRET IN FURY'S BRAIN IS CURRENTLY UP FOR AUCTION TO ANY TERRORIST WITH A MASTERCARD.
NOT EXACTLY SHIELD'S FINEST HOUR, GENERAL ROSS.
NO, COLONEL WRAITH. NOT OUR FINEST HOUR AT ALL. WHICH IS WHY, OF COURSE, WE'RE HERE AND TALKING TO WEAPON X.
WE WANT FURY BACK, THE MISSION COMPLETED AND THE MAN BEHIND THIS INDIAN GENOME THING WORKING FOR OUR TECH-DIVISION BY MIDNIGHT TONIGHT.
DO YOU THINK YOU CAN HELP?
ORDINARILY, I'D COMPLAIN ABOUT OUR USUAL LACK OF MANPOWER, SIR, BUT I THINK YOU'LL BE INTERESTED TO HEAR ABOUT SOME TALENTED, NEW RECRUITS WE PICKED UP RECENTLY --

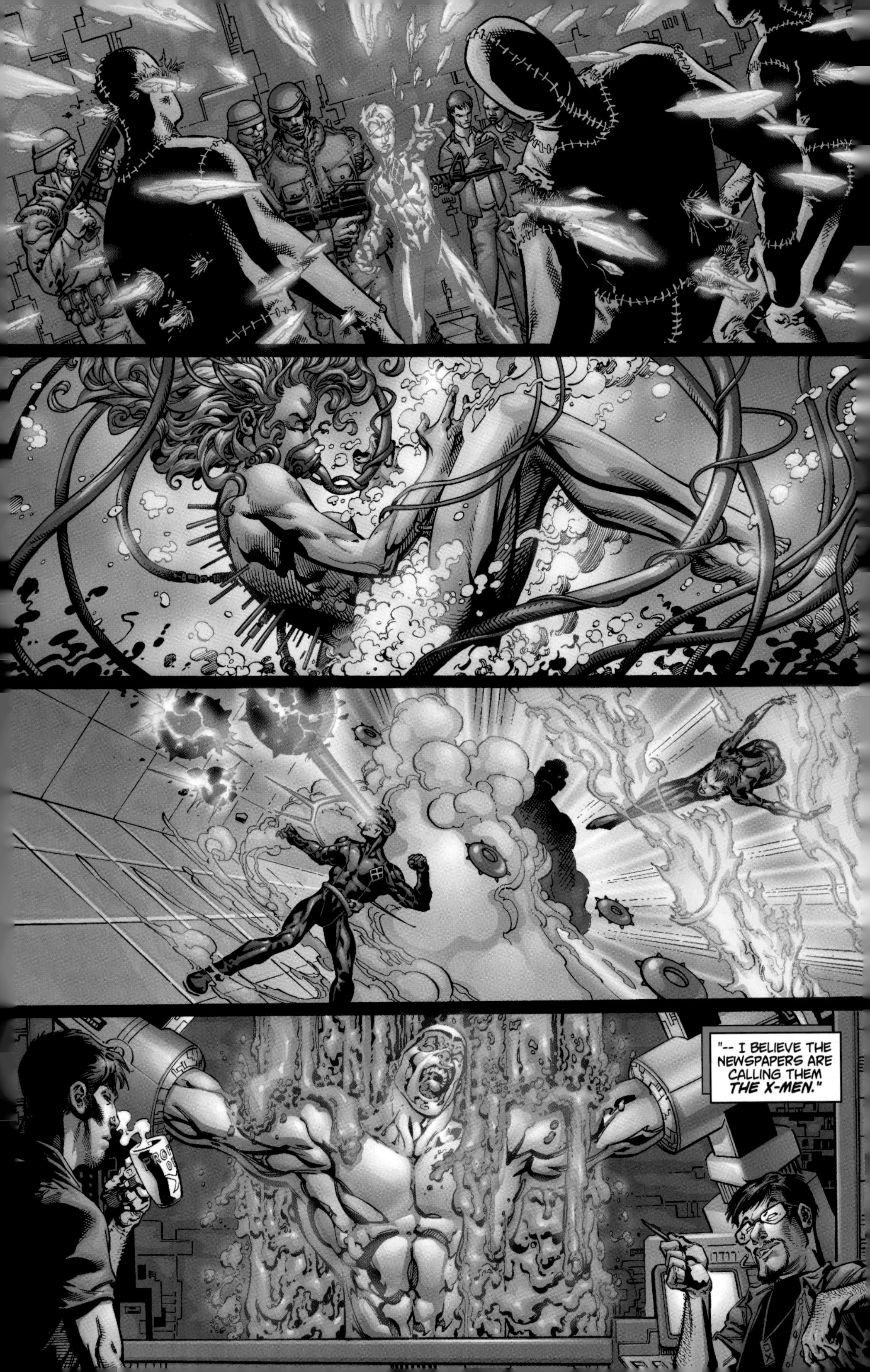
"-- I BELIEVE THE NEWSPAPERS ARE CALLING THEM THE X-MEN."

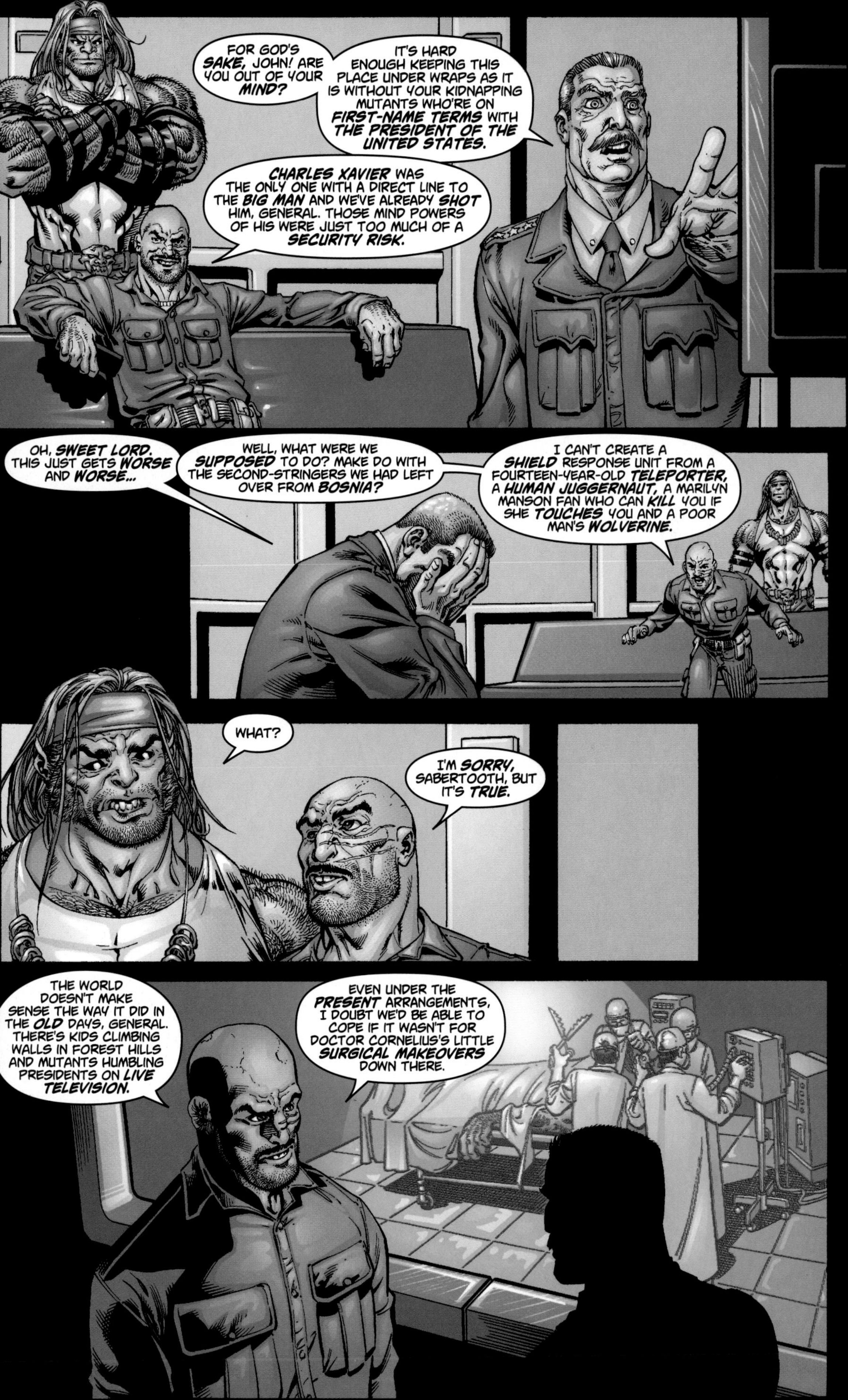
FOR GOD'S SAKE, JOHN! ARE YOU OUT OF YOUR MIND?
IT'S HARD ENOUGH KEEPING THIS PLACE UNDER WRAPS AS IT IS WITHOUT YOUR KIDNAPPING MUTANTS WHO'RE ON FIRST-NAME TERMS WITH THE PRESIDENT OF THE UNITED STATES.
CHARLES XAVIER WAS THE ONLY ONE WITH A DIRECT LINE TO THE BIG MAN AND WE'VE ALREADY SHOT HIM, GENERAL. THOSE MIND POWERS OF HIS WERE JUST TOO MUCH OF A SECURITY RISK.
OH, SWEET LORD. THIS JUST GETS WORSE AND WORSE...
WELL, WHAT WERE WE SUPPOSED TO DO? MAKE DO WITH THE SECOND-STRINGERS WE HAD LEFT OVER FROM BOSNIA?
I CAN'T CREATE A SHIELD RESPONSE UNIT FROM A FOURTEEN-YEAR-OLD TELEPORTER, A HUMAN JUGGERNAUT, A MARILYN MANSON FAN WHO CAN KILL YOU IF SHE TOUCHES YOU AND A POOR MAN'S WOLVERINE.
WHAT?
I'M SORRY, SABERTOOTH, BUT IT'S TRUE.
THE WORLD DOESN'T MAKE SENSE THE WAY IT DID IN THE OLD DAYS, GENERAL. THERE'S KIDS CLIMBING WALLS IN FOREST HILLS AND MUTANTS HUMBLING PRESIDENTS ON LIVE TELEVISION.
EVEN UNDER THE PRESENT ARRANGEMENTS, I DOUBT WE'D BE ABLE TO COPE IF IT WASN'T FOR DOCTOR CORNELIUS'S LITTLE SURGICAL MAKEOVERS DOWN THERE.

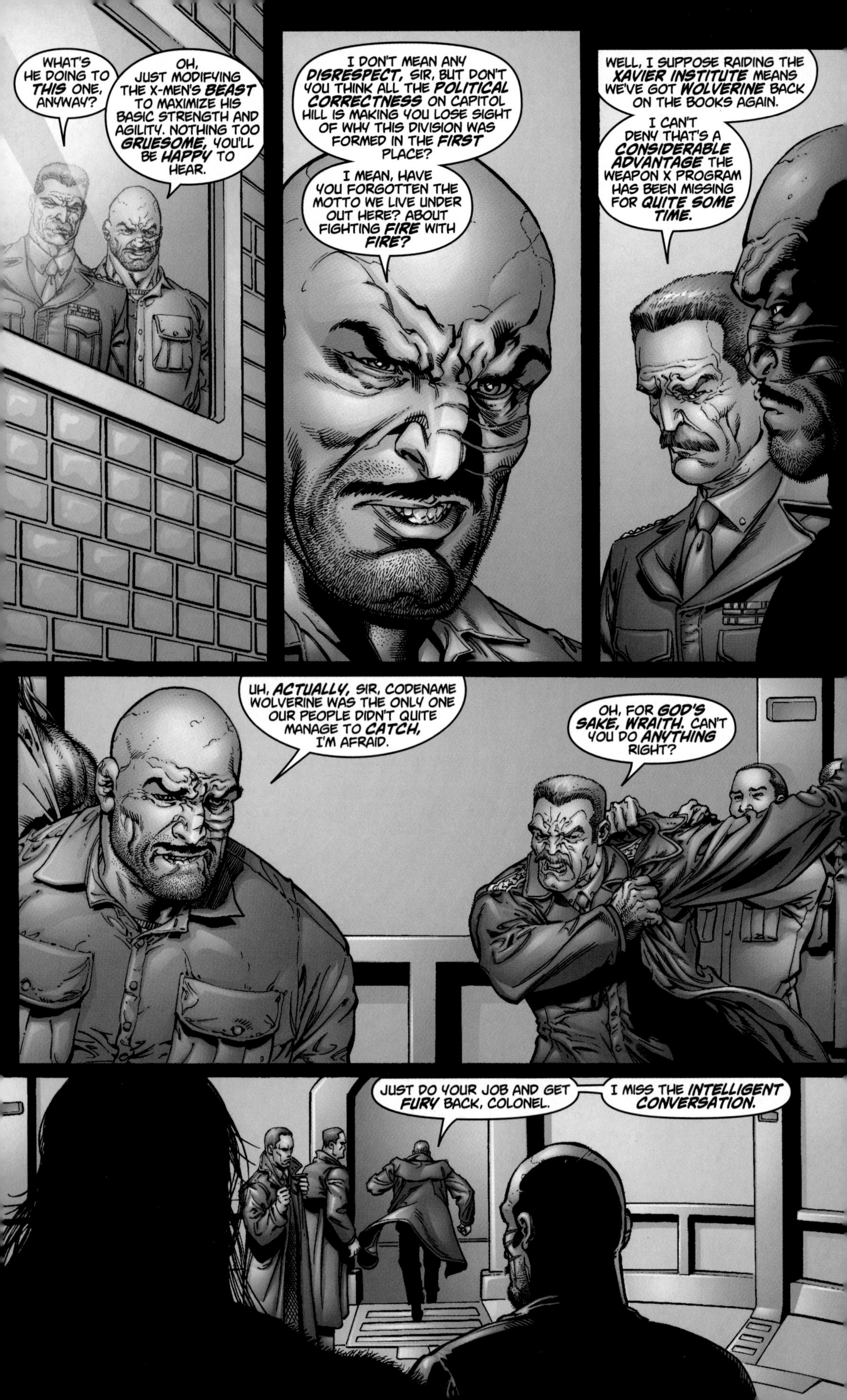
WHAT'S HE DOING TO THIS ONE, ANYWAY?
OH, JUST MODIFYING THE X-MEN'S BEAST TO MAXIMIZE HIS BASIC STRENGTH AND AGILITY. NOTHING TOO GRUESOME, YOU'LL BE HAPPY TO HEAR.
I DON'T MEAN ANY DISRESPECT, SIR, BUT DON'T YOU THINK ALL THE POLITICAL CORRECTNESS ON CAPITOL HILL IS MAKING YOU LOSE SIGHT OF WHY THIS DIVISION WAS FORMED IN THE FIRST PLACE?
I MEAN, HAVE YOU FORGOTTEN THE MOTTO WE LIVE UNDER OUT HERE? ABOUT FIGHTING FIRE WITH FIRE?
WELL, I SUPPOSE RAIDING THE XAVIER INSTITUTE MEANS WE'VE GOT WOLVERINE BACK ON THE BOOKS AGAIN.
I CAN'T DENY THAT'S A CONSIDERABLE ADVANTAGE THE WEAPON X PROGRAM HAS BEEN MISSING FOR QUITE SOME TIME.
UH, ACTUALLY, SIR, CODENAME WOLVERINE WAS THE ONLY ONE OUR PEOPLE DIDN'T QUITE MANAGE TO CATCH, I'M AFRAID.
OH, FOR GOD'S SAKE, WRAITH. CAN'T YOU DO ANYTHING RIGHT?
JUST DO YOUR JOB AND GET FURY BACK, COLONEL.
I MISS THE INTELLIGENT CONVERSATION.

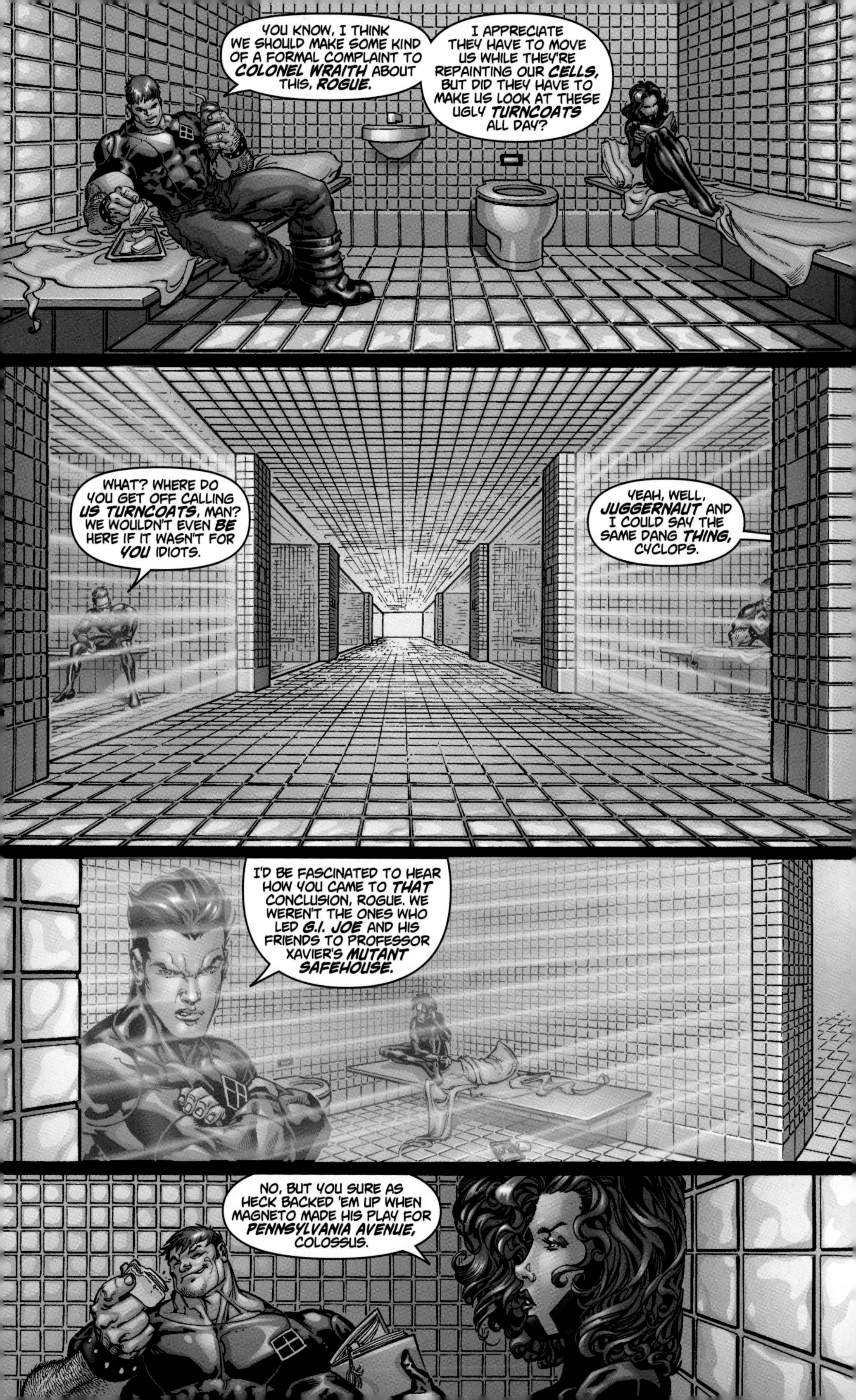

YOU KNOW, I THINK WE SHOULD MAKE SOME KIND OF A FORMAL COMPLAINT TO COLONEL WRAITH ABOUT THIS, ROGUE.
I APPRECIATE THEY HAVE TO MOVE US WHILE THEY'RE REPAINTING OUR CELLS, BUT DID THEY HAVE TO MAKE US LOOK AT THESE UGLY TURNCOATS ALL DAY?
WHAT? WHERE DO YOU GET OFF CALLING US TURNCOATS, MAN? WE WOULDN'T EVEN BE HERE IF IT WASN'T FOR YOU IDIOTS.
YEAH, WELL, JUGGERNAUT AND I COULD SAY THE SAME DANG THING, CYCLOPS.
I'D BE FASCINATED TO HEAR HOW YOU CAME TO THAT CONCLUSION, ROGUE. WE WEREN'T THE ONES WHO LED G.I. JOE AND HIS FRIENDS TO PROFESSOR XAVIER'S MUTANT SAFEHOUSE.
NO, BUT YOU SURE AS HECK BACKED 'EM UP WHEN MAGNETO MADE HIS PLAY FOR PENNSYLVANIA AVENUE, COLOSSUS.

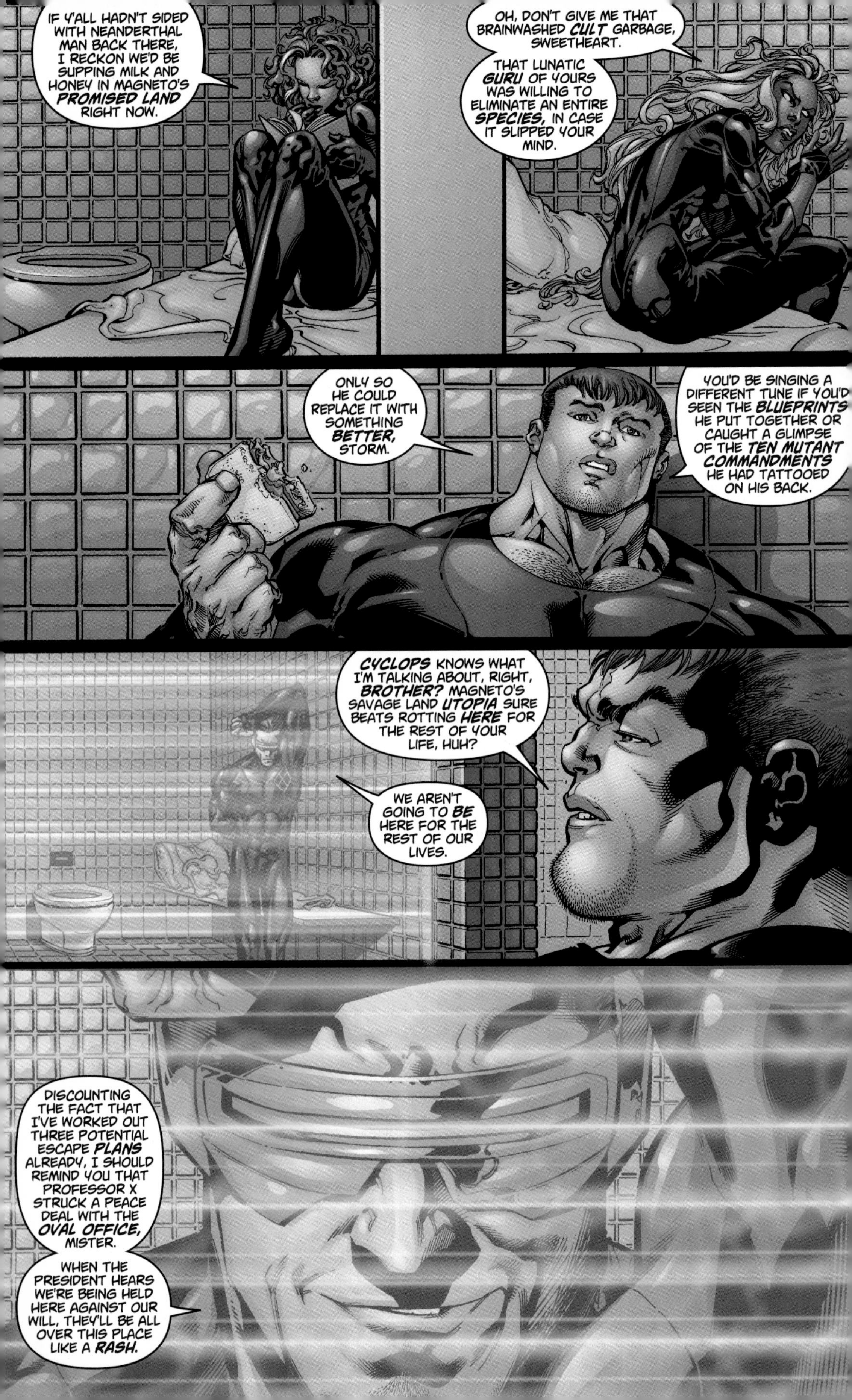
IF Y'ALL HADN'T SIDED WITH NEANDERTHAL MAN BACK THERE, I RECKON WE'D BE SUPPING MILK AND HONEY IN MAGNETO'S PROMISED LAND RIGHT NOW.
OH, DON'T GIVE ME THAT BRAINWASHED CULT GARBAGE, SWEETHEART.
THAT LUNATIC GURU OF YOURS WAS WILLING TO ELIMINATE AN ENTIRE SPECIES, IN CASE IT SLIPPED YOUR MIND.
ONLY SO HE COULD REPLACE IT WITH SOMETHING BETTER, STORM.
YOU'D BE SINGING A DIFFERENT TUNE IF YOU'D SEEN THE BLUEPRINTS HE PUT TOGETHER OR CAUGHT A GLIMPSE OF THE TEN MUTANT COMMANDMENTS HE HAD TATTOOED ON HIS BACK.
CYCLOPS KNOWS WHAT I'M TALKING ABOUT, RIGHT, BROTHER? MAGNETO'S SAVAGE LAND UTOPIA SURE BEATS ROTTING HERE FOR THE REST OF YOUR LIFE, HUH?
WE AREN'T GOING TO BE HERE FOR THE REST OF OUR LIVES.
DISCOUNTING THE FACT THAT I'VE WORKED OUT THREE POTENTIAL ESCAPE PLANS ALREADY, I SHOULD REMIND YOU THAT PROFESSOR X STRUCK A PEACE DEAL WITH THE OVAL OFFICE, MISTER.
WHEN THE PRESIDENT HEARS WE'RE BEING HELD HERE AGAINST OUR WILL, THEY'LL BE ALL OVER THIS PLACE LIKE A RASH.

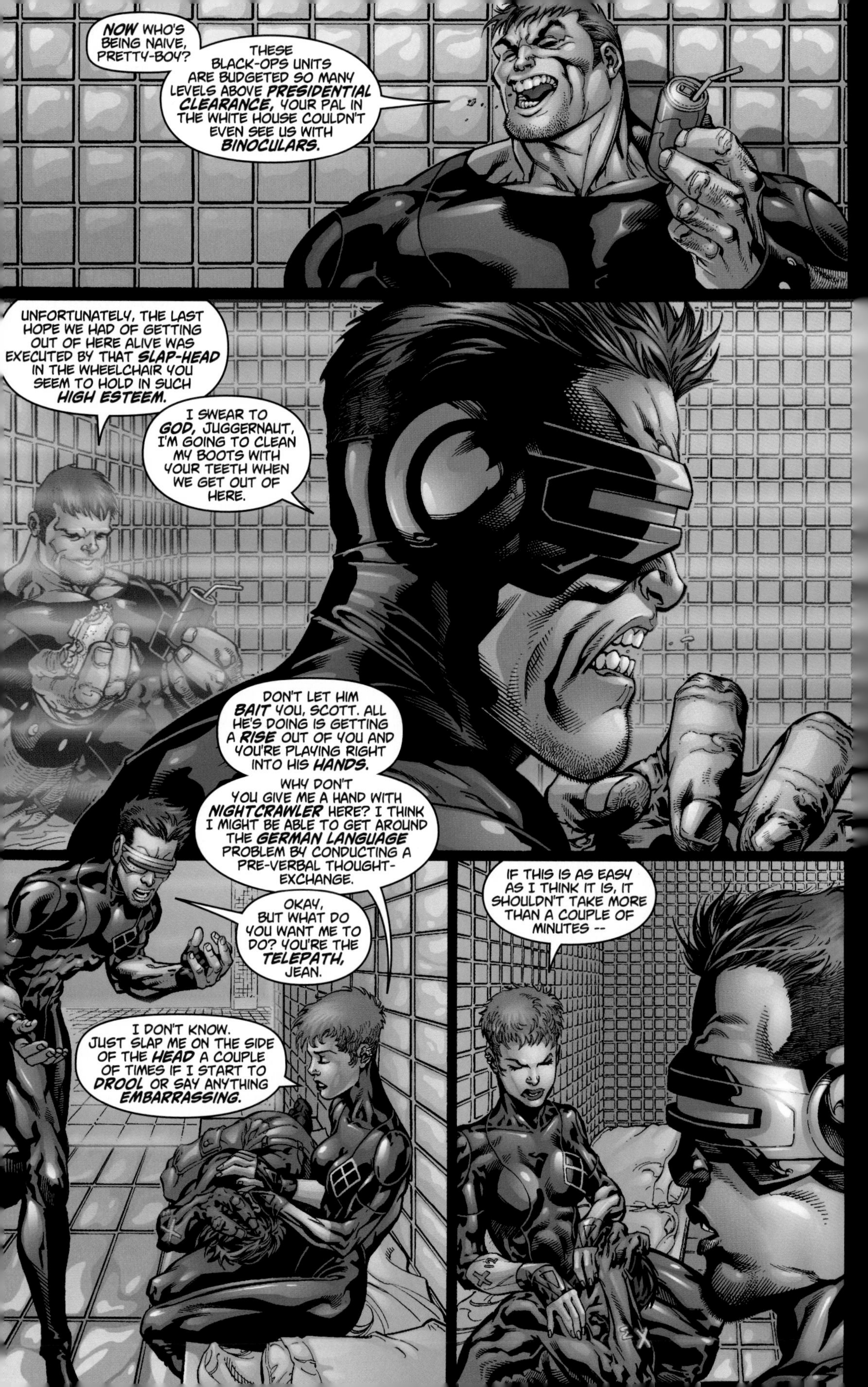
NOW WHO'S BEING NAIVE, PRETTY-BOY?
THESE BLACK-OPS UNITS ARE BUDGETED SO MANY LEVELS ABOVE PRESIDENTIAL CLEARANCE, YOUR PAL IN THE WHITE HOUSE COULDN'T EVEN SEE US WITH BINOCULARS.
UNFORTUNATELY, THE LAST HOPE WE HAD OF GETTING OUT OF HERE ALIVE WAS EXECUTED BY THAT SLAP-HEAD IN THE WHEELCHAIR YOU SEEM TO HOLD IN SUCH HIGH ESTEEM.
I SWEAR TO GOD, JUGGERNAUT, I'M GOING TO CLEAN MY BOOTS WITH YOUR TEETH WHEN WE GET OUT OF HERE.
DON'T LET HIM BAIT YOU, SCOTT. ALL HE'S DOING IS GETTING A RISE OUT OF YOU AND YOU'RE PLAYING RIGHT INTO HIS HANDS.
WHY DON'T YOU GIVE ME A HAND WITH NIGHTCRAWLER HERE? I THINK I MIGHT BE ABLE TO GET AROUND THE GERMAN LANGUAGE PROBLEM BY CONDUCTING A PRE-VERBAL THOUGHT-EXCHANGE.
OKAY, BUT WHAT DO YOU WANT ME TO DO? YOU'RE THE TELEPATH, JEAN.
I DON'T KNOW. JUST SLAP ME ON THE SIDE OF THE HEAD A COUPLE OF TIMES IF I START TO DROOL OR SAY ANYTHING EMBARRASSING.
IF THIS IS AS EASY AS I THINK IT IS, IT SHOULDN'T TAKE MORE THAN A COUPLE OF MINUTES --

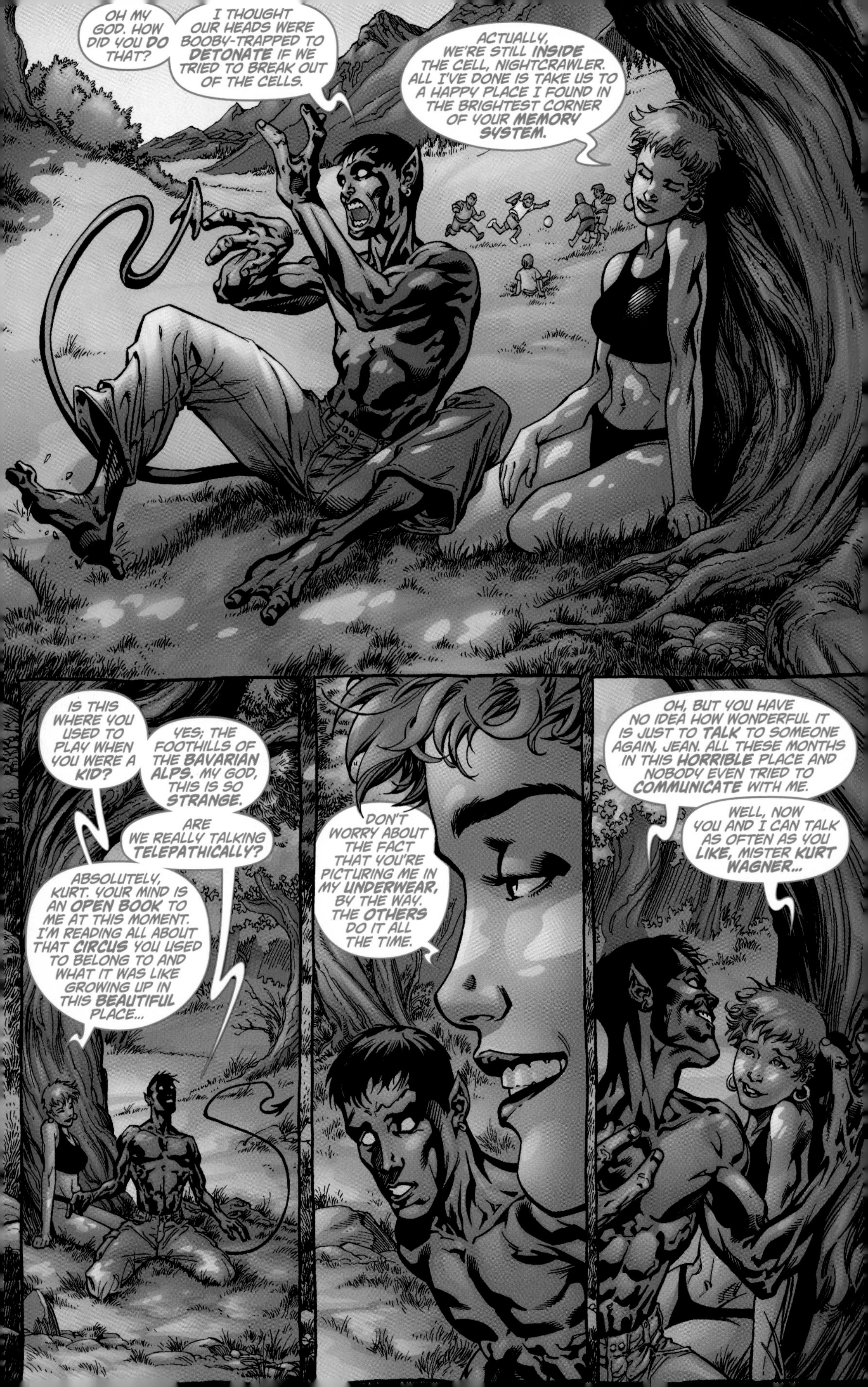
OH MY GOD. HOW DID YOU DO THAT?
I THOUGHT OUR HEADS WERE BOOBY-TRAPPED TO DETONATE IF WE TRIED TO BREAK OUT OF THE CELLS.
ACTUALLY, WE'RE STILL INSIDE THE CELL, NIGHTCRAWLER. ALL I'VE DONE IS TAKE US TO A HAPPY PLACE I FOUND IN THE BRIGHTEST CORNER OF YOUR MEMORY SYSTEM.
IS THIS WHERE YOU USED TO PLAY WHEN YOU WERE A KID?
YES; THE FOOTHILLS OF THE BAVARIAN ALPS. MY GOD, THIS IS SO STRANGE.
ARE WE REALLY TALKING TELEPATHICALLY?
ABSOLUTELY, KURT. YOUR MIND IS AN OPEN BOOK TO ME AT THIS MOMENT. I'M READING ALL ABOUT THAT CIRCUS YOU USED TO BELONG TO AND WHAT IT WAS LIKE GROWING UP IN THIS BEAUTIFUL PLACE...
DON'T WORRY ABOUT THE FACT THAT YOU'RE PICTURING ME IN MY UNDERWEAR, BY THE WAY. THE OTHERS DO IT ALL THE TIME.
OH, BUT YOU HAVE NO IDEA HOW WONDERFUL IT IS JUST TO TALK TO SOMEONE AGAIN, JEAN. ALL THESE MONTHS IN THIS HORRIBLE PLACE AND NOBODY EVEN TRIED TO COMMUNICATE WITH ME.
WELL, NOW YOU AND I CAN TALK AS OFTEN AS YOU LIKE, MISTER KURT WAGNER...

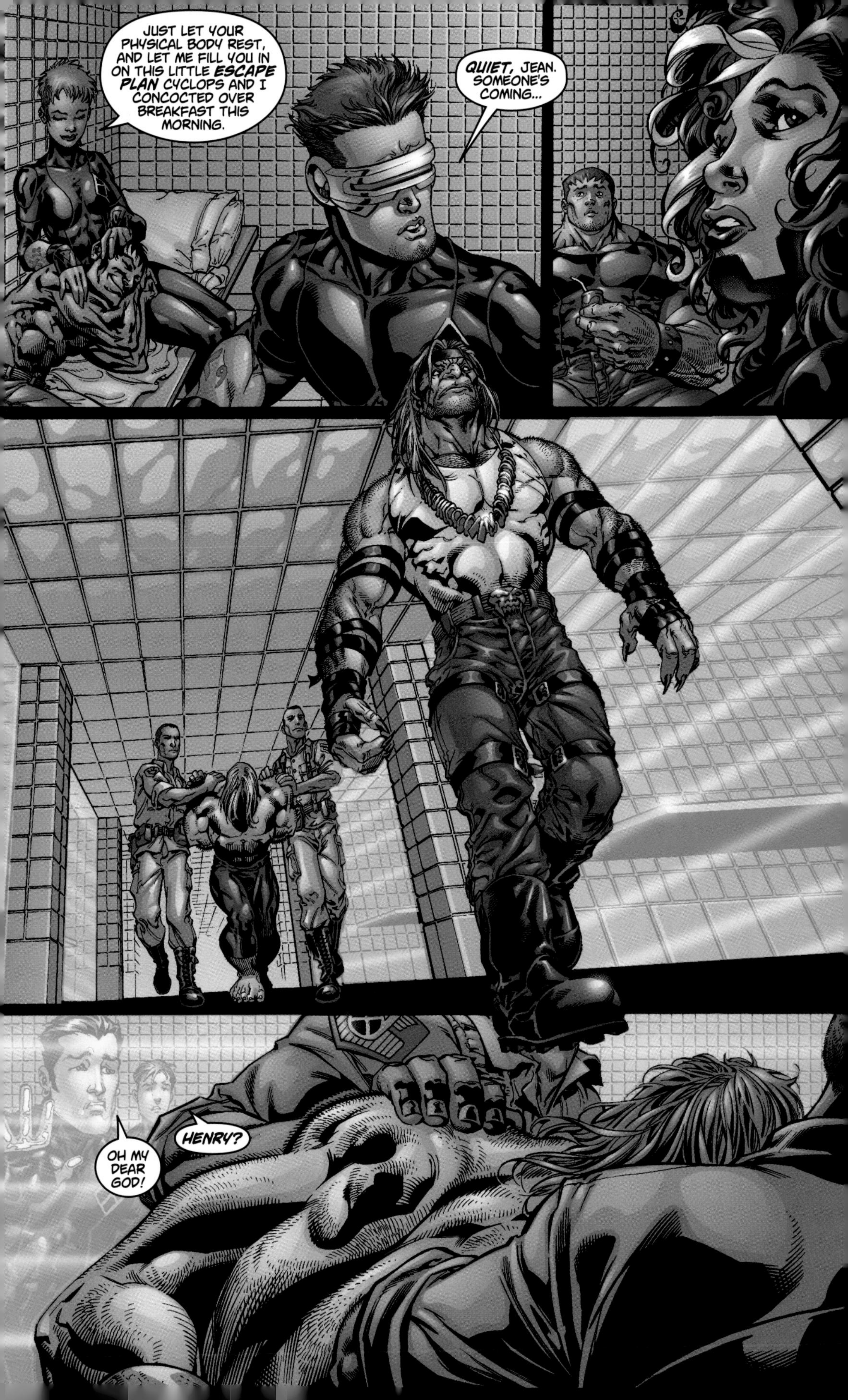
JUST LET YOUR PHYSICAL BODY REST, AND LET ME FILL YOU IN ON THIS LITTLE ESCAPE PLAN CYCLOPS AND I CONCOCTED OVER BREAKFAST THIS MORNING.
QUIET, JEAN. SOMEONE'S COMING...
HENRY?
OH MY DEAR GOD!

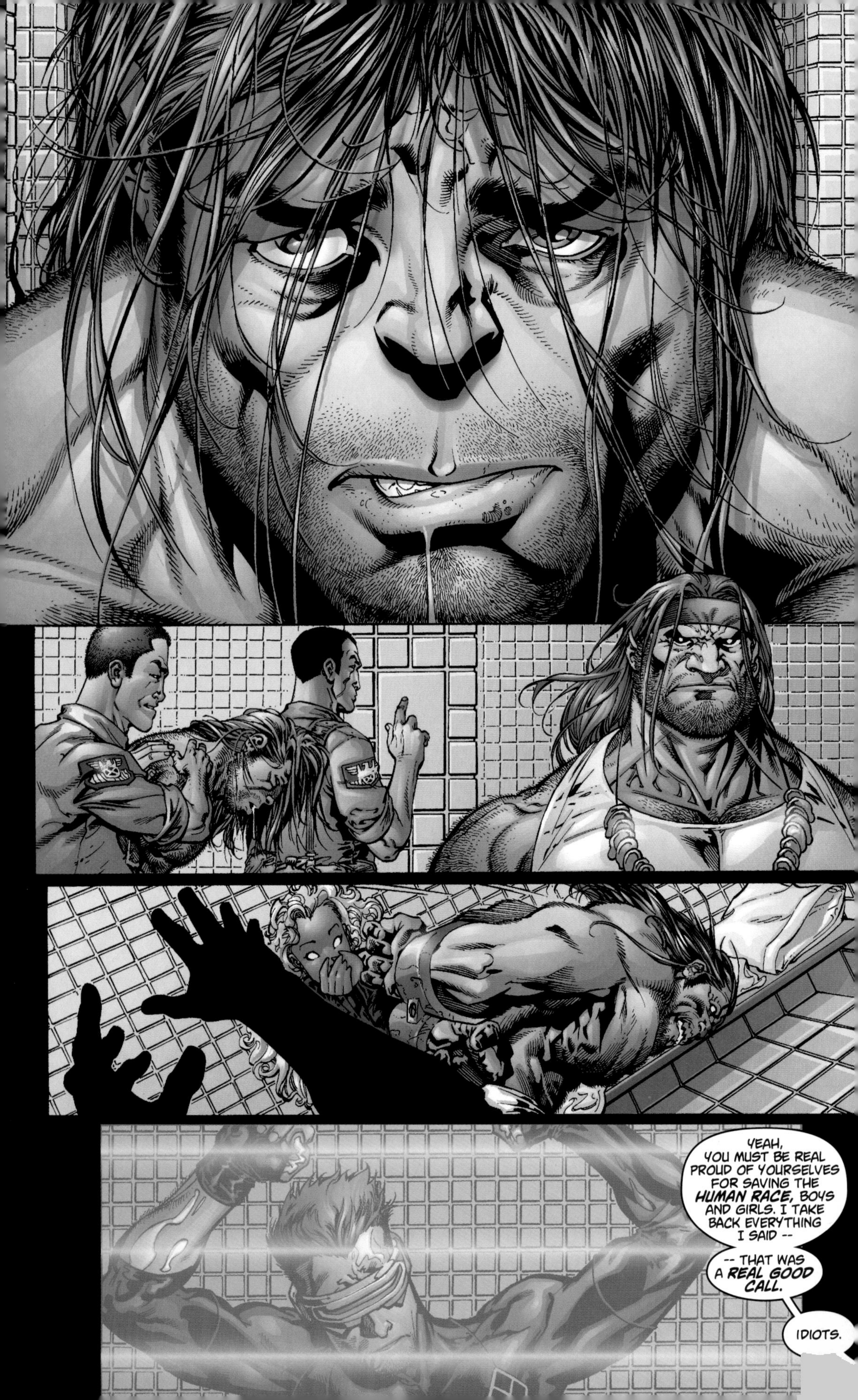
YEAH, YOU MUST BE REAL PROUD OF YOURSELVES FOR SAVING THE HUMAN RACE, BOYS AND GIRLS. I TAKE BACK EVERYTHING I SAID --
-- THAT WAS A REAL GOOD CALL.
IDIOTS.

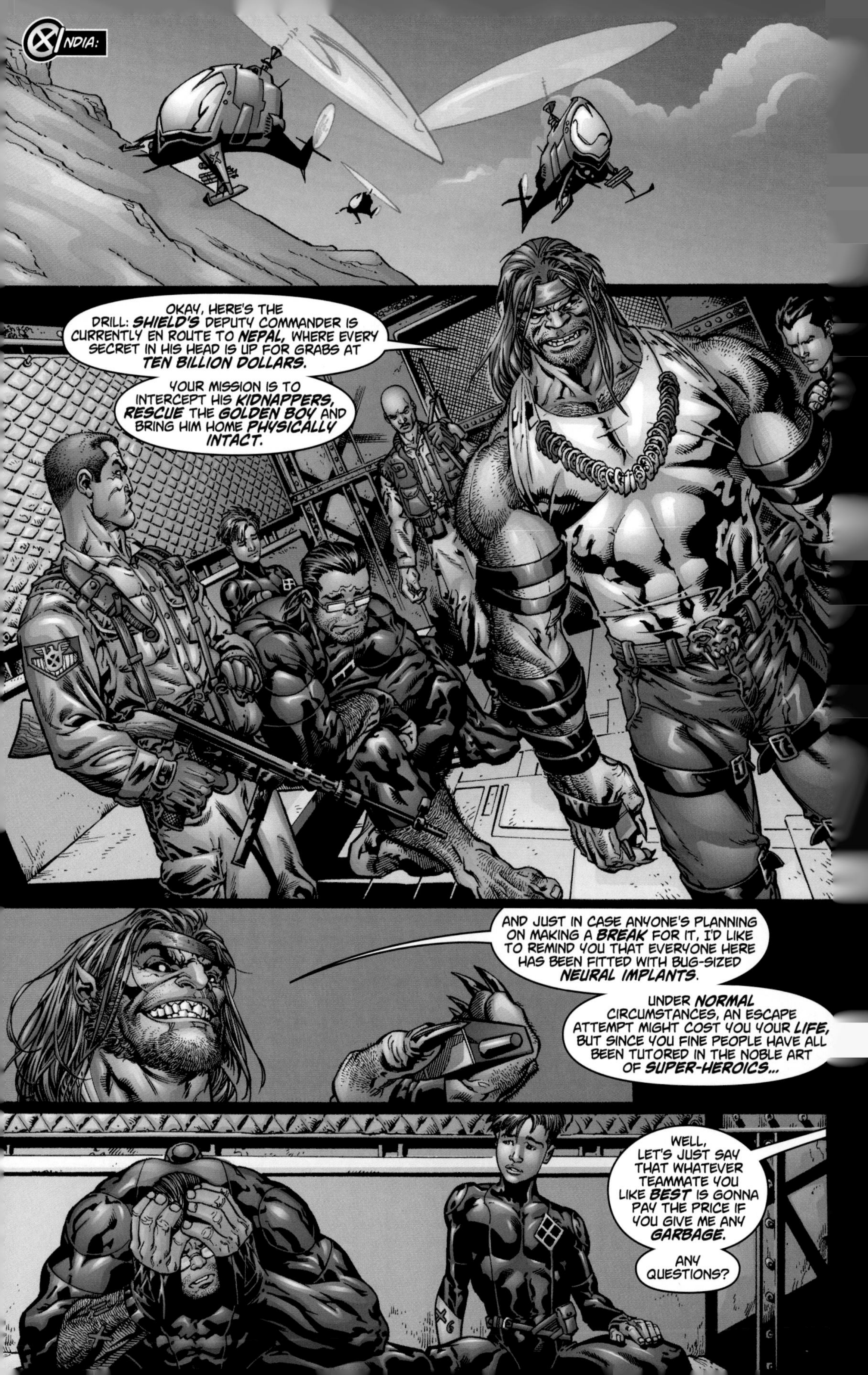

INDIA:
OKAY, HERE'S THE DRILL: SHIELD'S DEPUTY COMMANDER IS CURRENTLY EN ROUTE TO NEPAL, WHERE EVERY SECRET IN HIS HEAD IS UP FOR GRABS AT TEN BILLION DOLLARS.
YOUR MISSION IS TO INTERCEPT HIS KIDNAPPERS, RESCUE THE GOLDEN BOY AND BRING HIM HOME PHYSICALLY INTACT.
AND JUST IN CASE ANYONE'S PLANNING ON MAKING A BREAK FOR IT, I'D LIKE TO REMIND YOU THAT EVERYONE HERE HAS BEEN FITTED WITH BUG-SIZED NEURAL IMPLANTS.
UNDER NORMAL CIRCUMSTANCES, AN ESCAPE ATTEMPT MIGHT COST YOU YOUR LIFE, BUT SINCE YOU FINE PEOPLE HAVE ALL BEEN TUTORED IN THE NOBLE ART OF SUPER-HEROICS...
WELL, LET'S JUST SAY THAT WHATEVER TEAMMATE YOU LIKE BEST IS GONNA PAY THE PRICE IF YOU GIVE ME ANY GARBAGE.
ANY QUESTIONS?

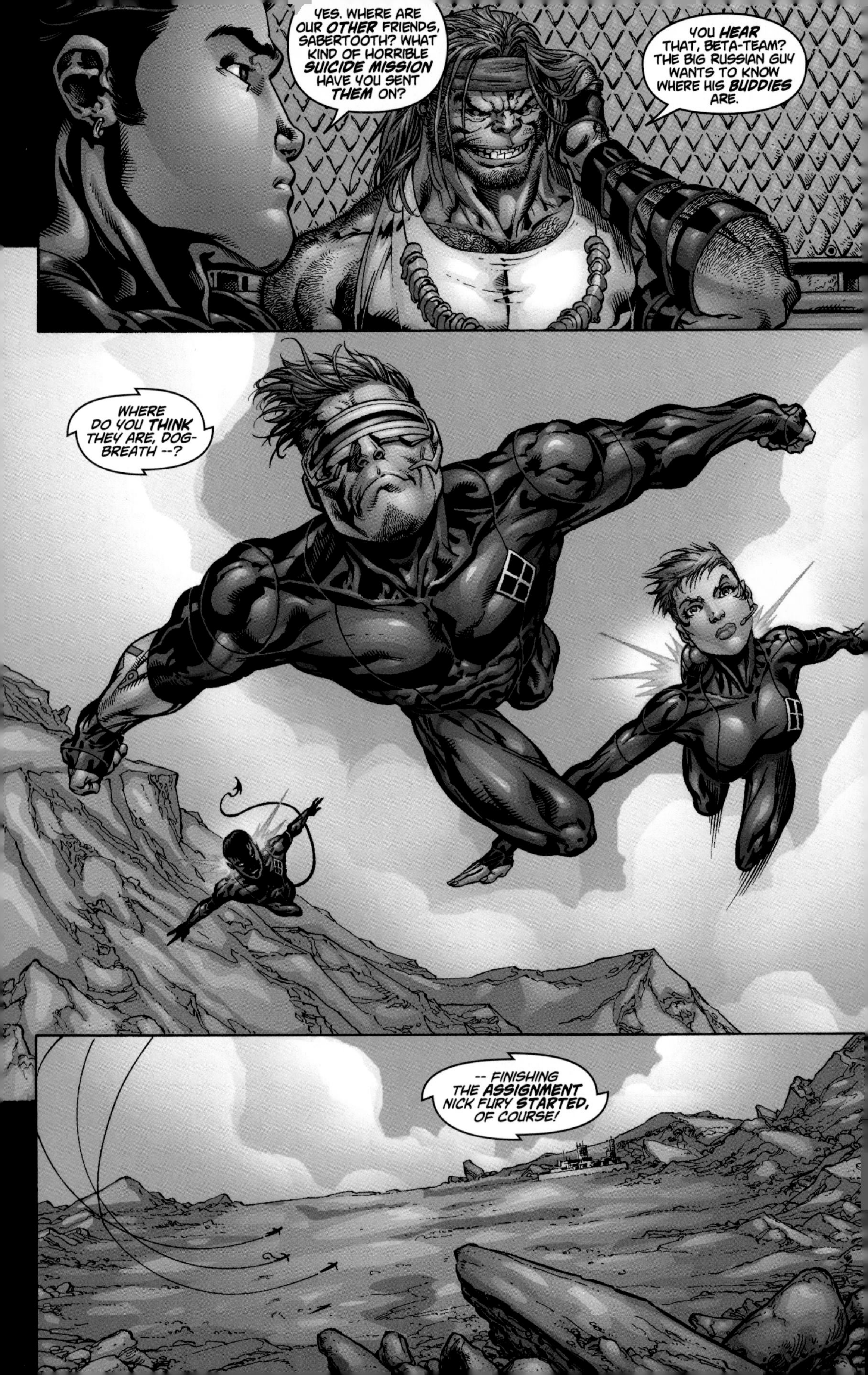
YES. WHERE ARE OUR OTHER FRIENDS, SABERTOOTH? WHAT KIND OF HORRIBLE SUICIDE MISSION HAVE YOU SENT THEM ON?
YOU HEAR THAT, BETA-TEAM? THE BIG RUSSIAN GUY WANTS TO KNOW WHERE HIS BUDDIES ARE.
WHERE DO YOU THINK THEY ARE, DOG-BREATH --?
-- FINISHING THE ASSIGNMENT NICK FURY STARTED, OF COURSE!

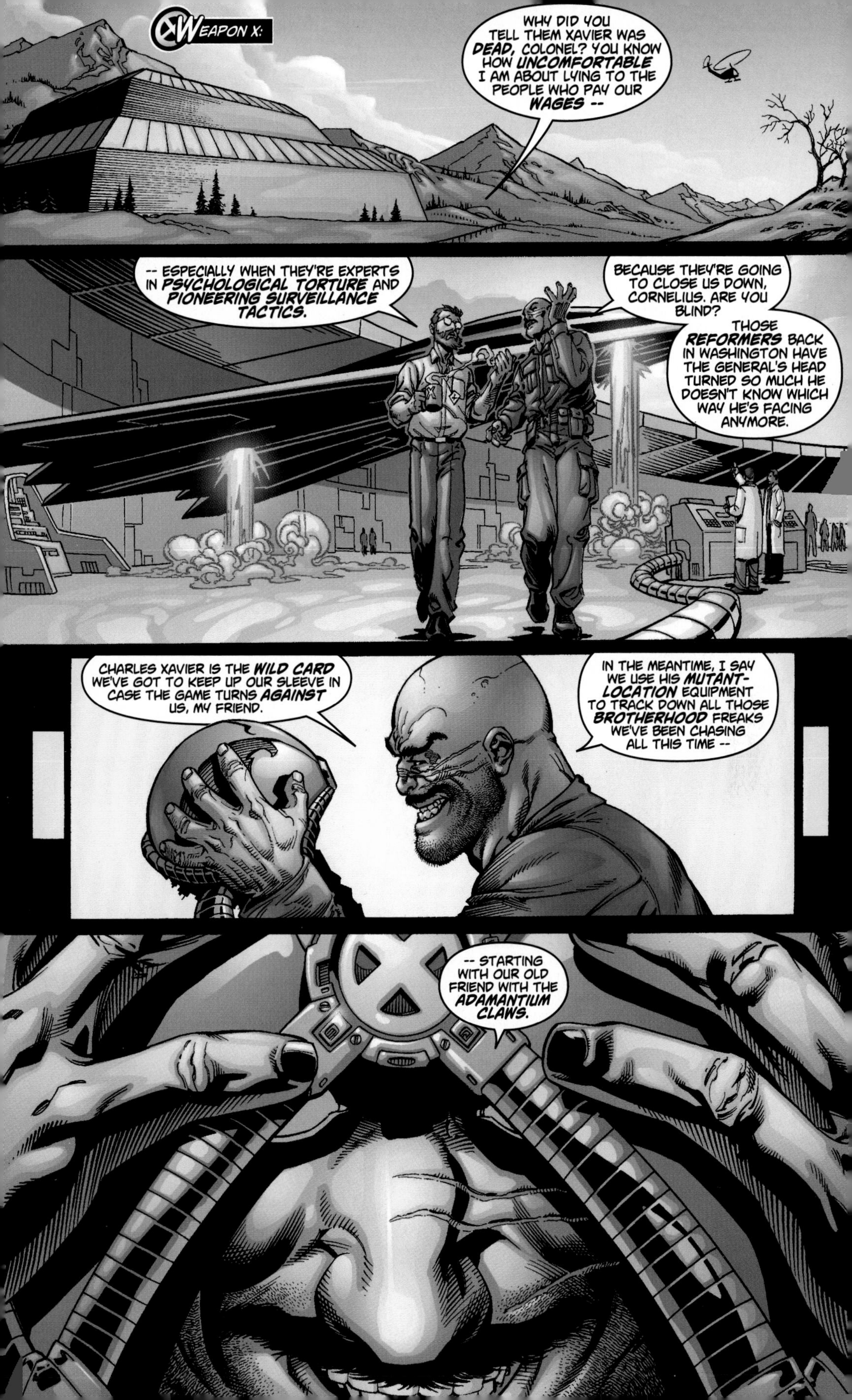
WEAPON X:
WHY DID YOU TELL THEM XAVIER WAS DEAD, COLONEL? YOU KNOW HOW UNCOMFORTABLE I AM ABOUT LYING TO THE PEOPLE WHO PAY OUR WAGES --
-- ESPECIALLY WHEN THEY'RE EXPERTS IN PSYCHOLOGICAL TORTURE AND PIONEERING SURVEILLANCE TACTICS.
BECAUSE THEY'RE GOING TO CLOSE US DOWN, CORNELIUS. ARE YOU BLIND?
THOSE REFORMERS BACK IN WASHINGTON HAVE THE GENERAL'S HEAD TURNED SO MUCH HE DOESN'T KNOW WHICH WAY HE'S FACING ANYMORE.
CHARLES XAVIER IS THE WILD CARD WE'VE GOT TO KEEP UP OUR SLEEVE IN CASE THE GAME TURNS AGAINST US, MY FRIEND.
IN THE MEANTIME, I SAY WE USE HIS MUTANT-LOCATION EQUIPMENT TO TRACK DOWN ALL THOSE BROTHERHOOD FREAKS WE'VE BEEN CHASING ALL THIS TIME --
-- STARTING WITH OUR OLD FRIEND WITH THE ADAMANTIUM CLAWS.

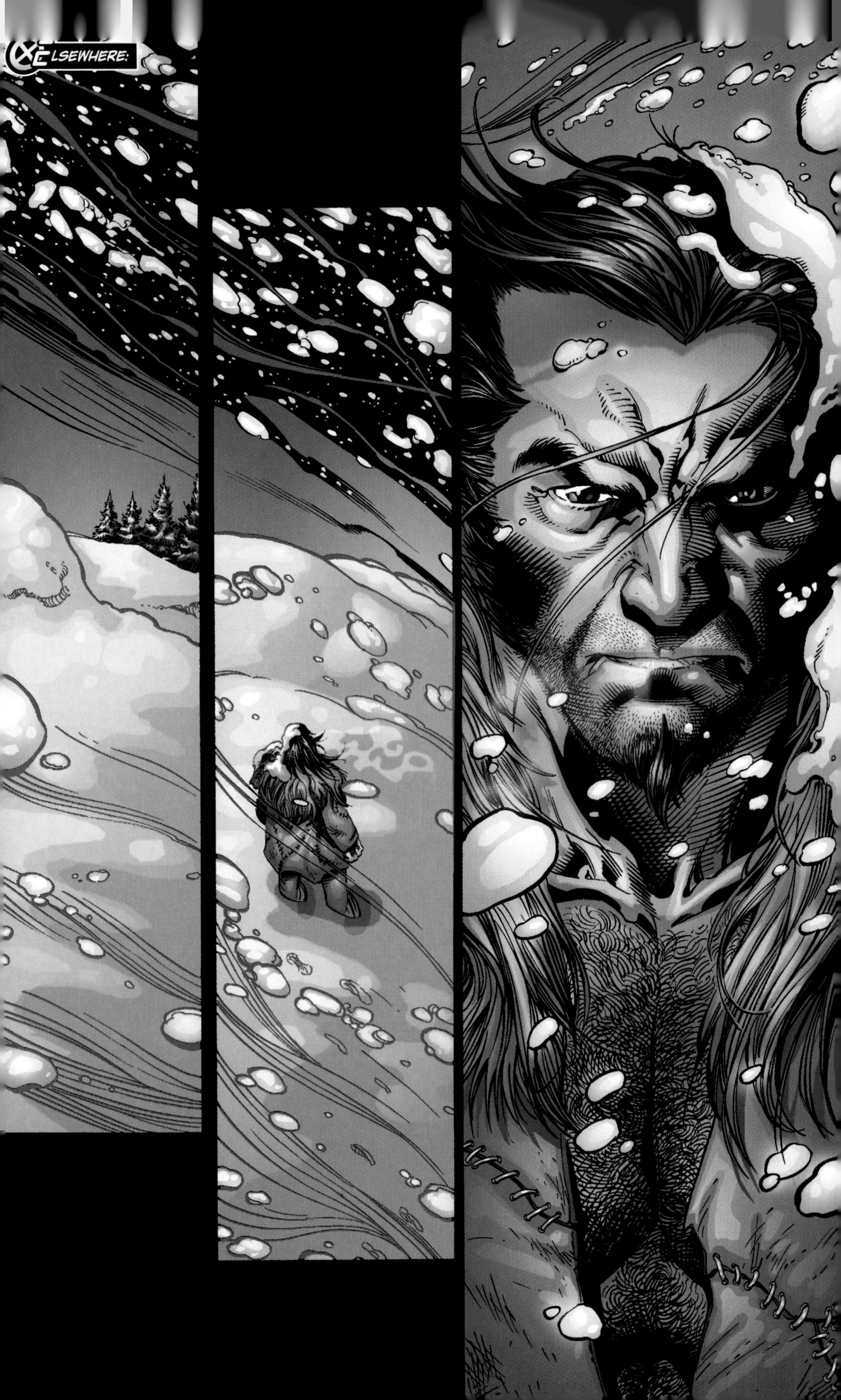
ELSEWHERE:

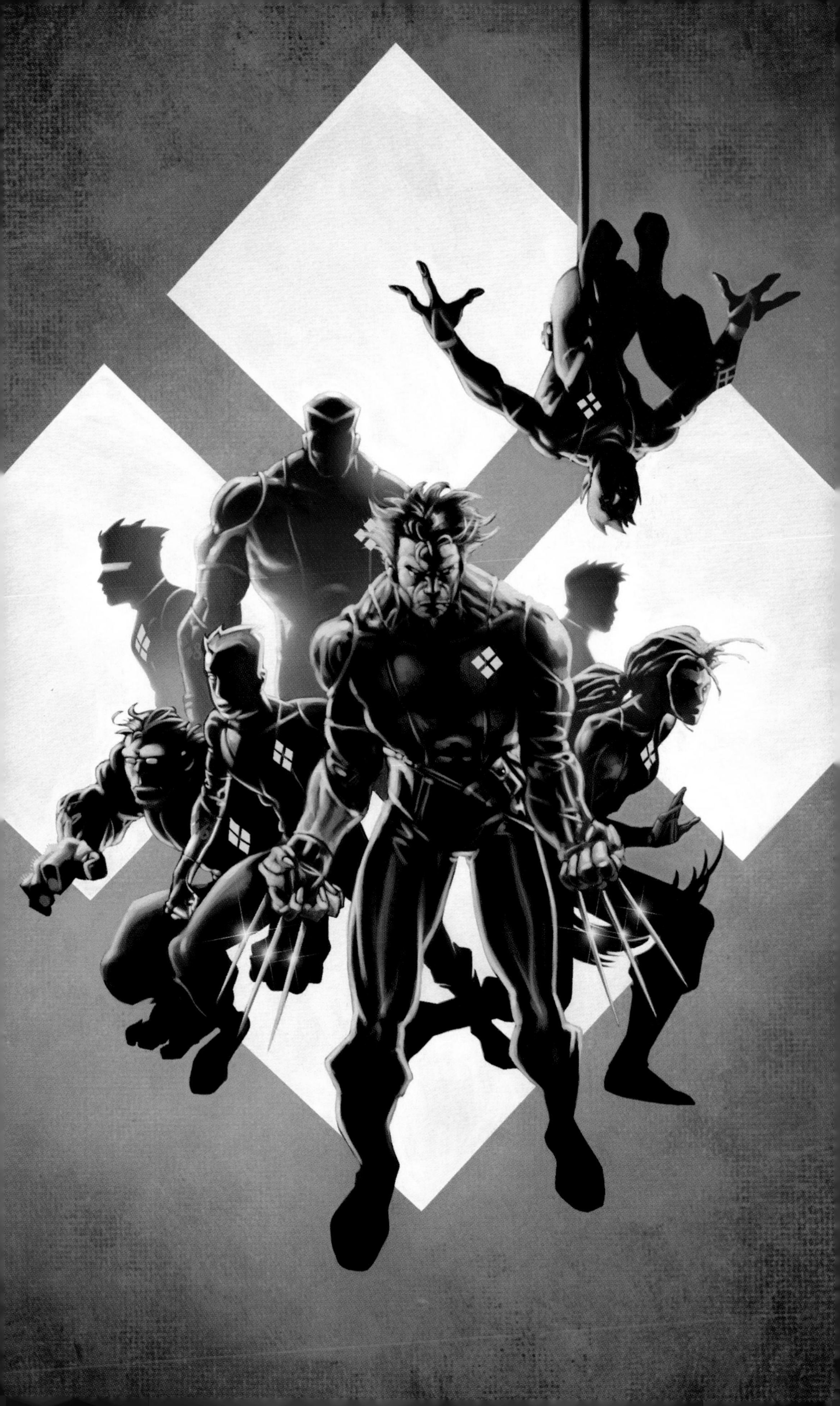

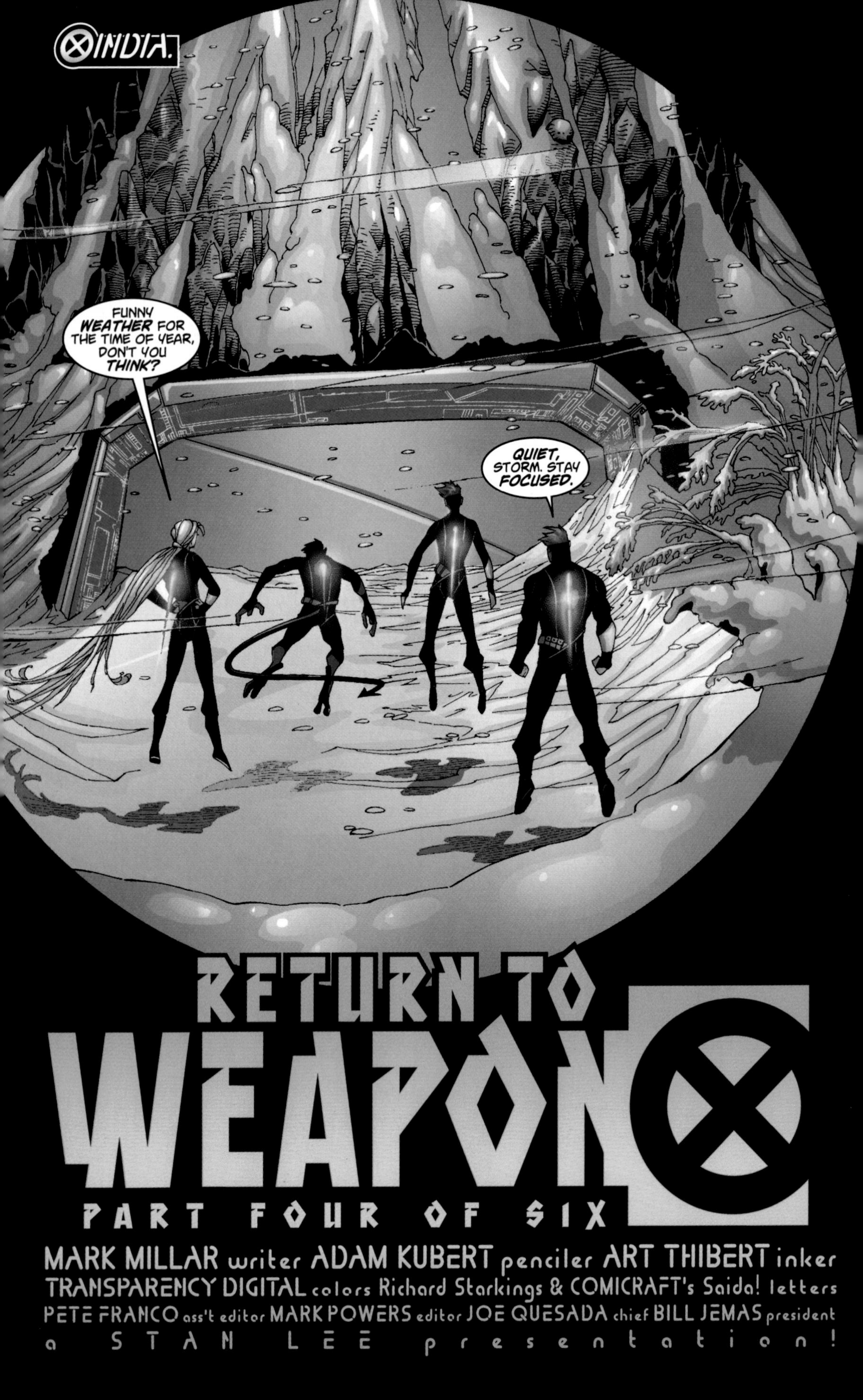

FUNNY WEATHER FOR THE TIME OF YEAR, DON'T YOU THINK?
QUIET, STORM. STAY FOCUSED.

RETURN TO WEAPON X

PART FOUR OF SIX

MARK MILLAR writer ADAM KUBERT penciler ART THIBERT inker
TRANSPARENCY DIGITAL colors Richard Starkings & COMICRAFT's Saida! letters
PETE FRANCO ass't editor MARK POWERS editor JOE QUESADA chief BILL JEMAS president
a STAN LEE presentation!

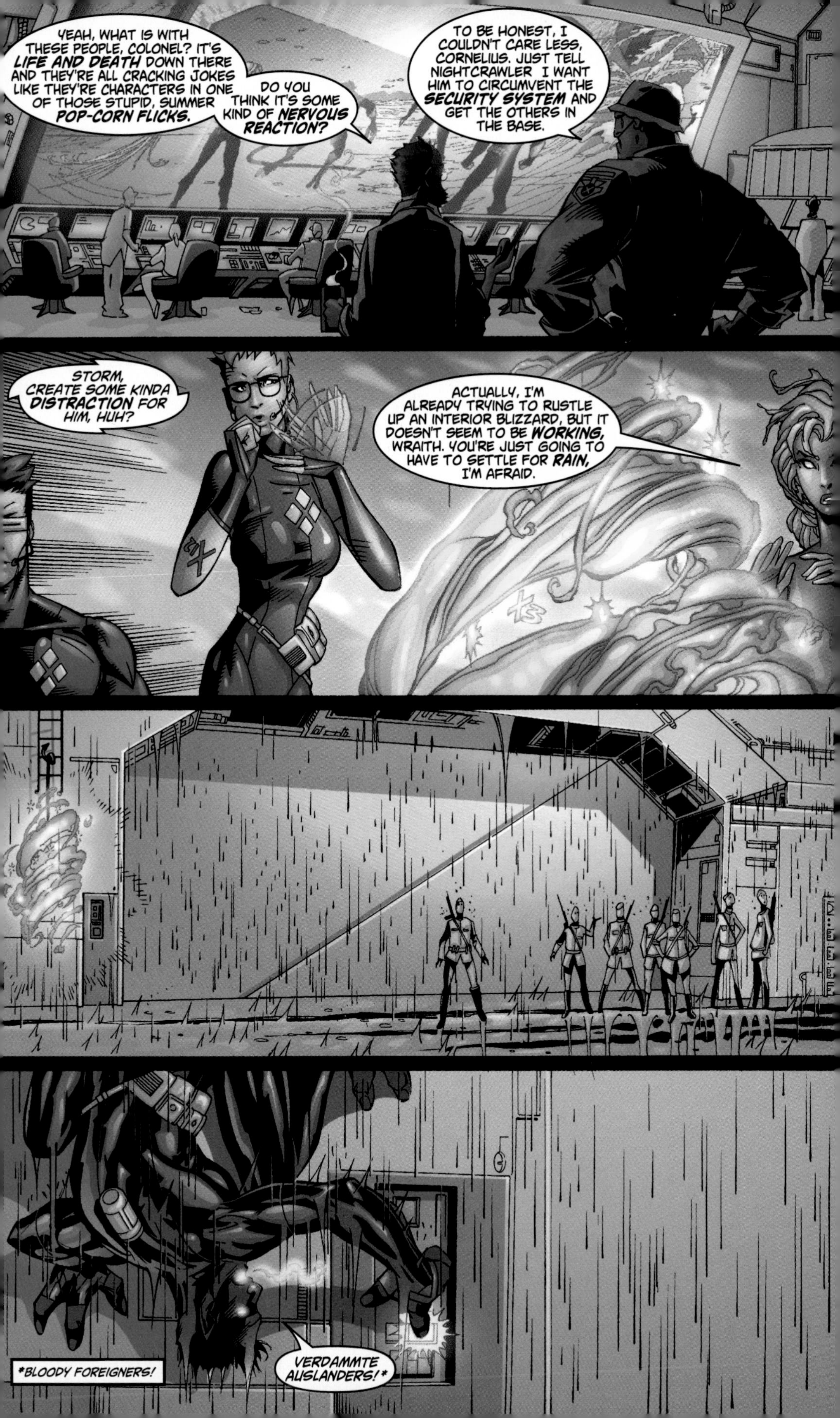

YEAH, WHAT IS WITH THESE PEOPLE, COLONEL? IT'S LIFE AND DEATH DOWN THERE AND THEY'RE ALL CRACKING JOKES LIKE THEY'RE CHARACTERS IN ONE OF THOSE STUPID, SUMMER POP-CORN FLICKS.
DO YOU THINK IT'S SOME KIND OF NERVOUS REACTION?
TO BE HONEST, I COULDN'T CARE LESS, CORNELIUS. JUST TELL NIGHTCRAWLER I WANT HIM TO CIRCUMVENT THE SECURITY SYSTEM AND GET THE OTHERS IN THE BASE.
STORM, CREATE SOME KINDA DISTRACTION FOR HIM, HUH?
ACTUALLY, I'M ALREADY TRYING TO RUSTLE UP AN INTERIOR BLIZZARD, BUT IT DOESN'T SEEM TO BE WORKING, WRAITH. YOU'RE JUST GOING TO HAVE TO SETTLE FOR RAIN, I'M AFRAID.
VERDAMMTE AUSLANDERS!*
*BLOODY FOREIGNERS!

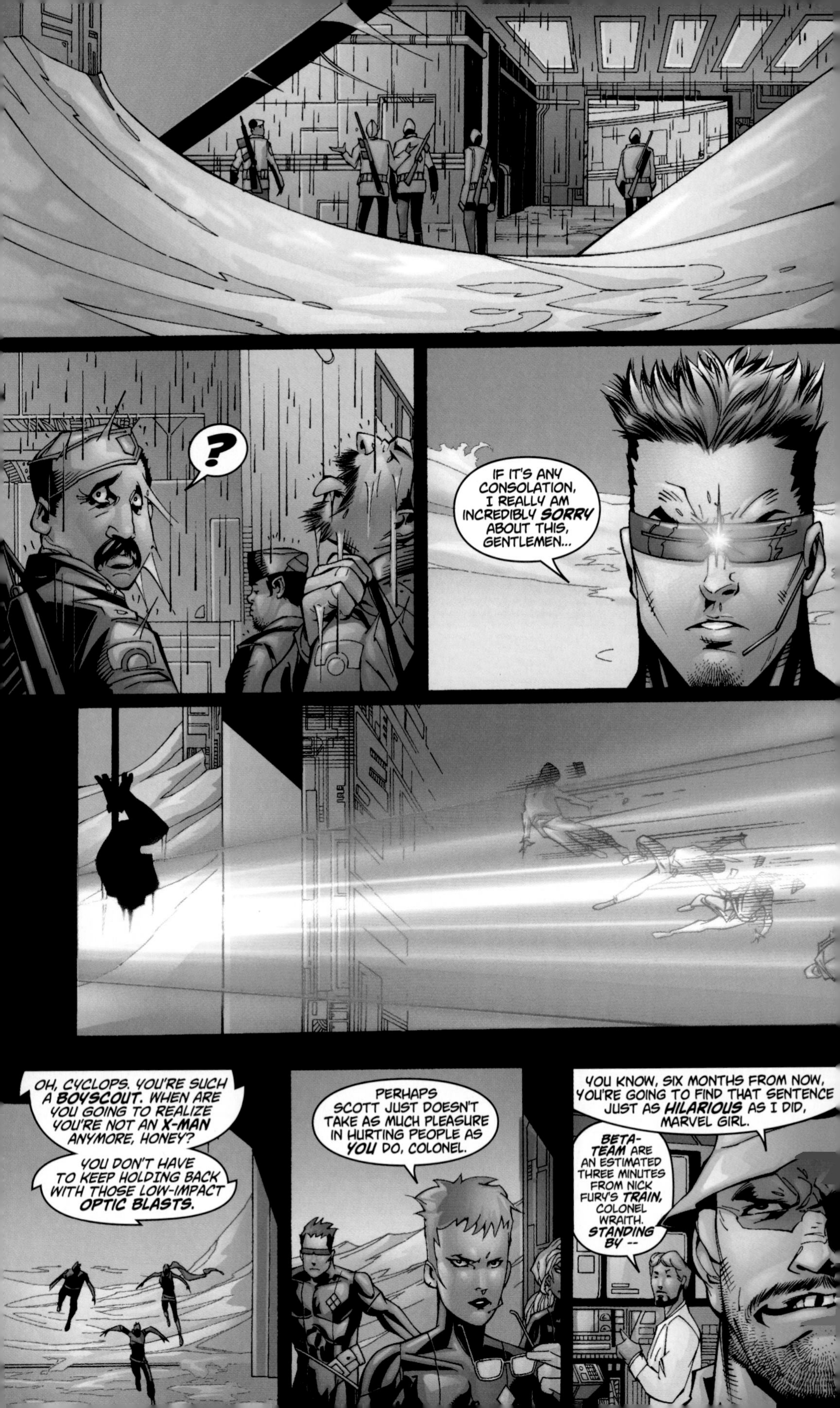
?
IF IT'S ANY CONSOLATION, I REALLY AM INCREDIBLY SORRY ABOUT THIS, GENTLEMEN...
OH, CYCLOPS. YOU'RE SUCH A BOYSCOUT. WHEN ARE YOU GOING TO REALIZE YOU'RE NOT AN X-MAN ANYMORE, HONEY?
YOU DON'T HAVE TO KEEP HOLDING BACK WITH THOSE LOW-IMPACT OPTIC BLASTS.
PERHAPS SCOTT JUST DOESN'T TAKE AS MUCH PLEASURE IN HURTING PEOPLE AS YOU DO, COLONEL.
YOU KNOW, SIX MONTHS FROM NOW, YOU'RE GOING TO FIND THAT SENTENCE JUST AS HILARIOUS AS I DID, MARVEL GIRL.
BETA-TEAM ARE AN ESTIMATED THREE MINUTES FROM NICK FURY'S TRAIN, COLONEL WRAITH. STANDING BY --

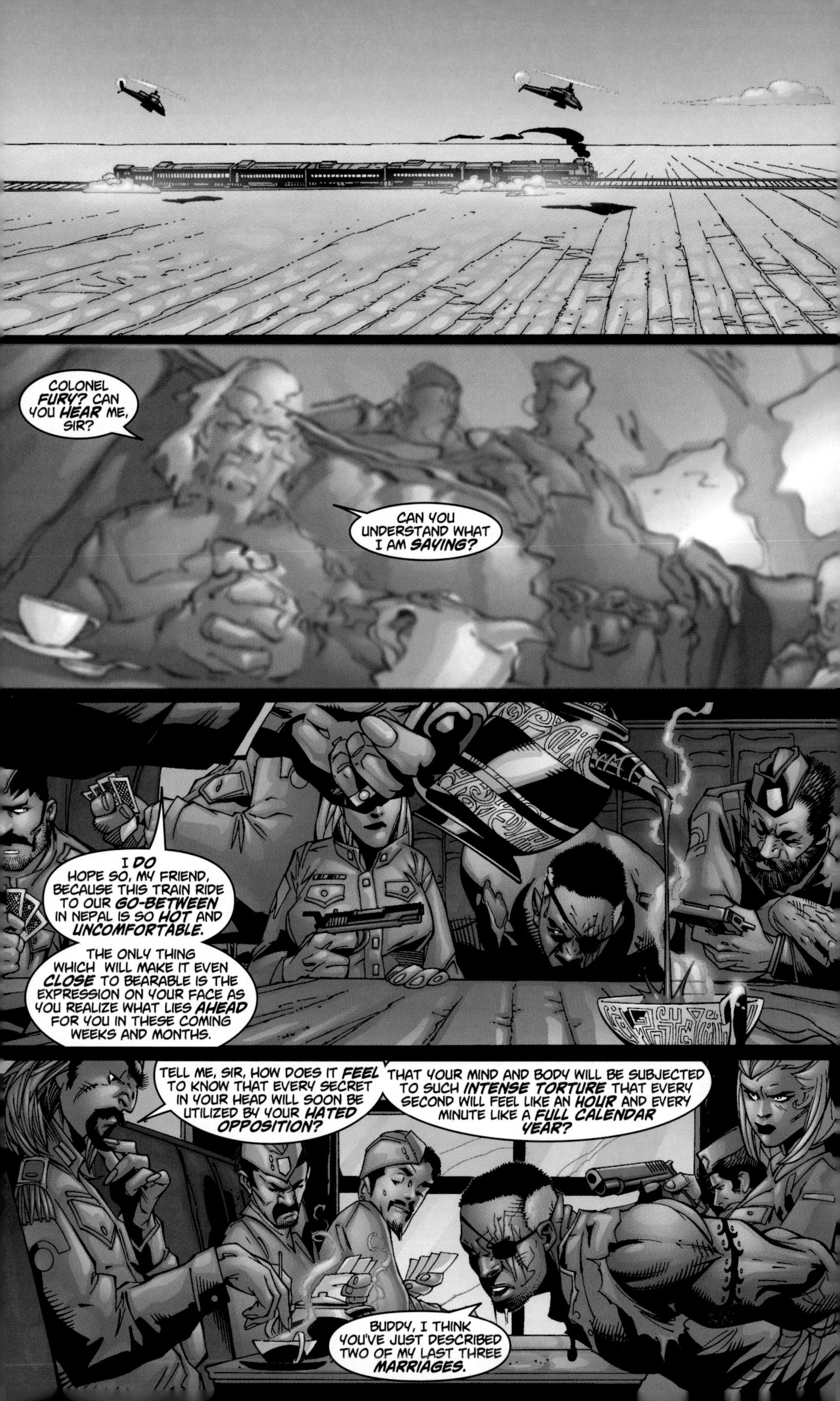
COLONEL FURY? CAN YOU HEAR ME, SIR?
CAN YOU UNDERSTAND WHAT I AM SAYING?
I DO HOPE SO, MY FRIEND, BECAUSE THIS TRAIN RIDE TO OUR GO-BETWEEN IN NEPAL IS SO HOT AND UNCOMFORTABLE.
THE ONLY THING WHICH WILL MAKE IT EVEN CLOSE TO BEARABLE IS THE EXPRESSION ON YOUR FACE AS YOU REALIZE WHAT LIES AHEAD FOR YOU IN THESE COMING WEEKS AND MONTHS.
TELL ME, SIR, HOW DOES IT FEEL TO KNOW THAT EVERY SECRET IN YOUR HEAD WILL SOON BE UTILIZED BY YOUR HATED OPPOSITION?
THAT YOUR MIND AND BODY WILL BE SUBJECTED TO SUCH INTENSE TORTURE THAT EVERY SECOND WILL FEEL LIKE AN HOUR AND EVERY MINUTE LIKE A FULL CALENDAR YEAR?
BUDDY, I THINK YOU'VE JUST DESCRIBED TWO OF MY LAST THREE MARRIAGES.

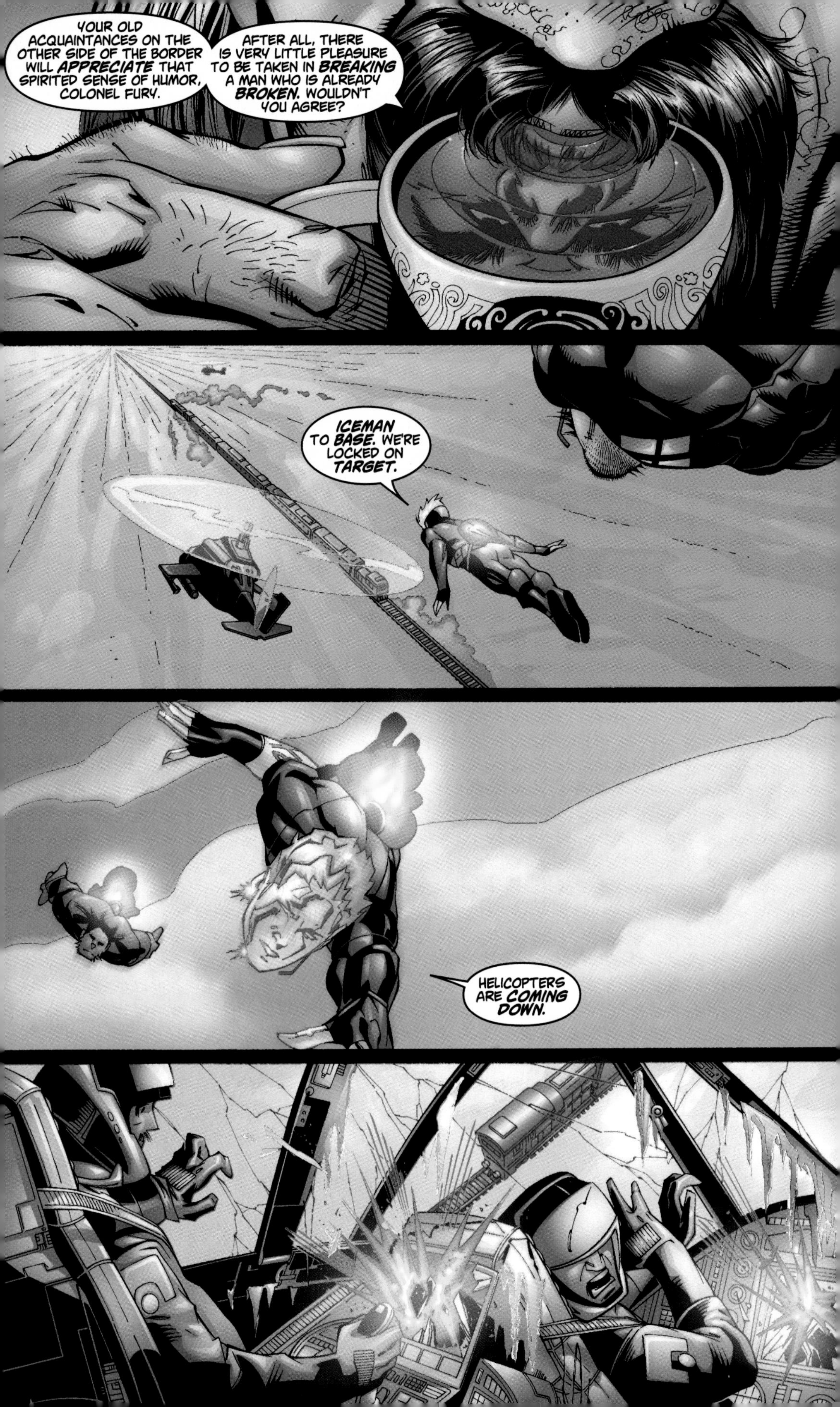

YOUR OLD ACQUAINTANCES ON THE OTHER SIDE OF THE BORDER WILL APPRECIATE THAT SPIRITED SENSE OF HUMOR, COLONEL FURY.
AFTER ALL, THERE IS VERY LITTLE PLEASURE TO BE TAKEN IN BREAKING A MAN WHO IS ALREADY BROKEN. WOULDN'T YOU AGREE?
ICEMAN TO BASE. WE'RE LOCKED ON TARGET.
HELICOPTERS ARE COMING DOWN.

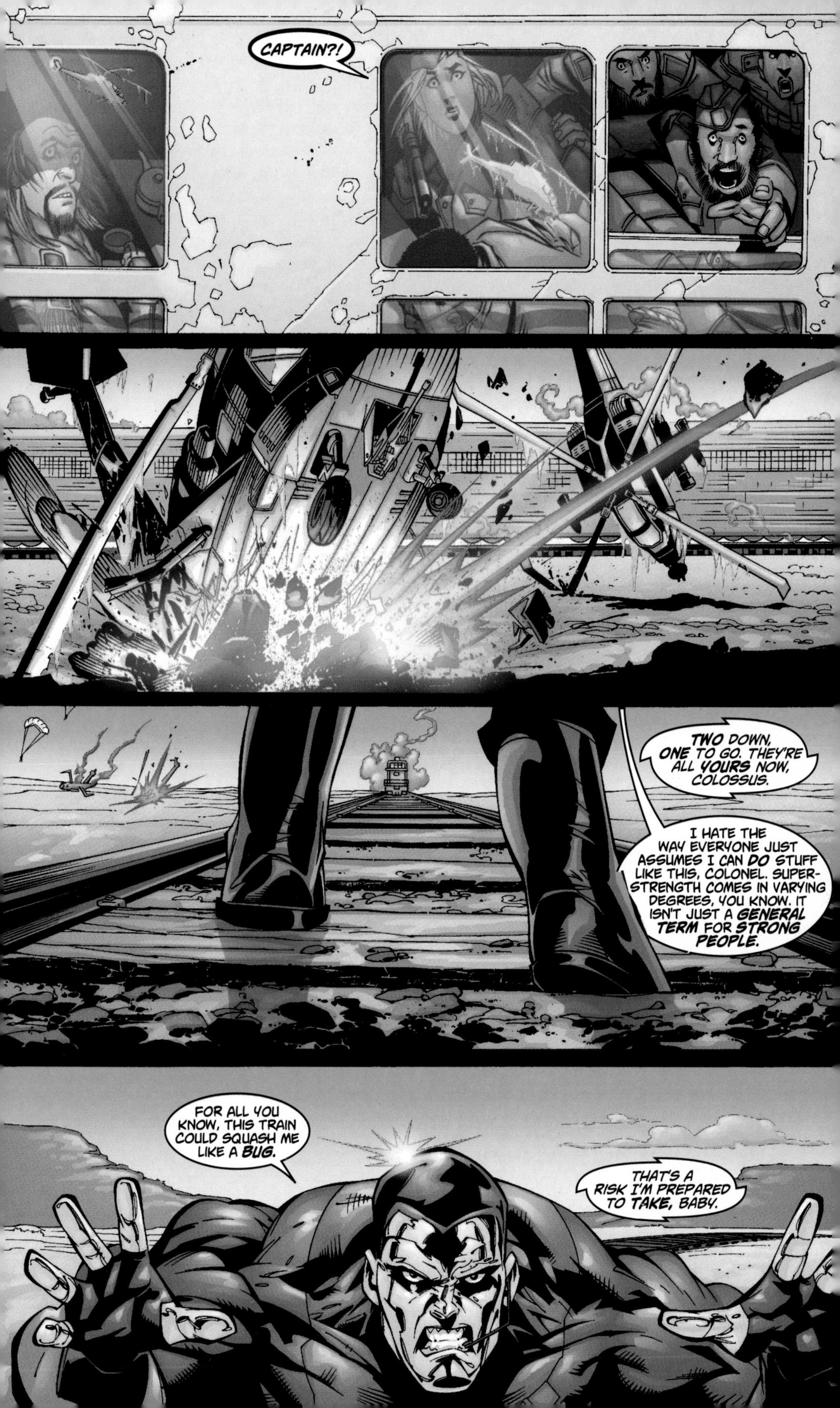
CAPTAIN?!
TWO DOWN, ONE TO GO. THEY'RE ALL YOURS NOW, COLOSSUS.
I HATE THE WAY EVERYONE JUST ASSUMES I CAN DO STUFF LIKE THIS, COLONEL. SUPER-STRENGTH COMES IN VARYING DEGREES, YOU KNOW. IT ISN'T JUST A GENERAL TERM FOR STRONG PEOPLE.
FOR ALL YOU KNOW, THIS TRAIN COULD SQUASH ME LIKE A BUG.
THAT'S A RISK I'M PREPARED TO TAKE, BABY.

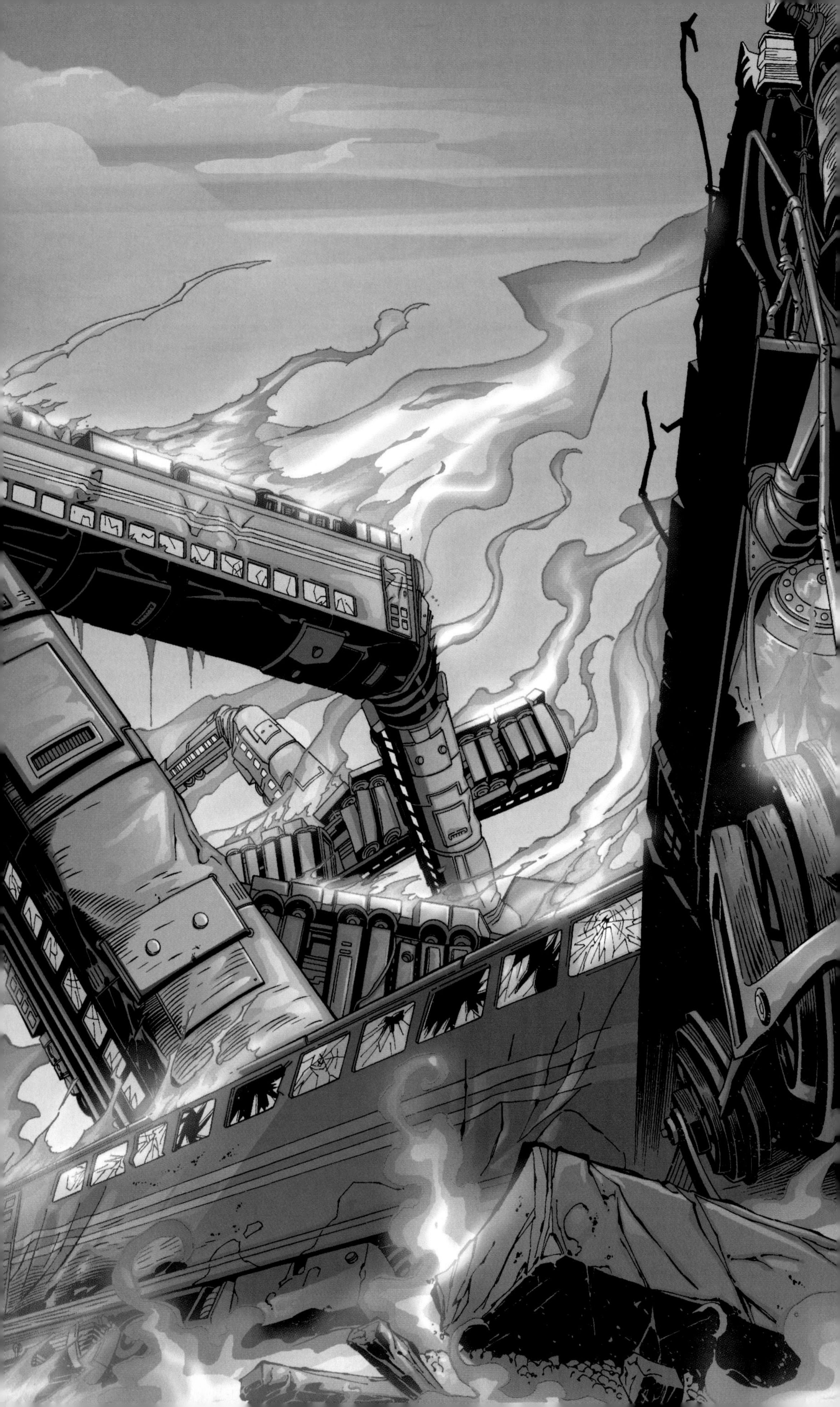

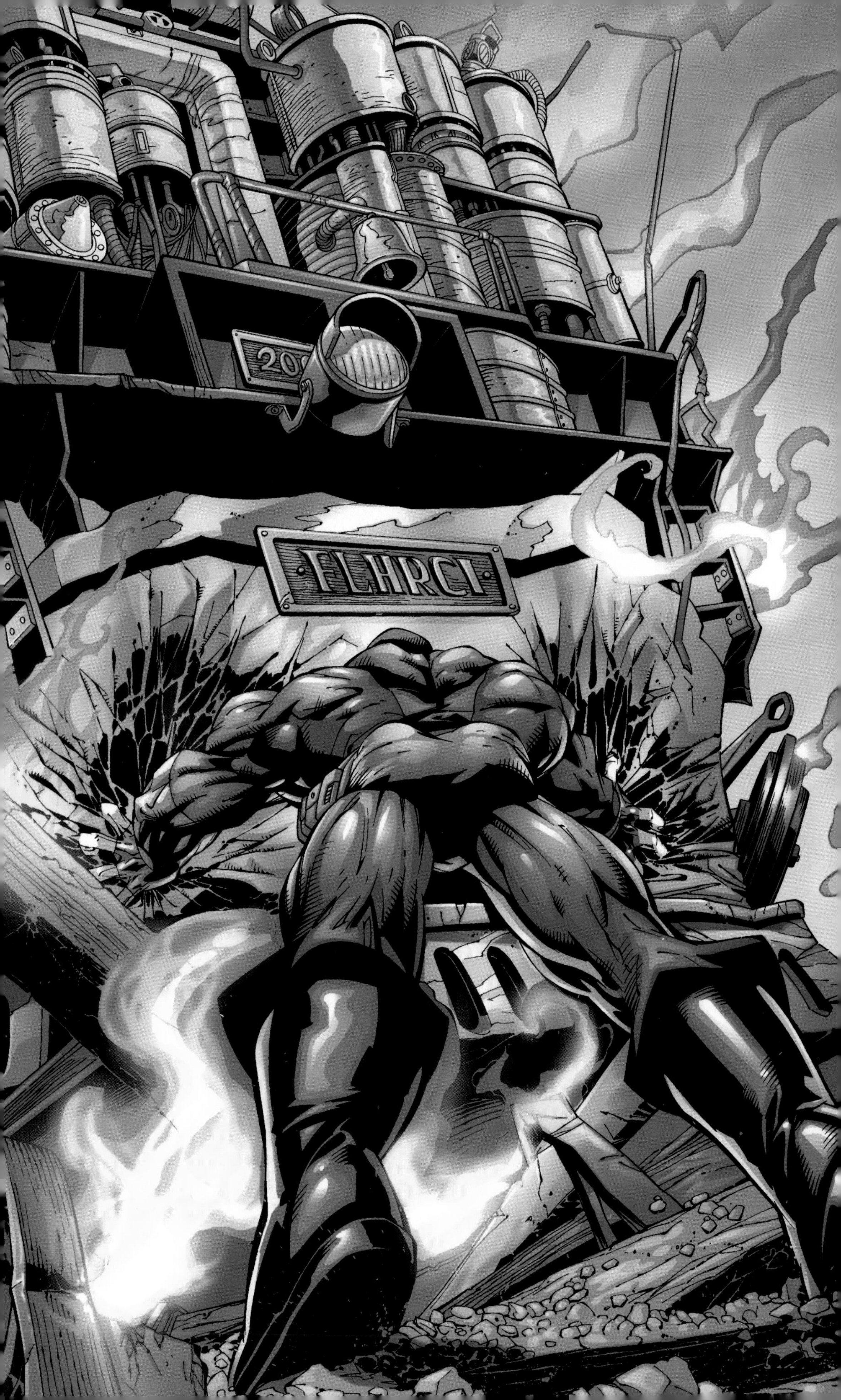
20
FLHRCI

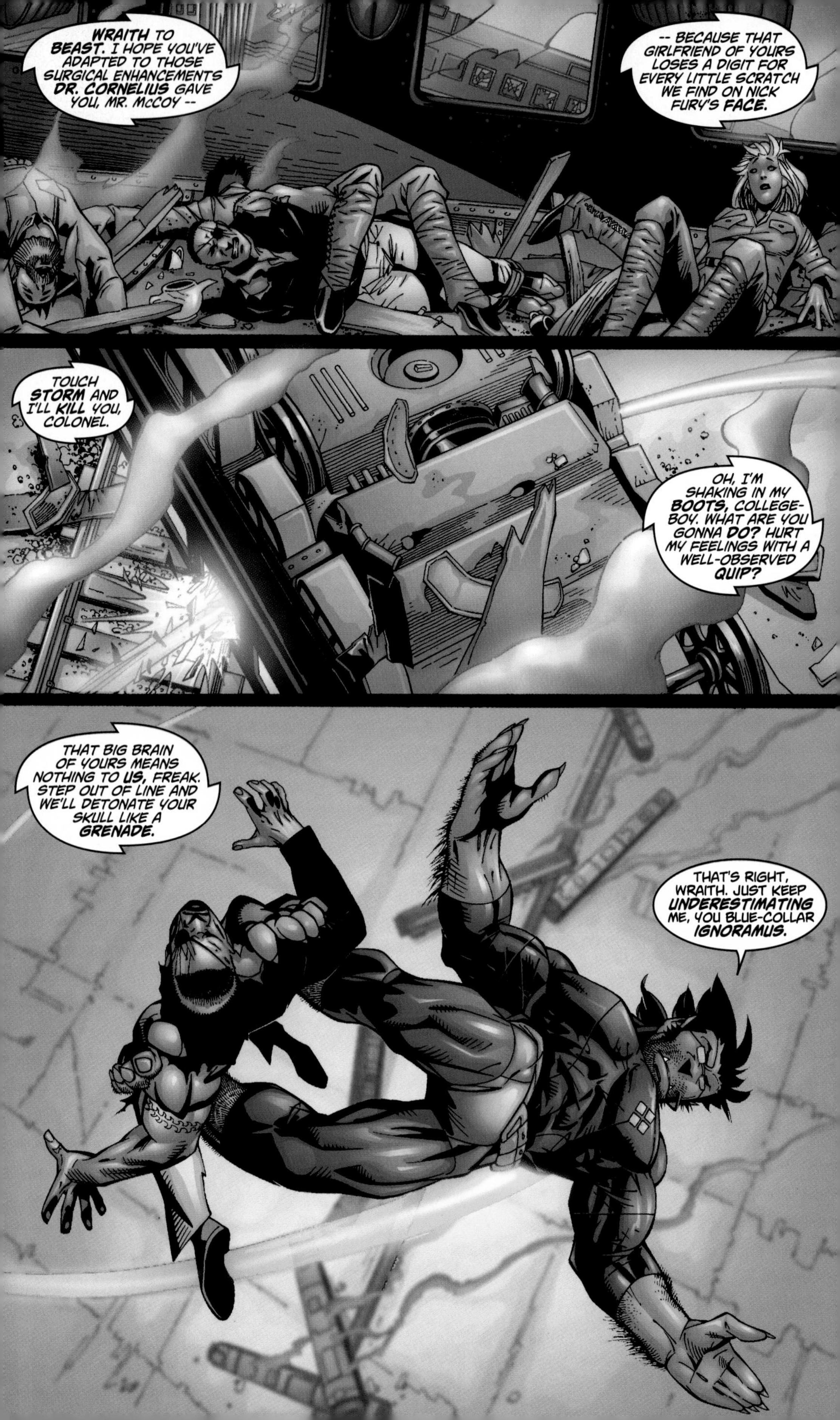
WRAITH TO BEAST. I HOPE YOU'VE ADAPTED TO THOSE SURGICAL ENHANCEMENTS DR. CORNELIUS GAVE YOU, MR. McCOY --
-- BECAUSE THAT GIRLFRIEND OF YOURS LOSES A DIGIT FOR EVERY LITTLE SCRATCH WE FIND ON NICK FURY'S FACE.
TOUCH STORM AND I'LL KILL YOU, COLONEL.
OH, I'M SHAKING IN MY BOOTS, COLLEGE-BOY. WHAT ARE YOU GONNA DO? HURT MY FEELINGS WITH A WELL-OBSERVED QUIP?
THAT BIG BRAIN OF YOURS MEANS NOTHING TO US, FREAK. STEP OUT OF LINE AND WE'LL DETONATE YOUR SKULL LIKE A GRENADE.
THAT'S RIGHT, WRAITH. JUST KEEP UNDERESTIMATING ME, YOU BLUE-COLLAR IGNORAMUS.

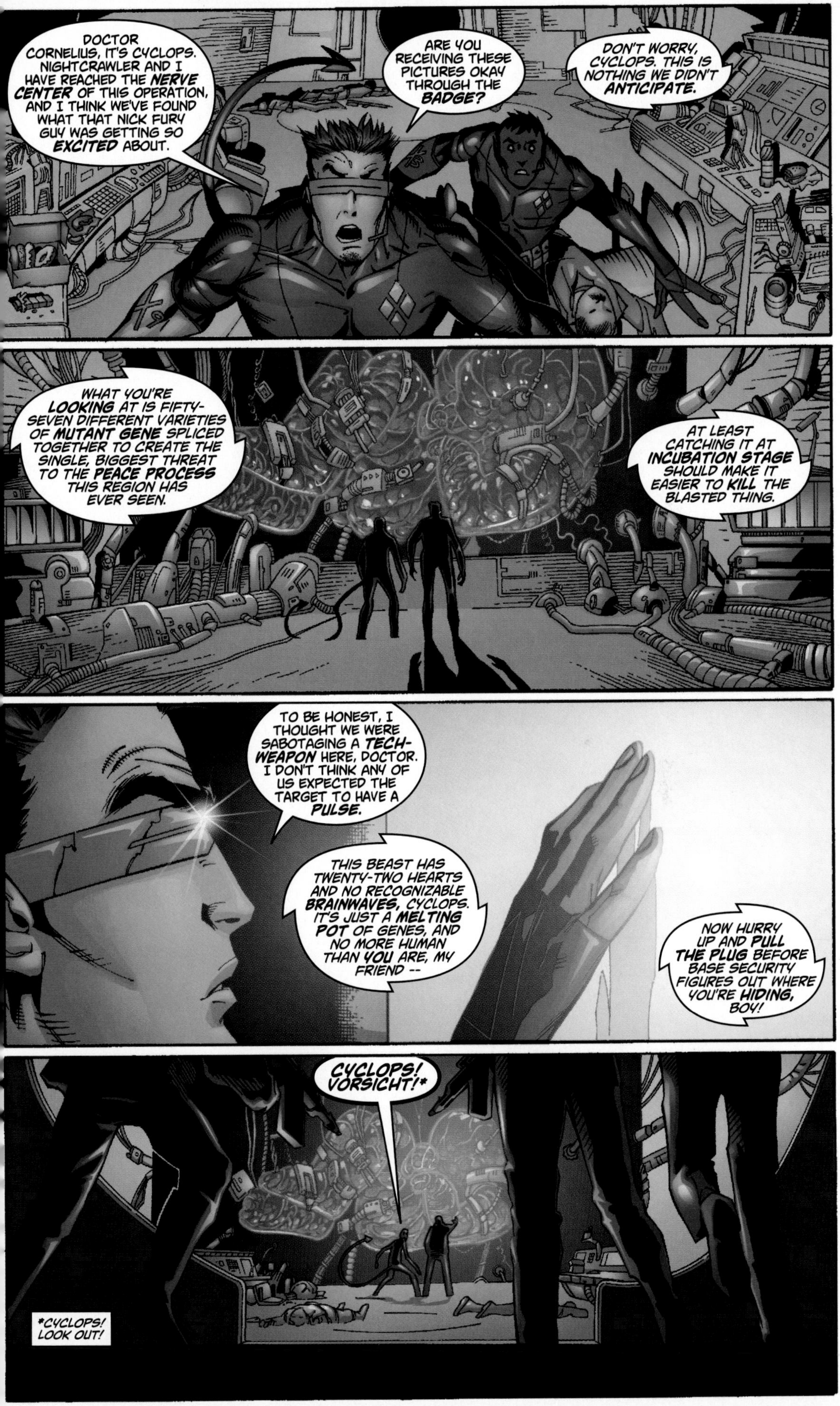
DOCTOR CORNELIUS, IT'S CYCLOPS. NIGHTCRAWLER AND I HAVE REACHED THE NERVE CENTER OF THIS OPERATION, AND I THINK WE'VE FOUND WHAT THAT NICK FURY GUY WAS GETTING SO EXCITED ABOUT.
ARE YOU RECEIVING THESE PICTURES OKAY THROUGH THE BADGE?
DON'T WORRY, CYCLOPS. THIS IS NOTHING WE DIDN'T ANTICIPATE.
WHAT YOU'RE LOOKING AT IS FIFTY-SEVEN DIFFERENT VARIETIES OF MUTANT GENE SPLICED TOGETHER TO CREATE THE SINGLE, BIGGEST THREAT TO THE PEACE PROCESS THIS REGION HAS EVER SEEN.
AT LEAST CATCHING IT AT INCUBATION STAGE SHOULD MAKE IT EASIER TO KILL THE BLASTED THING.
TO BE HONEST, I THOUGHT WE WERE SABOTAGING A TECH-WEAPON HERE, DOCTOR. I DON'T THINK ANY OF US EXPECTED THE TARGET TO HAVE A PULSE.
THIS BEAST HAS TWENTY-TWO HEARTS AND NO RECOGNIZABLE BRAINWAVES, CYCLOPS. IT'S JUST A MELTING POT OF GENES, AND NO MORE HUMAN THAN YOU ARE, MY FRIEND --
NOW HURRY UP AND PULL THE PLUG BEFORE BASE SECURITY FIGURES OUT WHERE YOU'RE HIDING, BOY!
CYCLOPS! VORSICHT!*
*CYCLOPS! LOOK OUT!

WHAT?

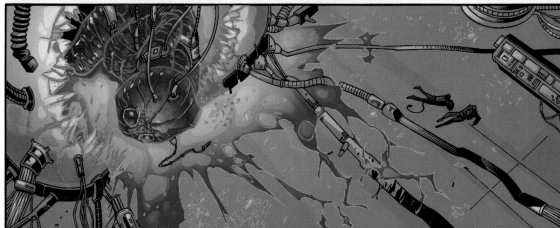

OH MY GOD!

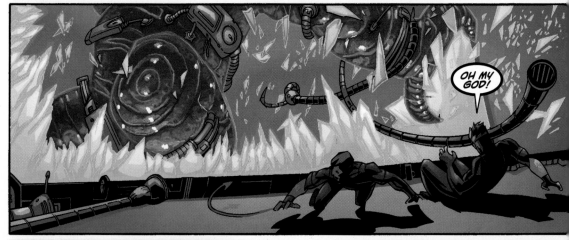

WHAT ARE YOU WAITING FOR, NIGHTCRAWLER? GET US OUT OF HERE, MAN!

*HIT THE DETONATOR, YOU IDIOT! HIT IT!

DRUEK AUF DEN ASLOESER! DRUEK ES!

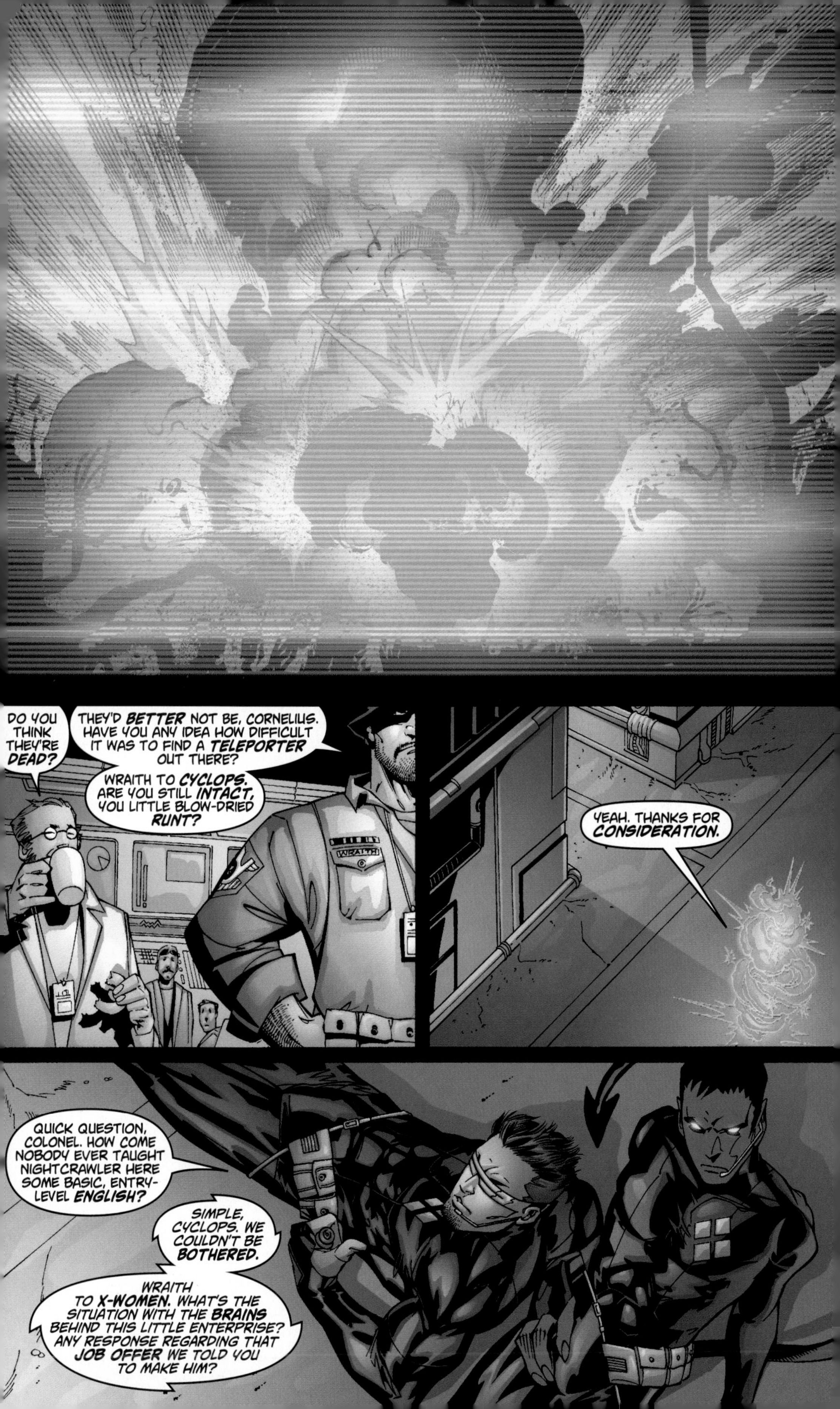

DO YOU THINK THEY'RE DEAD?
THEY'D BETTER NOT BE, CORNELIUS. HAVE YOU ANY IDEA HOW DIFFICULT IT WAS TO FIND A TELEPORTER OUT THERE?
WRAITH TO CYCLOPS. ARE YOU STILL INTACT, YOU LITTLE BLOW-DRIED RUNT?
WRAITH
YEAH. THANKS FOR CONSIDERATION.
QUICK QUESTION, COLONEL. HOW COME NOBODY EVER TAUGHT NIGHTCRAWLER HERE SOME BASIC, ENTRY-LEVEL ENGLISH?
SIMPLE, CYCLOPS. WE COULDN'T BE BOTHERED.
WRAITH TO X-WOMEN. WHAT'S THE SITUATION WITH THE BRAINS BEHIND THIS LITTLE ENTERPRISE? ANY RESPONSE REGARDING THAT JOB OFFER WE TOLD YOU TO MAKE HIM?

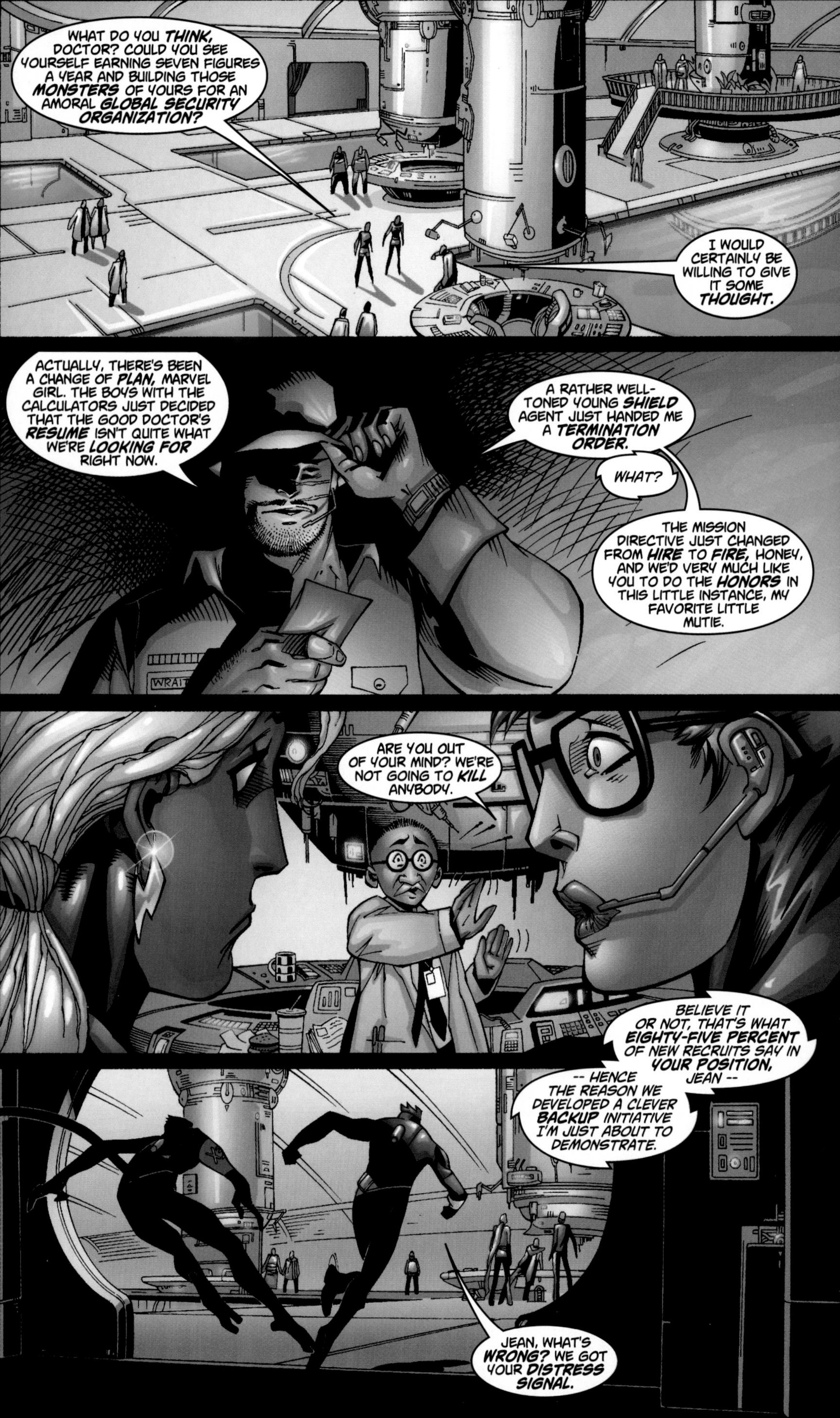
WHAT DO YOU THINK, DOCTOR? COULD YOU SEE YOURSELF EARNING SEVEN FIGURES A YEAR AND BUILDING THOSE MONSTERS OF YOURS FOR AN AMORAL GLOBAL SECURITY ORGANIZATION?
I WOULD CERTAINLY BE WILLING TO GIVE IT SOME THOUGHT.
ACTUALLY, THERE'S BEEN A CHANGE OF PLAN, MARVEL GIRL. THE BOYS WITH THE CALCULATORS JUST DECIDED THAT THE GOOD DOCTOR'S RESUME ISN'T QUITE WHAT WE'RE LOOKING FOR RIGHT NOW.
A RATHER WELL-TONED YOUNG SHIELD AGENT JUST HANDED ME A TERMINATION ORDER.
WHAT?
THE MISSION DIRECTIVE JUST CHANGED FROM HIRE TO FIRE, HONEY, AND WE'D VERY MUCH LIKE YOU TO DO THE HONORS IN THIS LITTLE INSTANCE, MY FAVORITE LITTLE MUTIE.
WRAIT
ARE YOU OUT OF YOUR MIND? WE'RE NOT GOING TO KILL ANYBODY.
BELIEVE IT OR NOT, THAT'S WHAT EIGHTY-FIVE PERCENT OF NEW RECRUITS SAY IN YOUR POSITION, JEAN --
-- HENCE THE REASON WE DEVELOPED A CLEVER BACKUP INITIATIVE I'M JUST ABOUT TO DEMONSTRATE.
JEAN, WHAT'S WRONG? WE GOT YOUR DISTRESS SIGNAL.

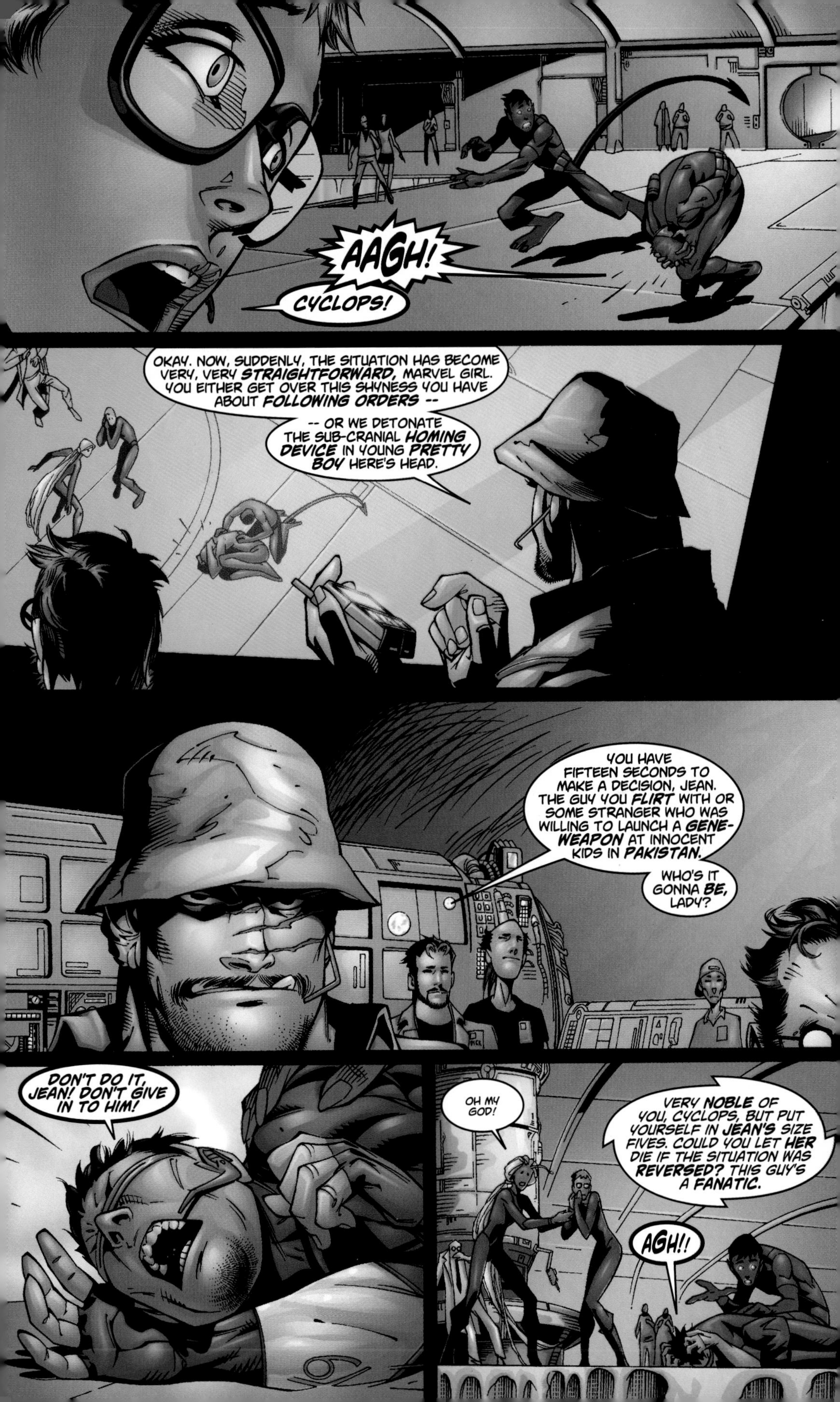
AAGH!
CYCLOPS!
OKAY. NOW, SUDDENLY, THE SITUATION HAS BECOME VERY, VERY STRAIGHTFORWARD, MARVEL GIRL. YOU EITHER GET OVER THIS SHYNESS YOU HAVE ABOUT FOLLOWING ORDERS --
-- OR WE DETONATE THE SUB-CRANIAL HOMING DEVICE IN YOUNG PRETTY BOY HERE'S HEAD.
YOU HAVE FIFTEEN SECONDS TO MAKE A DECISION, JEAN. THE GUY YOU FLIRT WITH OR SOME STRANGER WHO WAS WILLING TO LAUNCH A GENE-WEAPON AT INNOCENT KIDS IN PAKISTAN.
WHO'S IT GONNA BE, LADY?
DON'T DO IT, JEAN! DON'T GIVE IN TO HIM!
OH MY GOD!
VERY NOBLE OF YOU, CYCLOPS, BUT PUT YOURSELF IN JEAN'S SIZE FIVES. COULD YOU LET HER DIE IF THE SITUATION WAS REVERSED? THIS GUY'S A FANATIC.
AGH!!

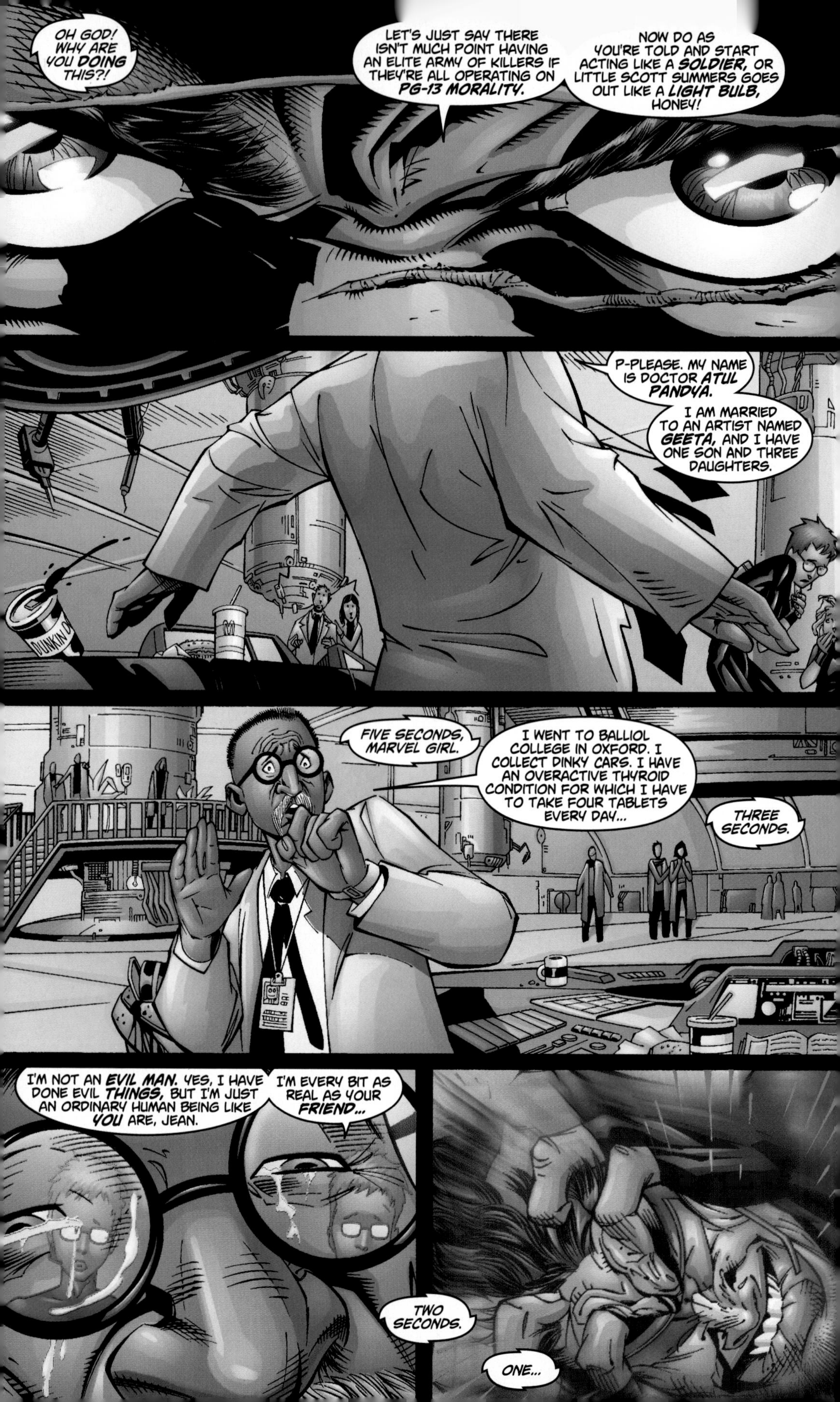
OH GOD! WHY ARE YOU DOING THIS?!
LET'S JUST SAY THERE ISN'T MUCH POINT HAVING AN ELITE ARMY OF KILLERS IF THEY'RE ALL OPERATING ON PG-13 MORALITY.
NOW DO AS YOU'RE TOLD AND START ACTING LIKE A SOLDIER, OR LITTLE SCOTT SUMMERS GOES OUT LIKE A LIGHT BULB, HONEY!
P-PLEASE. MY NAME IS DOCTOR ATUL PANDYA.
I AM MARRIED TO AN ARTIST NAMED GEETA, AND I HAVE ONE SON AND THREE DAUGHTERS.
DUNKIN D
FIVE SECONDS, MARVEL GIRL.
I WENT TO BALLIOL COLLEGE IN OXFORD. I COLLECT DINKY CARS. I HAVE AN OVERACTIVE THYROID CONDITION FOR WHICH I HAVE TO TAKE FOUR TABLETS EVERY DAY...
THREE SECONDS.
I'M NOT AN EVIL MAN. YES, I HAVE DONE EVIL THINGS, BUT I'M JUST AN ORDINARY HUMAN BEING LIKE YOU ARE, JEAN.
I'M EVERY BIT AS REAL AS YOUR FRIEND...
TWO SECONDS.
ONE...

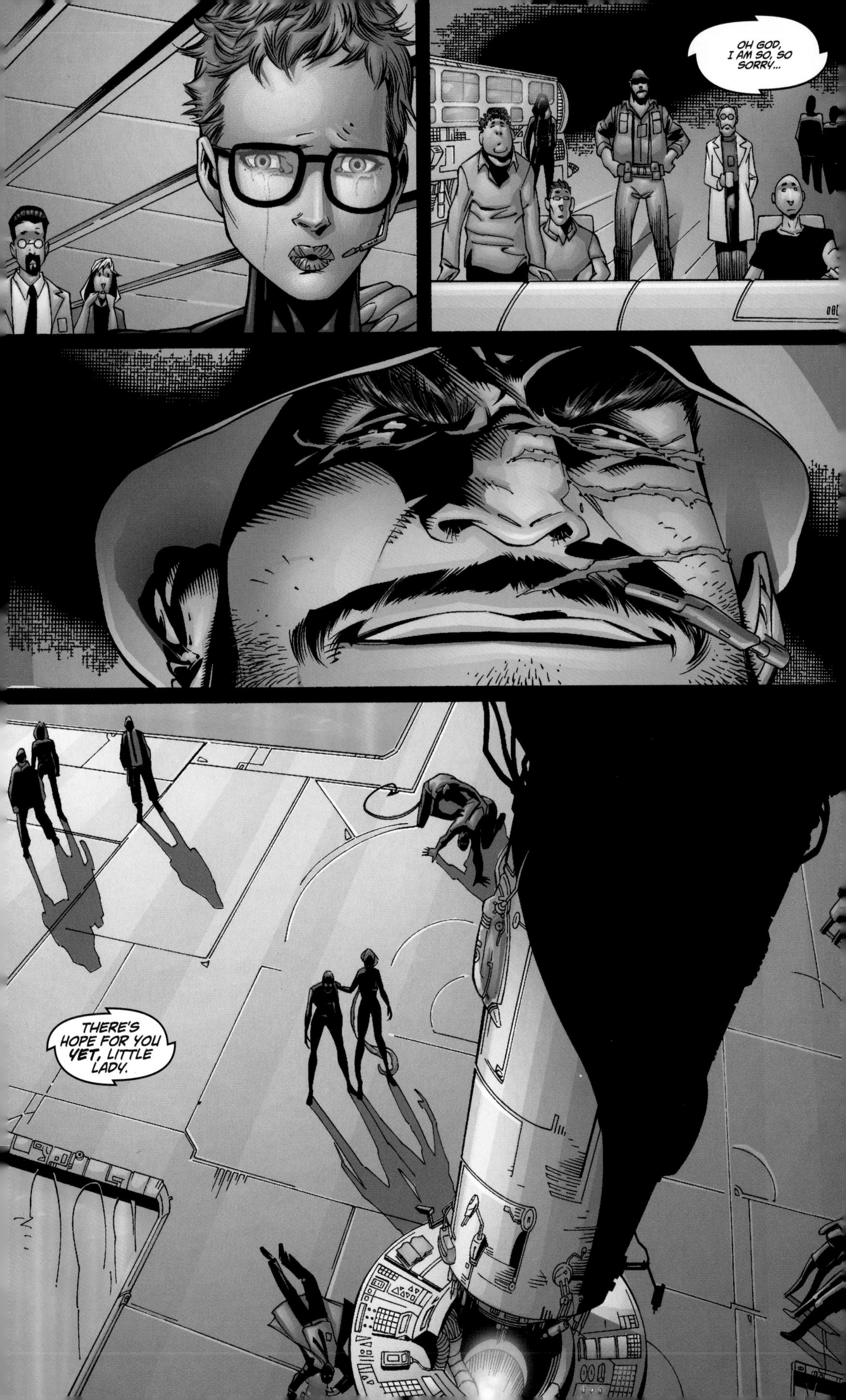
OH GOD, I AM SO, SO SORRY...
THERE'S HOPE FOR YOU YET, LITTLE LADY.

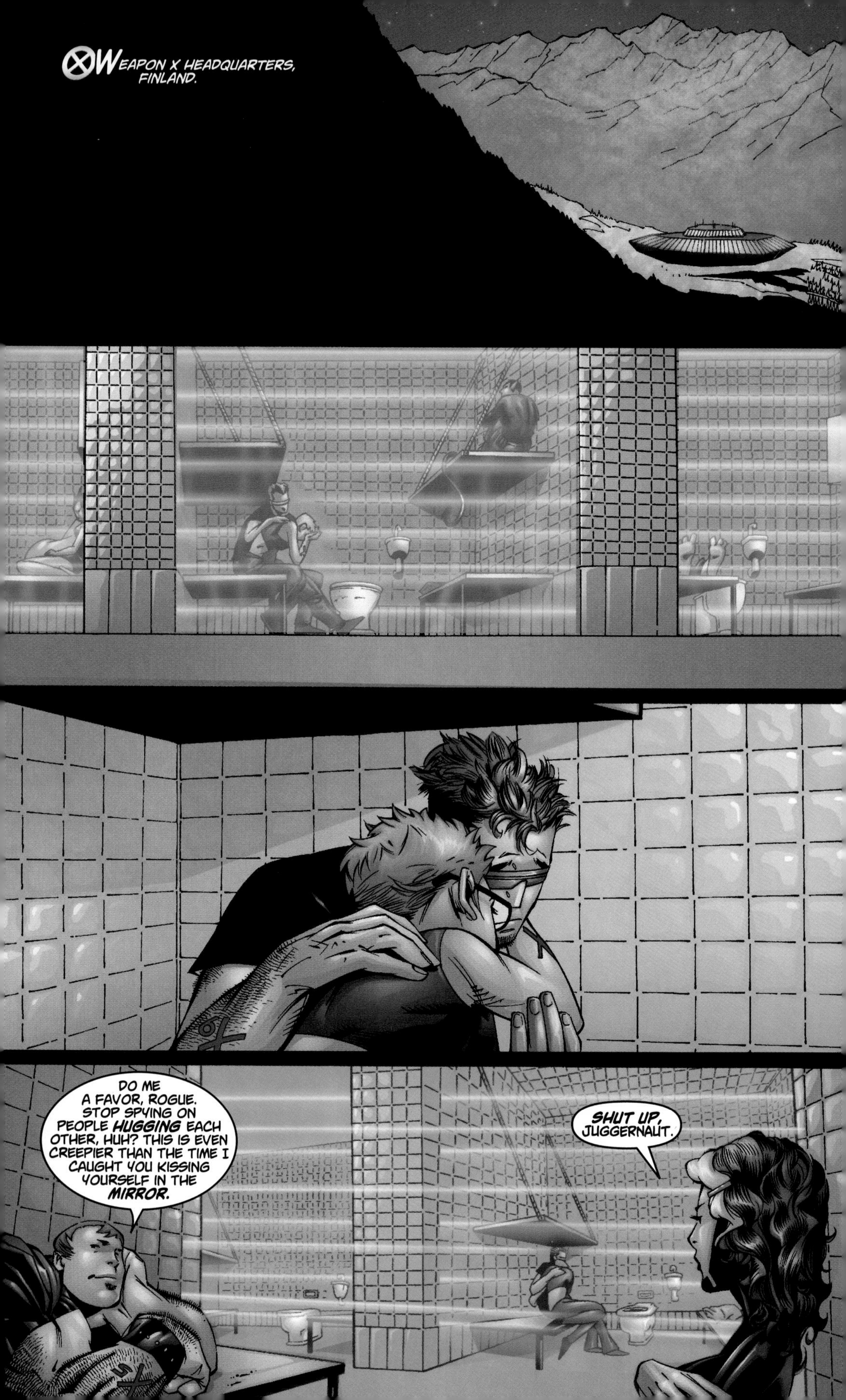
WEAPON X HEADQUARTERS,
FINLAND.
DO ME A FAVOR, ROGUE. STOP SPYING ON PEOPLE HUGGING EACH OTHER, HUH? THIS IS EVEN CREEPIER THAN THE TIME I CAUGHT YOU KISSING YOURSELF IN THE MIRROR.
SHUT UP, JUGGERNAUT.

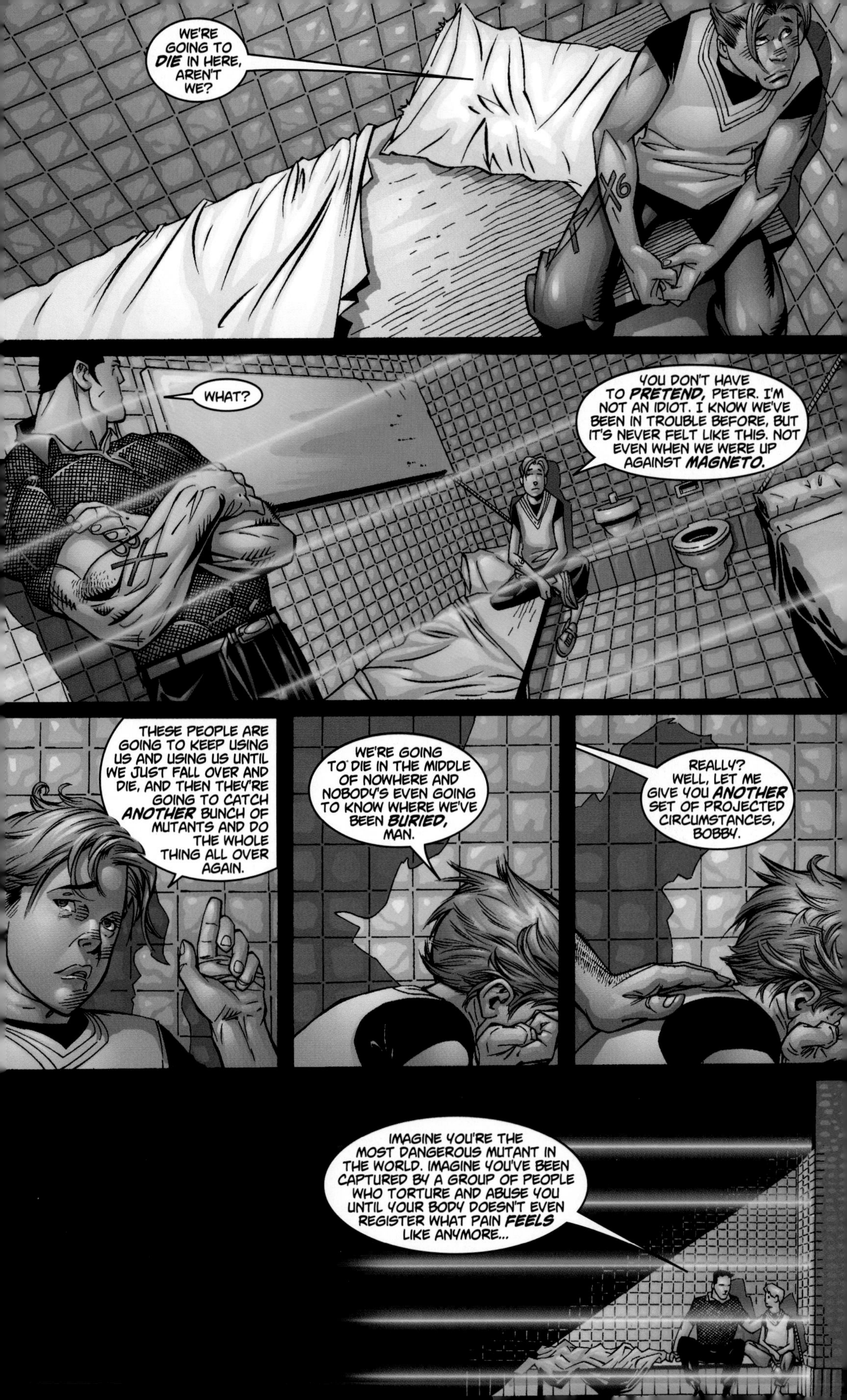
WE'RE GOING TO DIE IN HERE, AREN'T WE?
WHAT?
YOU DON'T HAVE TO PRETEND, PETER. I'M NOT AN IDIOT. I KNOW WE'VE BEEN IN TROUBLE BEFORE, BUT IT'S NEVER FELT LIKE THIS. NOT EVEN WHEN WE WERE UP AGAINST MAGNETO.
THESE PEOPLE ARE GOING TO KEEP USING US AND USING US UNTIL WE JUST FALL OVER AND DIE, AND THEN THEY'RE GOING TO CATCH ANOTHER BUNCH OF MUTANTS AND DO THE WHOLE THING ALL OVER AGAIN.
WE'RE GOING TO DIE IN THE MIDDLE OF NOWHERE AND NOBODY'S EVEN GOING TO KNOW WHERE WE'VE BEEN BURIED, MAN.
REALLY? WELL, LET ME GIVE YOU ANOTHER SET OF PROJECTED CIRCUMSTANCES, BOBBY.
IMAGINE YOU'RE THE MOST DANGEROUS MUTANT IN THE WORLD. IMAGINE YOU'VE BEEN CAPTURED BY A GROUP OF PEOPLE WHO TORTURE AND ABUSE YOU UNTIL YOUR BODY DOESN'T EVEN REGISTER WHAT PAIN FEELS LIKE ANYMORE...

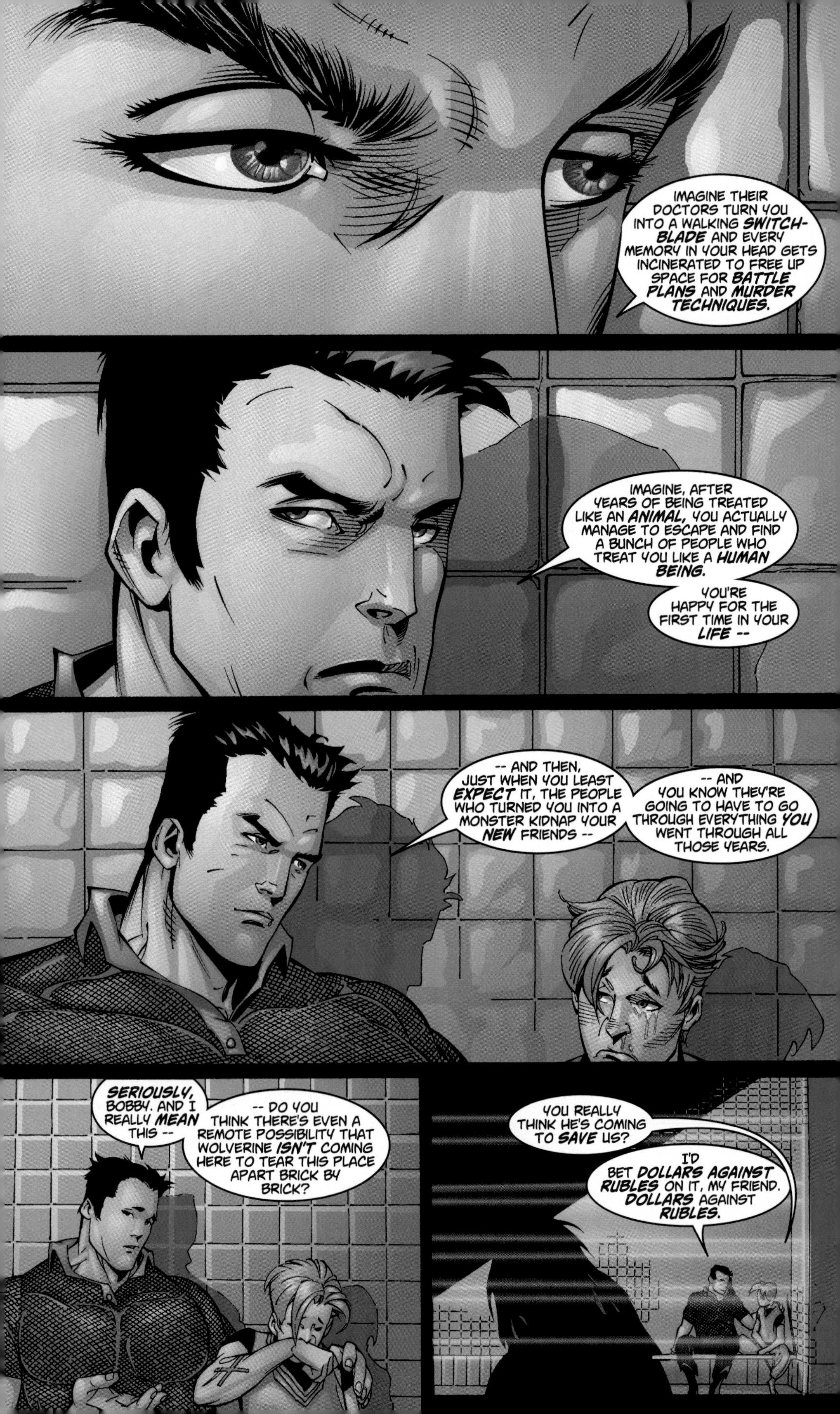
IMAGINE THEIR DOCTORS TURN YOU INTO A WALKING SWITCH-BLADE AND EVERY MEMORY IN YOUR HEAD GETS INCINERATED TO FREE UP SPACE FOR BATTLE PLANS AND MURDER TECHNIQUES.
IMAGINE, AFTER YEARS OF BEING TREATED LIKE AN ANIMAL, YOU ACTUALLY MANAGE TO ESCAPE AND FIND A BUNCH OF PEOPLE WHO TREAT YOU LIKE A HUMAN BEING.
YOU'RE HAPPY FOR THE FIRST TIME IN YOUR LIFE --
-- AND THEN, JUST WHEN YOU LEAST EXPECT IT, THE PEOPLE WHO TURNED YOU INTO A MONSTER KIDNAP YOUR NEW FRIENDS --
-- AND YOU KNOW THEY'RE GOING TO HAVE TO GO THROUGH EVERYTHING YOU WENT THROUGH ALL THOSE YEARS.
SERIOUSLY, BOBBY. AND I REALLY MEAN THIS --
-- DO YOU THINK THERE'S EVEN A REMOTE POSSIBILITY THAT WOLVERINE ISN'T COMING HERE TO TEAR THIS PLACE APART BRICK BY BRICK?
YOU REALLY THINK HE'S COMING TO SAVE US?
I'D BET DOLLARS AGAINST RUBLES ON IT, MY FRIEND. DOLLARS AGAINST RUBLES.

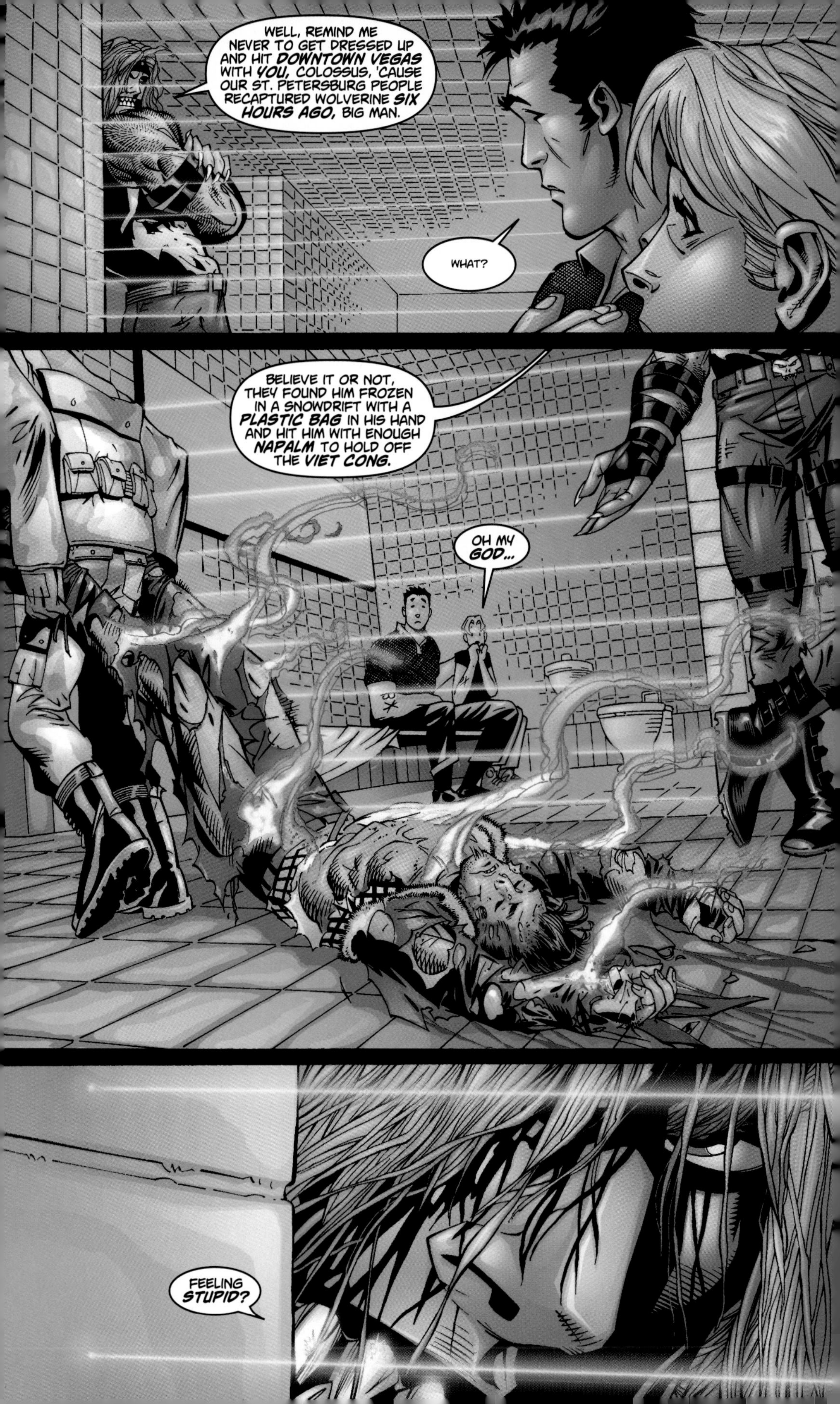
WELL, REMIND ME NEVER TO GET DRESSED UP AND HIT DOWNTOWN VEGAS WITH YOU, COLOSSUS, 'CAUSE OUR ST. PETERSBURG PEOPLE RECAPTURED WOLVERINE SIX HOURS AGO, BIG MAN.
WHAT?
BELIEVE IT OR NOT, THEY FOUND HIM FROZEN IN A SNOWDRIFT WITH A PLASTIC BAG IN HIS HAND AND HIT HIM WITH ENOUGH NAPALM TO HOLD OFF THE VIET CONG.
OH MY GOD...
FEELING STUPID?

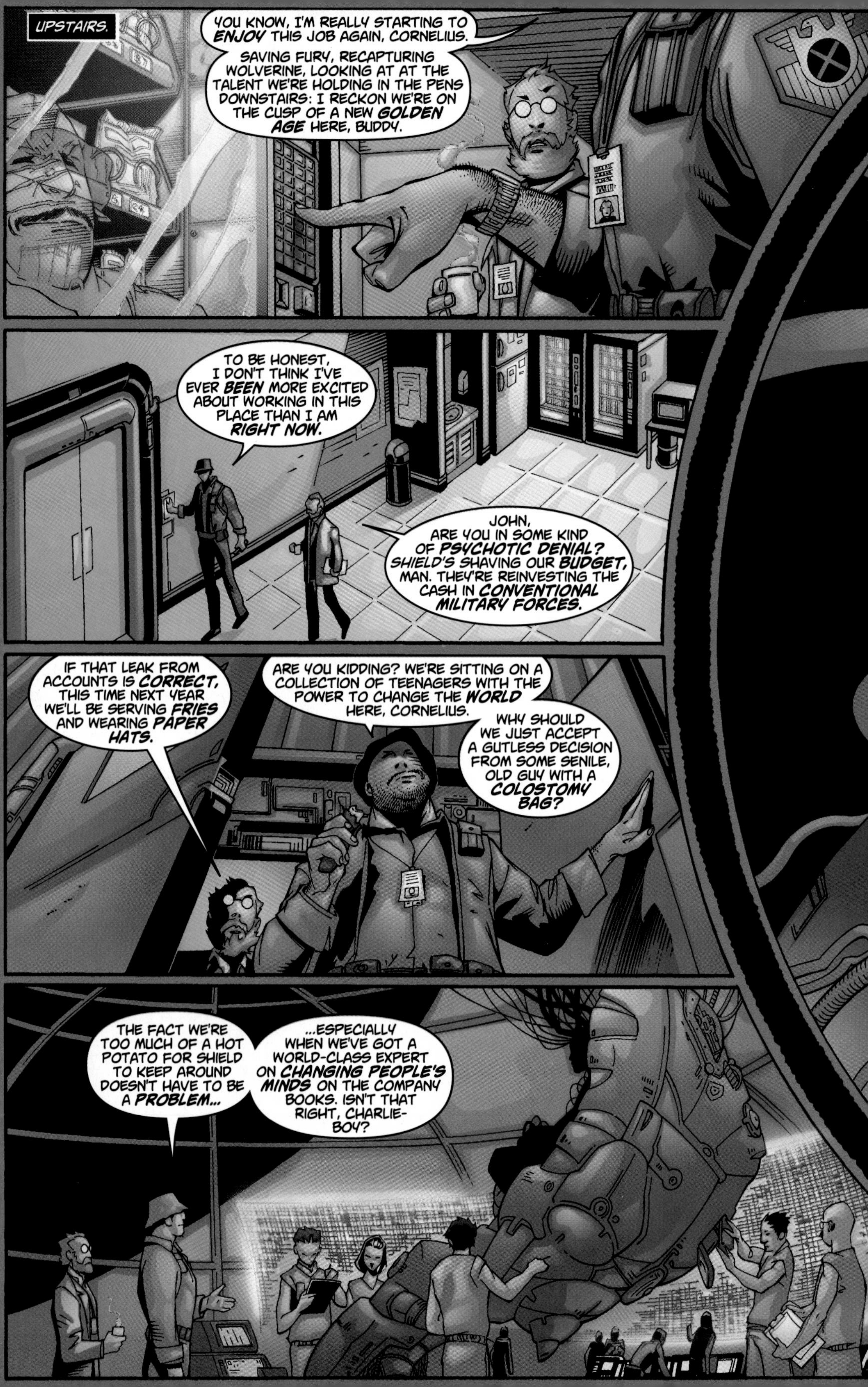
UPSTAIRS.
YOU KNOW, I'M REALLY STARTING TO ENJOY THIS JOB AGAIN, CORNELIUS.
SAVING FURY, RECAPTURING WOLVERINE, LOOKING AT AT THE TALENT WE'RE HOLDING IN THE PENS DOWNSTAIRS: I RECKON WE'RE ON THE CUSP OF A NEW GOLDEN AGE HERE, BUDDY.
TO BE HONEST, I DON'T THINK I'VE EVER BEEN MORE EXCITED ABOUT WORKING IN THIS PLACE THAN I AM RIGHT NOW.
JOHN, ARE YOU IN SOME KIND OF PSYCHOTIC DENIAL? SHIELD'S SHAVING OUR BUDGET, MAN. THEY'RE REINVESTING THE CASH IN CONVENTIONAL MILITARY FORCES.
IF THAT LEAK FROM ACCOUNTS IS CORRECT, THIS TIME NEXT YEAR WE'LL BE SERVING FRIES AND WEARING PAPER HATS.
ARE YOU KIDDING? WE'RE SITTING ON A COLLECTION OF TEENAGERS WITH THE POWER TO CHANGE THE WORLD HERE, CORNELIUS.
WHY SHOULD WE JUST ACCEPT A GUTLESS DECISION FROM SOME SENILE, OLD GUY WITH A COLOSTOMY BAG?
THE FACT WE'RE TOO MUCH OF A HOT POTATO FOR SHIELD TO KEEP AROUND DOESN'T HAVE TO BE A PROBLEM...
...ESPECIALLY WHEN WE'VE GOT A WORLD-CLASS EXPERT ON CHANGING PEOPLE'S MINDS ON THE COMPANY BOOKS. ISN'T THAT RIGHT, CHARLIE-BOY?

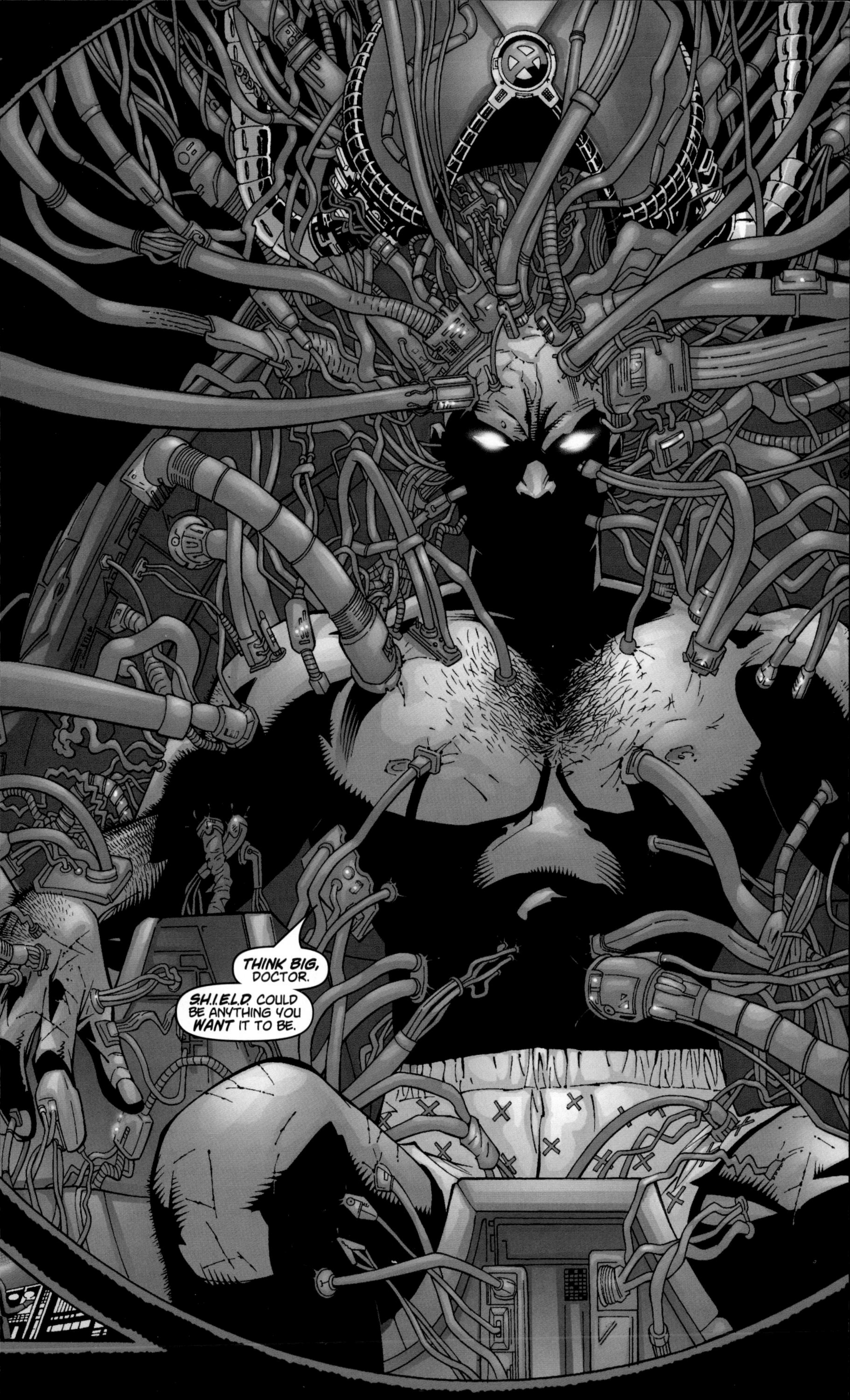
THINK BIG, DOCTOR.
S.H.I.E.L.D. COULD BE ANYTHING YOU WANT IT TO BE.

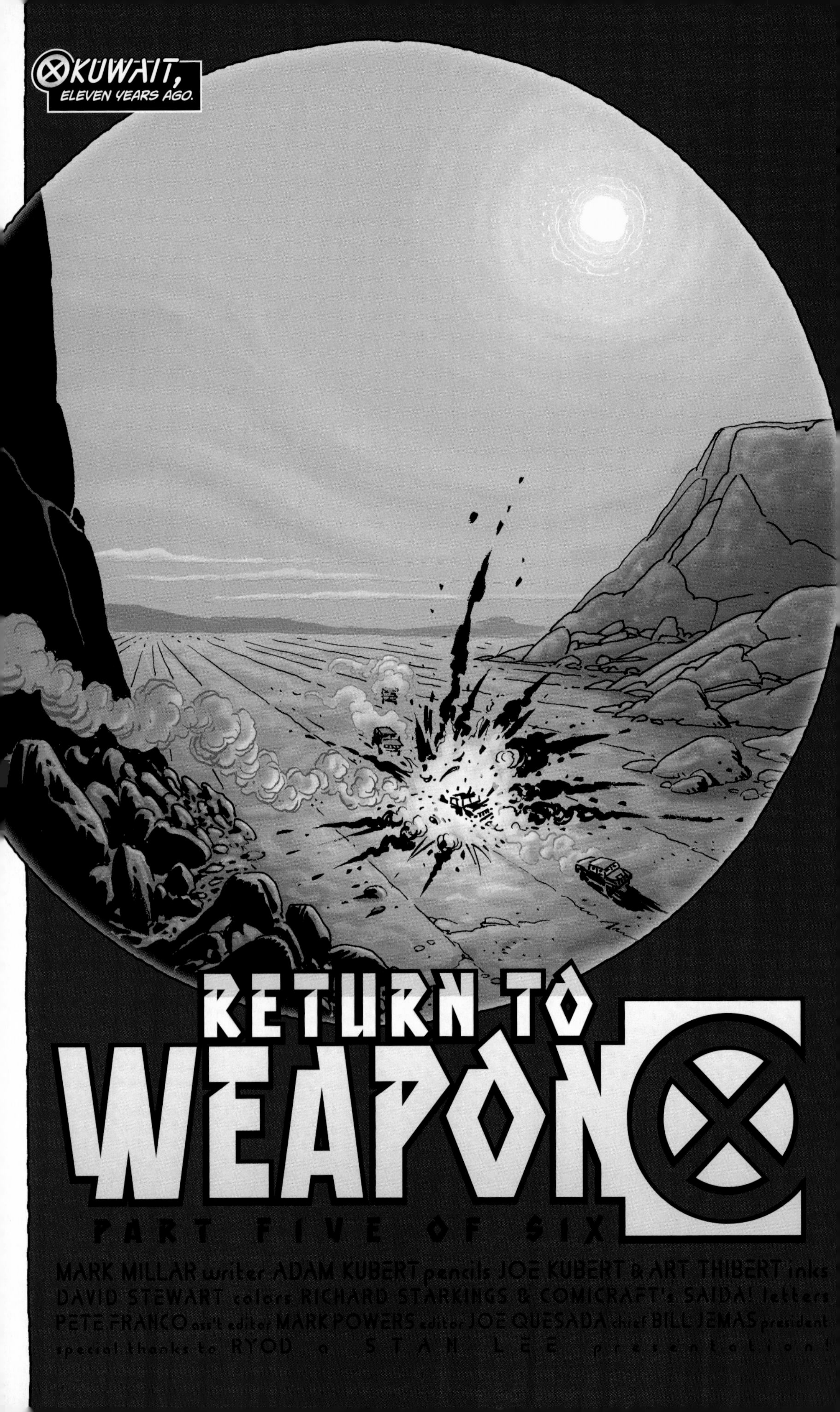
KUWAIT,
ELEVEN YEARS AGO.
RETURN TO
WEAPON X
PART FIVE OF SIX
MARK MILLAR writer ADAM KUBERT pencils JOE KUBERT & ART THIBERT inks
DAVID STEWART colors RICHARD STARKINGS & COMICRAFT's SAIDA! letters
PETE FRANCO ass't editor MARK POWERS editor JOE QUESADA chief BILL JEMAS president
special thanks to RYOD a STAN LEE presentation!

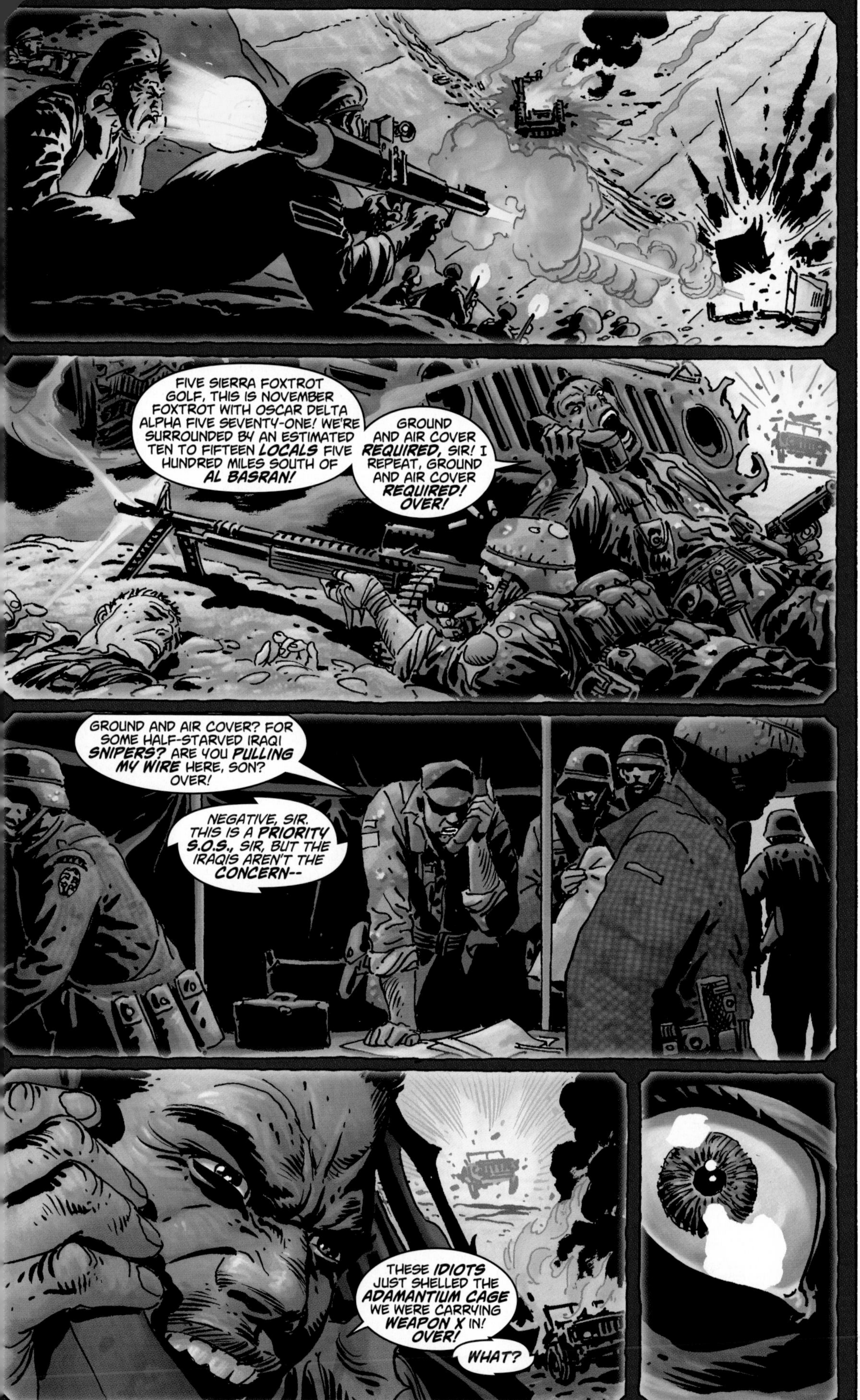
FIVE SIERRA FOXTROT GOLF, THIS IS NOVEMBER FOXTROT WITH OSCAR DELTA ALPHA FIVE SEVENTY-ONE! WE'RE SURROUNDED BY AN ESTIMATED TEN TO FIFTEEN LOCALS FIVE HUNDRED MILES SOUTH OF AL BASRAN!
GROUND AND AIR COVER REQUIRED, SIR! I REPEAT, GROUND AND AIR COVER REQUIRED! OVER!
GROUND AND AIR COVER? FOR SOME HALF-STARVED IRAQI SNIPERS? ARE YOU PULLING MY WIRE HERE, SON? OVER!
NEGATIVE, SIR. THIS IS A PRIORITY S.O.S., SIR, BUT THE IRAQIS AREN'T THE CONCERN--
THESE IDIOTS JUST SHELLED THE ADAMANTIUM CAGE WE WERE CARRYING WEAPON X IN! OVER!
WHAT?

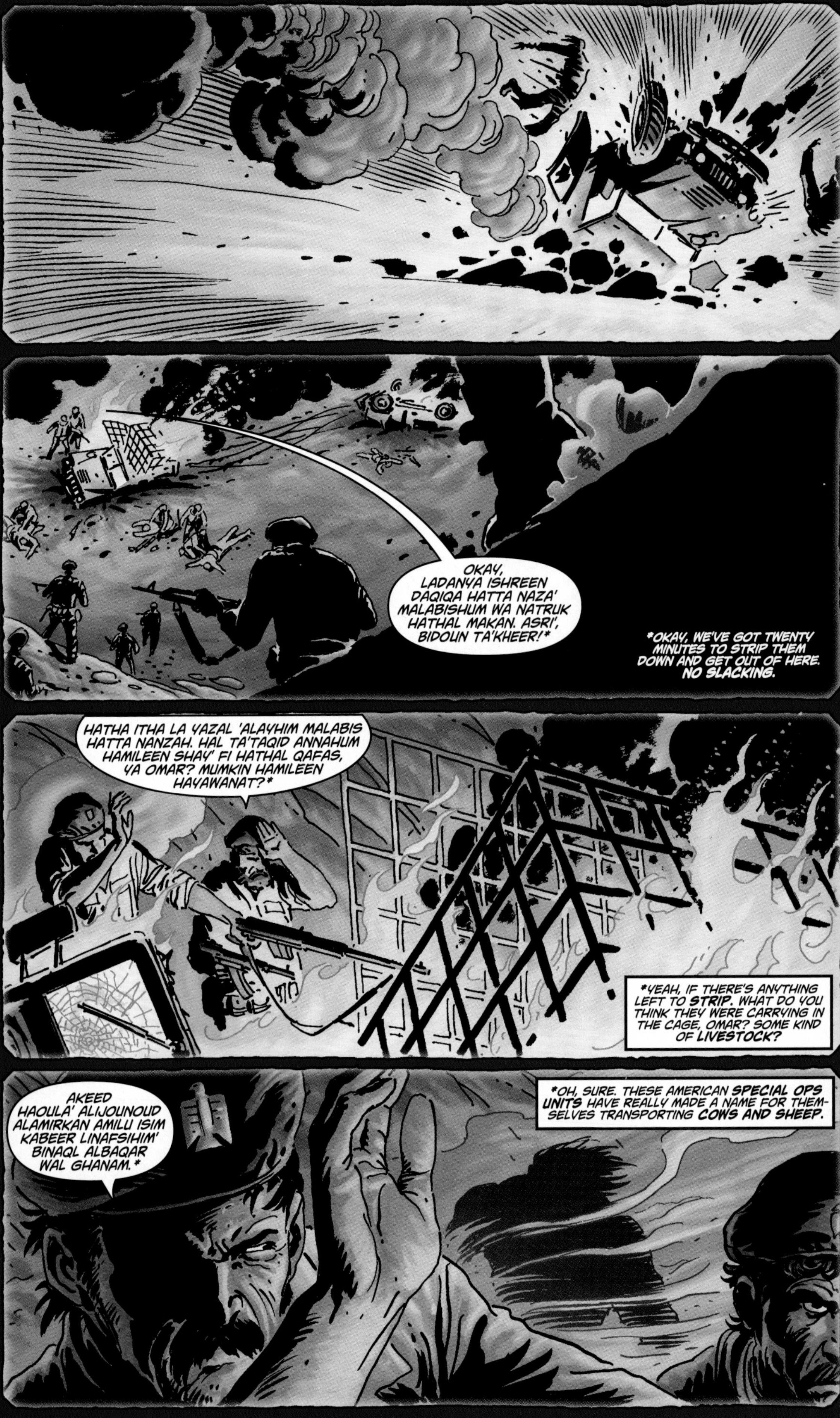

OKAY, LADANYA ISHREEN DAQIQA HATTA NAZA' MALABISHUM WA NATRUK HATHAL MAKAN. ASRI', BIDOUN TA'KHEER!*
*OKAY, WE'VE GOT TWENTY MINUTES TO STRIP THEM DOWN AND GET OUT OF HERE. NO SLACKING.
HATHA ITHA LA YAZAL 'ALAYHIM MALABIS HATTA NANZAH. HAL TA'TAQID ANNAHUM HAMILEEN SHAY' FI HATHAL QAFAS, YA OMAR? MUMKIN HAMILEEN HAYAWANAT?*
*YEAH, IF THERE'S ANYTHING LEFT TO STRIP. WHAT DO YOU THINK THEY WERE CARRYING IN THE CAGE, OMAR? SOME KIND OF LIVESTOCK?
AKEED HAOULA' ALIJOUNOUD ALAMIRKAN AMILU ISIM KABEER LINAFSIHIM' BINAQL ALBAQAR WAL GHANAM.*
*OH, SURE. THESE AMERICAN SPECIAL OPS UNITS HAVE REALLY MADE A NAME FOR THEMSELVES TRANSPORTING COWS AND SHEEP.

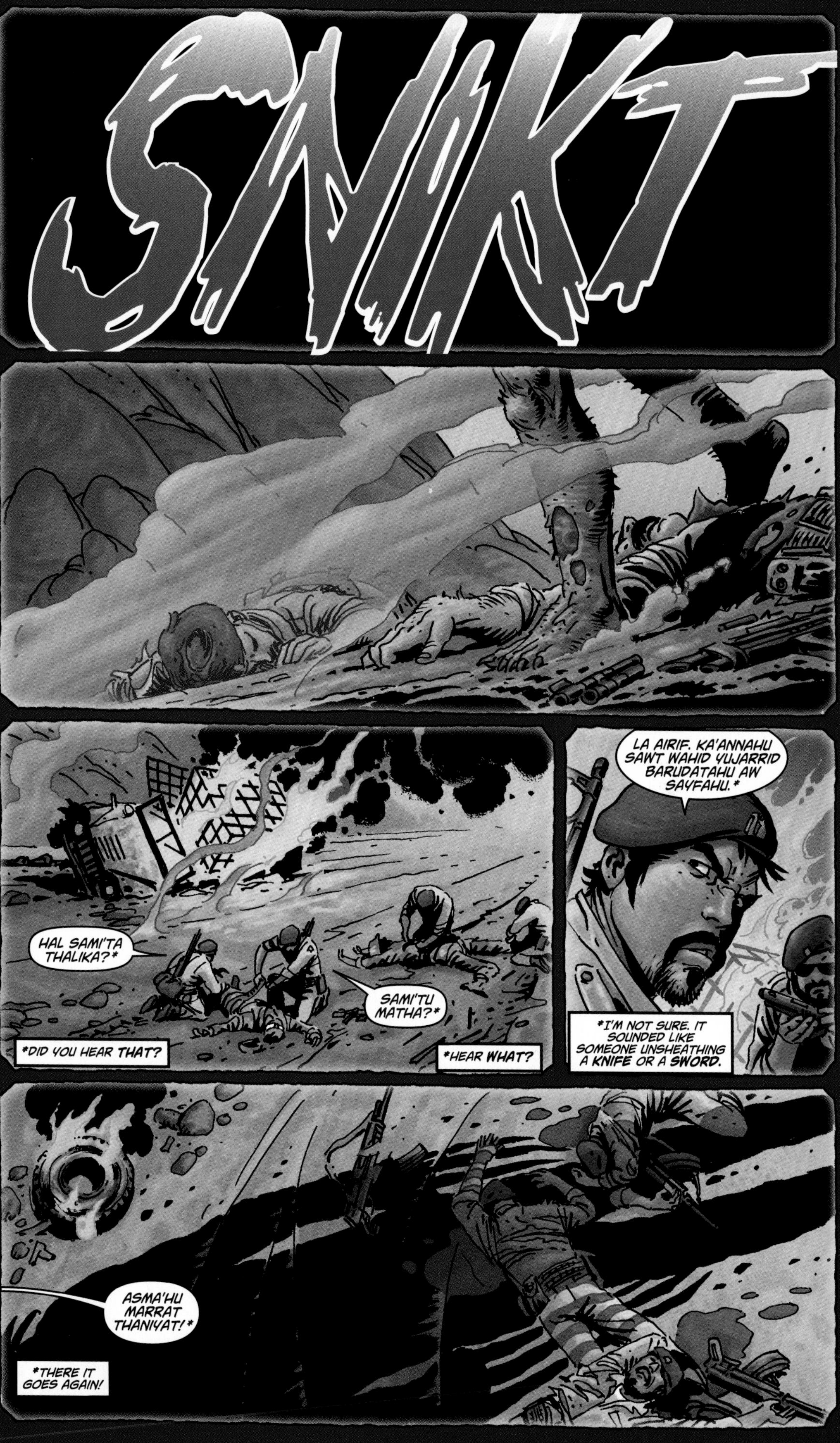
SNIKT
HAL SAMI'TA THALIKA?*
*DID YOU HEAR THAT?
SAMI'TU MATHA?*
*HEAR WHAT?
LA AIRIF. KA'ANNAHU SAWT WAHID YUJARRID BARUDATAHU AW SAYFAHU.*
*I'M NOT SURE. IT SOUNDED LIKE SOMEONE UNSHEATHING A KNIFE OR A SWORD.
ASMA'HU MARRAT THANIYAT!*
*THERE IT GOES AGAIN!

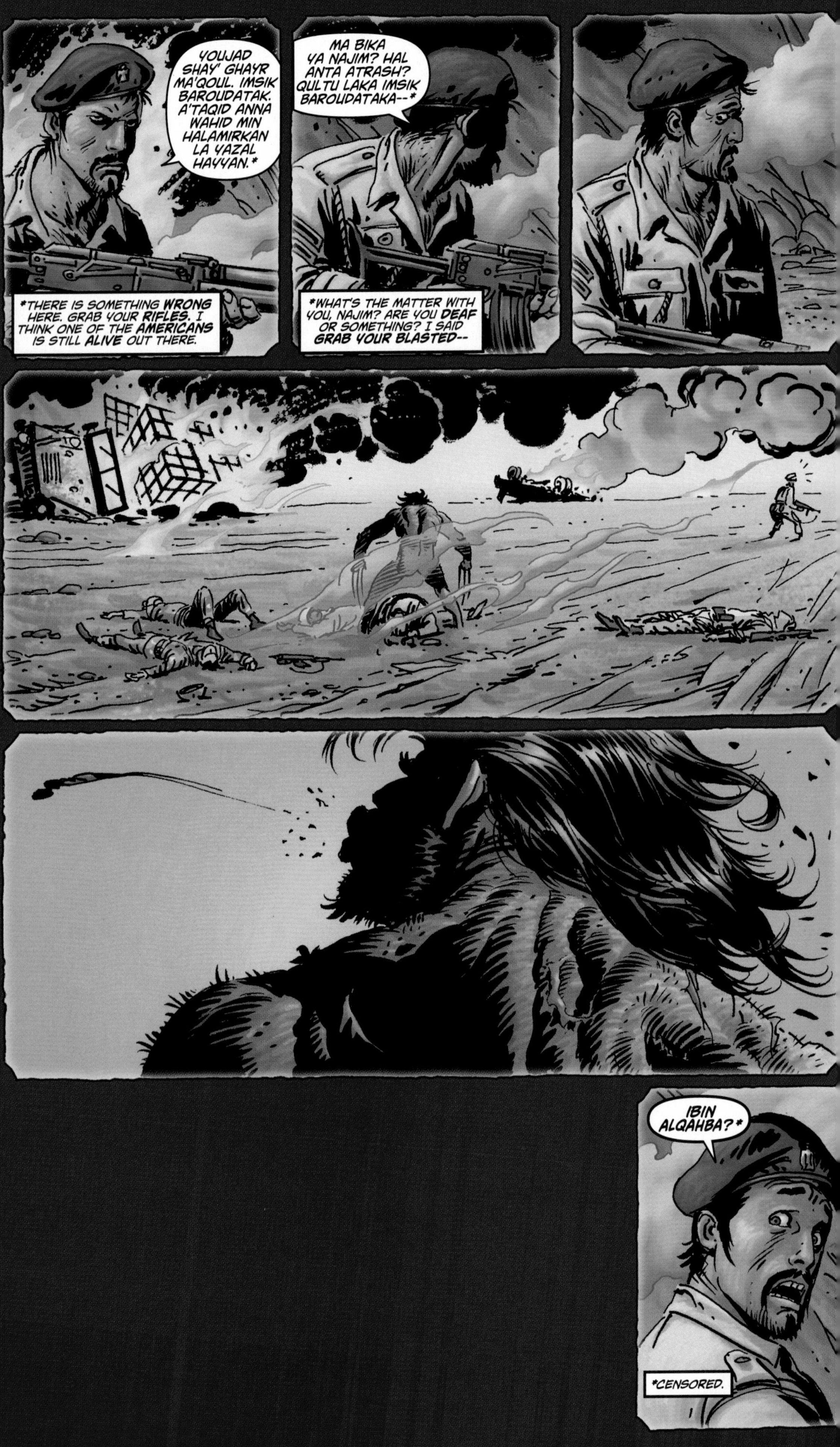
YOUJAD SHAY' GHAYR MA'QOUL. IMSIK BAROUDATAK. A'TAQID ANNA WAHID MIN HALAMIRKAN LA YAZAL HAYYAN.*
*THERE IS SOMETHING WRONG HERE. GRAB YOUR RIFLES. I THINK ONE OF THE AMERICANS IS STILL ALIVE OUT THERE.
MA BIKA YA NAJIM? HAL ANTA ATRASH? QULTU LAKA IMSIK BAROUDATAKA--*
*WHAT'S THE MATTER WITH YOU, NAJIM? ARE YOU DEAF OR SOMETHING? I SAID GRAB YOUR BLASTED--
IBIN ALQAHBA?*
*CENSORED.

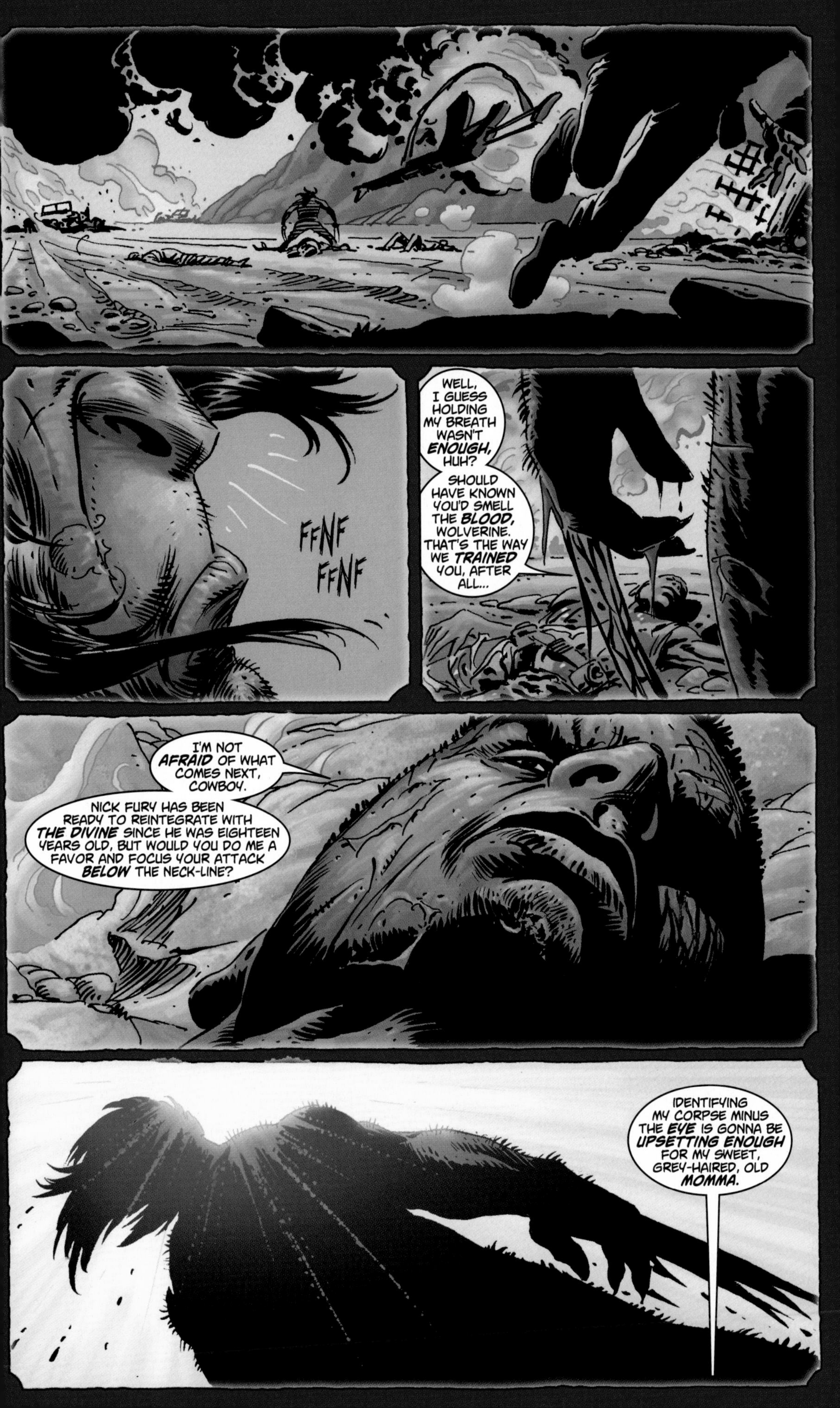
FFNF
FFNF
WELL, I GUESS HOLDING MY BREATH WASN'T ENOUGH, HUH?
SHOULD HAVE KNOWN YOU'D SMELL THE BLOOD, WOLVERINE. THAT'S THE WAY WE TRAINED YOU, AFTER ALL...
I'M NOT AFRAID OF WHAT COMES NEXT, COWBOY.
NICK FURY HAS BEEN READY TO REINTEGRATE WITH THE DIVINE SINCE HE WAS EIGHTEEN YEARS OLD, BUT WOULD YOU DO ME A FAVOR AND FOCUS YOUR ATTACK BELOW THE NECK-LINE?
IDENTIFYING MY CORPSE MINUS THE EYE IS GONNA BE UPSETTING ENOUGH FOR MY SWEET, GREY-HAIRED, OLD MOMMA.

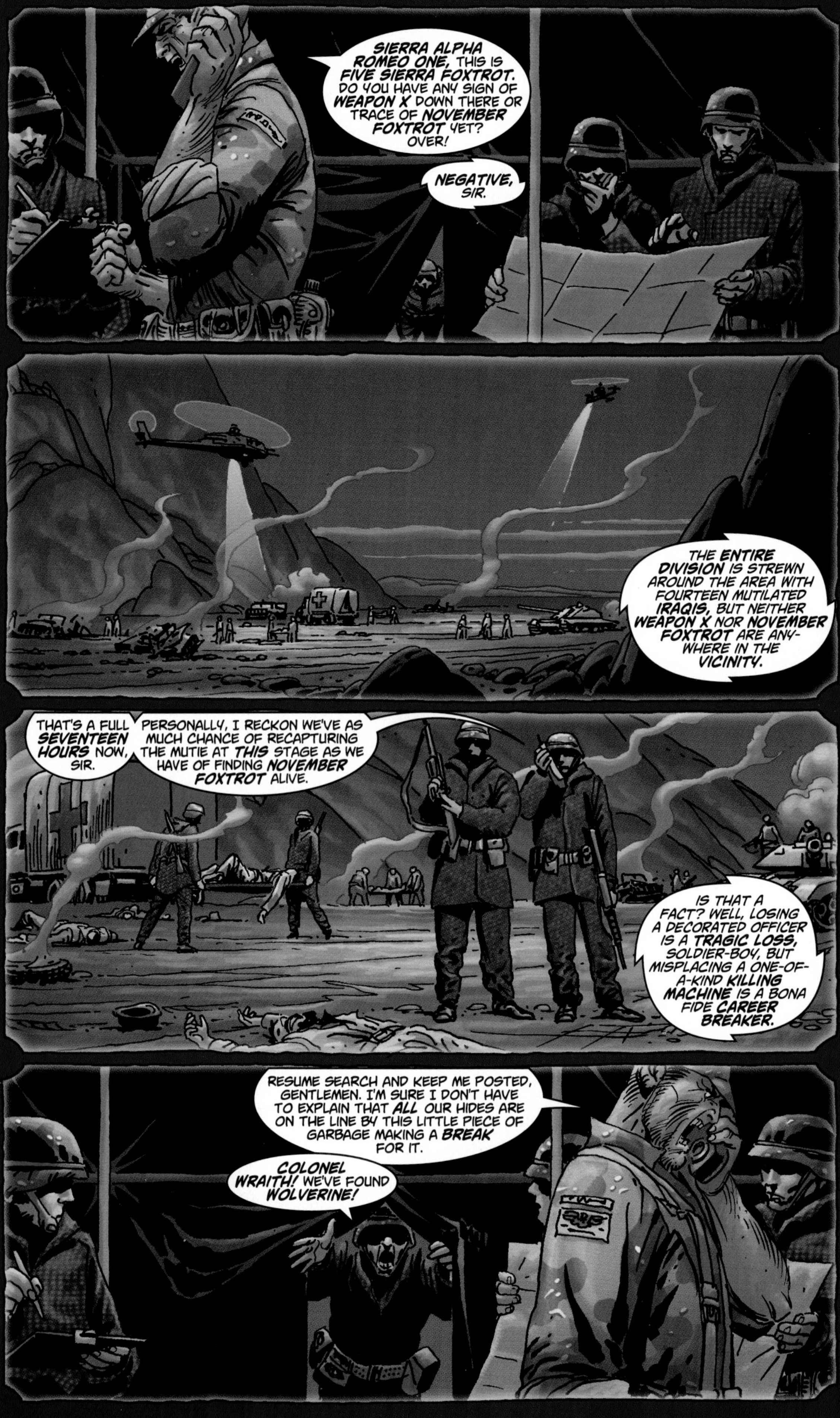
SIERRA ALPHA ROMEO ONE, THIS IS FIVE SIERRA FOXTROT. DO YOU HAVE ANY SIGN OF WEAPON X DOWN THERE OR TRACE OF NOVEMBER FOXTROT YET? OVER!
NEGATIVE, SIR.
THE ENTIRE DIVISION IS STREWN AROUND THE AREA WITH FOURTEEN MUTILATED IRAQIS, BUT NEITHER WEAPON X NOR NOVEMBER FOXTROT ARE ANY-WHERE IN THE VICINITY.
THAT'S A FULL SEVENTEEN HOURS NOW, SIR.
PERSONALLY, I RECKON WE'VE AS MUCH CHANCE OF RECAPTURING THE MUTIE AT THIS STAGE AS WE HAVE OF FINDING NOVEMBER FOXTROT ALIVE.
IS THAT A FACT? WELL, LOSING A DECORATED OFFICER IS A TRAGIC LOSS, SOLDIER-BOY, BUT MISPLACING A ONE-OF-A-KIND KILLING MACHINE IS A BONA FIDE CAREER BREAKER.
RESUME SEARCH AND KEEP ME POSTED, GENTLEMEN. I'M SURE I DON'T HAVE TO EXPLAIN THAT ALL OUR HIDES ARE ON THE LINE BY THIS LITTLE PIECE OF GARBAGE MAKING A BREAK FOR IT.
COLONEL WRAITH! WE'VE FOUND WOLVERINE!

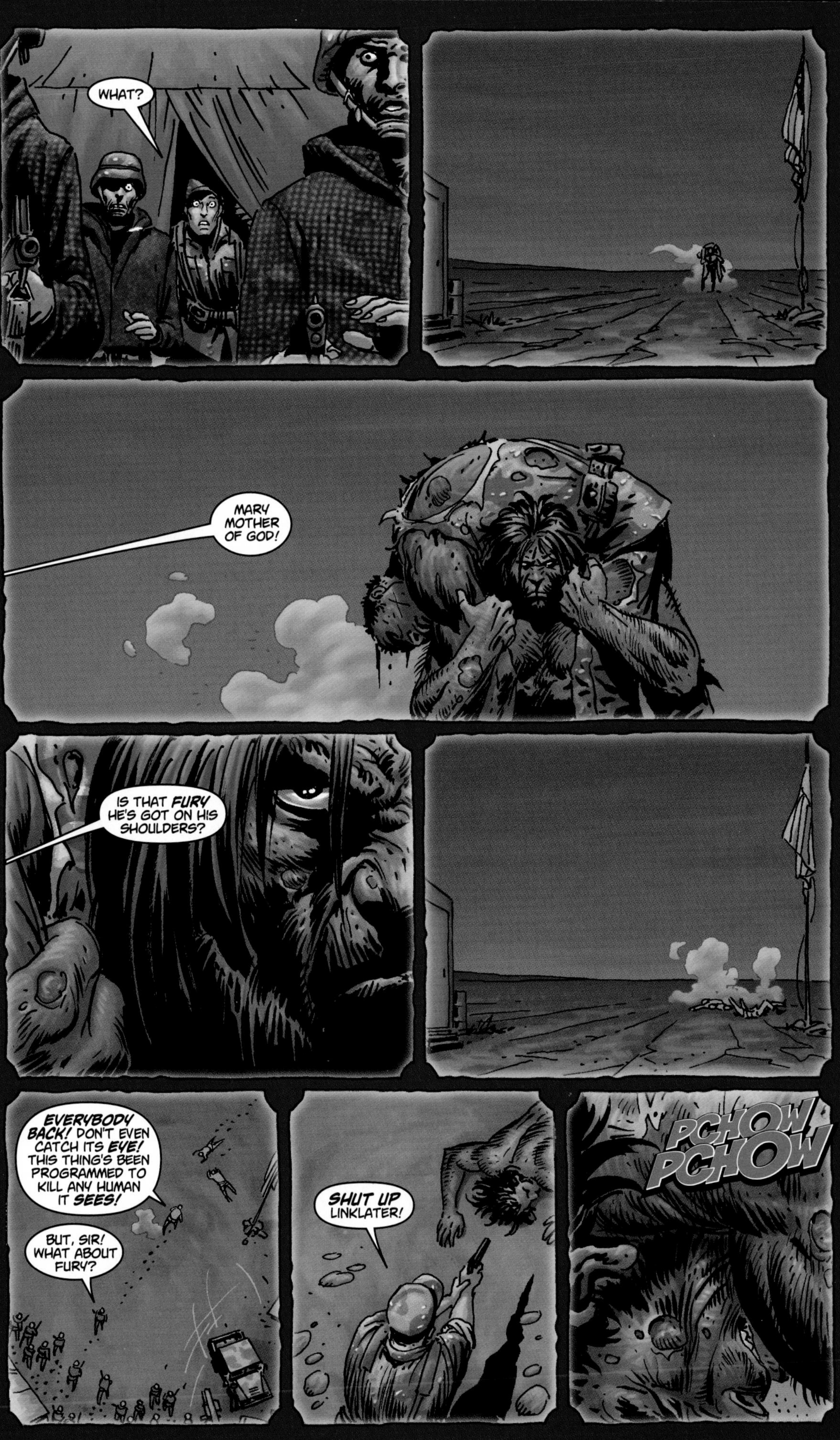
WHAT?
MARY MOTHER OF GOD!
IS THAT FURY HE'S GOT ON HIS SHOULDERS?
EVERYBODY BACK! DON'T EVEN CATCH ITS EYE! THIS THING'S BEEN PROGRAMMED TO KILL ANY HUMAN IT SEES!
BUT, SIR! WHAT ABOUT FURY?
SHUT UP LINKLATER!
PCHOW PCHOW

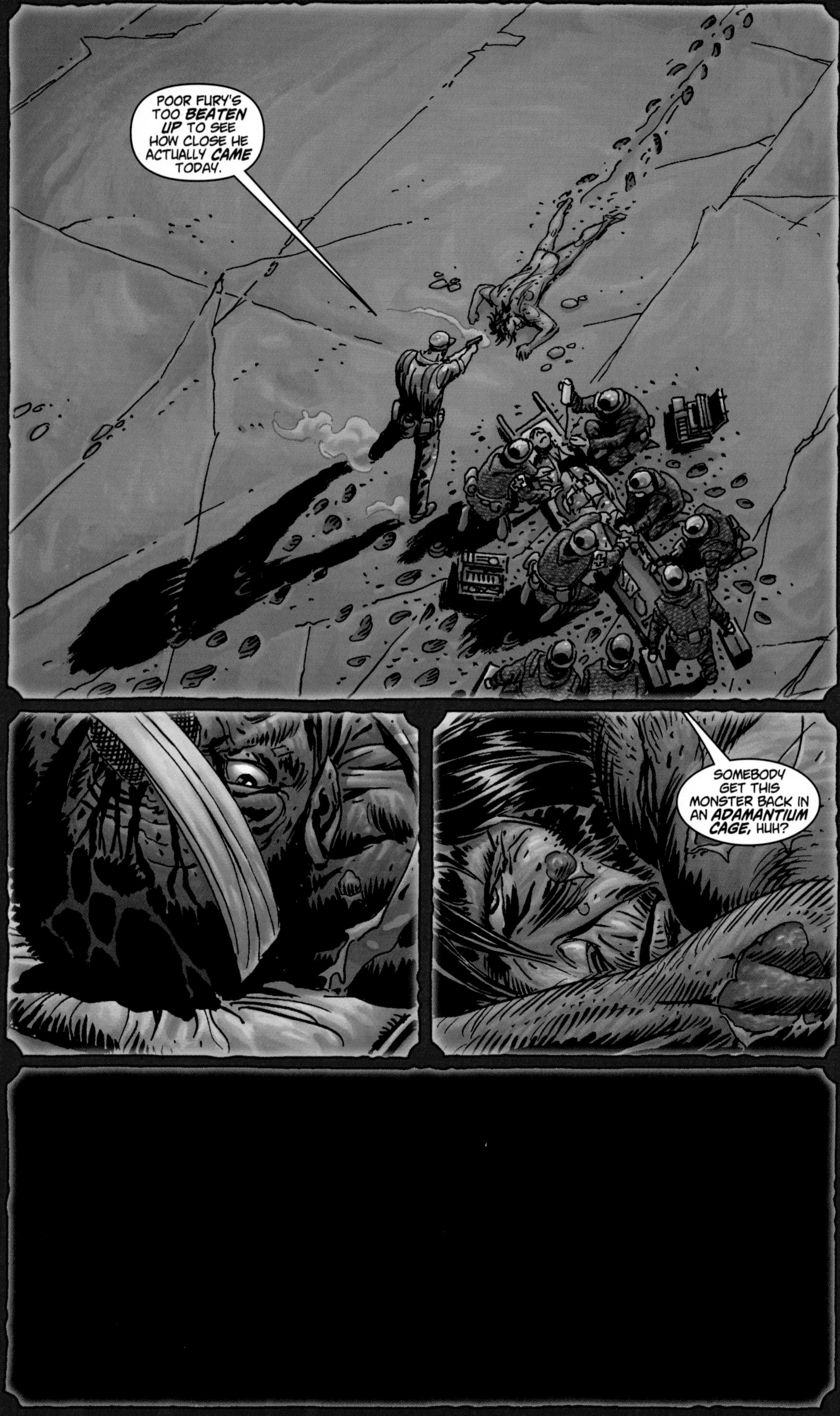
POOR FURY'S TOO BEATEN UP TO SEE HOW CLOSE HE ACTUALLY CAME TODAY.
SOMEBODY GET THIS MONSTER BACK IN AN ADAMANTIUM CAGE, HUH?

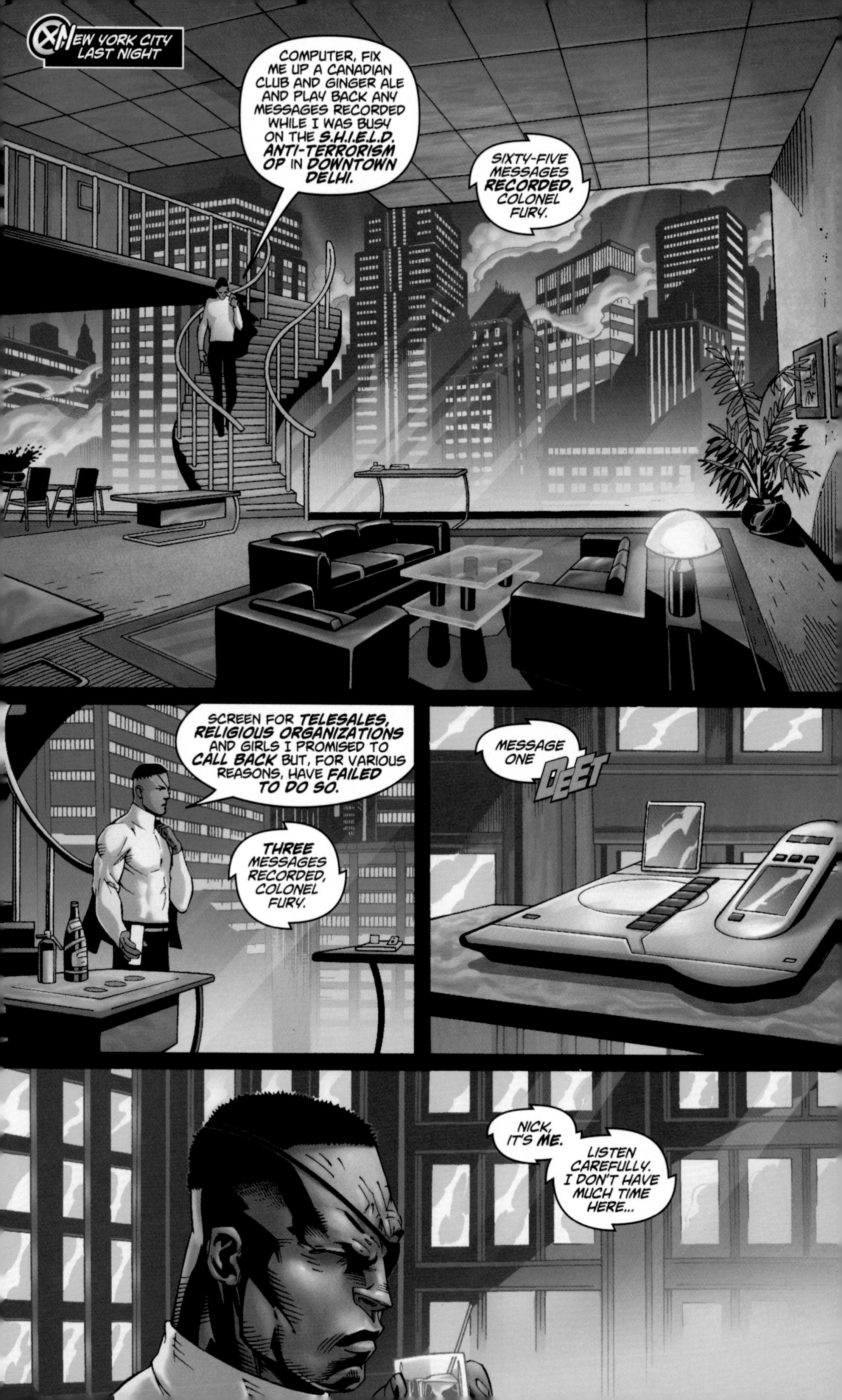
NEW YORK CITY
LAST NIGHT
COMPUTER, FIX ME UP A CANADIAN CLUB AND GINGER ALE AND PLAY BACK ANY MESSAGES RECORDED WHILE I WAS BUSY ON THE S.H.I.E.L.D. ANTI-TERRORISM OP IN DOWNTOWN DELHI.
SIXTY-FIVE MESSAGES RECORDED, COLONEL FURY.
SCREEN FOR TELESALES, RELIGIOUS ORGANIZATIONS AND GIRLS I PROMISED TO CALL BACK BUT, FOR VARIOUS REASONS, HAVE FAILED TO DO SO.
THREE MESSAGES RECORDED, COLONEL FURY.
MESSAGE ONE
DEET
NICK, IT'S ME.
LISTEN CAREFULLY. I DON'T HAVE MUCH TIME HERE...

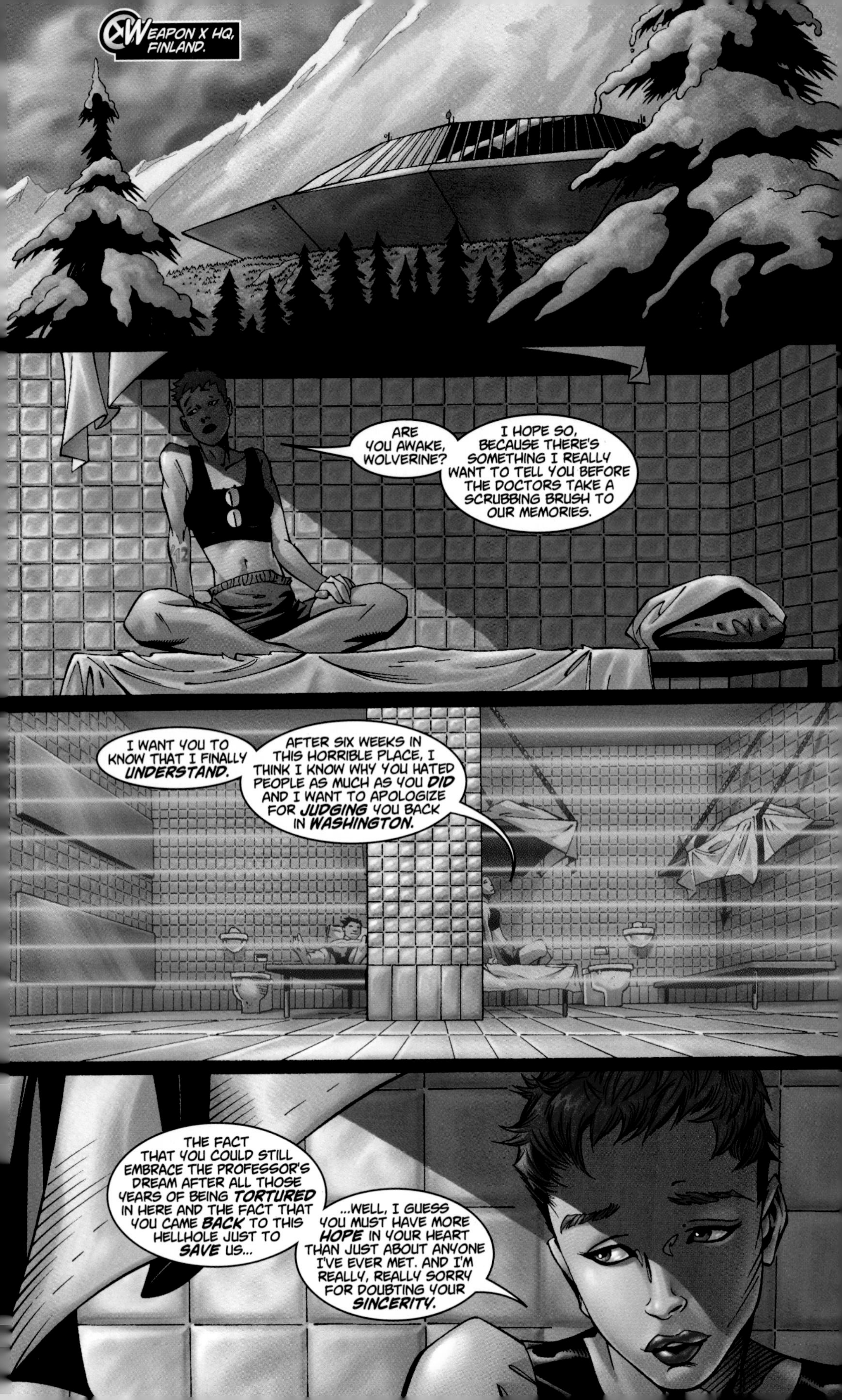
WEAPON X HQ, FINLAND.
ARE YOU AWAKE, WOLVERINE?
I HOPE SO, BECAUSE THERE'S SOMETHING I REALLY WANT TO TELL YOU BEFORE THE DOCTORS TAKE A SCRUBBING BRUSH TO OUR MEMORIES.
I WANT YOU TO KNOW THAT I FINALLY UNDERSTAND.
AFTER SIX WEEKS IN THIS HORRIBLE PLACE, I THINK I KNOW WHY YOU HATED PEOPLE AS MUCH AS YOU DID AND I WANT TO APOLOGIZE FOR JUDGING YOU BACK IN WASHINGTON.
THE FACT THAT YOU COULD STILL EMBRACE THE PROFESSOR'S DREAM AFTER ALL THOSE YEARS OF BEING TORTURED IN HERE AND THE FACT THAT YOU CAME BACK TO THIS HELLHOLE JUST TO SAVE US...
...WELL, I GUESS YOU MUST HAVE MORE HOPE IN YOUR HEART THAN JUST ABOUT ANYONE I'VE EVER MET. AND I'M REALLY, REALLY SORRY FOR DOUBTING YOUR SINCERITY.

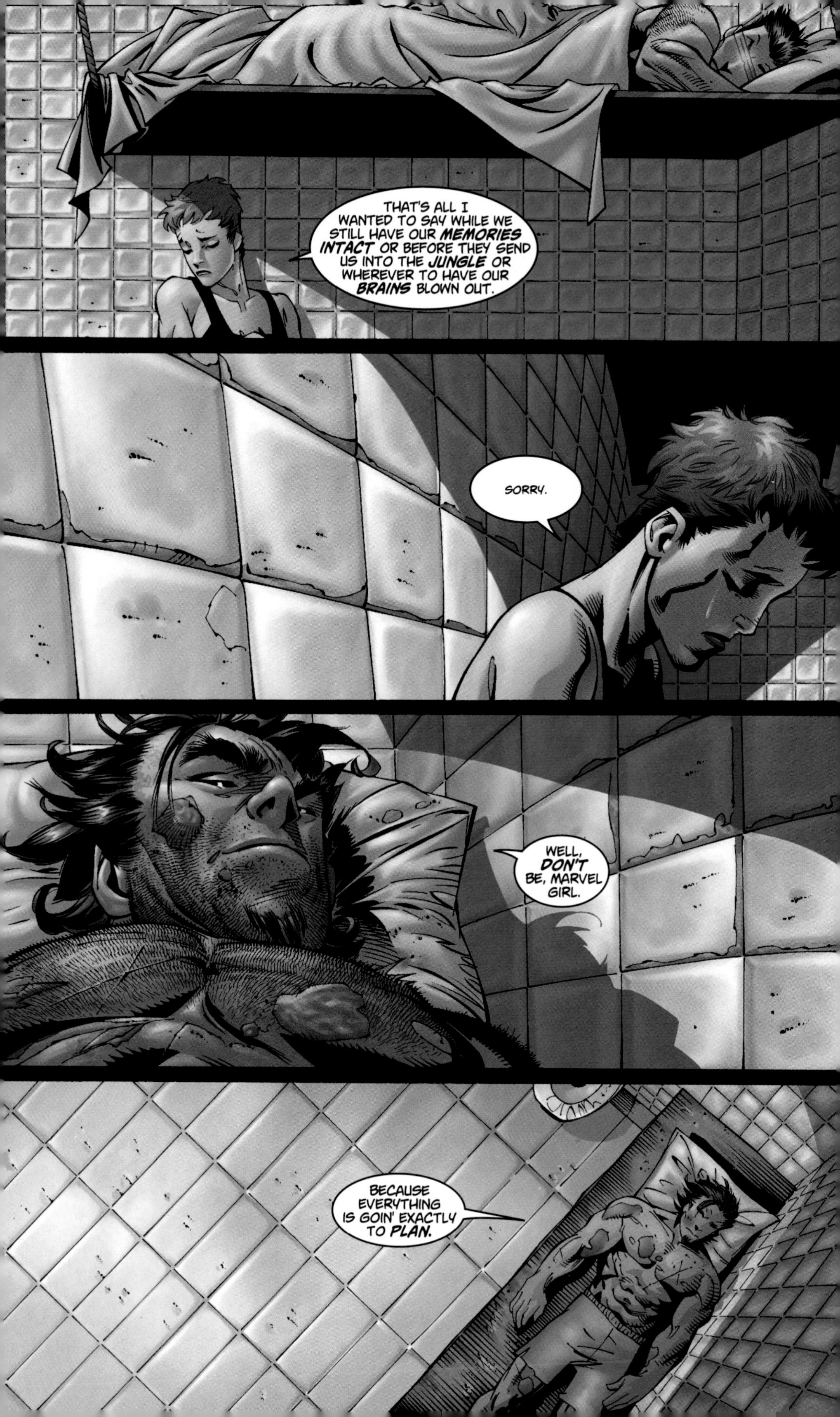
THAT'S ALL I WANTED TO SAY WHILE WE STILL HAVE OUR MEMORIES INTACT OR BEFORE THEY SEND US INTO THE JUNGLE OR WHEREVER TO HAVE OUR BRAINS BLOWN OUT.
SORRY.
WELL, DON'T BE, MARVEL GIRL.
BECAUSE EVERYTHING IS GOIN' EXACTLY TO PLAN.

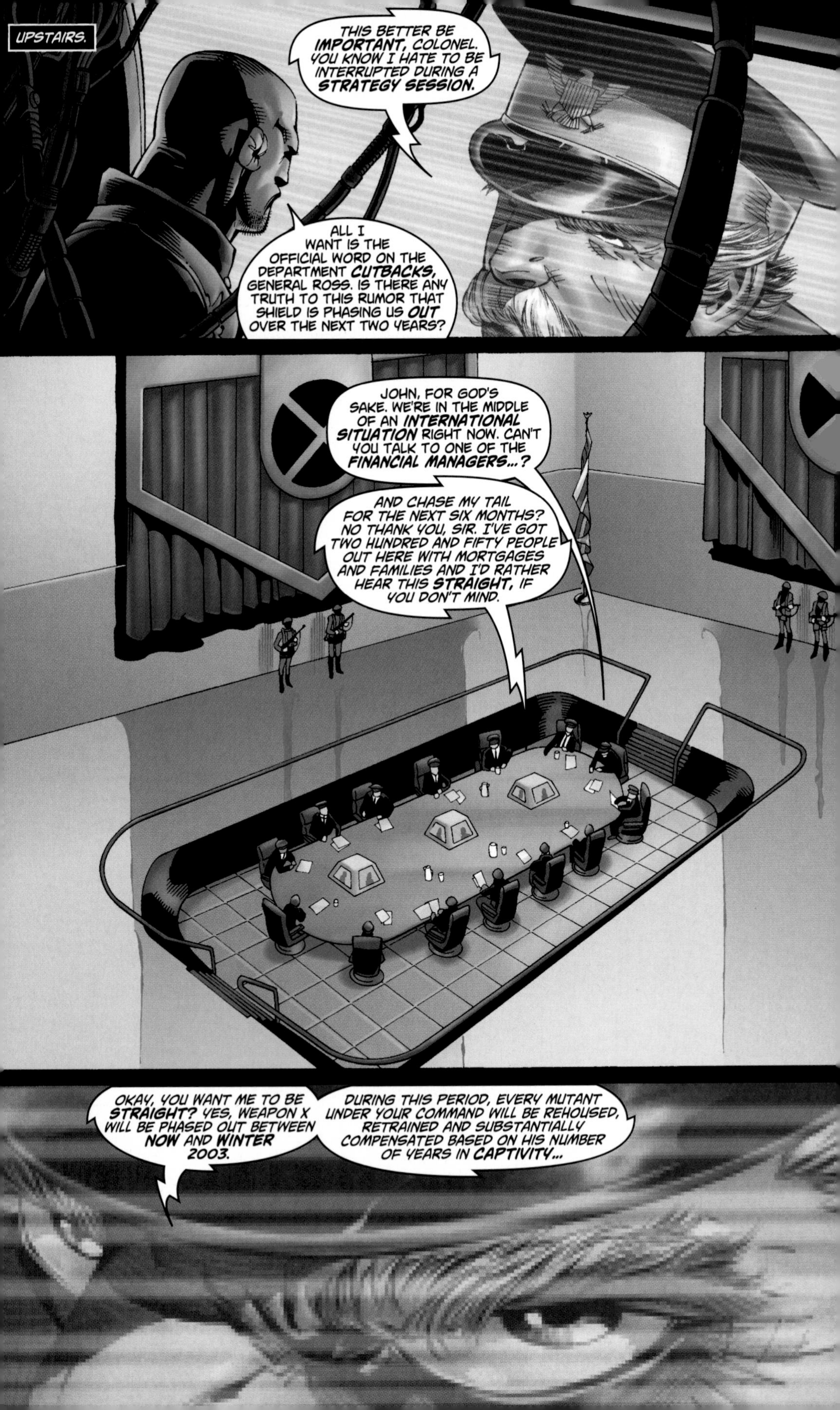
UPSTAIRS.
THIS BETTER BE IMPORTANT, COLONEL. YOU KNOW I HATE TO BE INTERRUPTED DURING A STRATEGY SESSION.
ALL I WANT IS THE OFFICIAL WORD ON THE DEPARTMENT CUTBACKS, GENERAL ROSS. IS THERE ANY TRUTH TO THIS RUMOR THAT SHIELD IS PHASING US OUT OVER THE NEXT TWO YEARS?
JOHN, FOR GOD'S SAKE. WE'RE IN THE MIDDLE OF AN INTERNATIONAL SITUATION RIGHT NOW. CAN'T YOU TALK TO ONE OF THE FINANCIAL MANAGERS...?
AND CHASE MY TAIL FOR THE NEXT SIX MONTHS? NO THANK YOU, SIR. I'VE GOT TWO HUNDRED AND FIFTY PEOPLE OUT HERE WITH MORTGAGES AND FAMILIES AND I'D RATHER HEAR THIS STRAIGHT, IF YOU DON'T MIND.
OKAY, YOU WANT ME TO BE STRAIGHT? YES, WEAPON X WILL BE PHASED OUT BETWEEN NOW AND WINTER 2003.
DURING THIS PERIOD, EVERY MUTANT UNDER YOUR COMMAND WILL BE REHOUSED, RETRAINED AND SUBSTANTIALLY COMPENSATED BASED ON HIS NUMBER OF YEARS IN CAPTIVITY...

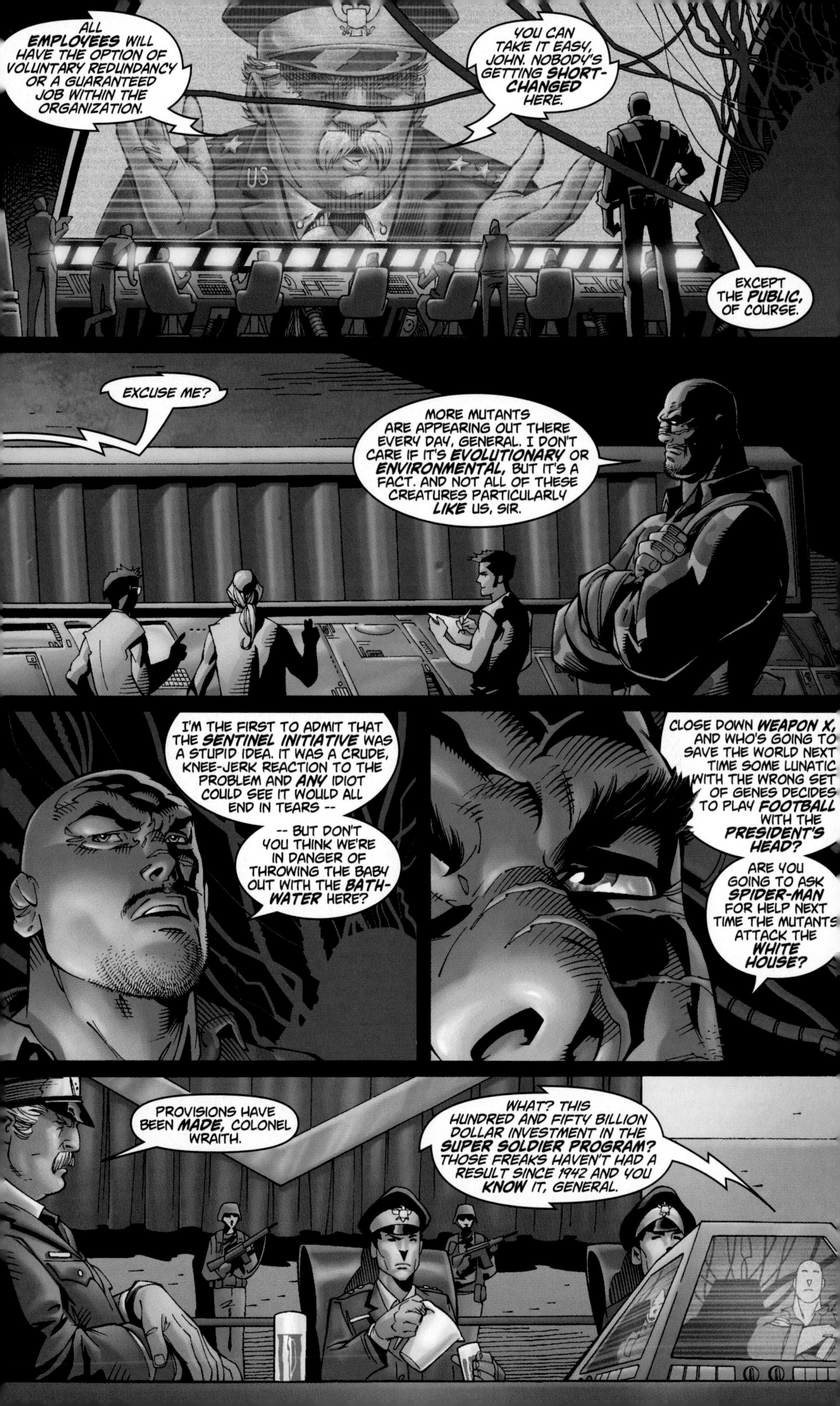

ALL EMPLOYEES WILL HAVE THE OPTION OF VOLUNTARY REDUNDANCY OR A GUARANTEED JOB WITHIN THE ORGANIZATION.
YOU CAN TAKE IT EASY, JOHN. NOBODY'S GETTING SHORT-CHANGED HERE.
US
EXCEPT THE PUBLIC, OF COURSE.
EXCUSE ME?
MORE MUTANTS ARE APPEARING OUT THERE EVERY DAY, GENERAL. I DON'T CARE IF IT'S EVOLUTIONARY OR ENVIRONMENTAL, BUT IT'S A FACT. AND NOT ALL OF THESE CREATURES PARTICULARLY LIKE US, SIR.
I'M THE FIRST TO ADMIT THAT THE SENTINEL INITIATIVE WAS A STUPID IDEA. IT WAS A CRUDE, KNEE-JERK REACTION TO THE PROBLEM AND ANY IDIOT COULD SEE IT WOULD ALL END IN TEARS --
-- BUT DON'T YOU THINK WE'RE IN DANGER OF THROWING THE BABY OUT WITH THE BATH-WATER HERE?
CLOSE DOWN WEAPON X, AND WHO'S GOING TO SAVE THE WORLD NEXT TIME SOME LUNATIC WITH THE WRONG SET OF GENES DECIDES TO PLAY FOOTBALL WITH THE PRESIDENT'S HEAD?
ARE YOU GOING TO ASK SPIDER-MAN FOR HELP NEXT TIME THE MUTANTS ATTACK THE WHITE HOUSE?
PROVISIONS HAVE BEEN MADE, COLONEL WRAITH.
WHAT? THIS HUNDRED AND FIFTY BILLION DOLLAR INVESTMENT IN THE SUPER SOLDIER PROGRAM? THOSE FREAKS HAVEN'T HAD A RESULT SINCE 1942 AND YOU KNOW IT, GENERAL.

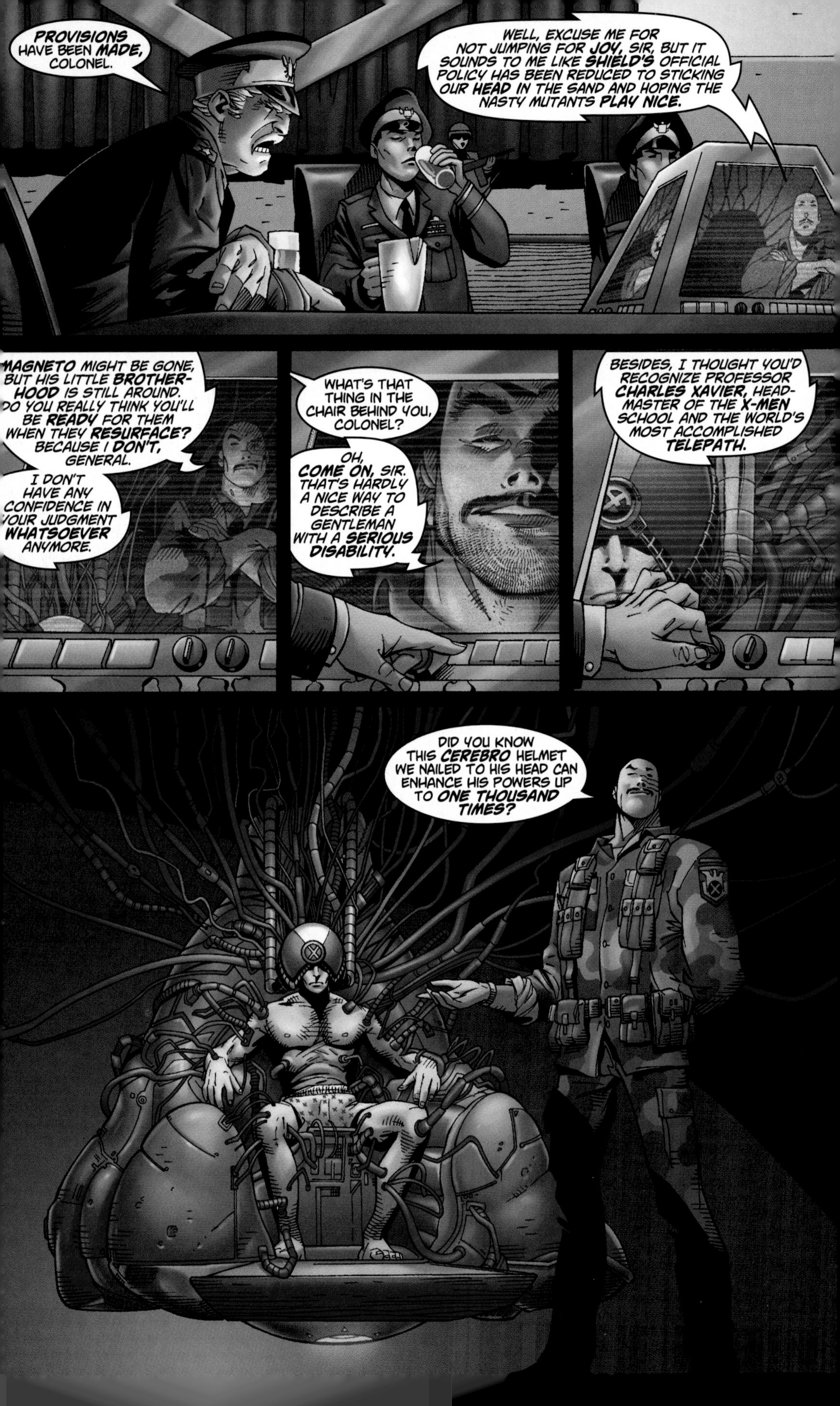

PROVISIONS HAVE BEEN MADE, COLONEL.
WELL, EXCUSE ME FOR NOT JUMPING FOR JOY, SIR, BUT IT SOUNDS TO ME LIKE SHIELD'S OFFICIAL POLICY HAS BEEN REDUCED TO STICKING OUR HEAD IN THE SAND AND HOPING THE NASTY MUTANTS PLAY NICE.
MAGNETO MIGHT BE GONE, BUT HIS LITTLE BROTHER-HOOD IS STILL AROUND. DO YOU REALLY THINK YOU'LL BE READY FOR THEM WHEN THEY RESURFACE? BECAUSE I DON'T, GENERAL.
I DON'T HAVE ANY CONFIDENCE IN YOUR JUDGMENT WHATSOEVER ANYMORE.
WHAT'S THAT THING IN THE CHAIR BEHIND YOU, COLONEL?
OH, COME ON, SIR. THAT'S HARDLY A NICE WAY TO DESCRIBE A GENTLEMAN WITH A SERIOUS DISABILITY.
BESIDES, I THOUGHT YOU'D RECOGNIZE PROFESSOR CHARLES XAVIER, HEAD-MASTER OF THE X-MEN SCHOOL AND THE WORLD'S MOST ACCOMPLISHED TELEPATH.
DID YOU KNOW THIS CEREBRO HELMET WE NAILED TO HIS HEAD CAN ENHANCE HIS POWERS UP TO ONE THOUSAND TIMES?

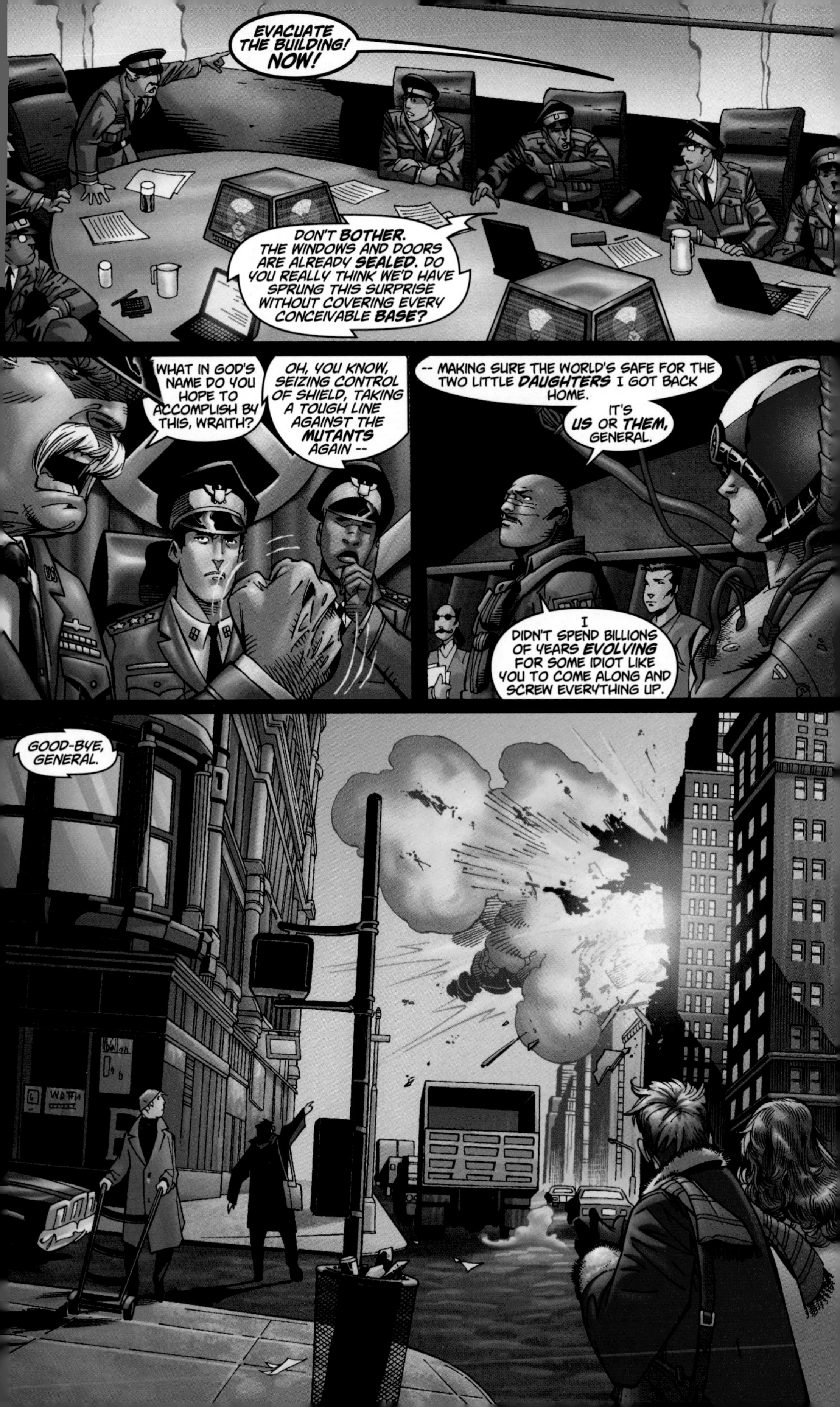
EVACUATE THE BUILDING! NOW!
DON'T BOTHER. THE WINDOWS AND DOORS ARE ALREADY SEALED. DO YOU REALLY THINK WE'D HAVE SPRUNG THIS SURPRISE WITHOUT COVERING EVERY CONCEIVABLE BASE?
WHAT IN GOD'S NAME DO YOU HOPE TO ACCOMPLISH BY THIS, WRAITH?
OH, YOU KNOW, SEIZING CONTROL OF SHIELD, TAKING A TOUGH LINE AGAINST THE MUTANTS AGAIN --
-- MAKING SURE THE WORLD'S SAFE FOR THE TWO LITTLE DAUGHTERS I GOT BACK HOME.
IT'S US OR THEM, GENERAL.
I DIDN'T SPEND BILLIONS OF YEARS EVOLVING FOR SOME IDIOT LIKE YOU TO COME ALONG AND SCREW EVERYTHING UP.
GOOD-BYE, GENERAL.

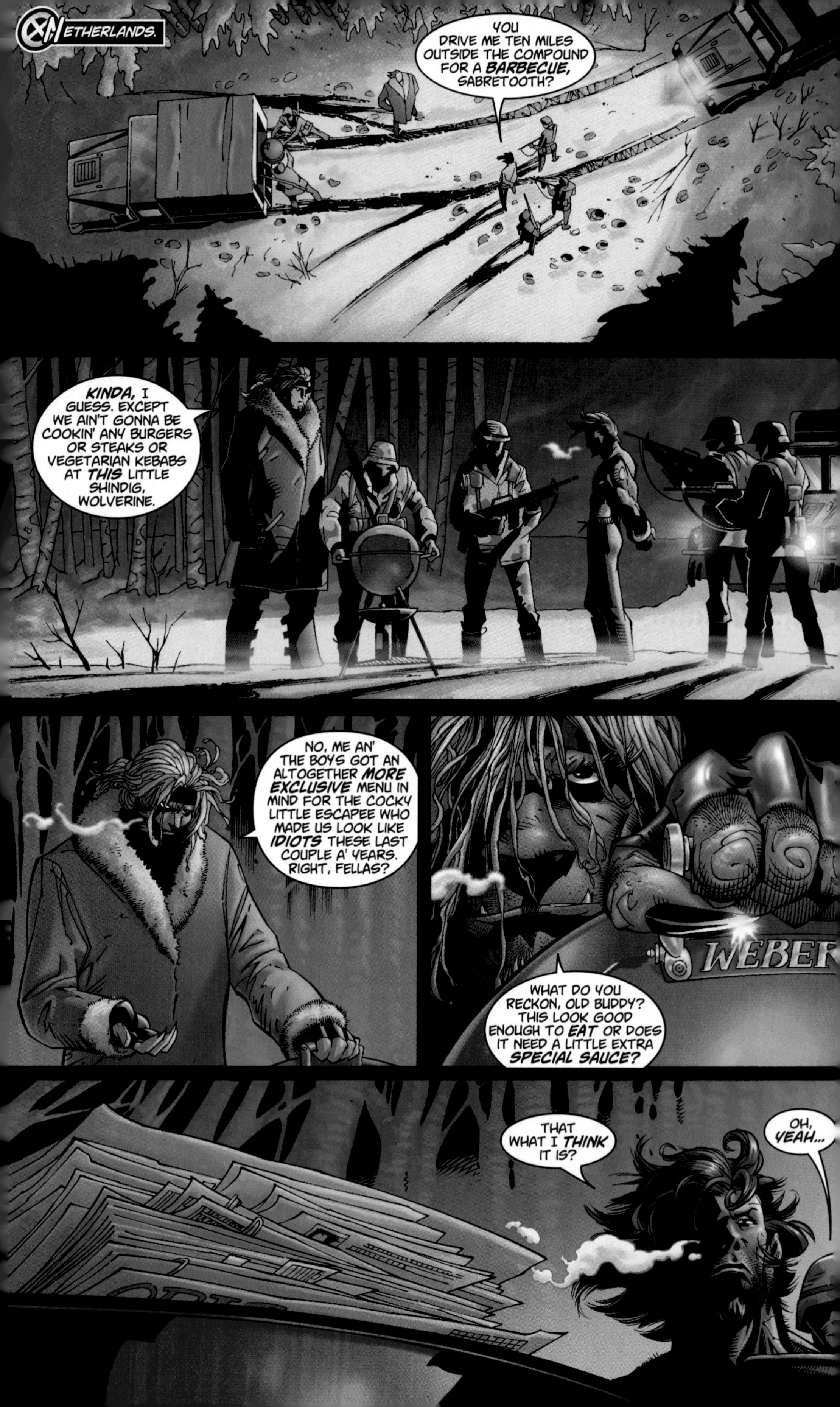
NETHERLANDS.
YOU DRIVE ME TEN MILES OUTSIDE THE COMPOUND FOR A BARBECUE, SABRETOOTH?
KINDA, I GUESS. EXCEPT WE AIN'T GONNA BE COOKIN' ANY BURGERS OR STEAKS OR VEGETARIAN KEBABS AT THIS LITTLE SHINDIG, WOLVERINE.
NO, ME AN' THE BOYS GOT AN ALTOGETHER MORE EXCLUSIVE MENU IN MIND FOR THE COCKY LITTLE ESCAPEE WHO MADE US LOOK LIKE IDIOTS THESE LAST COUPLE A' YEARS. RIGHT, FELLAS?
WEBER
WHAT DO YOU RECKON, OLD BUDDY? THIS LOOK GOOD ENOUGH TO EAT OR DOES IT NEED A LITTLE EXTRA SPECIAL SAUCE?
THAT WHAT I THINK IT IS?
OH, YEAH...

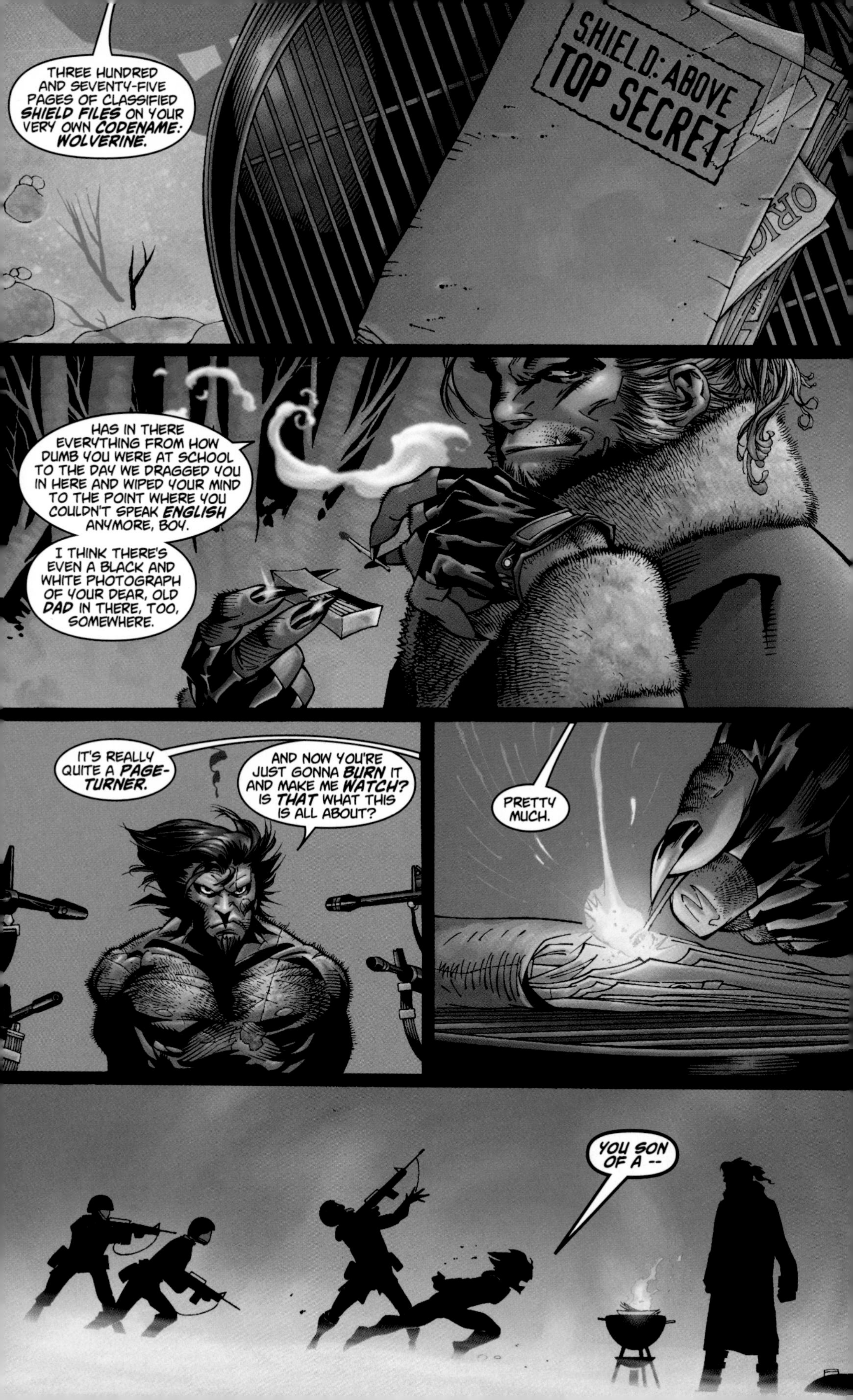

S.H.I.E.L.D: ABOVE TOP SECRET
THREE HUNDRED AND SEVENTY-FIVE PAGES OF CLASSIFIED SHIELD FILES ON YOUR VERY OWN CODENAME: WOLVERINE.
HAS IN THERE EVERYTHING FROM HOW DUMB YOU WERE AT SCHOOL TO THE DAY WE DRAGGED YOU IN HERE AND WIPED YOUR MIND TO THE POINT WHERE YOU COULDN'T SPEAK ENGLISH ANYMORE, BOY.
I THINK THERE'S EVEN A BLACK AND WHITE PHOTOGRAPH OF YOUR DEAR, OLD DAD IN THERE, TOO, SOMEWHERE.
IT'S REALLY QUITE A PAGE-TURNER.
AND NOW YOU'RE JUST GONNA BURN IT AND MAKE ME WATCH? IS THAT WHAT THIS IS ALL ABOUT?
PRETTY MUCH.
YOU SON OF A --

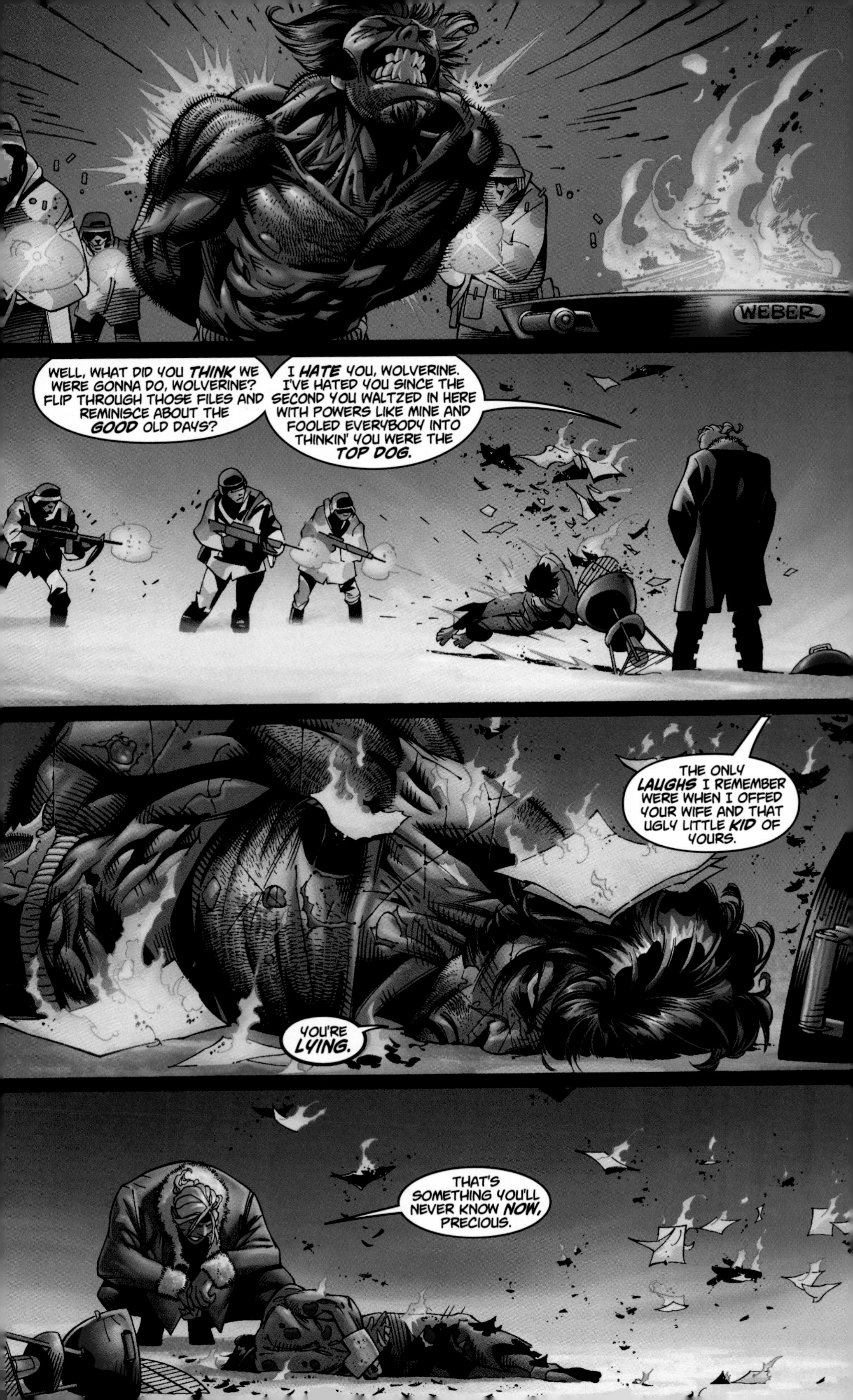
WEBER
WELL, WHAT DID YOU THINK WE WERE GONNA DO, WOLVERINE? FLIP THROUGH THOSE FILES AND REMINISCE ABOUT THE GOOD OLD DAYS?
I HATE YOU, WOLVERINE. I'VE HATED YOU SINCE THE SECOND YOU WALTZED IN HERE WITH POWERS LIKE MINE AND FOOLED EVERYBODY INTO THINKIN' YOU WERE THE TOP DOG.
THE ONLY LAUGHS I REMEMBER WERE WHEN I OFFED YOUR WIFE AND THAT UGLY LITTLE KID OF YOURS.
YOU'RE LYING.
THAT'S SOMETHING YOU'LL NEVER KNOW NOW, PRECIOUS.

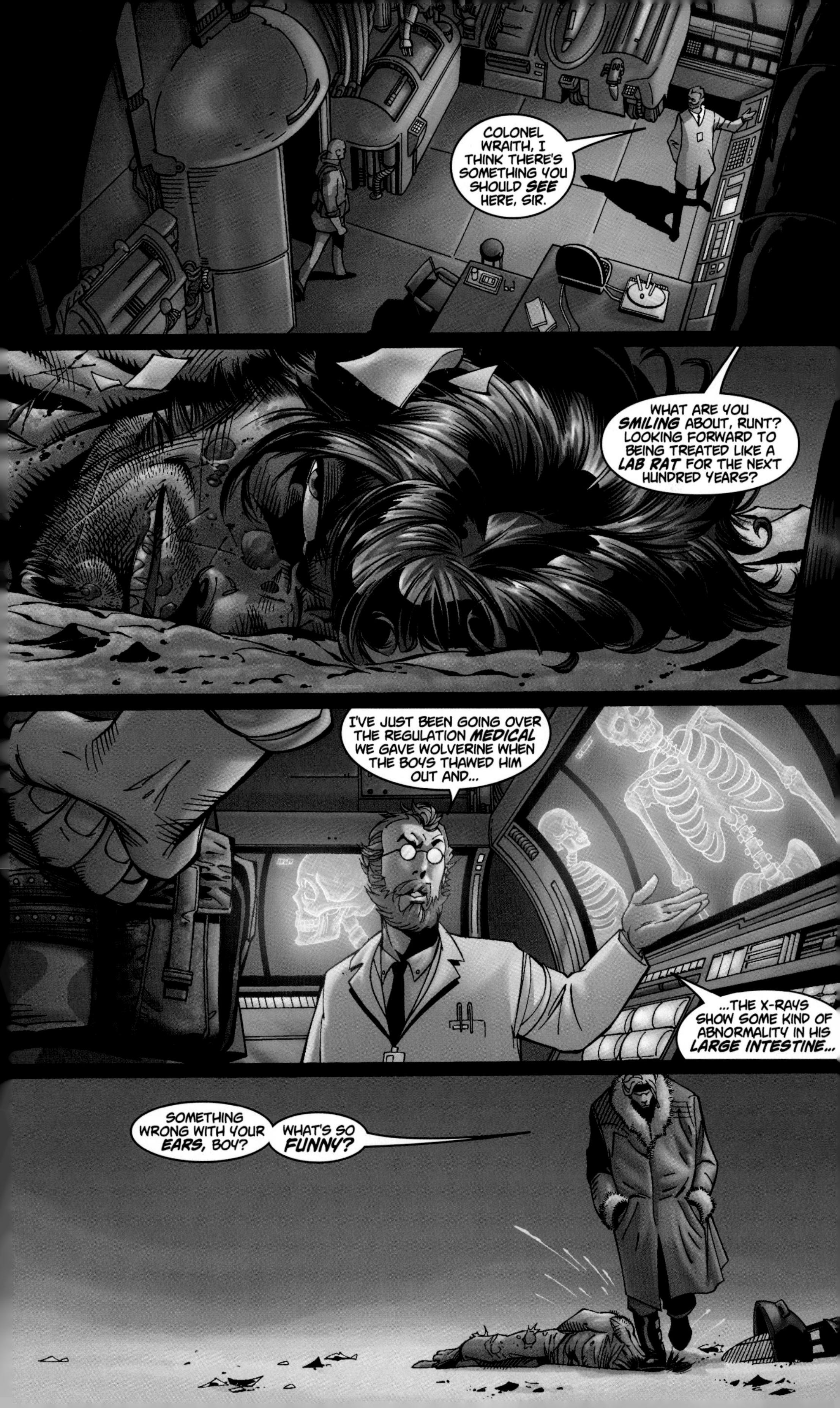
COLONEL WRAITH, I THINK THERE'S SOMETHING YOU SHOULD SEE HERE, SIR.
WHAT ARE YOU SMILING ABOUT, RUNT? LOOKING FORWARD TO BEING TREATED LIKE A LAB RAT FOR THE NEXT HUNDRED YEARS?
I'VE JUST BEEN GOING OVER THE REGULATION MEDICAL WE GAVE WOLVERINE WHEN THE BOYS THAWED HIM OUT AND...
...THE X-RAYS SHOW SOME KIND OF ABNORMALITY IN HIS LARGE INTESTINE...
SOMETHING WRONG WITH YOUR EARS, BOY?
WHAT'S SO FUNNY?

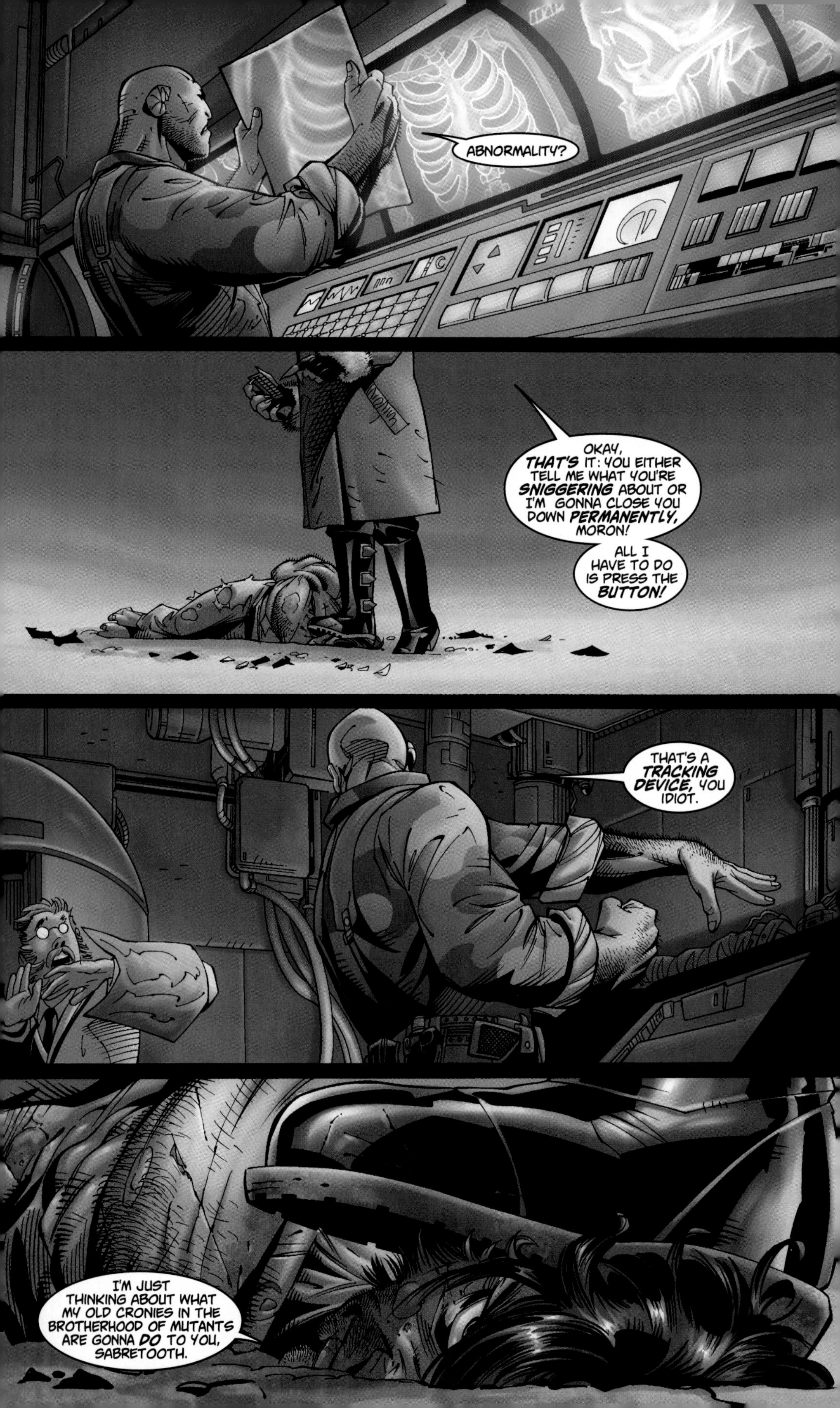
ABNORMALITY?
OKAY, THAT'S IT: YOU EITHER TELL ME WHAT YOU'RE SNIGGERING ABOUT OR I'M GONNA CLOSE YOU DOWN PERMANENTLY, MORON!
ALL I HAVE TO DO IS PRESS THE BUTTON!
THAT'S A TRACKING DEVICE, YOU IDIOT.
I'M JUST THINKING ABOUT WHAT MY OLD CRONIES IN THE BROTHERHOOD OF MUTANTS ARE GONNA DO TO YOU, SABRETOOTH.

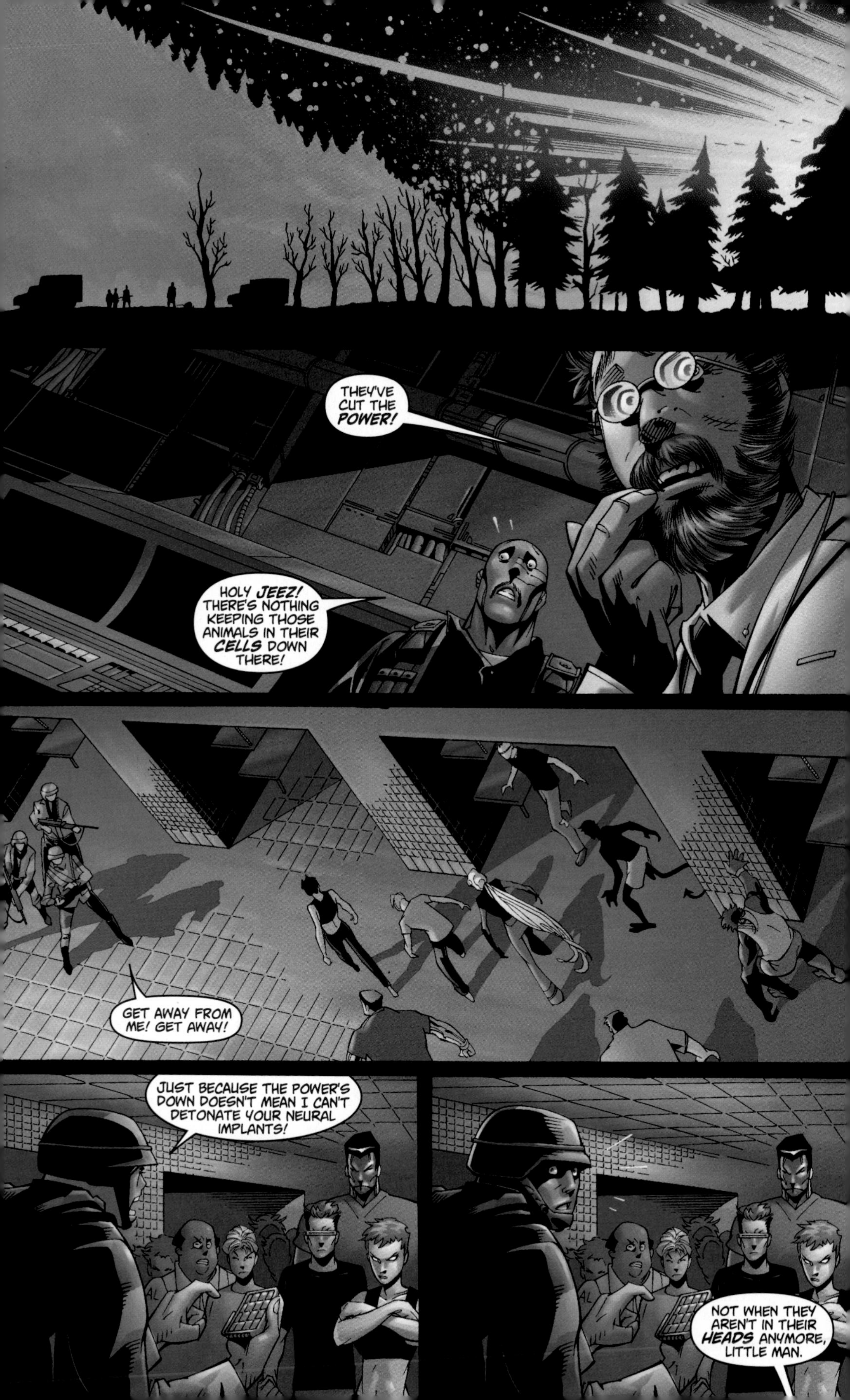
THEY'VE CUT THE POWER!
HOLY JEEZ! THERE'S NOTHING KEEPING THOSE ANIMALS IN THEIR CELLS DOWN THERE!
GET AWAY FROM ME! GET AWAY!
JUST BECAUSE THE POWER'S DOWN DOESN'T MEAN I CAN'T DETONATE YOUR NEURAL IMPLANTS!
NOT WHEN THEY AREN'T IN THEIR HEADS ANYMORE, LITTLE MAN.

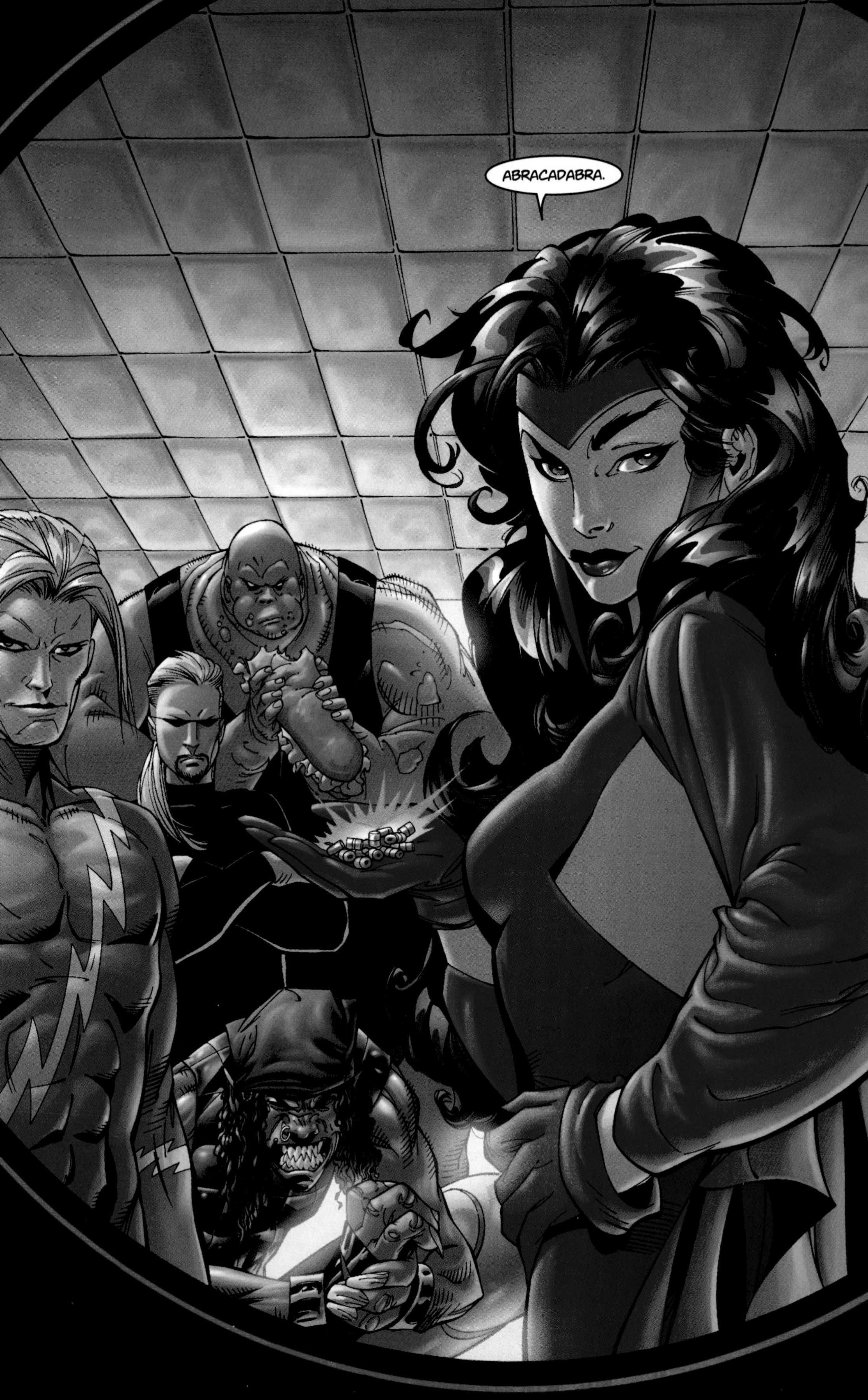
ABRACADABRA.

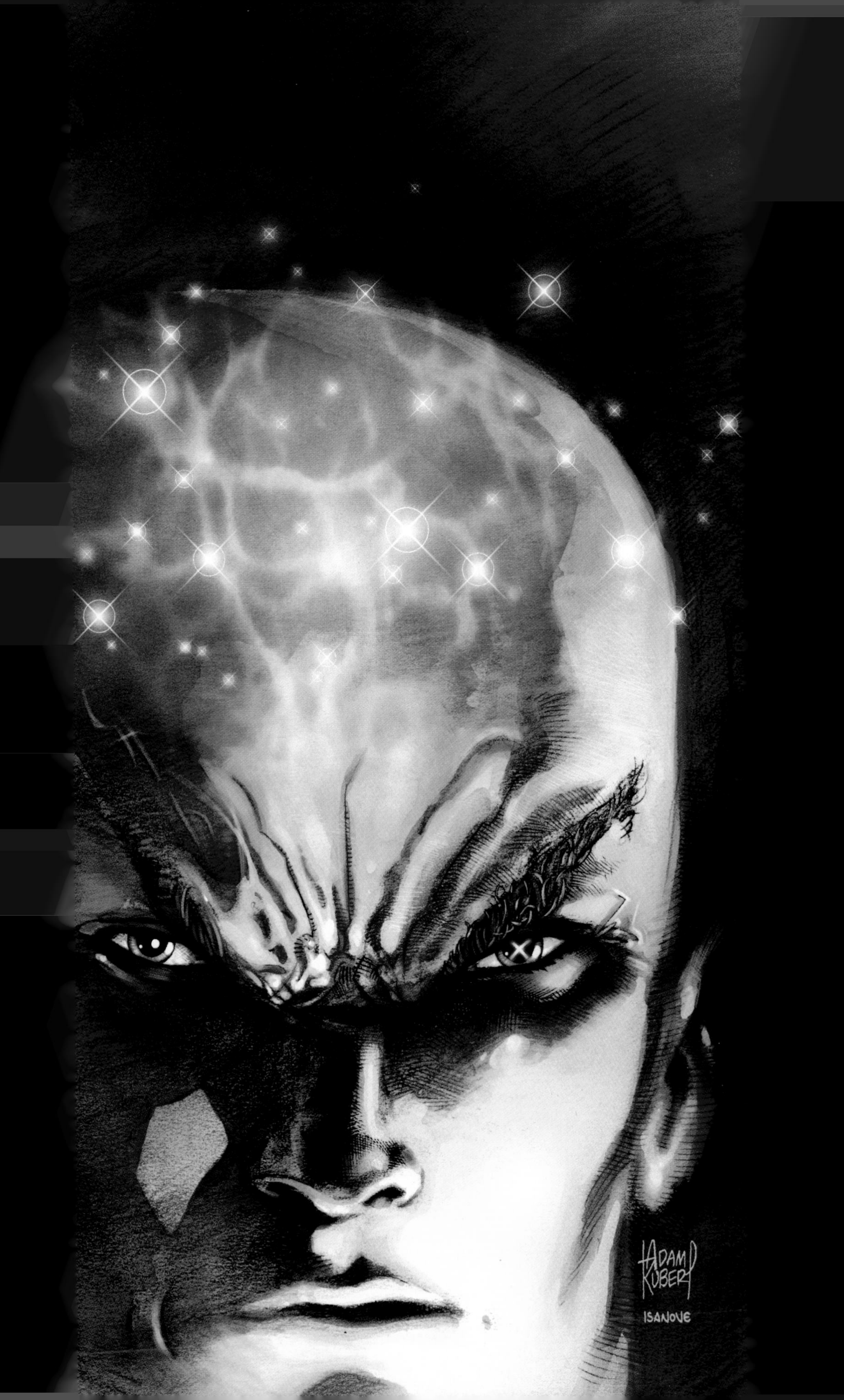
ADAM KUBERT
ISANOVE

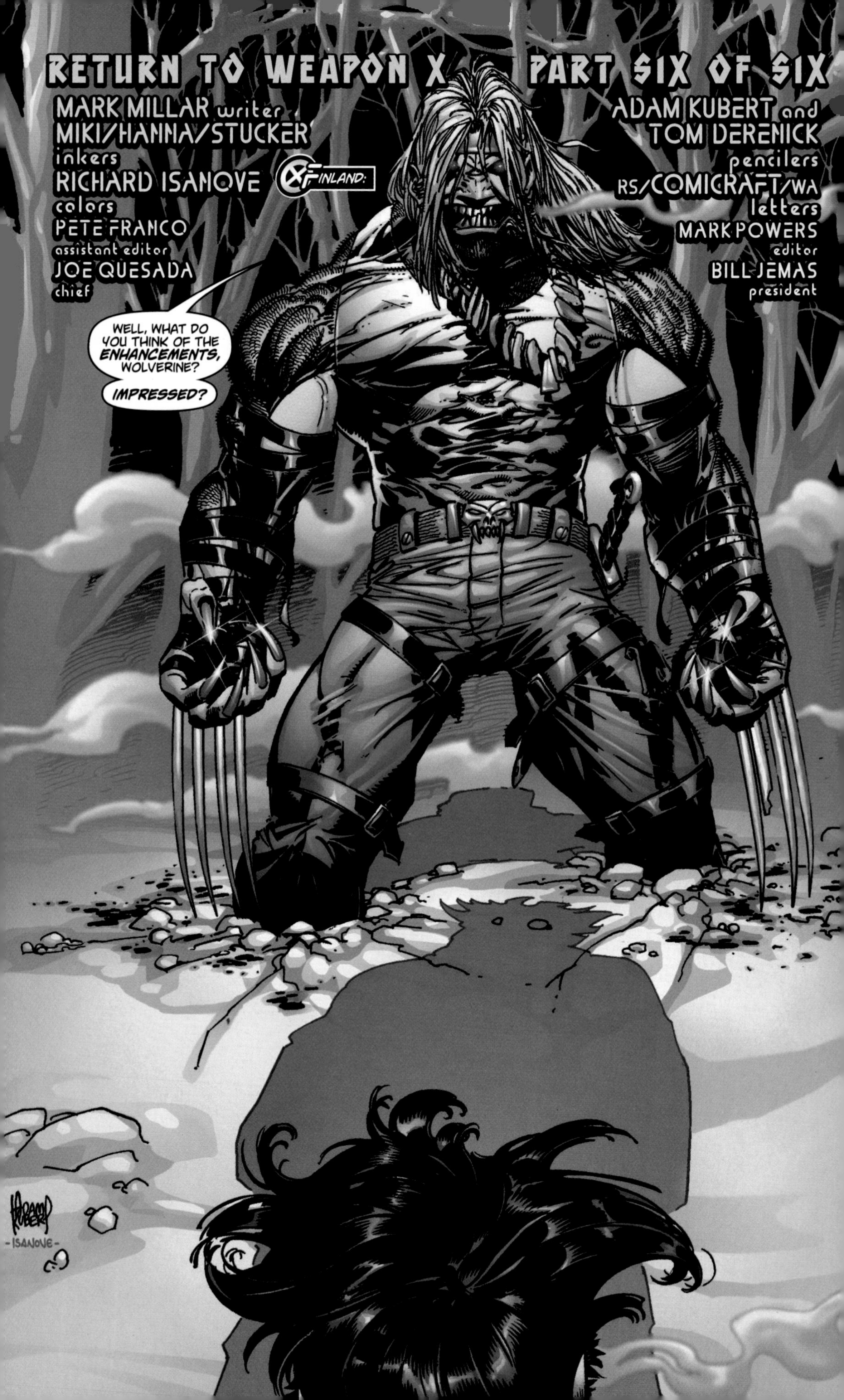

RETURN TO WEAPON X PART SIX OF SIX
MARK MILLAR writer
MIKI/HANNA/STUCKER inkers
RICHARD ISANOVE colors
PETE FRANCO assistant editor
JOE QUESADA chief
X-FINLAND:
ADAM KUBERT and TOM DERENICK pencilers
RS/COMICRAFT/WA letters
MARK POWERS editor
BILL JEMAS president
WELL, WHAT DO YOU THINK OF THE ENHANCEMENTS, WOLVERINE?
IMPRESSED?
ADAM KUBERT -ISANOVE-

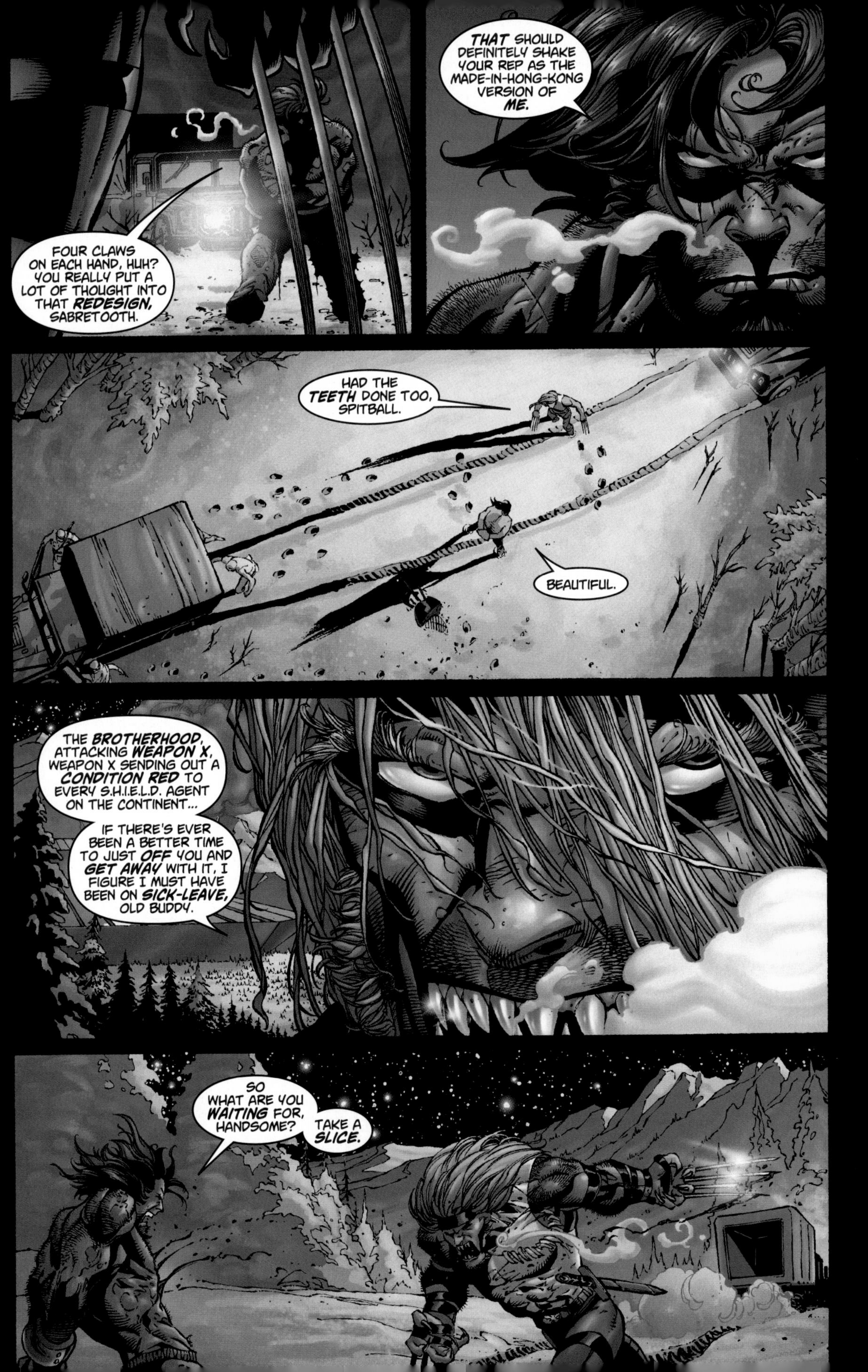
FOUR CLAWS ON EACH HAND, HUH? YOU REALLY PUT A LOT OF THOUGHT INTO THAT REDESIGN, SABRETOOTH.
THAT SHOULD DEFINITELY SHAKE YOUR REP AS THE MADE-IN-HONG-KONG VERSION OF ME.
HAD THE TEETH DONE TOO, SPITBALL.
BEAUTIFUL.
THE BROTHERHOOD, ATTACKING WEAPON X, WEAPON X SENDING OUT A CONDITION RED TO EVERY S.H.I.E.L.D. AGENT ON THE CONTINENT...
IF THERE'S EVER BEEN A BETTER TIME TO JUST OFF YOU AND GET AWAY WITH IT, I FIGURE I MUST HAVE BEEN ON SICK-LEAVE, OLD BUDDY.
SO WHAT ARE YOU WAITING FOR, HANDSOME?
TAKE A SLICE.

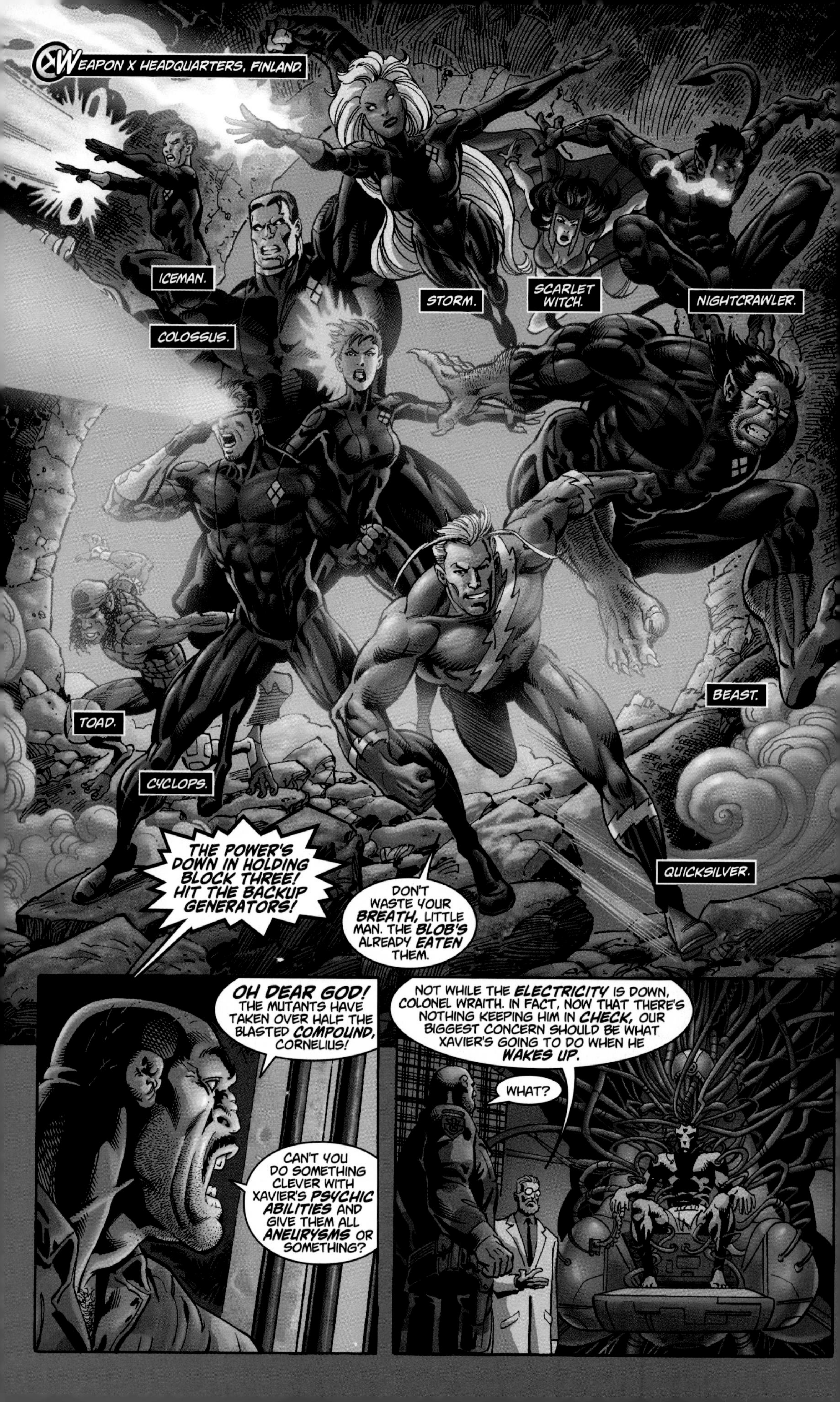
WEAPON X HEADQUARTERS, FINLAND.
ICEMAN.
COLOSSUS.
STORM.
SCARLET WITCH.
NIGHTCRAWLER.
BEAST.
TOAD.
CYCLOPS.
QUICKSILVER.
THE POWER'S DOWN IN HOLDING BLOCK THREE! HIT THE BACKUP GENERATORS!
DON'T WASTE YOUR BREATH, LITTLE MAN. THE BLOB'S ALREADY EATEN THEM.
OH DEAR GOD! THE MUTANTS HAVE TAKEN OVER HALF THE BLASTED COMPOUND, CORNELIUS!
CAN'T YOU DO SOMETHING CLEVER WITH XAVIER'S PSYCHIC ABILITIES AND GIVE THEM ALL ANEURYSMS OR SOMETHING?
NOT WHILE THE ELECTRICITY IS DOWN, COLONEL WRAITH. IN FACT, NOW THAT THERE'S NOTHING KEEPING HIM IN CHECK, OUR BIGGEST CONCERN SHOULD BE WHAT XAVIER'S GOING TO DO WHEN HE WAKES UP.
WHAT?

FREEZE, YOU FREAKS!

YOU KNOW, YOU REALLY SHOULDN'T GIVE ICEMAN *OPENINGS* LIKE THAT, MISTER.

WHAT MAKES YOU THINK HE'S GONNA WAKE UP?

WELL, WHY *SHOULDN'T* HE? THE ONLY THING THAT WAS LETTING US *CONTROL* HIM WERE THE *NEURAL CLAMPS,* AND NOW THAT THE *MACHINE* ISN'T WORKING...

...WELL, MY GUESS IS WE'VE GOT APPROXIMATELY FIVE TO TEN MINUTES TO GET *OUT* OF HERE.

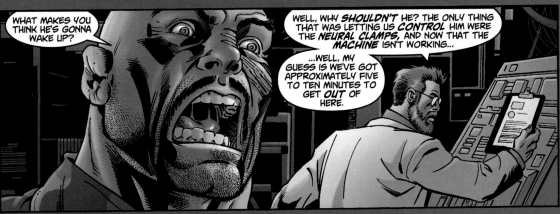

UNACCEPTABLE, CORNELIUS. ABSOLUTELY *OFF-THE-SCALE* UNACCEPTABLE...

WRAITH! WHAT ON EARTH ARE YOU *DOING?*

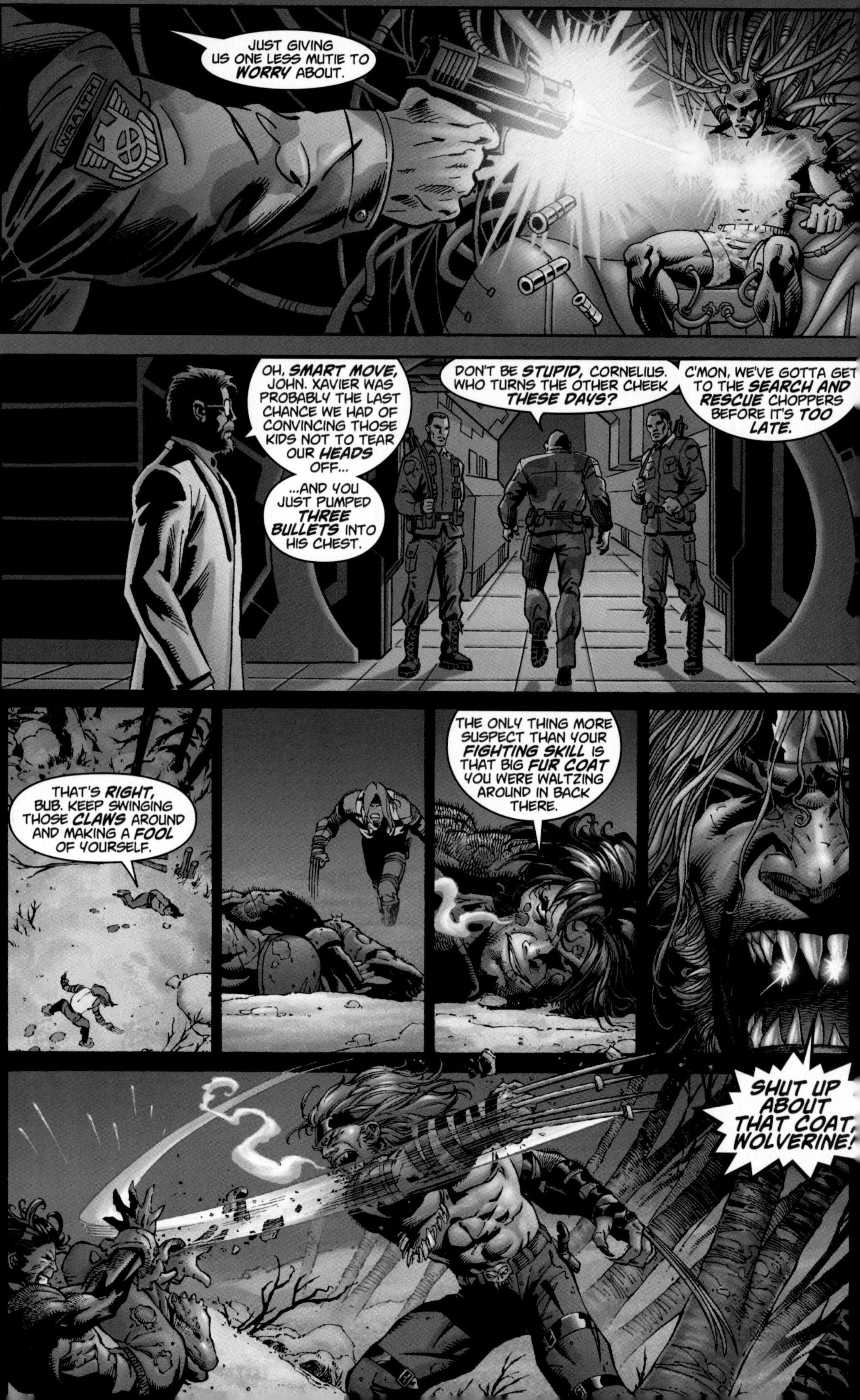
JUST GIVING US ONE LESS MUTIE TO WORRY ABOUT.
WRAITH
OH, SMART MOVE, JOHN. XAVIER WAS PROBABLY THE LAST CHANCE WE HAD OF CONVINCING THOSE KIDS NOT TO TEAR OUR HEADS OFF...
...AND YOU JUST PUMPED THREE BULLETS INTO HIS CHEST.
DON'T BE STUPID, CORNELIUS. WHO TURNS THE OTHER CHEEK THESE DAYS?
C'MON, WE'VE GOTTA GET TO THE SEARCH AND RESCUE CHOPPERS BEFORE IT'S TOO LATE.
THAT'S RIGHT, BUB. KEEP SWINGING THOSE CLAWS AROUND AND MAKING A FOOL OF YOURSELF.
THE ONLY THING MORE SUSPECT THAN YOUR FIGHTING SKILL IS THAT BIG FUR COAT YOU WERE WALTZING AROUND IN BACK THERE.
SHUT UP ABOUT THAT COAT, WOLVERINE!

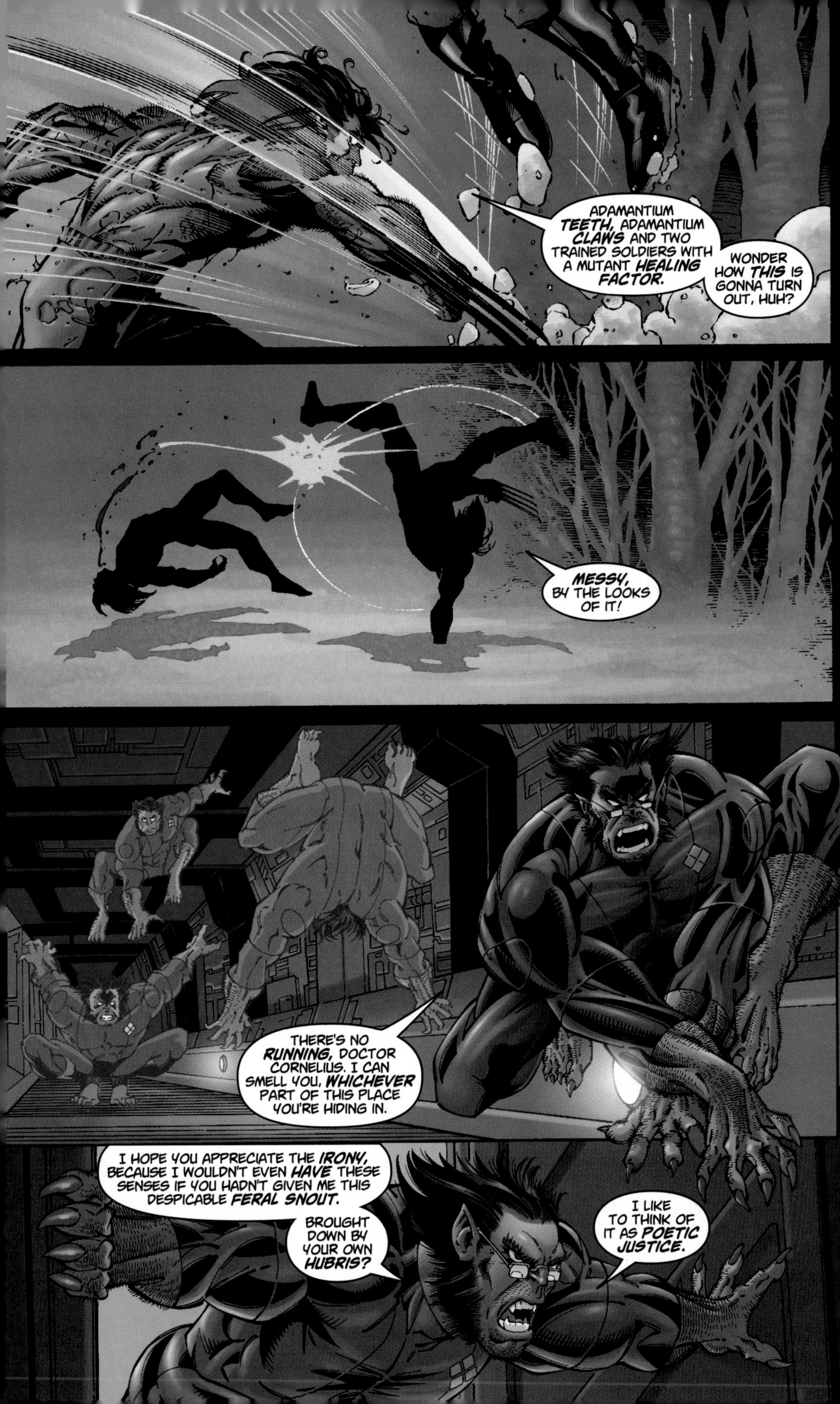
ADAMANTIUM TEETH, ADAMANTIUM CLAWS AND TWO TRAINED SOLDIERS WITH A MUTANT HEALING FACTOR.
WONDER HOW THIS IS GONNA TURN OUT, HUH?
MESSY, BY THE LOOKS OF IT!
THERE'S NO RUNNING, DOCTOR CORNELIUS. I CAN SMELL YOU, WHICHEVER PART OF THIS PLACE YOU'RE HIDING IN.
I HOPE YOU APPRECIATE THE IRONY, BECAUSE I WOULDN'T EVEN HAVE THESE SENSES IF YOU HADN'T GIVEN ME THIS DESPICABLE FERAL SNOUT.
BROUGHT DOWN BY YOUR OWN HUBRIS?
I LIKE TO THINK OF IT AS POETIC JUSTICE.

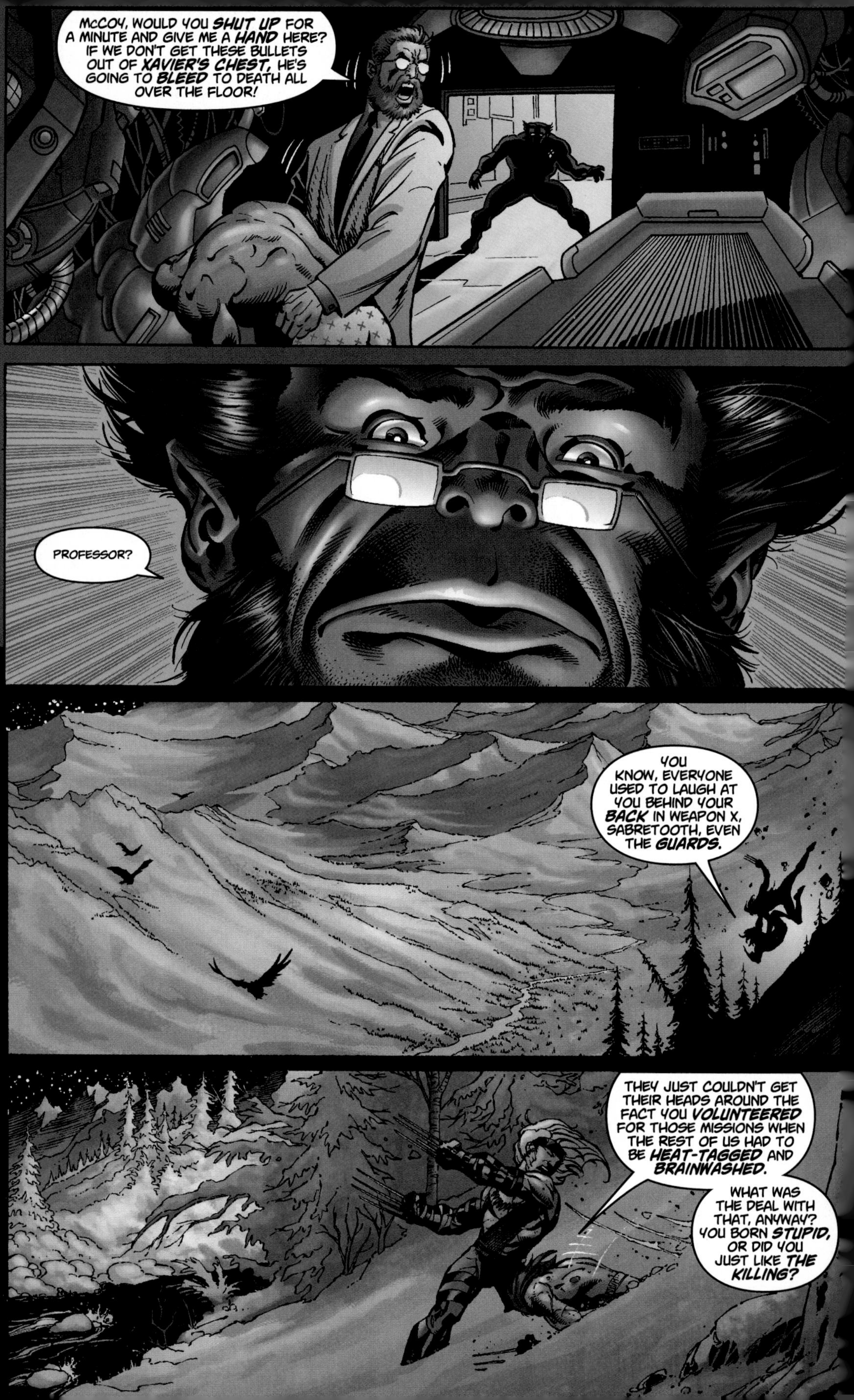
McCOY, WOULD YOU SHUT UP FOR A MINUTE AND GIVE ME A HAND HERE? IF WE DON'T GET THESE BULLETS OUT OF XAVIER'S CHEST, HE'S GOING TO BLEED TO DEATH ALL OVER THE FLOOR!
PROFESSOR?
YOU KNOW, EVERYONE USED TO LAUGH AT YOU BEHIND YOUR BACK IN WEAPON X, SABRETOOTH, EVEN THE GUARDS.
THEY JUST COULDN'T GET THEIR HEADS AROUND THE FACT YOU VOLUNTEERED FOR THOSE MISSIONS WHEN THE REST OF US HAD TO BE HEAT-TAGGED AND BRAINWASHED.
WHAT WAS THE DEAL WITH THAT, ANYWAY? YOU BORN STUPID, OR DID YOU JUST LIKE THE KILLING?

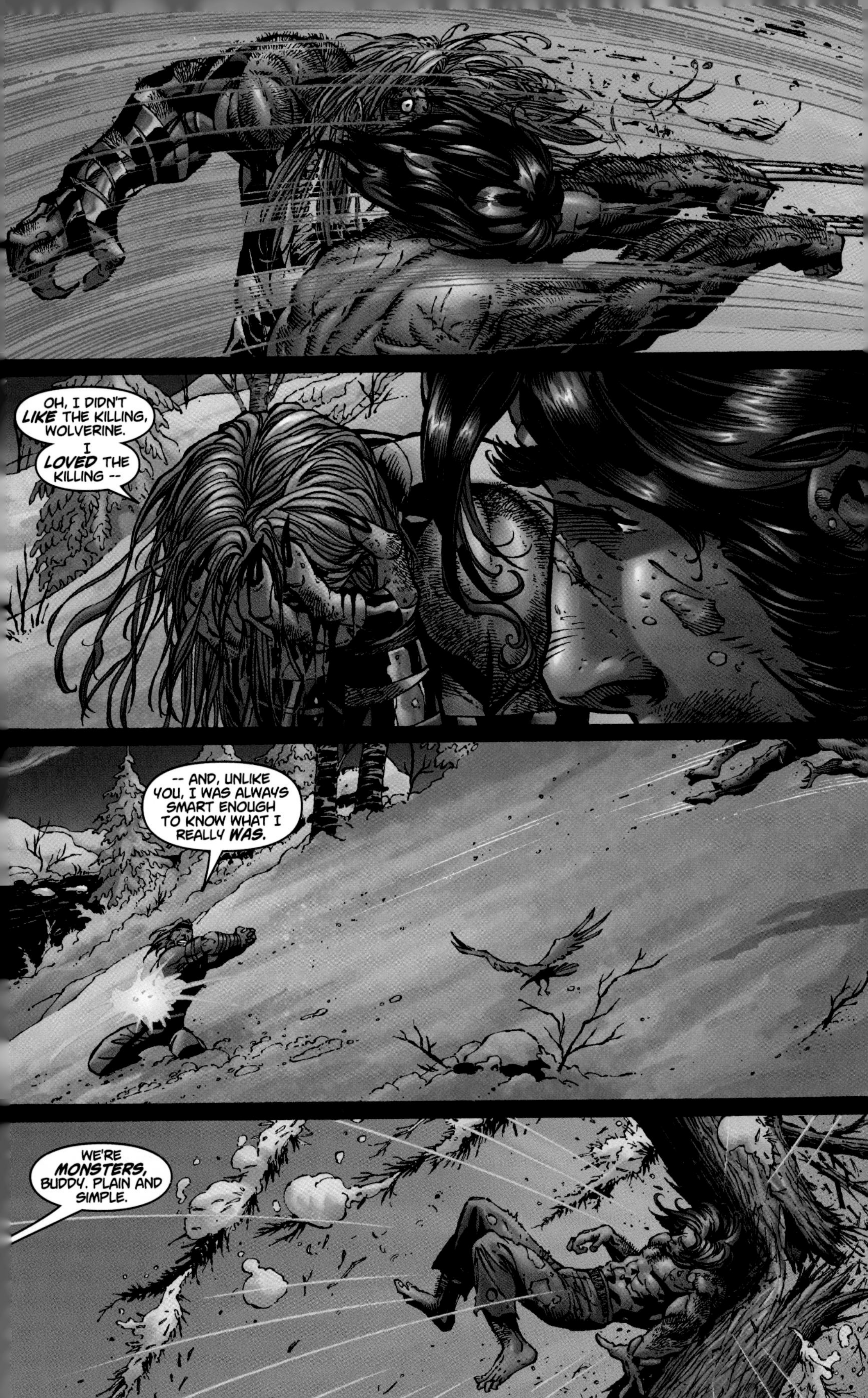
OH, I DIDN'T LIKE THE KILLING, WOLVERINE. I LOVED THE KILLING --
-- AND, UNLIKE YOU, I WAS ALWAYS SMART ENOUGH TO KNOW WHAT I REALLY WAS.
WE'RE MONSTERS, BUDDY. PLAIN AND SIMPLE.

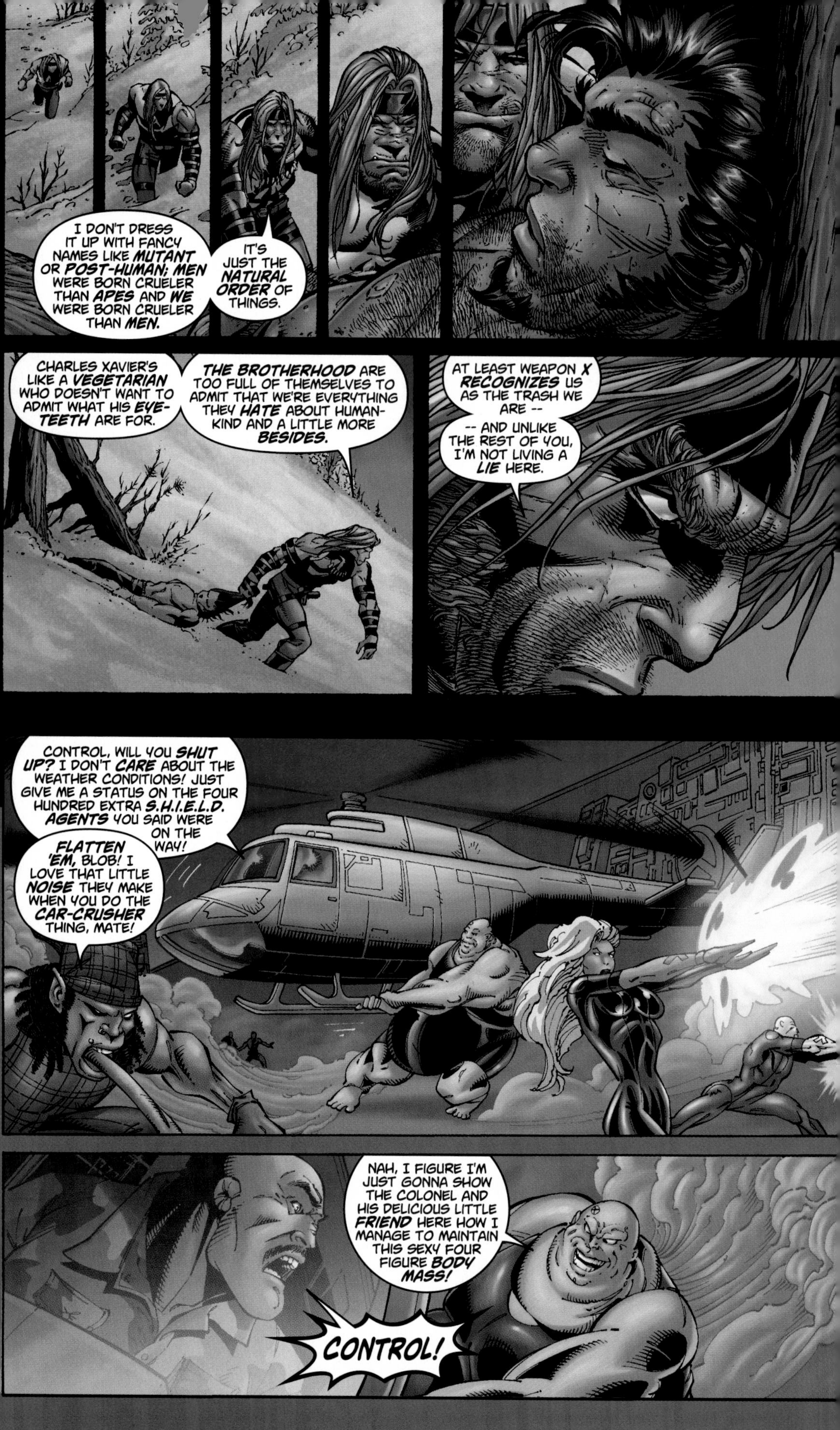
I DON'T DRESS IT UP WITH FANCY NAMES LIKE MUTANT OR POST-HUMAN; MEN WERE BORN CRUELER THAN APES AND WE WERE BORN CRUELER THAN MEN.
IT'S JUST THE NATURAL ORDER OF THINGS.
CHARLES XAVIER'S LIKE A VEGETARIAN WHO DOESN'T WANT TO ADMIT WHAT HIS EYE-TEETH ARE FOR.
THE BROTHERHOOD ARE TOO FULL OF THEMSELVES TO ADMIT THAT WE'RE EVERYTHING THEY HATE ABOUT HUMAN-KIND AND A LITTLE MORE BESIDES.
AT LEAST WEAPON X RECOGNIZES US AS THE TRASH WE ARE --
-- AND UNLIKE THE REST OF YOU, I'M NOT LIVING A LIE HERE.
CONTROL, WILL YOU SHUT UP? I DON'T CARE ABOUT THE WEATHER CONDITIONS! JUST GIVE ME A STATUS ON THE FOUR HUNDRED EXTRA S.H.I.E.L.D. AGENTS YOU SAID WERE ON THE WAY!
FLATTEN 'EM, BLOB! I LOVE THAT LITTLE NOISE THEY MAKE WHEN YOU DO THE CAR-CRUSHER THING, MATE!
NAH, I FIGURE I'M JUST GONNA SHOW THE COLONEL AND HIS DELICIOUS LITTLE FRIEND HERE HOW I MANAGE TO MAINTAIN THIS SEXY FOUR FIGURE BODY MASS!
CONTROL!

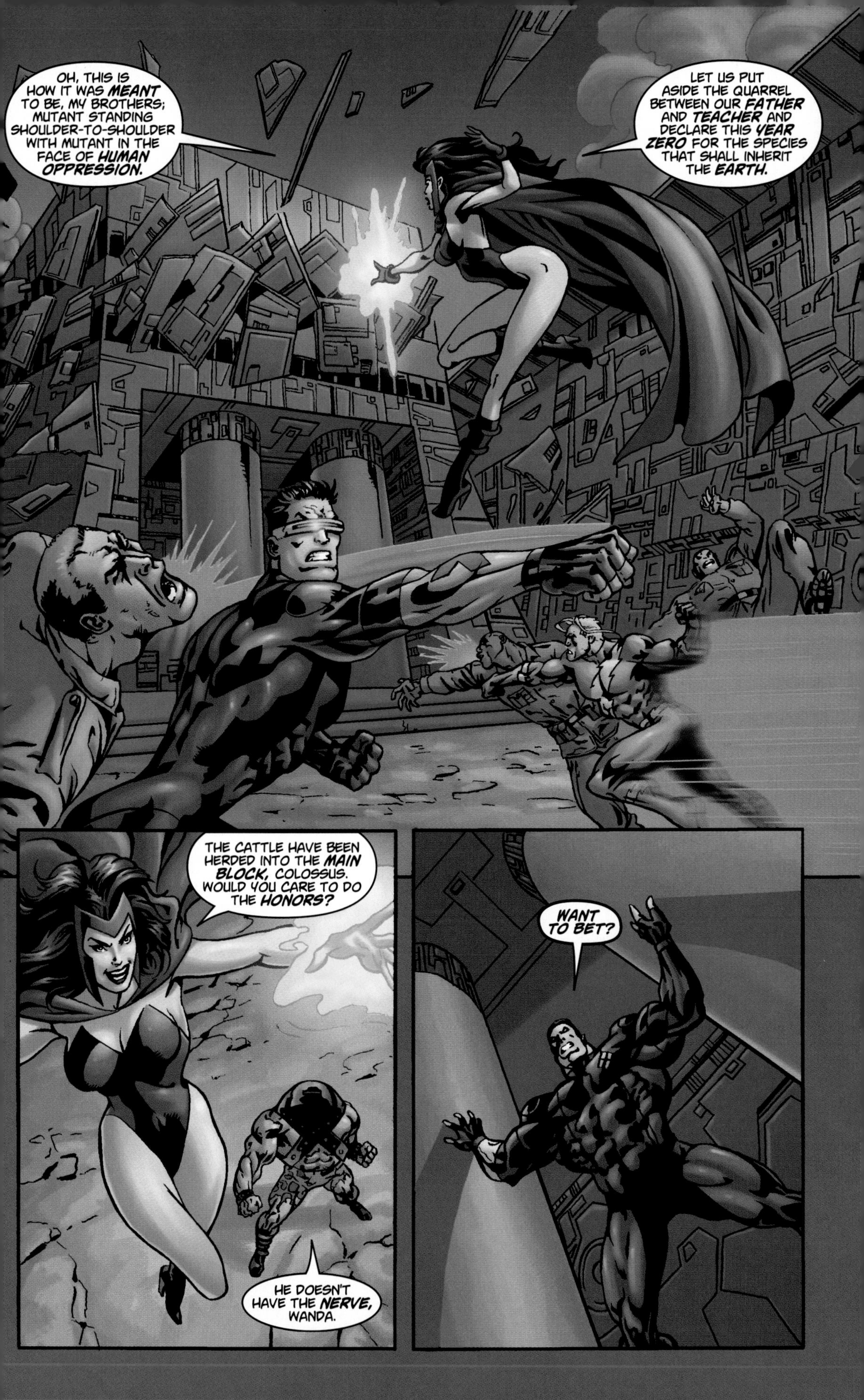
OH, THIS IS HOW IT WAS MEANT TO BE, MY BROTHERS; MUTANT STANDING SHOULDER-TO-SHOULDER WITH MUTANT IN THE FACE OF HUMAN OPPRESSION.
LET US PUT ASIDE THE QUARREL BETWEEN OUR FATHER AND TEACHER AND DECLARE THIS YEAR ZERO FOR THE SPECIES THAT SHALL INHERIT THE EARTH.
THE CATTLE HAVE BEEN HERDED INTO THE MAIN BLOCK, COLOSSUS. WOULD YOU CARE TO DO THE HONORS?
HE DOESN'T HAVE THE NERVE, WANDA.
WANT TO BET?

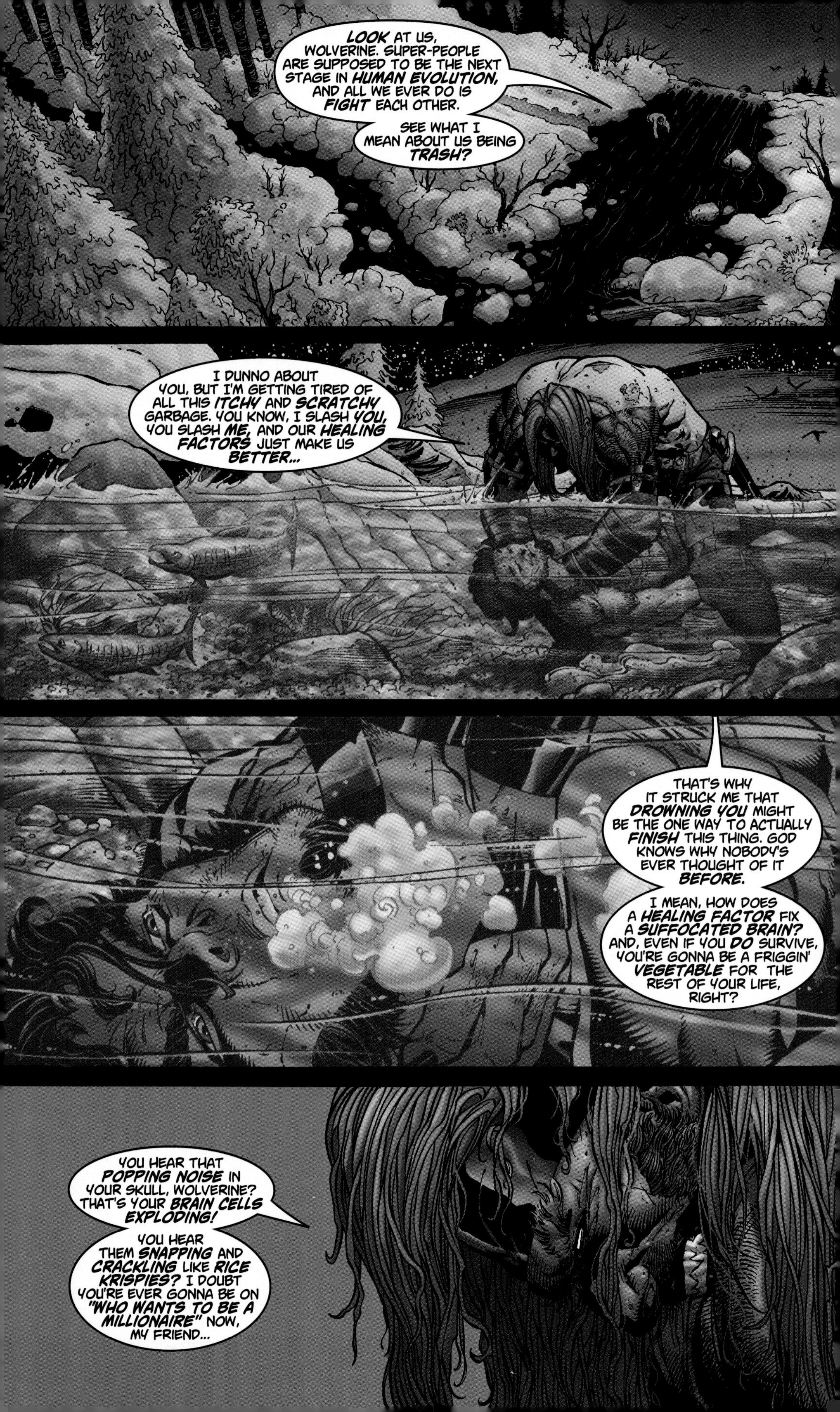
LOOK AT US, WOLVERINE. SUPER-PEOPLE ARE SUPPOSED TO BE THE NEXT STAGE IN HUMAN EVOLUTION, AND ALL WE EVER DO IS FIGHT EACH OTHER.
SEE WHAT I MEAN ABOUT US BEING TRASH?
I DUNNO ABOUT YOU, BUT I'M GETTING TIRED OF ALL THIS ITCHY AND SCRATCHY GARBAGE. YOU KNOW, I SLASH YOU, YOU SLASH ME, AND OUR HEALING FACTORS JUST MAKE US BETTER...
THAT'S WHY IT STRUCK ME THAT DROWNING YOU MIGHT BE THE ONE WAY TO ACTUALLY FINISH THIS THING. GOD KNOWS WHY NOBODY'S EVER THOUGHT OF IT BEFORE.
I MEAN, HOW DOES A HEALING FACTOR FIX A SUFFOCATED BRAIN? AND, EVEN IF YOU DO SURVIVE, YOU'RE GONNA BE A FRIGGIN' VEGETABLE FOR THE REST OF YOUR LIFE, RIGHT?
YOU HEAR THAT POPPING NOISE IN YOUR SKULL, WOLVERINE? THAT'S YOUR BRAIN CELLS EXPLODING!
YOU HEAR THEM SNAPPING AND CRACKLING LIKE RICE KRISPIES? I DOUBT YOU'RE EVER GONNA BE ON "WHO WANTS TO BE A MILLIONAIRE" NOW, MY FRIEND...

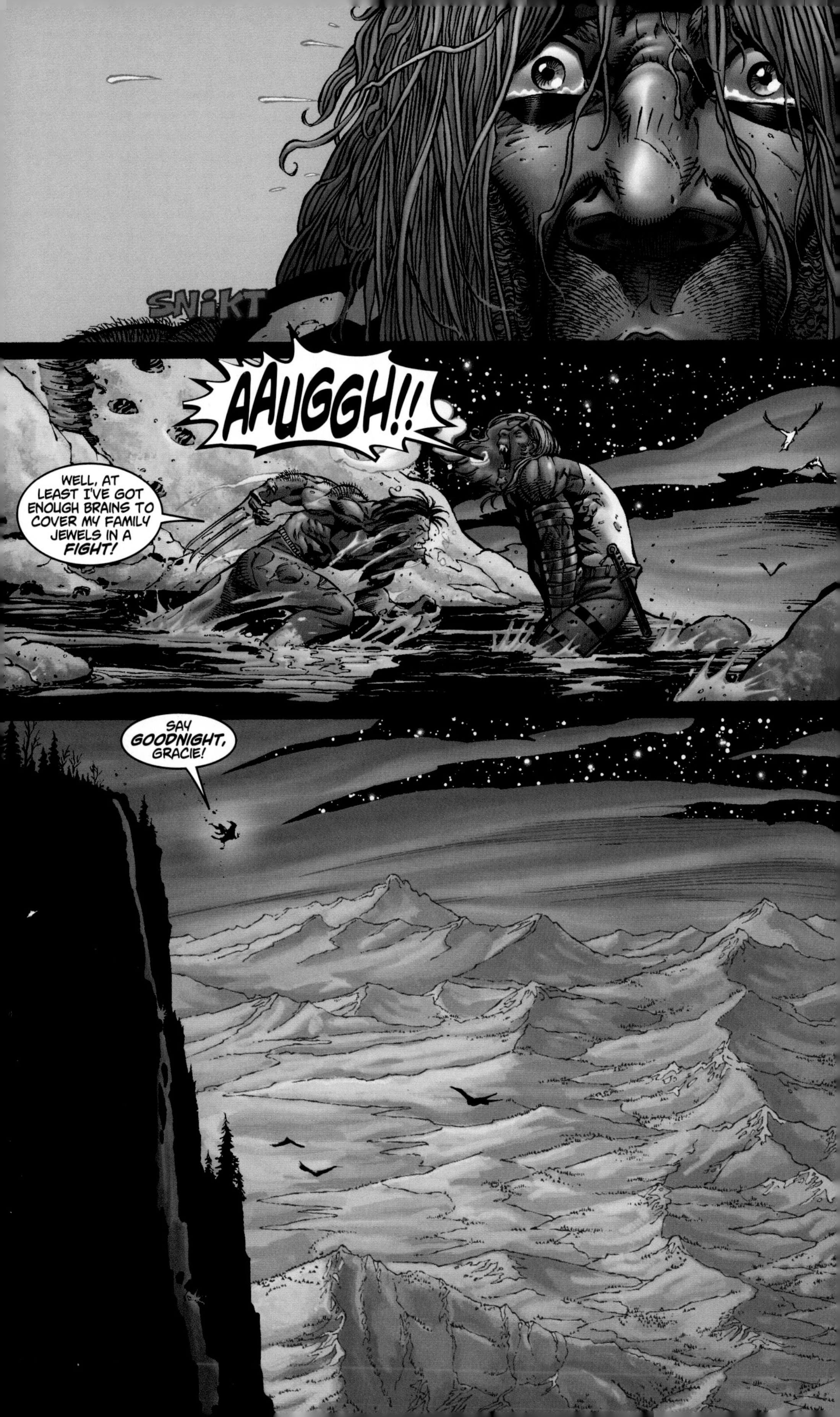
SNIKT
AAUGGH!!
WELL, AT LEAST I'VE GOT ENOUGH BRAINS TO COVER MY FAMILY JEWELS IN A FIGHT!
SAY GOODNIGHT, GRACIE!

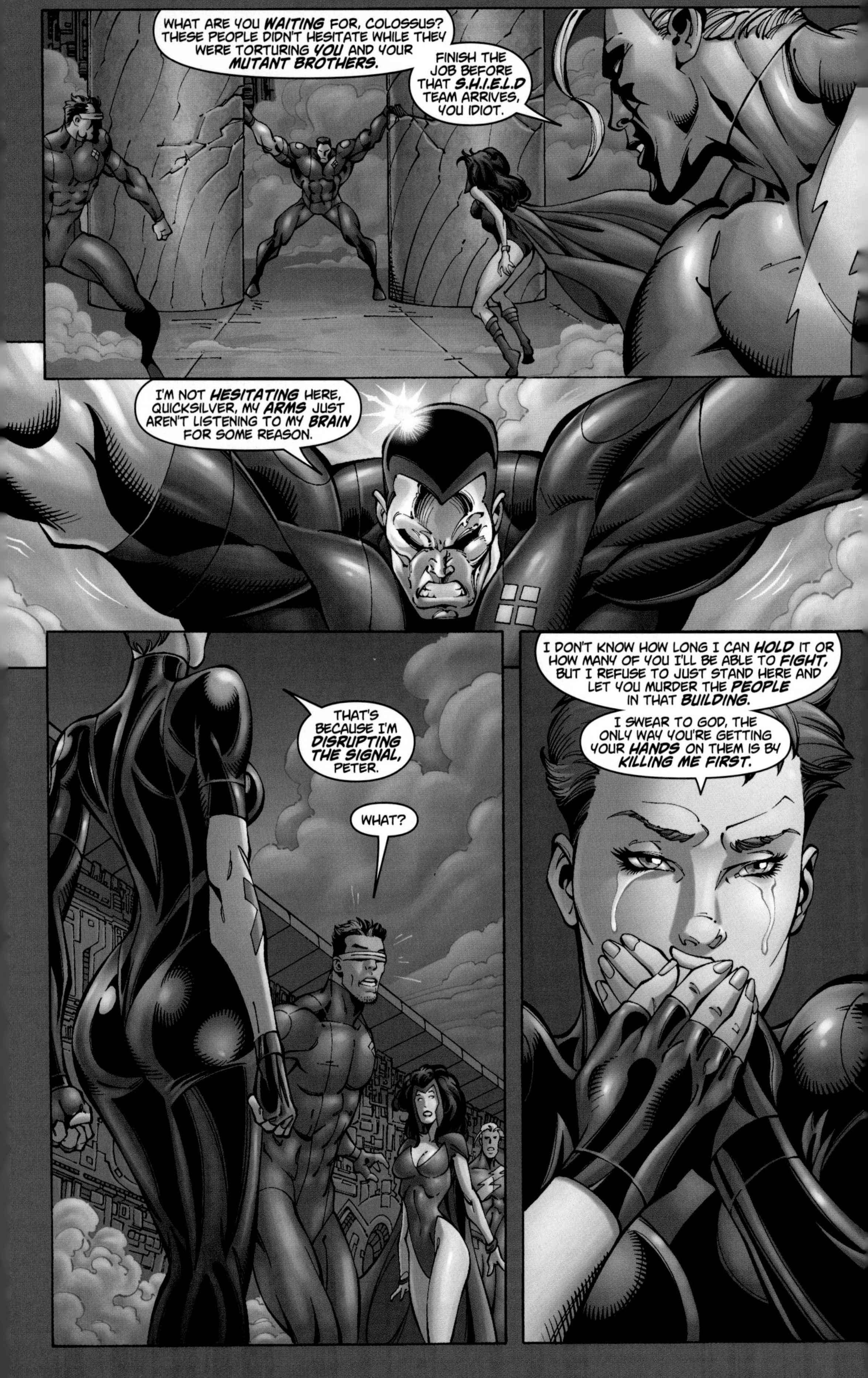
WHAT ARE YOU WAITING FOR, COLOSSUS? THESE PEOPLE DIDN'T HESITATE WHILE THEY WERE TORTURING YOU AND YOUR MUTANT BROTHERS.
FINISH THE JOB BEFORE THAT S.H.I.E.L.D TEAM ARRIVES, YOU IDIOT.
I'M NOT HESITATING HERE, QUICKSILVER, MY ARMS JUST AREN'T LISTENING TO MY BRAIN FOR SOME REASON.
THAT'S BECAUSE I'M DISRUPTING THE SIGNAL, PETER.
WHAT?
I DON'T KNOW HOW LONG I CAN HOLD IT OR HOW MANY OF YOU I'LL BE ABLE TO FIGHT, BUT I REFUSE TO JUST STAND HERE AND LET YOU MURDER THE PEOPLE IN THAT BUILDING.
I SWEAR TO GOD, THE ONLY WAY YOU'RE GETTING YOUR HANDS ON THEM IS BY KILLING ME FIRST.

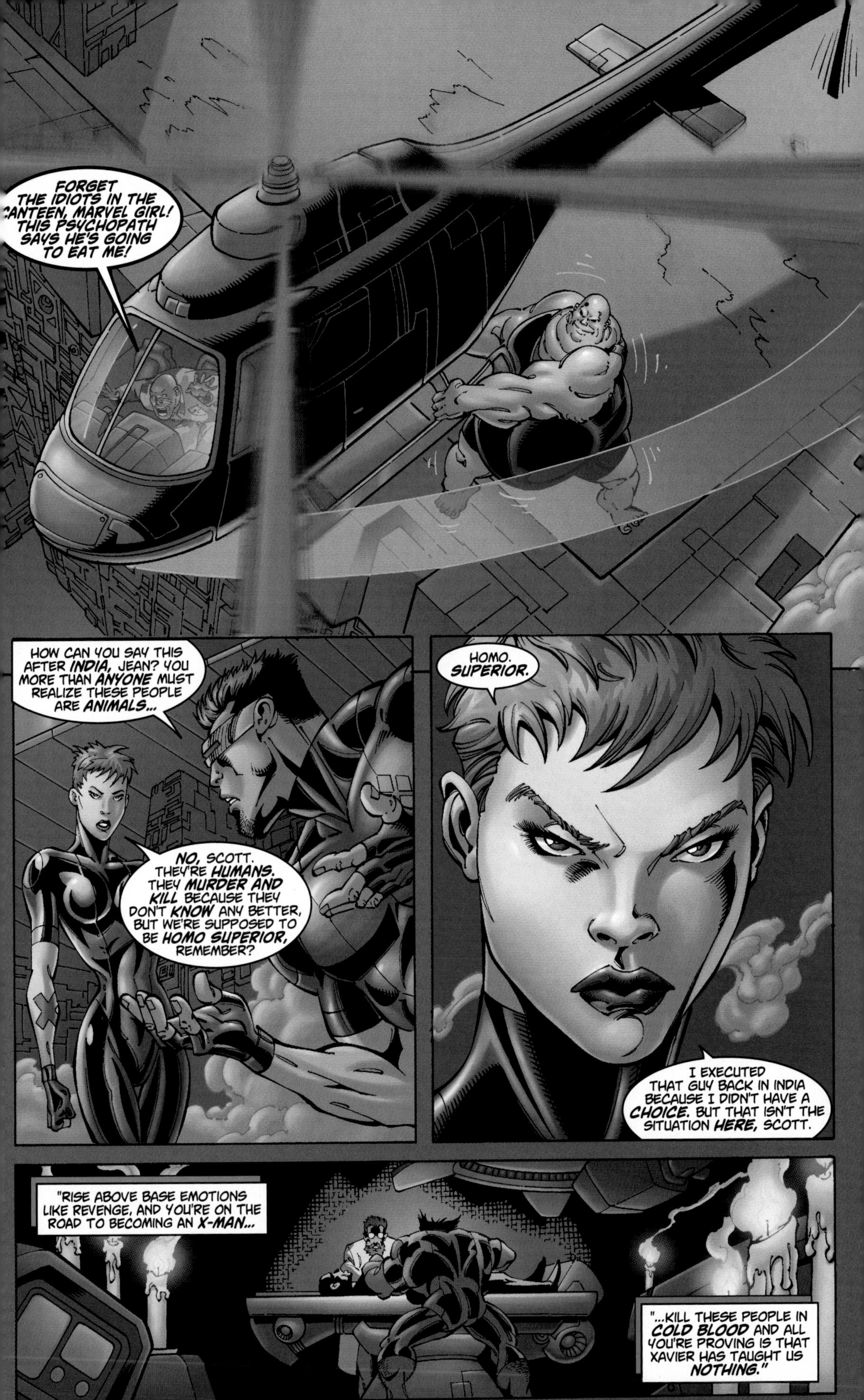
FORGET THE IDIOTS IN THE CANTEEN, MARVEL GIRL! THIS PSYCHOPATH SAYS HE'S GOING TO EAT ME!
HOW CAN YOU SAY THIS AFTER INDIA, JEAN? YOU MORE THAN ANYONE MUST REALIZE THESE PEOPLE ARE ANIMALS...
NO, SCOTT. THEY'RE HUMANS. THEY MURDER AND KILL BECAUSE THEY DON'T KNOW ANY BETTER, BUT WE'RE SUPPOSED TO BE HOMO SUPERIOR, REMEMBER?
HOMO. SUPERIOR.
I EXECUTED THAT GUY BACK IN INDIA BECAUSE I DIDN'T HAVE A CHOICE. BUT THAT ISN'T THE SITUATION HERE, SCOTT.
"RISE ABOVE BASE EMOTIONS LIKE REVENGE, AND YOU'RE ON THE ROAD TO BECOMING AN X-MAN...
"...KILL THESE PEOPLE IN COLD BLOOD AND ALL YOU'RE PROVING IS THAT XAVIER HAS TAUGHT US NOTHING."

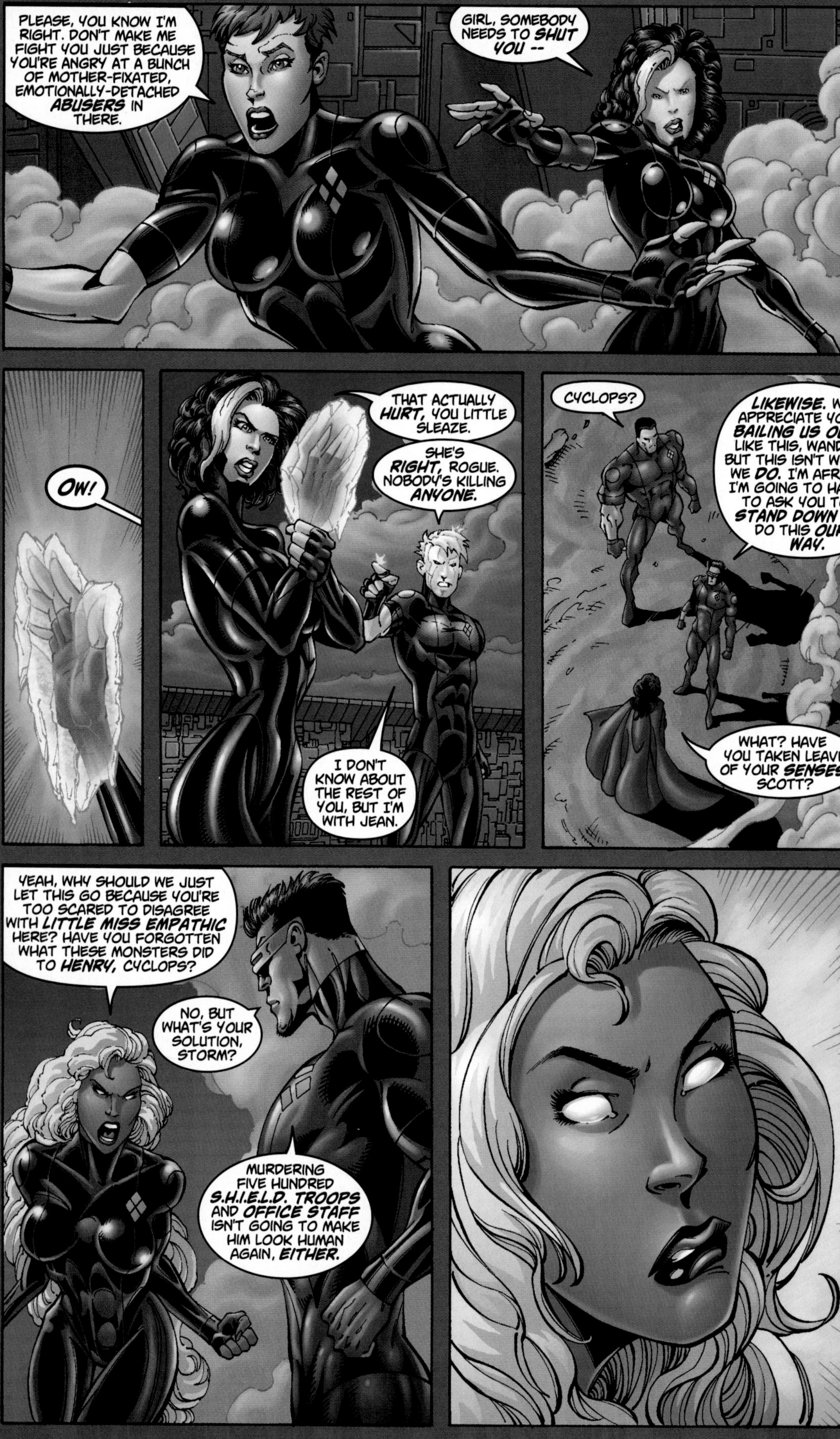
PLEASE, YOU KNOW I'M RIGHT. DON'T MAKE ME FIGHT YOU JUST BECAUSE YOU'RE ANGRY AT A BUNCH OF MOTHER-FIXATED, EMOTIONALLY-DETACHED ABUSERS IN THERE.
GIRL, SOMEBODY NEEDS TO SHUT YOU --
OW!
THAT ACTUALLY HURT, YOU LITTLE SLEAZE.
SHE'S RIGHT, ROGUE. NOBODY'S KILLING ANYONE.
I DON'T KNOW ABOUT THE REST OF YOU, BUT I'M WITH JEAN.
CYCLOPS?
LIKEWISE. WE APPRECIATE YOU BAILING US OUT LIKE THIS, WANDA, BUT THIS ISN'T WHAT WE DO. I'M AFRAID I'M GOING TO HAVE TO ASK YOU TO STAND DOWN AND DO THIS OUR WAY.
WHAT? HAVE YOU TAKEN LEAVE OF YOUR SENSES, SCOTT?
YEAH, WHY SHOULD WE JUST LET THIS GO BECAUSE YOU'RE TOO SCARED TO DISAGREE WITH LITTLE MISS EMPATHIC HERE? HAVE YOU FORGOTTEN WHAT THESE MONSTERS DID TO HENRY, CYCLOPS?
NO, BUT WHAT'S YOUR SOLUTION, STORM?
MURDERING FIVE HUNDRED S.H.I.E.L.D. TROOPS AND OFFICE STAFF ISN'T GOING TO MAKE HIM LOOK HUMAN AGAIN, EITHER.

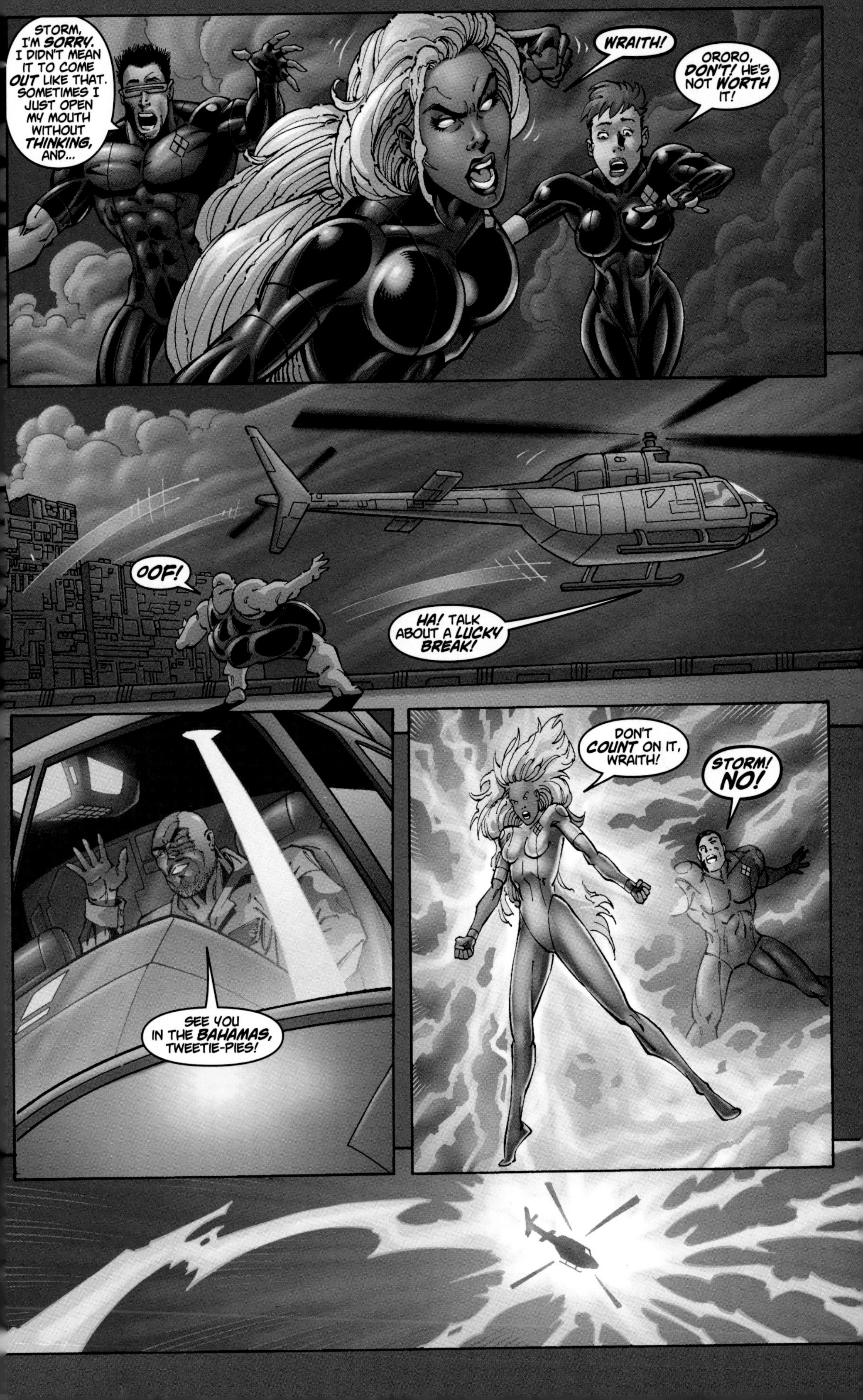
STORM, I'M SORRY. I DIDN'T MEAN IT TO COME OUT LIKE THAT. SOMETIMES I JUST OPEN MY MOUTH WITHOUT THINKING, AND...
WRAITH!
ORORO, DON'T! HE'S NOT WORTH IT!
OOF!
HA! TALK ABOUT A LUCKY BREAK!
SEE YOU IN THE BAHAMAS, TWEETIE-PIES!
DON'T COUNT ON IT, WRAITH!
STORM! NO!

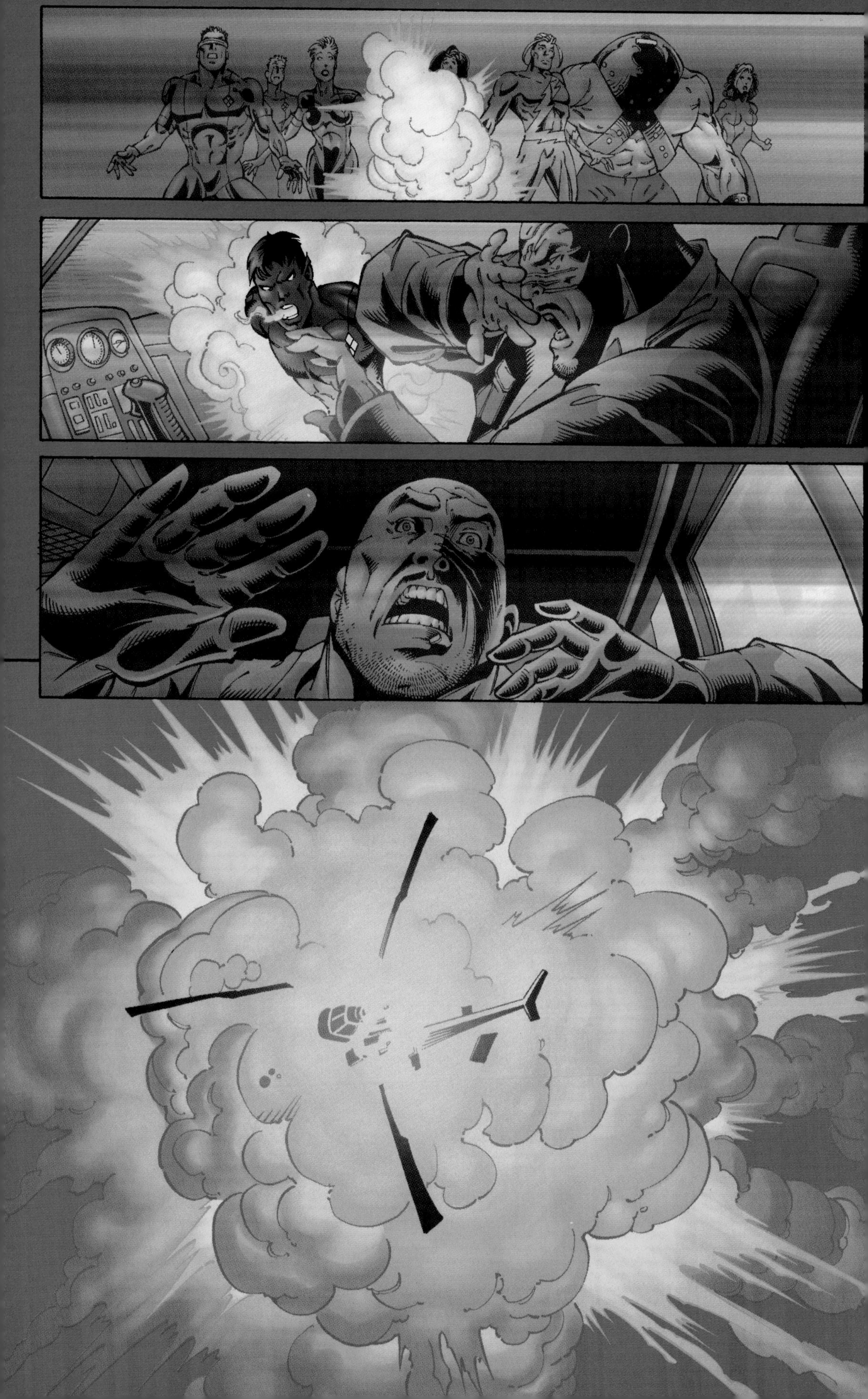

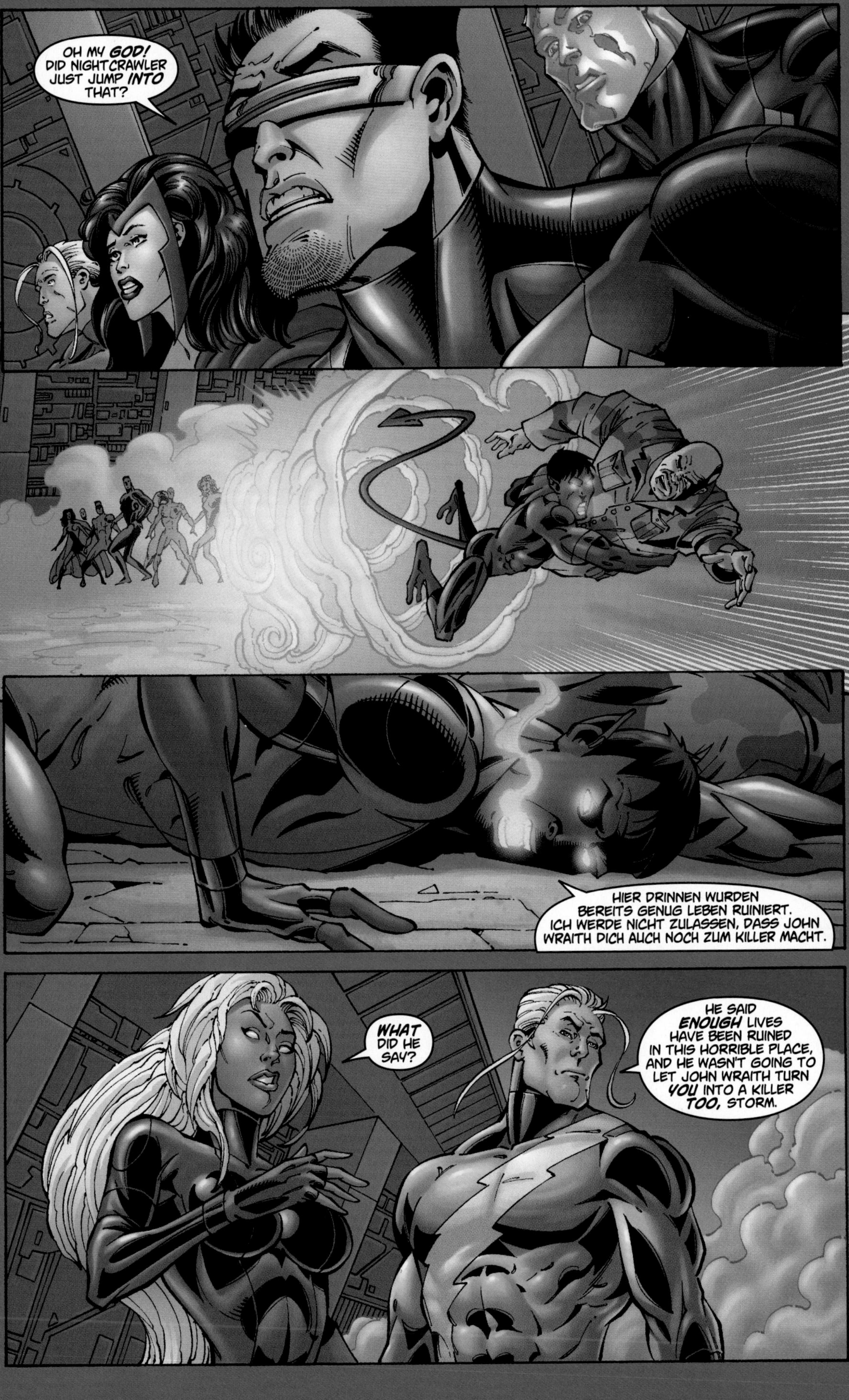
OH MY GOD! DID NIGHTCRAWLER JUST JUMP INTO THAT?
HIER DRINNEN WURDEN BEREITS GENUG LEBEN RUINIERT. ICH WERDE NICHT ZULASSEN, DASS JOHN WRAITH DICH AUCH NOCH ZUM KILLER MACHT.
WHAT DID HE SAY?
HE SAID ENOUGH LIVES HAVE BEEN RUINED IN THIS HORRIBLE PLACE, AND HE WASN'T GOING TO LET JOHN WRAITH TURN YOU INTO A KILLER TOO, STORM.

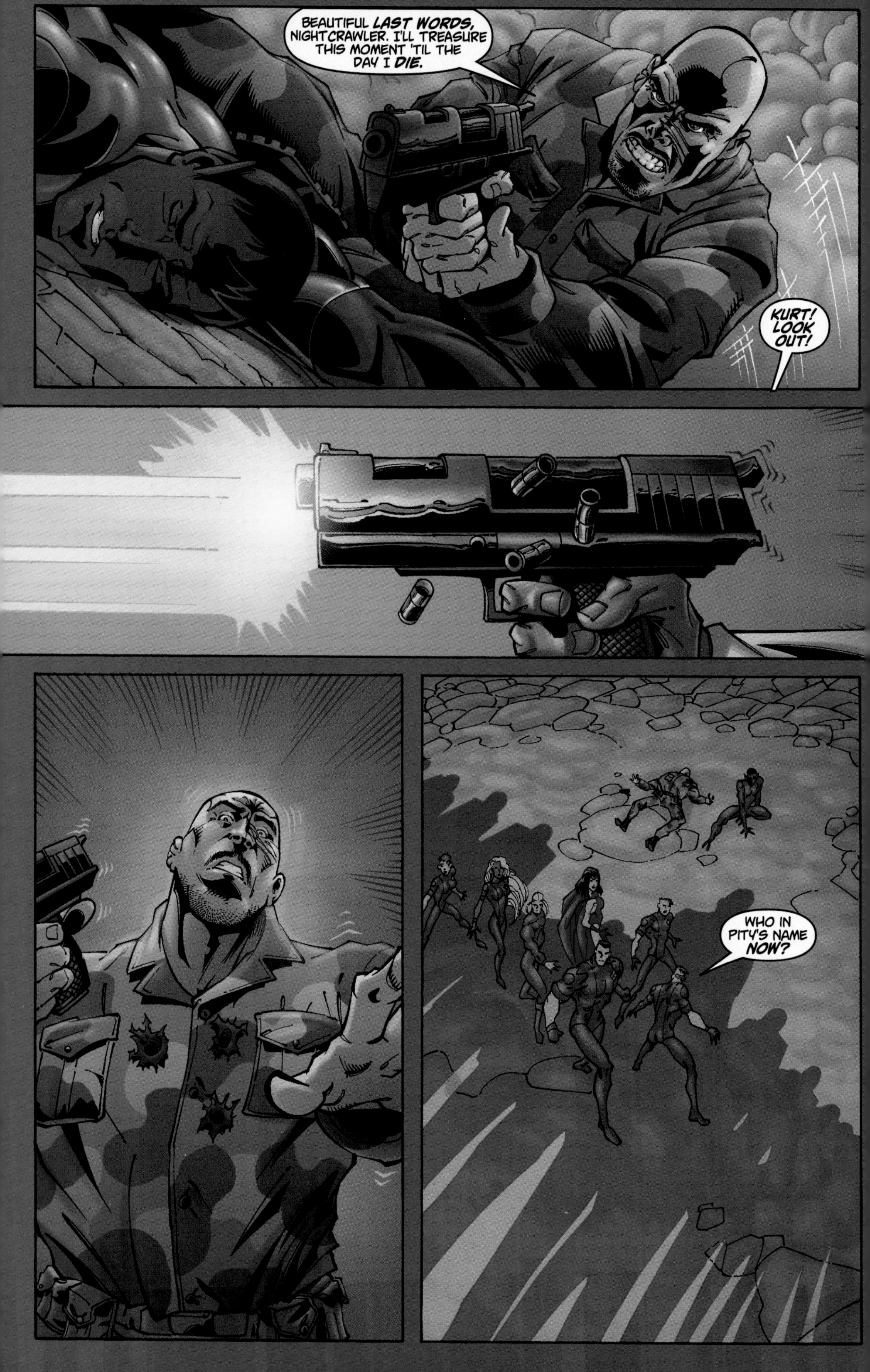
BEAUTIFUL LAST WORDS, NIGHTCRAWLER. I'LL TREASURE THIS MOMENT 'TIL THE DAY I DIE.
KURT! LOOK OUT!
WHO IN PITY'S NAME NOW?

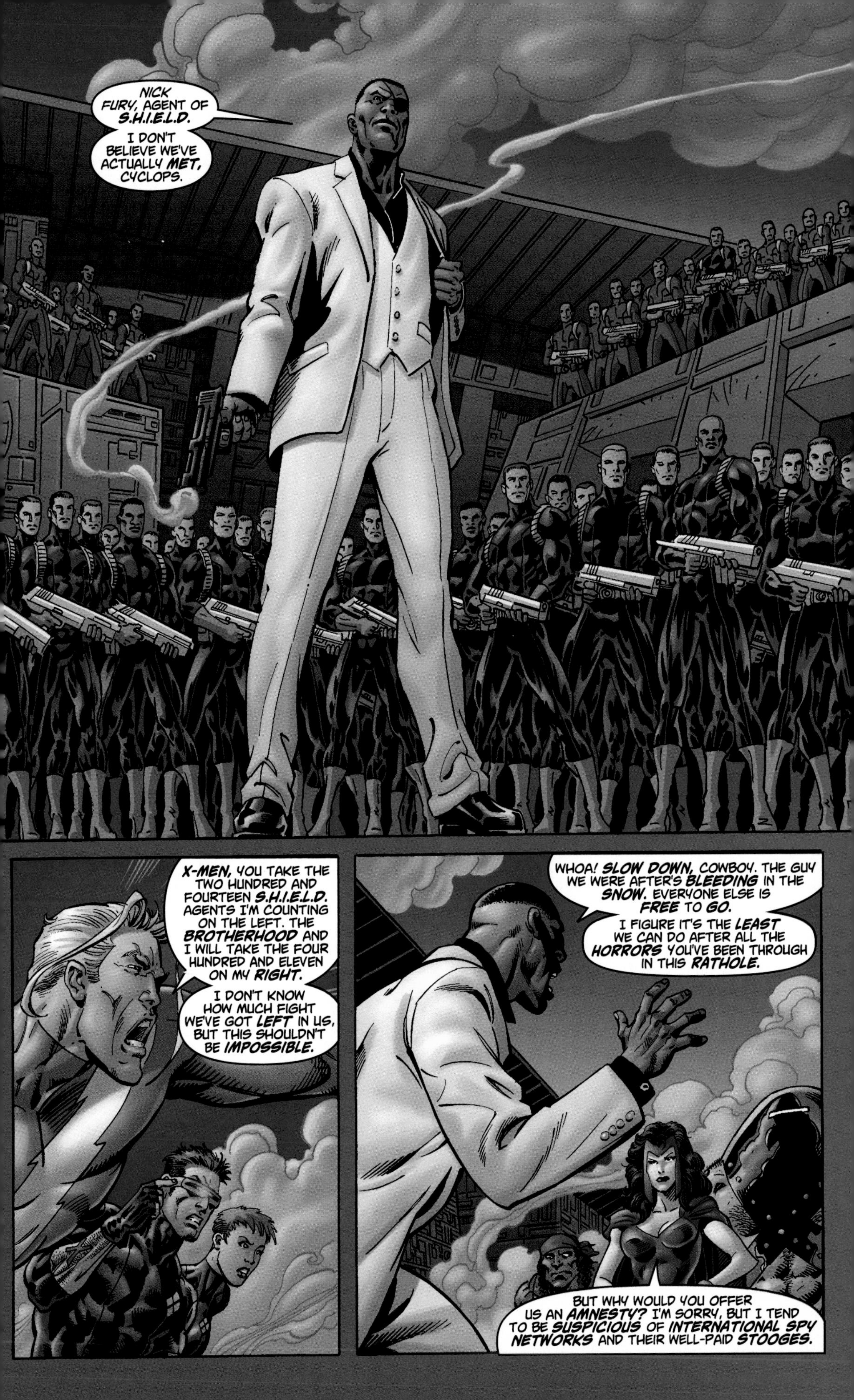
NICK FURY, AGENT OF S.H.I.E.L.D.
I DON'T BELIEVE WE'VE ACTUALLY MET, CYCLOPS.
X-MEN, YOU TAKE THE TWO HUNDRED AND FOURTEEN S.H.I.E.L.D. AGENTS I'M COUNTING ON THE LEFT. THE BROTHERHOOD AND I WILL TAKE THE FOUR HUNDRED AND ELEVEN ON MY RIGHT.
I DON'T KNOW HOW MUCH FIGHT WE'VE GOT LEFT IN US, BUT THIS SHOULDN'T BE IMPOSSIBLE.
WHOA! SLOW DOWN, COWBOY. THE GUY WE WERE AFTER'S BLEEDING IN THE SNOW. EVERYONE ELSE IS FREE TO GO.
I FIGURE IT'S THE LEAST WE CAN DO AFTER ALL THE HORRORS YOU'VE BEEN THROUGH IN THIS RATHOLE.
BUT WHY WOULD YOU OFFER US AN AMNESTY? I'M SORRY, BUT I TEND TO BE SUSPICIOUS OF INTERNATIONAL SPY NETWORKS AND THEIR WELL-PAID STOOGES.

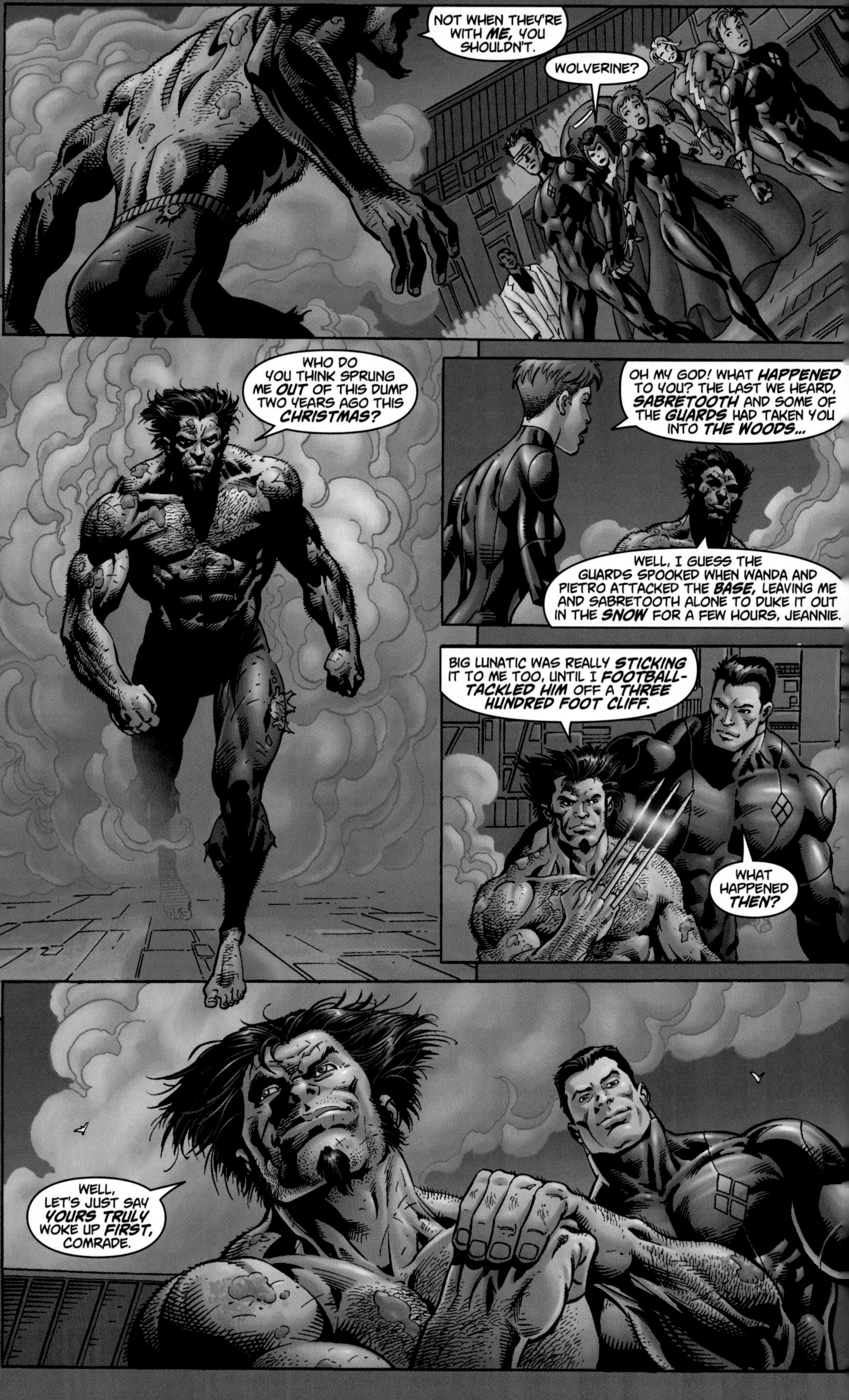
NOT WHEN THEY'RE WITH ME, YOU SHOULDN'T.
WOLVERINE?
WHO DO YOU THINK SPRUNG ME OUT OF THIS DUMP TWO YEARS AGO THIS CHRISTMAS?
OH MY GOD! WHAT HAPPENED TO YOU? THE LAST WE HEARD, SABRETOOTH AND SOME OF THE GUARDS HAD TAKEN YOU INTO THE WOODS...
WELL, I GUESS THE GUARDS SPOOKED WHEN WANDA AND PIETRO ATTACKED THE BASE, LEAVING ME AND SABRETOOTH ALONE TO DUKE IT OUT IN THE SNOW FOR A FEW HOURS, JEANNIE.
BIG LUNATIC WAS REALLY STICKING IT TO ME TOO, UNTIL I FOOTBALL-TACKLED HIM OFF A THREE HUNDRED FOOT CLIFF.
WHAT HAPPENED THEN?
WELL, LET'S JUST SAY YOURS TRULY WOKE UP FIRST, COMRADE.

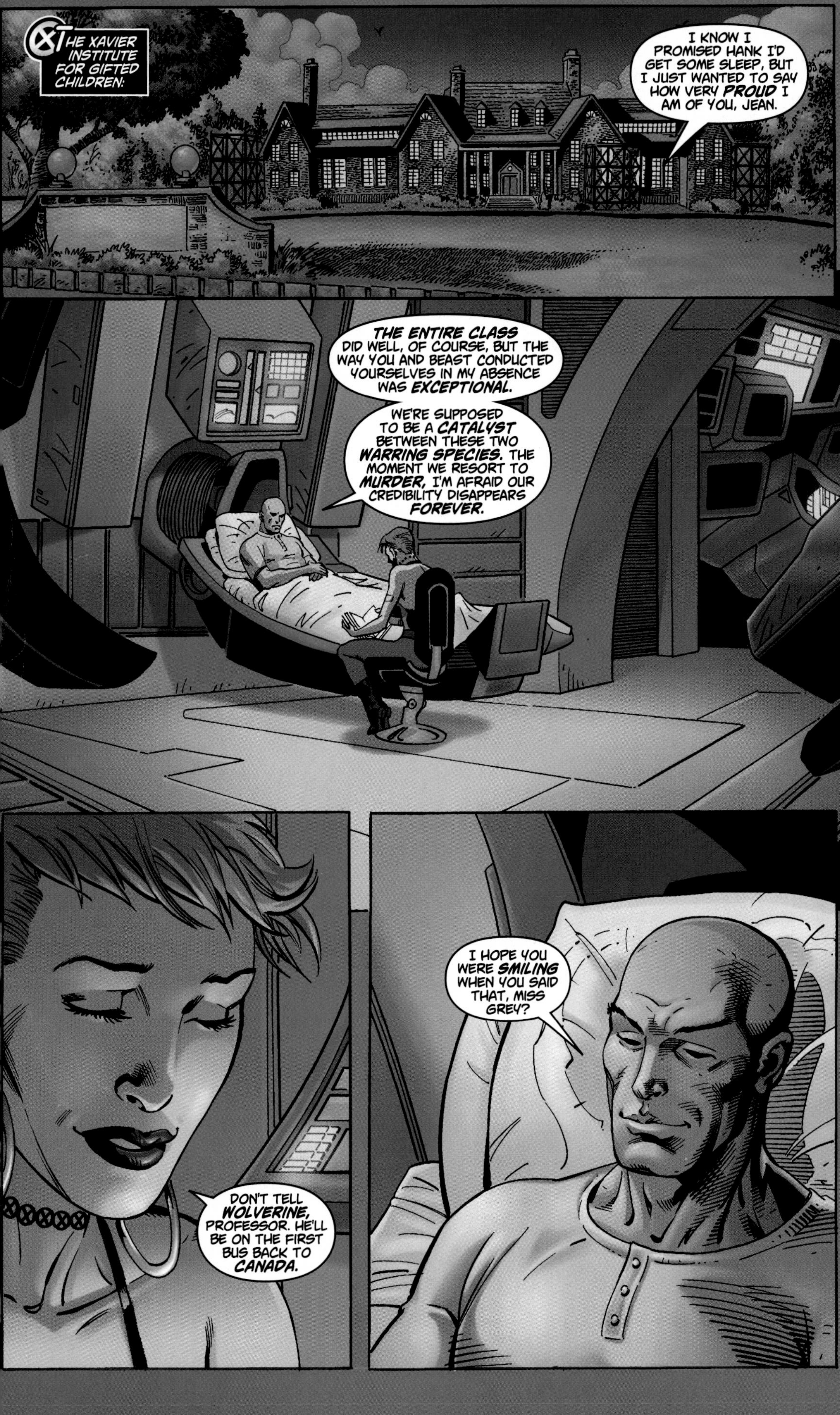
THE XAVIER INSTITUTE FOR GIFTED CHILDREN:
I KNOW I PROMISED HANK I'D GET SOME SLEEP, BUT I JUST WANTED TO SAY HOW VERY PROUD I AM OF YOU, JEAN.
THE ENTIRE CLASS DID WELL, OF COURSE, BUT THE WAY YOU AND BEAST CONDUCTED YOURSELVES IN MY ABSENCE WAS EXCEPTIONAL.
WE'RE SUPPOSED TO BE A CATALYST BETWEEN THESE TWO WARRING SPECIES. THE MOMENT WE RESORT TO MURDER, I'M AFRAID OUR CREDIBILITY DISAPPEARS FOREVER.
DON'T TELL WOLVERINE, PROFESSOR. HE'LL BE ON THE FIRST BUS BACK TO CANADA.
I HOPE YOU WERE SMILING WHEN YOU SAID THAT, MISS GREY?

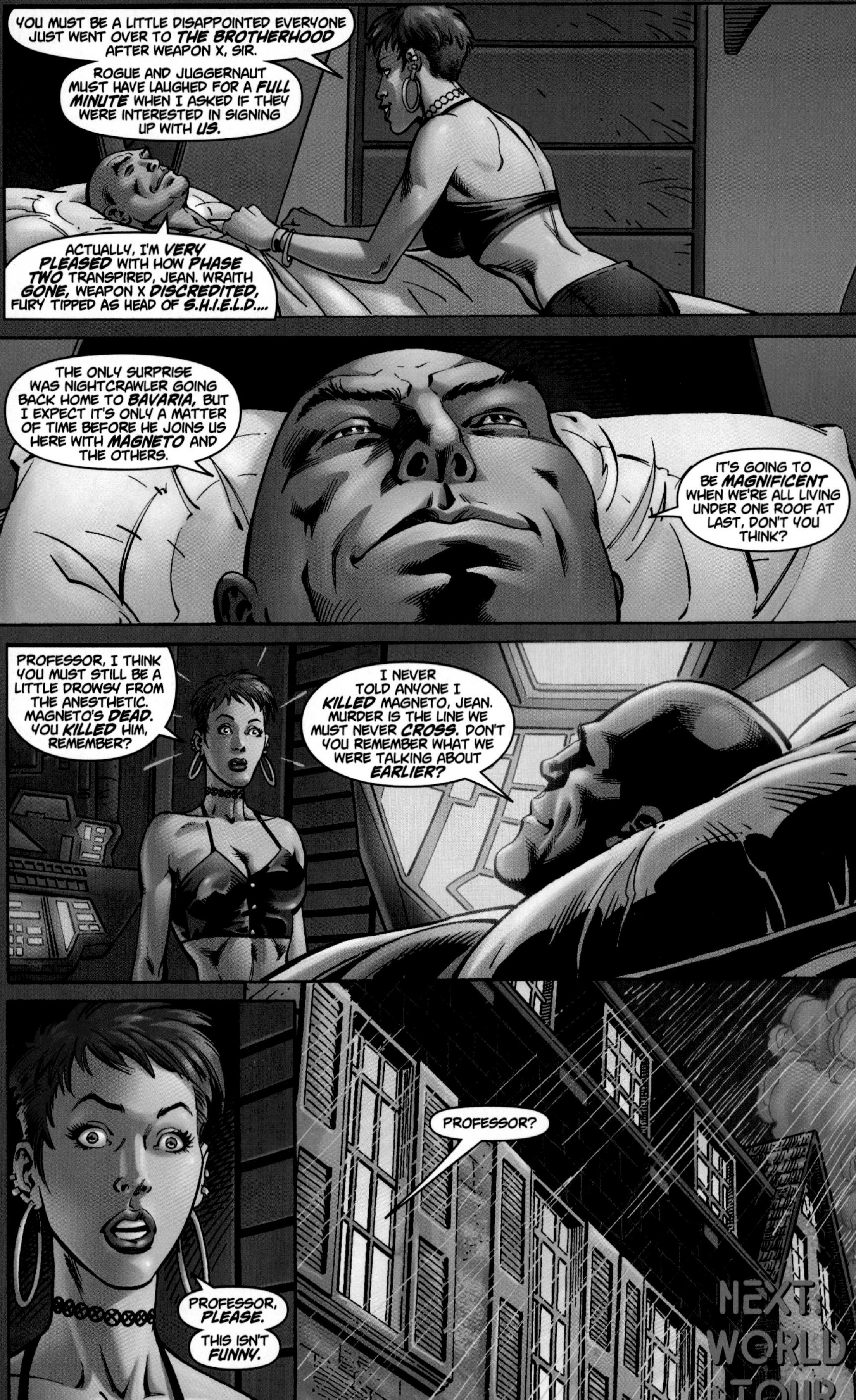

YOU MUST BE A LITTLE DISAPPOINTED EVERYONE JUST WENT OVER TO THE BROTHERHOOD AFTER WEAPON X, SIR.
ROGUE AND JUGGERNAUT MUST HAVE LAUGHED FOR A FULL MINUTE WHEN I ASKED IF THEY WERE INTERESTED IN SIGNING UP WITH US.
ACTUALLY, I'M VERY PLEASED WITH HOW PHASE TWO TRANSPIRED, JEAN. WRAITH GONE, WEAPON X DISCREDITED, FURY TIPPED AS HEAD OF S.H.I.E.L.D....
THE ONLY SURPRISE WAS NIGHTCRAWLER GOING BACK HOME TO BAVARIA, BUT I EXPECT IT'S ONLY A MATTER OF TIME BEFORE HE JOINS US HERE WITH MAGNETO AND THE OTHERS.
IT'S GOING TO BE MAGNIFICENT WHEN WE'RE ALL LIVING UNDER ONE ROOF AT LAST, DON'T YOU THINK?
PROFESSOR, I THINK YOU MUST STILL BE A LITTLE DROWSY FROM THE ANESTHETIC. MAGNETO'S DEAD. YOU KILLED HIM, REMEMBER?
I NEVER TOLD ANYONE I KILLED MAGNETO, JEAN. MURDER IS THE LINE WE MUST NEVER CROSS. DON'T YOU REMEMBER WHAT WE WERE TALKING ABOUT EARLIER?
PROFESSOR?
PROFESSOR, PLEASE.
THIS ISN'T FUNNY.
NEXT: WORLD TOUR